THE LIFE OF

IAN CURTIS

TORN APART

MICK MIDDLES & LINDSAY READE

OMNIBUS PRESS

LONDON / NEW YORK / PARIS / SYDNEY / COPENHAGEN / BERLIN / MADRID / TOKYO

Copyright © 2006 Omnibus Press
This edition © 2009 Omnibus Press
(A Division of Music Sales Limited)

Cover designed by Fresh Lemon

ISBN: 978.1.84772.508.0
Order No: OP52547

The Author hereby asserts his/her right to be identified as the author of this work in accordance with
Sections 77 to 78 of the Copyright, Designs and Patents Act 1988.

All rights reserved. No part of this book may be reproduced in any form or by any electronic or
mechanical means, including information storage or retrieval systems, without permission in writing
from the publisher, except by a reviewer who may quote brief passages.

Exclusive Distributors
Music Sales Limited,
14/15 Berners Street,
London, W1T 3LJ.

Music Sales Corporation,
257 Park Avenue South,
New York, NY 10010, USA.

Macmillan Distribution Services,
56 Parkwest Drive
Derrimut, Vic 3030,
Australia.

All uncredited photographs from the Curtis Family Collection. Used by kind permission.

Every effort has been made to trace the copyright holders of the photographs in this book but one or
two were unreachable. We would be grateful if the photographers concerned would contact us.

Typeset by Phoenix Photosetting, Chatham, Kent
Printed by the MPG Books Group

A catalogue record for this book is available from the British Library.

Visit Omnibus Press on the web at www.omnibuspress.com

"If it be now, 'tis not to come; if it be not to come, it will be now; if it be not now, yet it will come: the readiness is all." Hamlet

For Doreen

"Every life is the story of a collapse. If biographies are so fascinating, it is because the heroes, and the cowards quite as much, strive to innovate in the art of the debacle." – Paul Morley, *Nothing.*

Contents

Introduction & Acknowledgements

Joy Division was the finest live band I have ever seen, and I have seen a fair few: Led Zeppelin, The Who, The Stooges, Grateful Dead, The Rolling Stones, Metallica and many more. That might seem like an outrageous claim for a short lived band from Macclesfield and Salford whose legacy barely stretched beyond two albums and whose image would forever be encapsulated in monochrome images of them huddled together in the Stockport snow.

But there is one reason, and only one, why I will always regard Joy Division as the finest. No disrespect to Bernard Sumner, Peter Hook and Steve Morris – gargantuan figures to a man – but the reason is very simple: Ian Curtis. I close my eyes every now and again and I see him; and I see a beam of light and a big open heart of emotion and some kind of pain, a howling from that sound. Genesis P-Orridge, catching sight of Joy Division for the first time at Hemel Hempstead Pavilion, noted that Curtis seemed separated from the others by a bolt of lightening. It sounds fantastical – but I saw it also.

I hovered around Joy Division for a while and always found Ian Curtis disarmingly courteous. It was difficult to square the man on stage with the man eating pies in the pub. Something remarkable happened here.

When the chance came to work with Lindsay, who was much closer to the characters involved than I was, it just felt like a gift. I had read every word on Joy Division and had written a few of them myself but I never really got close to what it was that happened back then. Not until now.

The roots of this book stretch back about five years, to a time when an enduring – and productive – friendship formed from a series of interviews between the co-authors. So my thanks to Lindsay for special times and tofu. Throughout this period, a vague notion of a book changed shape and form a number of times before being seized upon by Chris Charlesworth, who hurtled us both in the same direction.

There are a number of people I need to thank, notably Steve Burke, Kevin Cummins, Steve Diggle, Michael Eastwood, Mike Finney, Paul Hanley, Alan Hempsall, Chris Hewitt, Clinton Heylin, Jake Kennedy, Dave McCullough, Joe Matera, Mike Nicholls, Martin O'Neill, David Quantick, Martin Ryan, Peter Saville, Richard Searling, Chris Seivey, Colin Sharp, David Sultan (for the discography and gig listing) and Ian Wood. In memory of Derek Brandwood and Rob Gretton.

Mick Middles, January 2006.

Researching and co-writing this book turned out to be quite a journey. When I first embarked on it, I had no real idea of the direction it would take. Actually, that's not strictly true. I was sure I did know but, as it turned out, some of the people I had assumed would talk to me refused, and those I had thought would remain silent – either because, as in the case of Annik Honoré, they hadn't spoken about Ian for 25 years, or because, as in the case of Ian's mum, sister Carole and Aunt Barbara, I had never met and had no way of finding – recounted their memories in ways I could never have imagined.

The greatest pleasure of the journey was travelling with companions like these and having the opportunity to reawaken long lost or barely established friendships with many faces from my past. At some point along the way, I realised that the book had a life of its own and I began to see myself more as some kind of transmitter than a biographer. I like to think that the spirit of that life came from Ian. The most extraordinary thing for me about being involved with this book has been getting to know Ian so well. That was the best surprise and a genuine pleasure.

I would like to offer enormous thanks to all the people I interviewed who brought this book to life: Larry Cassidy, Carole Curtis, Doreen Curtis, Bob Dickinson, Alan Erasmus, David Holmes, Annik Honoré, Pete Johnson, Jeremy Kerr, Barbara Lloyd, Terry Mason, Paul Morley, Genesis P-Orridge, Mark Reeder, Vini Reilly, Tosh Ryan, Pete Shelley, Tony Wilson, Alan Wise and Kevin Wood. Also Martin Hannett for his invaluable contribution.

I can't thank Annik enough for sharing her story and her private letters. Her great dignity and the tender love that she and his family have for Ian is a wonderful tribute to him. Terry Mason provided a tremendous amount of detail about life with the band and made me laugh every time we met. He reminded me of how much fun there was in Ian's life. When I first met Ian's mum she said that she was unhappy that her son's life was so often described as tragic. It wasn't, she emphasised. He had a very happy life and there were many good times. Just because it was cut short doesn't negate that. He was always joking, she said.

A special word of thanks to Mick Middles for his support and encouragement which proved invaluable to my work on this book. Sincere thanks also to Chris Charlesworth for his help and editorial input, for giving space when it was needed and for grabbing hold of the helm when the ship was steering towards the rocks.

Sadly, no matter how many films are made and books are written about Ian, nothing can bring him back – but we sincerely dedicate this book to his precious memory.

Lindsay Reade, January 2006.

CHAPTER ONE

Memories Of A Child's Past

"They (Ian's family) count more than anyone else, more than Debbie, me or the group. To lose a child is just the worst that can happen to one. His mum's life must have been broken. Unlike Debbie or myself whose life carried on, even if it remains a wound. I know it has influenced my whole life because it made me lose lots of confidence and frightened to hurt anyone or be hurt. There is always a price to pay. But it has also made me a more sensitive and careful person." – Annik Honoré

Ian Kevin Curtis was born into a close, loving, respectable, working-class family on St Swithin's Day – July 15 – in 1956. This is the day when legend has it that if it rains it will continue to do so for the next 40 days, or if it is fine then the sun will shine for a similar period. His mother remembers that it didn't rain. The place of birth was Basford House, a cottage hospital in Old Trafford that was popular among local pregnant mothers, especially the Peter Pan ward with its large stained glass windows and images of author J. M. Barrie's most famous creation, the boy who never grew up. The baby weighed in at 9lb 4oz, above average, but there were no birthing problems.

Ian's parents had been married for almost four years when their first child was born. His mother, formerly Doreen Hughes, tied the knot with Kevin Curtis on August 9, 1952. Doreen was 21, soon to be 22 on August 15, her new husband five years older. The service was held at St. John's Church in Old Trafford, the same church where Ian would be christened, and was followed by a reception at the Star Café in Chorlton. Doreen had met Kevin on a blind date when she was 18, introduced by her friend Edna whose boyfriend worked alongside him in the Railway Police, as today's British Transport Police was then known. Edna had a photo of Doreen that was taken on an outing to Southport and had shown it to Kevin. Suitably impressed, he suggested a foursome be arranged and they all went to the Imperial, a cinema in Brook's Bar, on the borders of Old Trafford and Chorlton. Doreen doesn't remember which film they saw.

The couple courted for four years. Kevin was working shift hours at Guide Bridge and Doreen would catch two buses – one into Piccadilly and one out – to meet him at 10pm when he came off work. At the time she worked as a shorthand typist for the Henry Wells Oil Company in Salford, latterly known as Germ Lubricants.

The newlyweds honeymooned on Canvey Island, off the southern coastline of Essex. Doreen's Auntie Ivy – her favourite aunt – owned a bungalow there that was loaned to them, and years later it became the scene of many happy family holidays. Ivy had an upright piano and taught Ian to sing 'My Old Man's A Dustman', Lonnie Donegan's music-hall styled 1960 UK chart topper.

When they were first married, Doreen and Kevin lived with Doreen's parents at 156 Stamford Street in Old Trafford. This house has remained in the family for decades and was much loved by Ian who when he was old enough enjoyed sliding down the banisters. It was here that Ian and his wife Debbie would come to live, with his grandparents, immediately after they were married, when Ian first began singing with the band that became Joy Division.

At Stamford Street during the Second World War the occupants were often obliged to flee outside to the tin underground Anderson shelter – complete with bunk beds – in the back garden. The bomb shelter was provided by the Government because Old Trafford was constantly being targeted by the German Luftwaffe, which was intent on destroying the many munitions and military hardware factories at nearby Trafford Park. Before the family was given the shelter, when the terrifying noise of the air-raid warning sounded they would sit on the cellar steps beneath the stairs to the main house, which was considered the safest place to be in the event of a direct hit. Doreen can remember hearing the drone from the Doodlebugs and the day that the church in their street was blown up, shattering all the windows of their house. Because of the danger to the child that Doreen then was, she was evacuated to Hale but she didn't like it one bit. The household to which she was billeted was very posh – the husband was a Colonel and there was a grand piano in one room – and Doreen cried for her mother. After only a week there she was reunited with her parents at Old Trafford. "Well if we go – we'll all go together," said Doreen's mother.

Meanwhile, Kevin Curtis – her future son-in-law – was doing war service in the Navy. After several years of action, his ship, *HMS Valiant*, was torpedoed, and the severity of his injuries, mainly burns, led to a six-month spell in Bath hospital, after which he was awarded several medals for bravery. Not only was he a war hero but he also had a talent for writing that may well have been passed on to Ian. He wrote plays and short stories[1].

Heroism seems to run in Ian's family on both parental lines. Doreen's grandfather, Thomas Mansfield, was in the Merchant Navy and was part of the Dardanelles campaign during the First World War. Hit by an explosion and buried in the sand, he was crippled for life and spent the rest of his days in a wheelchair. Returning home from the war with green outfits for everyone, he discovered that his wife, Doreen's mum's mother, had died suddenly (in her forties) during his absence. He concluded that green clothes brought bad luck and threw the outfits away, declaring that none of his kin would ever wear green again, a family tradition that continues to this day. He later moved in with Doreen's family at Barton Road in Stretford, their home before the move to Old Trafford in 1938–39. Although Doreen was only five when her granddad died, she remembers her mum telling her how he would sit the little girl on his knee and sing the famous Irish folk-song:

I'll tell my ma when I get home
The boys won't leave the girls alone
They pull my hair and they break my comb
I'll tell my ma when I get home

Despite – or perhaps because of – his disability, Doreen's grandfather Thomas campaigned for pensions and helped the poor receive benefits they might not otherwise have realised they were entitled to. He liked a bet and followed his dreams. Once he had a dream about peeling potatoes in the army and the next day bet on a horse called 'Spud Murphy' which won. Another time he dreamt he rode across a field of daffodils in his wheelchair but when he looked back they weren't crushed. He bet on 'False Alarm' the

---

[1] A short story by Kevin Curtis is re-produced as an appendix at the end of this book. It appears to be an autobiographical account of his war experience, with an interesting twist. Coincidentally, one of Kevin's fellow officers in the story is called Hooky!

next day and that won too. Kevin's father, grandfather Curtis, also served his country heroically and was wounded in the First World War whilst in the artillery.

Doreen's sister Barbara was born on Whit Sunday when Doreen was nearly 14. She recalls that at the age of five she had whooping cough and Kevin bought her a little toy horse. When Ian was born Barbara was only 12, more of an elder sister than an aunt, and because of this she became extremely devoted to him.

Kevin and Doreen Curtis had already moved out of Old Trafford to 26 Balmoral Crescent, in an overspill estate in Hurdsfield, Macclesfield, before their first baby arrived. However, in order not to lose her eligibility for a maternity bed at Basford House, Doreen and Kevin stayed for six weeks at her mother's house in Stamford Street for Ian's birth. It appears he had a sweet face when he was born, so much so that the midwife commented on it when she saw him. "He has musical hands," she said. "Long fingers. I'd like to meet him when he's 21."

Following his arrival they all settled in at Balmoral Crescent, a two-bedroomed house with a garden in the leafy suburbs. A traditional Cheshire market town on the borders of the Pennines, Macclesfield's industrial history was built largely on its silk mills. Traditionally working class – many three-storey weavers cottages remain to this day – its deprivations are somewhat exaggerated by its proximity to the wealth of Cheshire, with Prestbury lying two miles away and Alderley Edge five miles. Macclesfield had an air of respectability in the Seventies though, and it has now become more a suburb or commuter town of Manchester rather than a town in its own right. Kevin was able to catch the train from Macclesfield to Manchester – one of the perks of his job in the Transport Police was free train travel – or ride into work on his moped.

Auntie Ivy in Canvey Island fostered children and had acquired a very expensive pram from one of the children's well-to-do parents. Delivered to Manchester by train was a lovely new Marmet high pram which became Ian's carriage. Barbara remembers the pride she felt wheeling him about in it.

Another much loved Aunt was Auntie Nell, Kevin's sister, who had glamorous film star looks and three little dogs that resembled the Shih Tzu variety. "Ian had a pair of short red ladybird trousers," recalls Doreen. "He used to go to Nell's to stay the night and the dog used to swing on them. She had three dogs, Jasmin, Kylie and Tamboo. He loved them. He'd only be aged two or three. He loved animals. He brought a white mouse home one day to Balmoral Crescent. We got him a little cage for it. He had hamsters too, one of which was called Marmeduke."

There was also Felix the cat and Gulliver the Guinea-pig at Balmoral. Ian seemed drawn to all animals and would in time befriend a neighbour's sausage dog – a dachshund – when they lived in Macclesfield and walk it by the canal. The family eventually obtained from a dog's refuge a large Doberman they called Ricki which became Ian's companion to the end of his life.

When Ian was four, his sister Carole was born. Doreen gave Ian an engine as like most little boys he was mad on trains, and told him it was a gift from his new little sister. This may have influenced Ian's attitude towards his sister as he and Carole were always very close, rarely arguing or fighting in the way siblings so often do.

Aunt Barbara visited every weekend and during the school holidays, staying with the Curtis family wherever they were. The whole tribe would often spend weekends together at Stamford Street. "He loved that house at 156 Stamford Street," says Aunt Barbara. "It had a garden at the back and a cobbled street. When my dad was due back he'd say, 'Granddad will be here in a minute on his bike'. He'd run down to meet him and his granddad would put him on the bike and wheel him back up the path."

From the very beginning, Ian loved attending school. His first, from the age of four and a half to seven, was Trinity Square Infants, a church school in Macclesfield. The Victorian building, appropriately placed next to a church, is now demolished. "It needed knocking down," says Pete Johnson, who first met Ian when they were both four-and-a-half and became his closest childhood friend. "It was a really old building with outside lavatories – open to the elements, uncovered. It seemed great at the time. The school was attached to the church. Looking at the photographs, it's almost like looking at Victorian photographs because it was quite a poor area then, Macclesfield. Mention it now and everyone thinks of it as being upmarket but I remember it as being quite poor. It was a long time ago – 40 odd years but I was friends with Ian as early as that."

From there he went on to Hurdsfield County Primary and he attended Sunday School and was also a member of the Cubs group which was tied to the church. Later he was confirmed at the church with Pete Johnson, and a picture of his confirmation can be seen on the website of Joy Division Central.

As children, Pete and Ian used to write stories together and Ian's family have a book called *Who Zoo?* with a dedication at the front 'To: "HAMMY" From Pete "Captain Miracle".' Pete Johnson's title was taken from the

Marvel comics popular at the time and Ian's nickname probably originated from a schoolboy joke that he bore a resemblance to a hamster because of his chubby cheeks.

Pete was in the same class as Ian at Trinity Square Infant School. He lived in Hurdsfield, on Hurdsfield Road, and today describes Ian as "living on the estate", which he thought was really glamorous. From where he lived he could walk round to Balmoral Crescent to play with Ian. "We went up into the Hurdsfield school just as it was built," he says, "a brand, spanking new school which they've now knocked down again. They built another one on the other side."

For the first few years Ian and Pete were in different classes since the annual intake of pupils was sufficiently large to necessitate two for each year, but this never impacted on a friendship which remained strong throughout their time together at Hurdsfield and later at secondary school. While at the primary school they would play together most days after classes ended and also at weekends.

Looking back on that friendship at a distance of forty years, Pete retains a vivid impression of Ian's quality as a leader. "He was always a leader of everything but in a very quiet way, not in a dominating way."

"Things like… it must have been the time of the election – '64, I guess – and we had our own school election. They had mock elections and hustings and three or four candidates who would take part and then we'd vote for the candidates who had made up their own parties. Ian put himself forward as a candidate – he was the leader of the 'Curt-servative' party! No relation to Conservative – I've heard a lot of rubbish over the years about Ian's extreme right wing views. He never had any political views as far as I remember him. I became quite political later on in my teens, I joined the local Labour party and then a socialist, militant party. Ian never had any views about that at all. I never heard him express a political view in his life. The 'Curt-servative' party was a popular party – Ian was only eight at the time so it probably didn't have policies but it had his charisma."

Pete and Ian attended the same three schools all the way through to secondary school, King's Grammar, whereupon they were joined by a friend called Paul Heapy. Another close friend was Tony Nuttall, who lived in nearby Balmoral Crescent, although he was a bit younger than Ian. Tony's mum, Edna, was very friendly with Doreen, and Ian's dad regularly took Ian and Tony to the Speedway at Belle Vue where his hero was a rider called Ivan Maugers. Ian and Tony also liked to go caddying at Prestbury Golf Club and Carole recalls that they once found jobs on Bailey's milk farm, where they bottled milk, and that they also went round door to door delivering football coupons to those who did the pools. Pete did a Littlewoods pools round on the estate, so they may have had rival rounds though he never knew. Ian's mum recalls the names of two other boys with whom Ian was friendly: Alan Firkin and Harvey Potts. Pete remembers Harvey Potts and thinks that Ian's mother's recollection of the "three musketeers", as she called them, would be Ian, Harvey and himself at early junior school.

Ian was fascinated by history and loved to read history books. He liked to draw knights in armour and cowboys and Indians.[1] Like most little boys growing up in the Fifties he followed the adventures of Davy Crockett, the American frontiersman turned politician and hero of the Alamo, and knew its theme song: 'Davy, Davy Crockett, King of the Wild Frontier – Born on a mountain top in Tennessee, killed a bear when he was only three'. Predictably, therefore, Ian loved the Lone Ranger, the masked lawman with a secret identity who upheld justice on the wild frontier, and Tonto, his man-of-few-words Red Indian sidekick. As a teenager he developed an all consuming interest in Richard the Lionheart, the Knights Templar and the Crusades.

"He always loved castles, Ian," says his sister Carole.

Doreen: "Yes he loved them. He used to go to the top of Conway Castle. We used to go to London for the day a lot."

Carole: "We used to go round the museums, the history museum. He liked anything to do with history. In these books they try to imply he's a Nazi[2] but he never showed any interest in Germany apart from a historic point of view. He wasn't even particularly interested in the Second World War. He loved the knights, King Arthur."

Barbara: "He had his sword and shield and he drew pictures of the knights."

Doreen: "I used to joke with him that he'd been a knight in the past… laughing with him. He thought he had been. He was really obsessed with it."

Barbara: "He went on a trip with Nell with her husband Ray's school.[3] They went to some castle and she said he was saying 'I know there's a

---

[1] See Ian's sketch of two Davy Crockett characters in their racoon hats with a cowboy and Indian.

[2] Carole is referring to erroneous suggestions in books and magazine articles that the Nazi connotations of the name Joy Division implied that the members of the band had Nazi sympathies.

[3] Ian's Aunt Nell's husband Ray was a senior master at Ancoats.

passage up there and over that way'. It was as though he knew his way around. She thought he must have been there before."

"He had a passion for a while on chivalry and heraldry," says Pete Johnson. "He'd read up all about Richard the Lionheart. He'd be absolutely fascinated and would go on for hours. He was very proud of the fact – whether it's true or not – that Curtis came from the chivalric word for courteous. That was what he said. And he *was* always courteous – likeable, friendly, open. No one ever had a bad word for him.

"When we were at Hurdsfield we had schools – or teams. They were based on castles and named after the roads around the school. There was Ludlow, Carisbrook, Arundel and Conway, I think. They mixed these teams across the classes so we'd all each belong to one of these. I was Carisbrook, I can't remember what Ian was. But I remember one time they organised a coach trip where we would go and visit all the castles. It took about a week. Arundel is in West Sussex, Carisbrook is in the Isle of Wight – we went all around staying in youth hostels. So it was Ian and I again. He had a real interest in history and would do his own reading. He wouldn't just do what was expected in class, he would find his own bits – like the chivalry thing, he'd get his own book and read up on it and enthuse as well. He was great at enthusing other people."

Whilst Ian's love of history was, perhaps, unusual in a boy so young, there was one particular childhood activity he shied away from that is a highlight of the year for most young children – Guy Fawke's Night.

Doreen: "He didn't like fireworks. He didn't like the bangs. And if he had a sparkler we used to have to tie it on a big stick for him."

Barbara: "Yes, so it'd be miles away... like the length of a broomstick."

Doreen: "When we had the bonfires at Macclesfield we couldn't get him out of the house to go with the other kids."

Barbara: "He looked through the window."

Doreen: "I wondered if it was because when I was expecting him we went to Nell's to a party and I sat on a balloon and burst it. I often wonder if it was because of that. I don't think he'd have liked to have gone to war."

Although Ian has been portrayed as a Manchester City fan, his family cast doubts on this. "I wouldn't have put him down as a City fan," said Carole. "I was – I even hoped I might be the next Mrs Colin Bell when I was 14! I'd have known if Ian was. As a young boy he was more of a United fan. He got their programmes. Debbie[1] says he was a City fan but she's got a picture

---

[1] Debbie Curtis, Ian's widow.

of him in her book wearing a United top. We've got an autograph book with Matt Busby and George Best and the rest of United – my dad got it for Ian when the United team were on one of his trains. He would have watched City and United and enjoyed both."

Doreen: "We saw Ian and his dad in the crowd of a United game once on TV. I could tell it was Kevin because he had a white mac on."

Around the time Ian passed his examination for King's School the family moved to a brand new first floor flat at 11 Park View. Although they lost their garden, they gained an all-important third bedroom. The block of flats, opposite Victoria Park and the High School, is now demolished, the site remaining at the rear of Arigi's, the furniture department store. Carole was seven or eight at the time of the move.

Carole: "He had posters on the wall of his bedroom at the flat. He had a Jimi Hendrix one and a picture of a toreador that my Auntie Nell had brought back from Spain."

Doreen: "One of those Spanish matadors. She wrote a book about them and I typed it. He didn't go to Spain. He didn't like to fly."

Weekends were mostly spent with the extended family. "We always went to Old Trafford to my nana's," says Carole. "We used to stay over a lot, when we were kids. We had a great time, making our own fun, exploring and going to the park, playing tennis. We used to pretend there was a witch called Zelda that lived in the middle room and Ian and I would write letters to her and post them behind the large marble fire place."

Ian and his friends often played by the Huddersfield canal. He liked fishing, and the family would occasionally go there for a picnic. On one visit to the canal Carole, who was then about eight or nine, fell in, an incident recalled by the family in some detail, not least because it occurred the same day that her Aunt Barbara brought her new beau, soon to become her fiancé, home to meet the family.

As well as speedway, Ian liked to watch the wrestling on ITV on Saturday afternoons, an hour's worth of good-natured rough-and-tumble which more perceptive eyes could see was played more for laughs and drama than as a serious competitive sport. Ian enjoyed the fun, and was always looking out for his hero Mick McManus.

Doreen: "He was always happy and bubbly. He liked to have a laugh and was full of jokes."

Carole: "He used to like all the joke shops."

Doreen: "He liked that fella…"

Carole: "Freddie 'Parrot Face' Junior."

The slapstick comedian Freddie 'Parrot Face' Davis sported a trademark bowler hat pulled down over his ears and his catchphrase, said with a lisp, was, "I'm sick, sick, sick up to here."

Carole: "He'd say 'I tort I taw a pussy cat'. Ian used to take him off."

Doreen: "That was his party piece. He used to stand against the wall and pull a bowler hat down over his head and make his hat bob up and down."

Carole: "At these Christmas parties he was always up on stage doing his Lonnie Donegan impersonations – 'My old man's a dustman'."

Ian was among the first generation of British children to grow up with a television set in the home, and probably took it for granted, unlike previous generations. His mother and father had a TV when they lived at Stafford Street and brought it with them to Balmoral Crescent, which was quite unusual in the early Fifties.

Doreen can recall Ian watching the *Tonight* show presented by Cliff Michelmore, a BBC news programme that went out in the early evening five nights a week and ran for eight years from 1957. Despite being rather young to be interested in the news Ian loved the theme music, a brief but sprightly orchestral fanfare. Whenever it came on Ian would shout out to his mother to come and watch 'Mr Da Da', his name for the bespectacled Mitchelmore, based on the 'da da' sound of the music.

Dr Who was also a must-see. Ian once told his impressionable younger sister that the Daleks had taken over Macclesfield Town Hall. Later, the anarchic cult comedy *Monty Python's Flying Circus* was another favourite.

Though they were unusually amicable towards one another for young siblings, there were ways in which Ian and Carole were notably different. "Carole was very independent," says Doreen. "Ian was a bit softer when he was younger. She would dress herself when she was young and do more things. I'd do more for Ian. They always got on well. No jealousy."

Carole: "I was always the noisy one in the early teenage years, loud in general with lots of friends. Kids that hang about in the streets, in the park, I was one of them, just a fiesty kid really. We didn't do horrible things. Ian was quiet. Music-wise we had nothing in common whatsoever. When we went to see them at the Apollo [in 1979] – Ian had got us free passes for the Sunday, they did two nights there – me and my friend Gail went, we were all excited. Then we started wondering if we'd get last orders in after listening to this racket. That's sacrilege really isn't it? But it just wasn't our music at all. We weren't into that. At that age we were into Seventies disco music. The punk era passed us by."

Despite the free rail travel they enjoyed, the family did own a car, albeit briefly. "When Nell went to Tenerife and sold up we bought her car off her," says Doreen. "It got set on fire in a garage. I came home from work one day and saw the fire engines. We'd put the car up for sale because Kevin had got one from Ladbrokes. A chap had been up to look at it. Some kids set fire to it so we never got a thing for it. Brian (Barbara's husband) had put a radio in it and it had new tyres as well."

Holidays were spent at Canvey Island but as Ian grew older the family ventured abroad. One of their happiest trips was a visit to Switzerland, where they stayed in a town called Davros. Ian's Auntie Barbara joined the four of them and remembers saving up for the special journey.

Doreen: "We went to Canvey Island a lot. We got free passes on the train. First class… we always went first class. With him (Kevin) being an Inspector. We got so much off for abroad as well. We went to Austria and Switzerland travelling by night. We got off at Basle station for breakfast. We went to Lichenstein, the little principality between Austria and Switzerland. It had a castle and a count."

Barbara can remember other trips, including visits to Wales where her husband Brian would ply his trade as a church organ builder. "He used to go and tune the organs for the churches," she explains. "[They were] the pipe organs that his company had put in, or he'd renew them. Sometimes, when Brian had the south Wales round, Ian would go with him for the weekend. Ian would hold the notes for Brian while he did the tuning. He liked playing the organ. They had good fun, staying in B&Bs for the night or there was one occasion on a trip to Porthcawl when I went too and all the hotels were fully booked – something was going on – and we ended up sleeping in the car for the night. Ian thought that was great. He was spread on the back seat with his big jacket over him."

Ian's fascination with history and history books ran over to theology and divinity. Auntie Nell used to joke that Ian would go for the cloth. Doreen, however, thought Ian would more likely become a lawyer or a history teacher.

Carole: "Nothing would surprise you with Ian. You expected the unexpected with him, I think. Whatever he did, you'd just think, well that's our Ian. When he started off with his music it was of no surprise to anybody."

"He was very polite," adds Carole of her younger brother.

Doreen: "Very loving. Very thoughtful."

Aunt Barbara: "For a lad he was very thoughtful."

Carole: "And he was very different. It's hard to describe him to someone. We just accepted him for what he was."

Doreen: "He was kind of way ahead. He loved the family but he was different. When he was on the phone he'd be back and forth, back and forth talking to somebody. He'd walk up and down in his bedroom. He was very tidy but he'd be back and forth."

Barbara: "He wouldn't stand still the way we'd stand still. He was always walking. He'd do it in his nana's front room – pacing."

Carole: "He was just different. It's really hard to explain. Whatever he said he'd do, he'd do. If he'd have said he was going to be an actor he would have been an actor. He would have definitely have made his mark at whatever he was going to do. I always knew that he'd be talked about."

CHAPTER TWO

I Was Looking For A Friend

"These are your friends from childhood, through youth..." – Ian Curtis

In 1966, when Ian was 11, he and his friend Pete Johnson transferred from co-educational Hurdsfield to boys-only King's School in Cumberland Street, Macclesfield, a big transition for them both. "Hurdsfield School was really friendly, with small classes but King's was a brutalising environment where you lost your first name," says Pete. "There was a high level of physical brutality at King's – a lot of beatings went on for very minor things."

Ian and Pete both passed the entrance examination and ended up in the same class at King's, where only a minority of pupils received the scholarships that Ian and Pete managed to attain. The majority of the boys there came up through fee-paying preparatory schools, a situation that soon caused Pete to realise that, economically, his family was relatively poor. This had never occurred to him before going to King's, where most of his fellow-pupils seemed to him to come from rich and privileged backgrounds, at least by his standards. In reality they were probably simply from aspiring middle-class families, but it was also disconcerting for them that most of the pupils Ian and Pete studied alongside had already spent two years learning languages, Latin and French, and were already familiar with the teachers. Ian and Pete both went from being the top of their classes at Hurdsfield to being at the bottom at King's.

"All the people who came from external schools ended up sitting at the back, playing games," says Pete. "The boys from the preparatory school knew each other and dominated the front of the class and the teachers seemed to pay more attention to them than the pupils at the back, with no-one evidently picking up on the fact that these children, who presumably did well at their previous schools, were suddenly completely failing or just disengaged.

"I remember feeling really angry, I think more than Ian did, at all these rich kids, spoilt people; envious really... and also angry that I was feeling inferior or dirty or scruffy... that I wasn't good enough. And also feeling very scared. Eventually we got through that but it was quite brutalising. Ian was quite good at managing all that in some ways. And in some ways he would just sit at the back with me. He was always very bright. I used to copy things from him in class. He was always so quick on the uptake. He was intellectually very sharp.

"Then there was the gender thing. Just at the time when you are becoming interested in the opposite sex you are locked into seven years with boys and male teachers. The only woman teacher we had to call 'Sir'! You had to – is it any surprise we were all screwed up really?

"I remember that being a very sad time, leaving Hurdsfield and going to this big place. Not many of us got through to King's from there. The others either went to the Central School – which was seen as the pits – and Broken Cross that was somewhere in between."

Coming from a similar background and being simultaneously thrown into the new environment at King's certainly brought Ian and Pete closer together. "We knew each other in this class when no-one else did," says Pete. "We walked home together for the first bit of the journey before we went off [on our separate ways]. I think Ian got through that period better than I did. He made new friends and then he started the football team."

Ian played rugby at King's School – "He didn't like it though. It was rough, rugby," says Doreen Curtis – but was far more interested in football.

"Throughout school and then later on we had a football team that Ian set up," says Pete Johnson. "He was the captain. His ambition was to try to get us into a local football league. This was a 13-year-old boy, we didn't have a kit, we didn't have a pitch and he nearly got us in. He got 11 people together and would push us all to be doing that kind of thing. He had tremendous enthusiasm... putting the players together, hiring a pitch, hiring a strip. I ran up a programme on an old portable keyboard. He was doing all the work and was clearly the captain and well respected."

"There were three of us – me and Ian and Paul Heapy," remembers Pete. "Paul was also in our class at King's. The three of us were friends for quite a while. We'd do spoof Superman comic hero things. We all had characters. Ian was Hammy, partly because of the fat cheeks he had at the time. I was Captain Miracle. We wrote these stories that were just packed full of puns. There was one about a ballet dancer called 'Maggot Fountain' [based after Margot Fontaine who was the most famous ballerina of the era]. We had to rescue her – using lots of puns on the way, and we'd always win through because we were super-heroes. Hammy was the only one that could be a superstar as himself (as he was, of course!). We each contributed these stories and shared them with the other.

"He was always doing a whole range of things. I knew his Macclesfield side but he also had a strong Manchester side. He was mad on the Belle Vue Aces Speedway [motorbikes and scrambling]. A real Ivan Mauger fan. Being Ian he organised a speedway on bicycles for us. There was a bit on Hurdsfield Estate which had a kind of *cul de sac* and a circular track and he organised a whole meet! Everyone had their bikes and Ian would give them points. He was just brilliant."

Up to the age of 12, Ian had shown little more than a passing interest in pop music but in view of his ever-widening interests they weren't that surprised when, inspired by the prospect of winning a competition on TV, he started up a band.

"When we were about 12 there was a television competition," says Pete. "It was a TV show where they had auditions for young bands. Ian wrote in and said he'd like us to be on this show. We didn't really have a band. Well, there was a band, there were four of us and we were called Treacle Teapot. The four members were Ian and I, Alan Firkin and I think Steve Moss was the other one. We only had two instruments. There was an old upright piano at my house and Ian had a little ukulele– a cheap £5 imitation guitar type thing. The others didn't have anything at all so we had makeshift drums and things. We sat around plinking away. I don't know if we had a singer but Ian was the leader of it all. He never said, 'I'm the leader of it'… it's just that he had initiative – he organised it, he had drive and he could see where he wanted to be.

"I was dreading the TV coming back and telling us we might be on the show next week. We had half of one song, which was the chorus. It was called 'Four Days To Go'. I think it had three chords. I thought Treacle Teapot was quite a cool name… that was the best thing we had going for us."

Ian's sister remembers a group that would have been a later incarnation than this one. "Tony Nuttall played drums," says Carole. "Ian had a mouth organ, a harmonica – that was his first instrument and a Jews harp. He had a guitar but you never saw him learn to play it."

Ian's growing interest in music was matched by his love of drama and he took part in plays at King's. He even attended a week-long drama course in Anglesey, and at its close all the family, including Auntie Barbara, went to see him perform in the play, although they don't recall what it was.

Ian and Pete appeared in the school plays together, as well as productions by a local amateur dramatic society. In one play at King's they both played Scottish prostitutes, no girls being available for such roles at this single-sex school. The play, set in Edinburgh, was about Burke and Hare, the notorious body snatchers, and the doctor John Knox. It featured medical students who would pay body snatchers to dig up freshly buried corpses on which to practise their medical skills.

"I don't think they were very big parts," says Pete. "The body snatchers ran out of freshly interred bodies and so they actually killed people. The prostitutes were the victims – or at least Ian was."

Pete recalls that his character was more cautious and told his fellow prostitute [Ian] not to go with these people. Ian was therefore murdered but Pete's character, more timid and less trusting, managed to escape. Perhaps the experience explains why Ian wasn't in as many plays as Pete, who stuck with it and went on to appear in productions all the way through school.

Pete and Ian went to Anglesey to *HMS Conway* for a week's residential drama course when they were 15. He's forgotten the plays but remembers the experiences they shared during that week. "It was a training facility for the Navy but actually on land, not on board ship… a rough and ready building. Loads of children went but there were only two from King's at any one time so me and Ian went. You'd have fencing lessons [in relation to stage fencing], and drama lessons generally and choreography. It culminated in a play that was staged on the final night."

Pete doesn't recall spending much time with Tony Nuttall, Ian's friend from Balmoral Crescent. "Ian kept us separate really," he replied. "He kept separate friendships. Tony was quite a bit younger and he went to another school. It was like a different set of friends that Ian compartmentalised. I think I felt a bit jealous about Tony because I probably wanted to be Ian's only best friend but he obviously had two best friends for different occasions. Tony was more with the Manchester side of Ian's life. They went to speedway and so on. It didn't really work: I know one time when Ian and I and Paul Heapy were out and Tony came along and, well, I didn't get on with Tony really. It just never really worked so it was probably quite right to keep us separate. I could never see Tony joining in with some of the things

I liked to do with Ian – such as writing scripts and stories and things. Ian liked doing lots of different things – maybe that's why Ian kept us separate."

Pete agrees that to some extent he might have been Ian's intellectual sparring partner, a co-author and inspiration for words. Nevertheless, most of Pete's memories of Ian seem to be from playing outside – cricket during summer months in the park, football in winter. He does recall a Saturday job that the threesome shared for a time: "I got a holiday/Saturday job at Fine Fare Supermarket in Macclesfield, and persuaded Ian and Paul to work there as well. I remember one time when we got called into the office, after we'd been to the pub at lunchtime, and told not to do it again. We were called into the office a week later for the same offence, even though we hadn't been drinking on this occasion – clearly we were having too good a time."

Pete never witnessed Ian losing his temper. "Ian was only ever angry with me once. I sent him a death threat. This was at Hurdsfield so I must have been about 10 or 11 and my mother had this old manual typewriter. I thought it would be a really good joke to do a kind of spoof death threat to Ian, which I did, saying something like 'Unless you do such and such you will be... whatever'. I put it through his letter box anonymously and I imagined him opening it up and thinking, 'Oh this is interesting, I wonder who this is from?' [Of] course his dad was a copper and took this very seriously. I'd almost expected him to come into school and say, 'Guess what happened over the weekend?' but actually what he did say was that his dad was really upset about this letter. So I told him that I'd done it – thinking he'd be laughing but he was clearly a bit unhappy about it. It didn't last long though. Perhaps I'd done it too well."

Like most schools of its type there were regular outbreaks of bullying at King's, and Ian was not immune though he developed his own effective way of dealing with it. Pete: "There was one lunch time when we were playing football at school. Boys grow up at different stages and the ones that spurt up two foot higher than the others tend to bully the smaller or younger ones. There was one real thug in our age group. He came up to us when Ian was playing football with me and he just punched Ian in the face very hard.[1]

"Ian's response to this was... he said, 'Oh thanks a lot Dave, that tooth was a bit loose anyway and it needed to be coming out'. He said it in a way that wasn't sarcastic and it wasn't kind of riling – it was almost as if it was quite genuine. I guess that was part of his way of getting away from conflict

---

[1] Asked the reason for this, Pete replied: "Just 'cos he could."

– just by accepting it. He didn't rise to the bait but also he didn't craven and try and get out of the way either.

"There were times when we were walking in the street and young males would pick on you but Ian would just walk on and just ignore it."

Unlike Ian, Pete was in the choir at Hurdsfield Church, but like most boys in their early teenage years playing football with Ian was far more fun. Pete now assumes that he took confirmation simply because he was in the choir and it was expected of choristers to do so, and now thinks that it was he who might have persuaded Ian to do the same. As far as he is aware, Ian never went to church before or since. Both lads had to endure six sessions of preparation beforehand, ostensibly learning about what it meant to be confirmed. This relatively rigorous training might have stood Ian in good stead when he subsequently applied to join the Civil Service.

Pete: "I remember the choirmaster telling us that when he was confirmed the bishop put his hand on his head and he could feel this tingle going right through him. I remember being a bit disappointed because I didn't feel this tingle. I don't know whether Ian did. We were all dressed up and the girls wore these remarkable shrouds… really weird."

Fuelled by his awareness of the economic divide between himself and Ian, and the other boys in their classes at King's, Pete would became attracted to socialism and revolutionary theory later in life. Ian, however, seems to have been less traumatised by the class divide than his best friend, and showed no particular interest in left-wing politics. He didn't see its relevance to his own life and, in any case, had a whole range of other interests.

"I did continue to hang around extreme left-leaning groups for a while, but I think meeting in the pub was probably the main motivating factor for me. Ian never had any views about that at all. I never heard him express a political view in his life. I was put off the LPYS when I went to university – they were dominated by ex-public school types going on about the working classes."

Ian's lack of political motivation might explain why the pair began to drift apart in their mid-teens. By then Pete had realised that the only way out of his situation, and the only way out of Macclesfield, was to go to university. As the boys grew older, the corporal punishment at King's declined and the class divide levelled out somewhat; hence Pete was able to concentrate more on his studies, the prerequisite to a college education. Ian, on the other hand, was less inclined towards academic ambition and had begun to enjoy himself socially. He had started to seek out female company and was among the first in his class to have a steady girlfriend. Simultaneously, he began to take a greater interest in music and the arts in general.

Pete is inclined to think that Ian's nature made him more attractive to girls than most other boys. "I think he probably was. I don't know. He was interesting and confident and did things that I couldn't imagine doing. Like... he entered a junior talent contest in Manchester as a stand-up comedian when he was about 13.[1] I was full of admiration for him. I think he did quite well. It was only some junior talent competition somewhere, but still really impressive. It was a great upbringing."

Nonetheless, Ian began to turn more and more towards music.

"After Treacle Teapot Ian got a lot more interested in music," says Pete, "so we were in half-formed bands and you'd end up at someone's house. I can't remember if Ian had a bass guitar or not. I got an electric guitar – I think Ian did as well. My brother was older than me and he was a music fanatic, he built his own soundproof booth in the attic. I don't think we had an amplifier between us. We'd go round people's houses with our guitars and make a bit of a noise but we never really knew what we were doing. Ian had a friend who lived in Prestbury who also had a guitar and we'd go round and play a few chords and mess about. Then we would wander around Prestbury in a desultory way trying to get a packet of crisps from a posh restaurant."

Though Ian's pre-occupation with music while Pete concentrated on his studies caused them to eventually drift apart, the pair still remained on good terms.

"The final bit of us coming back together was probably when we about about 16 or 17," says Pete. "This would be early sixth form. I think Ian started off here and started 'A' levels but didn't last long. There were a few of us there who, by that stage, were a bit like the 'in crowd', Ian, Oliver Cleaver and a few others and myself. This group also included Kelvin Briggs, or 'Bessie' as he was known at the time, who was in our first year class at King's, having been in the Junior School, and Ian and I got to know him better later on, as a member of the circle including Oliver Cleaver, and a few others. Kelvin was fun, and open to experience, but was essentially decent and principled – a good choice for best man. We were into Lou Reed and Bowie and all that kind of gender interesting stuff. That was quite a good time. I remember feeling that things were improving now generally – we had more freedom, we'd go drinking in the park with a bottle of vodka. Then we'd start playing bowls and everyone else would go off because we were a bit too boisterous."

★   ★   ★

[1] This may well have been his Freddie 'Parrot Face' Davis impersonation.

It was around this time that there occurred a drug-related incident, which Pete remembers well. "Ian and another boy had been out – there weren't many drugs around in those days, certainly where we were – [and] those two had been sniffing dry cleaning fluid and taking pills. It scared the life out of me. I was unsettled by it. I think they just did it for fun. Ian and I were both in detention one night when Ian started to drop off from the effects of the pills he'd taken. He hadn't known what they were and ending up having to have his stomach pumped."

Tellingly, Ian was suspended after this incident while the other boy was not. "He was well off and his father was a headmaster," says Pete. "He was given psychiatric counselling and given a chance."

Pete is convinced that the different treatment meted out to the two boys was due entirely to their differing backgrounds, as opposed to the fact that one boy might have said he'd taken an overdose while the other said it was just for fun. "It was a class thing," he says. "He was very bright and ended up getting three 'A's and is now a media consultant."

Soon after that Ian more or less disappeared from Pete's life, although on the odd occasions when they did come across one another they always got on well.

"He was always incredibly polite. He'd be talking about music and I'd have no idea about it. Our musical interests diverged – I was into Frank Zappa and jazz by then. I liked Soft Machine and Yes and a lot of prog rock. Ian was more interested in rawness – such as Iggy Pop. We'd always talk music and I was aware that I was letting him down because I wasn't aware of the people he talked about. He was always polite and never dismissive though. I felt his views carried more weight than mine – because he was Ian!"

Long after their relationship had faded it came as something of a shock to Pete to learn about Ian's starring role in Joy Division. "I was really surprised later on – I'd heard of Joy Division and their music before I knew that Ian was in the band," he says. "It was only when someone said 'That's Ian Curtis…' I never knew that was the way he was going to be going. I was knocked out that Ian could do that and very proud of him. But I had no idea and wouldn't have recognised it from hearing him singing. It was almost like that was another bit of Ian entirely that I had yet to know."

Pete did maintain his own interest in music after school, but it was a far cry from the world of intense introspection that Joy Division would eventually inhabit. He played CIU clubs with a covers band, performing songs by Gary Numan. Tamla Motown groups and The Beatles. "Gary Numan didn't go down too well," he recalls. "They said, 'Why do you play that zoomy music?'"

Pete hasn't been able to listen to Joy Division since Ian's death despite enjoying it while the group was active. Although he never got on with punk, he found Joy Division "very musical".

He isn't in contact nowadays with anyone who knew Ian. He had one conversation with Paul Heapy, coincidentally about a month after Ian died. "He burst into tears when I told him. I asked him if he was ringing about Ian and he obviously hadn't heard. Then I left the area and lost touch with everyone. Part of the difficult thing was that everyone else had some kind of a view on it [why he'd committed suicide]. I remember not telling people that I knew him. Someone said that he'd hanged himself on a lamppost like Mussolini and all this stuff about the group being extreme right-wing."

And Pete Johnson scoffs at that, as does everyone who knew the real Ian Curtis. "One of the things about Ian was that you could not have predicted fame early one, simply because he seemed so balanced," he adds of the best friend he had as a child.

CHAPTER 3

I Remember When We Were Young

"It was a good time to be 16 and 17," – Pete Johnson

In the present era of PlayStations, extreme sports and 100-plus cable TV channels vying for the attention of teenagers, pop music has become just one of many potential distractions, but in the early Seventies, when Ian Curtis was beginning to look around and see what was out there, pop music held a fascination that was uniquely captivating, especially those performers who were pushing at the boundaries, leaving the Sixties behind them in a quest for something new. At the head of this pack was David Bowie.

"Ian was mad on David Bowie," says Doreen. "He had his hair cut the same. Spiked up on top and longer at the side. Nell took him to Vidal Sassoon. He got some awful red satin trousers. I remember thinking 'Oh my God!'"

Carole: "I borrowed them once and some of our Ian's silver platform boots for a play at school when I was going to be Gary Glitter. And I went to see David Cassidy in Ian's black jeans with studs on the back – because David Cassidy had a pair like that. Ian lent me them. I must have been skinny then… blimey."

Doreen: "She had a crush on David Cassidy."

Carole: "Ian used to wear my fun fur jacket in the glam rock days. He had blue eye shadow in the drawer and Miners black nail polish. He only messed about with make up – he wouldn't sit round the house with make-up on or even particularly go out. I think it was just an experiment, bit of a laugh really."

Ian's parents may not have been altogether thrilled with their son's interest in the glittery end of the rock spectrum, but they wisely took the view that an overt critical reaction would only serve to make their son dig in his heels even deeper.

Doreen: "Kevin said to me 'Leave him, the phase will pass. The more you get on to them, the worse they are.'"

"It was a good time to be 16 and 17," says Pete Johnson, "[what with] the music that was around and the glam rock generally. We all played with it a bit. Ian did enjoy that side of it. He was always a bit more fashion conscious than most people. He'd wear these kind of two-tone trousers, kind of purply-green. He was always interested in that kind of stuff but he was never vain, never posing in these clothes. He was never really bothered what people thought of him. One of his personas was to play a bit stupid. He'd make out he was a bit thicker than he was. And he would take pleasure in people responding to him like that."

Fashion or no fashion, to attempt any level of androgyny on the streets of Macclesfield in 1972 would have been bound to attract attention from the less liberal members of the community. Glam rock was something that had started to happen in the music papers and then on *Top Of The Pops*. It could be found in small club enclaves in most of the cities of Britain, but it wasn't something that was particularly easy to take out onto the provincial streets.

Ian was apparently wearing Carole's fun fair jacket when he was first spotted by Deborah Woodruff, at the time the girlfriend of Ian's close friend, Tony Nuttall. He must have made an extraordinary sight. Though Liverpool born, Deborah had also grown up in Macclesfield and got to know Ian through hanging out at his Victoria Park home whilst dating Tony.

Ian's Bowie fixation reached a new level during 1972, as Bowie's Ziggy Stardust Tour passed through Manchester's Hardrock venue on no less than four occasions. The Hardrock was a purpose built venue, now a B&Q, in Stretford. A soulless, modern monstrosity, originally intended to provide scampi-in-a-basket disco evenings for the large local housing estates, almost by accident it found itself hosting some of the most legendary gigs in early Seventies Manchester. These included Chuck Berry, Roxy Music, Cockney Rebel/Be Bop Deluxe – also attended by Ian – and, most famously of all, Ziggy Stardust, which had a profound effect on the city. Many of the young punks of the 1977 would come to cite one of these Ziggy gigs as their initial tasting of rock's extraordinary power.

In September, the awestruck Curtis even managed to push through to the dressing room and, despite failing to catch a word with the man himself, passed sheets of paper around which were autographed by various members of The Spiders From Mars, Bowie's backing band.

Ziggy Stardust returned to Manchester at the close of December 1972 for two gigs, both of which Ian attended, the second of which accompanied by Deborah. This night was, in fact, their first date – Ian was 16 and Debbie was 15. The Ziggy show was a powerful, sexual, vivacious performance that would later be regarded as one of the pivotal moments of rock history. Whether planned or by chance, it was quite an occasion for a first date.

This particular tour hurtled David Bowie into orbit as rock's newest and most colourful superstar, simultaneously rendering much of the established rock world of the early Seventies dour by comparison. It certainly had a profound effect on Ian, whose love of Bowie would never wane even if, during the years ahead, his attention was seized by numerous other seismic cultural explosions. One, which occurred almost simultaneously was the feature film *Cabaret*, and Debbie would later tell the writer Jon Savage that, when she started to see Ian, they saw the film "a dozen times".

This certainly hints at some kind of obsession, although it was the kind of film that encouraged multi-viewing. *Cabaret*'s stylish romanticising of the seedy glamour and anti-Nazi satire in the Kit-Kat Club, a downbeat Thirties Berlin night-spot, became intrinsically linked with the unfolding glam and Bowie scene. The unforgettable hi-camp routines of Joel Grey and Liza Minnelli immediately struck a chord with the new breed of Bowie fans. Intriguingly, both David Bowie and Iggy Pop would later cite the film as a major influence in bringing a Germanic influence to their *Low* and *Idiot* periods which, in turn, would heavily influence the embryonic lyricism of Ian Curtis.

In 1973 the Curtis family moved from Macclesfield to New Moston. Auntie Nell lived just around the corner and knew a family who wanted to sell a house there. Debbie sent some flowers for Doreen when the move took place.

Although a very bright student, with nine 'O' levels at King's to his credit, Ian was becoming disenchanted with academic life. He did consider taking 'A' levels in his favourite subjects, History and Divinity, but seems to have abandoned the idea before he'd hardly started. "We always thought he'd go to university but he wanted to work. I thought he would have made a good lawyer," says Doreen. So he got a job – after fairly rigorous interviews – working for the civil service. No sooner had this house move taken place than Ian was posted to Woodford, which was some distance away. He had to take a bus into Piccadilly Station (or London Road as it was sometimes called), followed by a train out to Cheadle, or somewhere near there, and then another bus. This was expensive, arduous and time consuming.

"As we got older most of Ian's weekends were spent with Debbie, usually at our house in Manchester," says Carole. "Surprisingly to us, Debbie wrote that her mum never liked Ian, which would account for the fact that they were always at ours. They'd spend their time in his room, listening to music or getting ready to go into town. I was always left with the impression that it was Debbie pulling the strings in that relationship. She was really shy but she used to nudge him to give him instructions – such as to go and sit in the other room. They were just young kids."

They would all have tea together and there was never any friction although Kevin did once suggest that Ian should think about his mother more because, as well as working full-time she was taking care of the meals and cleaning for everyone. He was worried she was being run ragged and thought the pair might give her a break for once and have tea at Debbie's parents. Notwithstanding, the couple would spend hours in Ian's downstairs room, which had been made into a kind of bed-sitter with a writing bureau and a radiogram on which Ian would play his beloved records.

"As well as David Bowie he liked Lou Reed," said Carole. "He had a green Lou Reed tee-shirt – my friend Vivien asked him if she could have it when he'd finished with it. He liked Andy Warhol – he had a picture of him on his wall. And Jimi Hendrix – he liked him and had a picture of him as well. I seem to remember he liked Mick Jagger and The Rolling Stones – he had that album with the lips and the tongue. I think he liked Rod Stewart or The Faces as it was then."

In terms of age and cultural awareness, Ian Curtis was perfectly placed to welcome the new Lou Reed into his vision. As such, on September 27, 1973, he took Debbie to her second gig: the Liverpool Empire date of Reed's highly controversial Rock'n'Roll Animal Tour. The controversy lay with Reed's reworking of favourite old Velvet Underground songs, such as 'Heroin', 'Sweet Jane' and 'White-Light – White Heat'. The bleached-haired, glammed–up Reed could now be seen fronting a large scale tradi-tional rock band with the Detroit guitars of Steve Hunter and Dick Wagner drafted in from Alice Cooper's band. Not everyone enjoyed this new rock sounding Reed. Bowie fans drawn to Reed via Bowie's production of

Reed's *Transformer* album felt let down by the solid rock sound. Equally unhappy, perhaps, were the ageing Velvet Underground fans who saw the transition as little short of sacrilege.

Mick Middles recalls reminiscing with Ian Curtis about the Lou Reed gig, in Portland Bars, Manchester, in 1978. "The memory of this conversation is vivid because I told Ian about the legendary Lou Reed gig at Manchester's Free Trade Hall, which was actually part of the Sally Can't Dance Tour," he says. "Ian fell absolutely spellbound as I informed him of the infamous riot which ensued following the gig's conclusion. Elements of the crowd, unhappy with Reed's refusal to appear for the encore, attempted to storm the stage and grasp the equipment. By contrast, Ian stated that the Liverpool Empire gig, despite the controversy, had seemed rather tame and he wished he'd been to the Free Trade Hall. Nevertheless, he still claimed it to have been one of the finest gigs he had seen."

Ian lived at New Moston for two or three years but only worked at Woodford for about one of those. This same house was also where Ian lived for the last two weeks of his life. He wrote a letter at that time describing the garden and their dog Ricki, a Manchester terrier (a miniature mongrel that looks like a Doberman). It had been Carole who had longed for a dog and got her wish when the family finally moved to a house with a large garden.

Ian worked at Rare Records after leaving Woodford and while he was living in this house, a form of employment that provided him with a further excuse, if one was needed, to continue to develop his musical knowledge. Even for his interview he apparently spent time scouring the music press, honing his knowledge of the bands of the day. The job was as sales assistant at Rare Records, but there is some debate about the location of the store. Some clearly recall the site to have been on John Dalton Street, latterly the site of The Romans Italian restaurant. However, others remember Rare Records was situated on a corner of King Street West (in between Deansgate and Butter Lane). Nonetheless, it was a curiously misnamed shop because, in the subterranean 'pop department', there didn't appear too many records that might be considered rare.

Mark Reeder, a regular visitor to the store, recalls its unusual appeal. "Rare Records was dingy and gloomy and you went downstairs and sat in telephone boxes where you listened to records. They (the records) were just hard to get. Lots of back catalogue but the really, really rare records you could never find."

That stated, a lovely old-fashioned ambience was maintained at all times. Ian was quite correct to pore over the music press prior to his interview, as

Rare Records was staffed by quietly helpful, ferociously knowledgeable, mostly long-haired men who would always be found perusing *Melody Maker*, the most musicianly of all the music papers, on the counter. As such, Rare Records became one of the essential ports of call for any young Mancunian seeking to blow a chunk of their wage on any album of the moment. Recalling shops like Rare Records from the megastore/Amazon governed perspective of the 21st Century is akin to entering a lovely nostalgic dream.

Carole remembered that while Ian was there she had a friend who liked Alice Cooper. Ian kindly brought a huge cardboard cut out of Cooper home on the bus for her! She also recalled: "I was still at school when Ian worked there. I went to a party and a girl's older brother was playing this LP that I'd never heard of before. One of the songs was called 'Life Is A Three-ringed Circus' and it was a bit like a Stylistics type of thing. I don't know who it was but I came home and told our Ian about it and he actually got it for me from Rare Records."

It's easy to see how Ian would find himself relishing his new role. One of the endearing aspects of a trip to Rare Records would be the chance to 'talk music' with staff who were, at all times, enthusiastic and knowledgeable. It provided an opportunity for Ian to meet like-minded people and forge lasting friendships. Such was the case with Ian and Mark Reeder, whose friendship was set to continue throughout Ian's life.

Mark Reeder: "I don't actually remember where I met Ian. I just knew him from Rare Records, because he worked there. We'd just talk about music and other things as well. He'd recommend things and I'd listen to them. We'd just chat about music and things that were being released. Record shop blah blah blah really. That was how I first got to talk to him."

Ian's stint at Rare Records would see him fleetingly and, of course, unknowingly, in contact with many of those who would drive the local music scene that flourished in later years. Given the size of the music megastores of today, it is difficult to perceive that just two or three miniscule city centre record shops would be remembered so fondly by practically every serious music fan in the city at the time.

Photographer Kevin Cummins, later to become – alongside Anton Corbijn – one of two lens-men who would most famously evoke the essence of Joy Division, also recalls Ian from his days in the shop: "Well we all used to go down to Rare Records, didn't we?" he says. "That's how we recognised Ian when he first started fronting the band. It was that kid from Rare Records who used to talk about reggae. Manchester was a very small place back then… in some respects it still is. You just had to be there to be part of the scene… although we didn't quite know what a scene was."

Bob Dylan biographer Clinton Heylin has a rather different memory of Rare Records and a fairly antagonistic encounter with an assistant he feels sure was Ian Curtis.

Clinton Heylin: "Oh it was definitely Ian. I can picture him now and I remembered him when I was lucky enough to catch Joy Division live. I had purchased a single from Rare Records. Now I am extremely fastidious about my record collecting and I always like things to be right. I remember getting home and realising that the single should have been housed in a picture sleeve. It may sound silly, but it annoyed me because I knew, full well, what these shops would do. They would take the records out of the collectable picture sleeve and put them in a plain white one. I'm not suggesting that it was Ian who did that… but he was the unfortunate who was behind the counter at the time. The thing is, at one point I leant over the counter and grabbed him by the scarf. I recall this vividly. I know it was Ian and I also know something else… it was definitely a Manchester United scarf he was wearing."

Mark Reeder's own musical career, which would see him briefly 'employed' as an early bass player in Mick Hucknall's Frantic Elevators before decamping for a productive life in the German and European record industry, began in a similar establishment. Virgin Records on Lever Street was an extraordinary place. Small, dark, tight, more often than not, smoke-filled, it held an appealing Bohemian atmosphere.

Mark Reeder: "When I went to work at Virgin Records on Lever Street, I stopped going to Rare Records. I could get all the records I wanted to get through Virgin. Ian would come in and it was like seeing an old face. He was someone I'd talk to. He came in during his dinner hour. That's how I got to know him. We liked things that were a bit on the edge. We weren't looking at the charts or anything."

Virgin Records would certainly have held a fascination for Ian. At all times it seemed edgy and filled with characters sitting in corners, listening to all manner of eclectic music. It was managed by Daryl Edwards, who became the proprietor of a rock/punk club called Stoneground – later to become the Mayflower – on Hyde Road. Inside the store were a few old aircraft seats with headphones attached, and a noticeboard covered with hastily scrawled notes, mostly classified adverts for openings such as "… bass player wanted for progressive acid band…" In later years, Howard Devoto would famously use this board while in the process of assembling Magazine.

Anybody harbouring thoughts of starting a band, however distant that might be, would have enjoyed the prevailing musicianly banter of the Lever Street Virgin Records.

Following his stint within the gentle confines of Rare Records Ian decided to strike out on his own. Whether it was a spark of entrepreneurial spirit (typical of Ian, who had shown a similar independent spirit as a child), or a simple desire to strike out alone remains unclear, but he briefly utilised his music knowledge via a spell selling LPs at Butter Lane Antique Market in Manchester (off King St. West). Many of the LPs were Ian's own but Auntie Nell had given him a good supply after a clear out and he bought a few to sell on as well. Carole thought he must have bought some from other dealers. "He didn't want to be stuck in a nine-to-five job – most people don't want that and this was something that interested him," she says. "I was working in town – at ICL then, you used to go downstairs to the market and there were antiques there as well. He had all his records laid out. I think his was the only record stall there. I went in my dinner hour with my friend Gail. The Village Barbers was opposite – Ian used to go there to get his hair cut. It wasn't successful at all. Obviously he didn't make any money and that's why he had to finish doing it 'cos he needed something to live on. But he'd have been quite happy living on nothing and just selling his records."

No doubt it also provided Ian with plenty of opportunity to pass the time of day with like-minded Manchester music fans but since it provided little in the way of income he was left with no choice but to gravitate through a series of interviews that would lead him back to the ambition-crushing safety of life as a civil servant.

Nonetheless, Ian's interest in music had forged another important friendship which began in a similar environment around this time.

Vini Reilly: "I first met Ian at a music shop called Reno's on Oxford Road – there's still a music shop there now by the railway bridge by Oxford Road station. We used to go down and look at the guitars. Ian and I had a mutual friend – Eugene Ryan. Eugene was a civil servant. I was a civil servant – or I had been, I'd been sacked by then. Ian was a civil servant at that time. I was serving petrol and working as a parks gardener. Ian and I had both been clerical officers – that was the grade we were at, at that point. Eugene knew Ian because he worked with him and he'd told him about me. Eugene served petrol with me. Both Ian and me knew him quite well. Eugene was a huge music fan and I think Ian was a bit of a hero to Eugene and I was a bit of a hero to Eugene. So anyway we met in the basement of Reno's. Eugene introduced us to each other. He thought Ian was an amazing vocalist and I was an amazing guitarist and that we should meet."

Ian Curtis and Debbie Woodruff became engaged in April 1974 and an engagement party was held at the bride-to-be's family home, a bungalow in Sutton, Macclesfield. "We had met Audrey and Bob (Deb's parents) before this," says Doreen. "We went up one night and Debbie introduced us."

Carole was 14 at the time and remembered sitting on the wall outside with her friend Gail while Jill, Debbie's sister, gave them alcoholic drinks that they probably shouldn't have had. Doreen and Kevin Curtis didn't drink alcohol (Kevin was driving in any case) but they entered into the spirit and joined in the dancing. Other members of Ian's family present were Nell and Ray, and Barbara and Brian. Doreen and Carole recall everyone enjoying themselves.

Nevertheless, the Curtis family all felt that Ian was far too young to be getting married. As Carole remembered: "I just thought why get married at such a young age. I couldn't understand it. It wasn't as if they had to. I remember my dad saying, 'What you getting married for? You're throwing your life away'. Ian said, 'We're not, it's what we want to do.' But I still think he just wanted to cram everything in because he knew he wasn't long for this world. He crammed everything in in such a short time."

However insistent Ian may have been to his father that this was what he wanted, he confided pre-marital doubts to others. His mother remembers that he told his Auntie Nell the day before that he didn't want to go through with it (but he said that it was too late, everything was done). Furthermore, Ian confided to Lindsay Reade during the last weeks of his life that he had a foreknowledge, immediately prior to the wedding, that there would be another woman – and therefore, as marriage would be wrong, seriously considered calling it off even at this late stage.

Lindsay and Carole both feel that Ian seemed to have some kind of vision, that he could see into the future. His mother felt he had a kind of knowing way about him, as reflected in his interest in Knights as a child. "… not in a morbid way," says Carole. "Just messing about really – but he used to say that he'd die young – that he'd be like them, you know Jimi Hendrix."

Clairvoyant or not, there was certainly a degree of doubt nestling beneath the couple's outward happiness. It may have been simply down to the fact that they married young, without true thought to the progression of their marital ambitions. It was Pete Shelley who, when quizzed about the relationships that crowded his songs, perceptively noted that: "Love is not two people looking at one another, it is two people looking ahead in the same direction."

With Ian casting hopeful glances to a vague future with a rock band, it seems unlikely that they were enjoying a united vision of the future.

The marriage of Ian Curtis to Deborah Woodruff took place at St Thomas's Church, Henbury, on the fringe of Macclesfield on a sunny day – August 23, 1975. "It was a nice church, high up, a nice setting," remembers Doreen. Ian was just 19 and Debbie 18.

Carole spent the night before at Debbie's house in Sutton while Ian stayed with his best man, Kelvin Briggs. Ian's friendship with Kelvin had begun at King's School but went on for some years thereafter. "He was lovely Kelvin – a really nice lad," remembers Carole. "We met him and Ian the day before at the Leigh Arms [in Adlington on the Silk Road into Macclesfield]. My dad must have taken us and then they dropped us off at Audrey's [Debbie's mother]."

"Yes, you stayed in Macc," Doreen went on. "Kevin's brother's wife Margaret came down from Blackpool [Kevin's brother Harold had died] and came in the car with us."

Carole and Jill, Debbie's sister, were both bridesmaids. Carole remembers going to the hairdressers with Debbie on the morning of the big day (although Carole didn't have her hair done there, she always did her own).

It was pretty much the typical young Cheshire marriage of the mid-Seventies, with bulbous ties, blow-dried hair, and the kind of clothing that always seemed destined to add a comedic touch to wedding photos of the era, before fading quickly to a fashion faux pas. Ian's pin-striped suit came from Jonathan Silver, who had the Lord John shops and was a friend and sponsor of David Hockney.

There is nothing to suggest that there was anything abnormal whatsoever about either the marriage ceremony or the relationship. The choice of a Haydn hymn that included the theme of the German National Anthem apparently reflected a fondness for Germanic culture and history that was shared by both Ian and Debbie.

The reception was held at the Bull's Head in the centre of Macclesfield, where a sit-down meal was served. On the menu was coq-au-vin and Doreen recalls her Aunt Nell being amazed that Debbie's Liverpudlian family didn't know what it was. Like all local weddings, the event was covered in the regional newspaper – "Couple honeymoon in Paris" read the archetypal headline – together with a small picture.

Despite the comparative austerity of the time, and Ian's pre-marital doubts along with his burgeoning desire to break out of a predestined routine on some level, there can be no question that the couple were in love. The prospect of marriage would have been seen as a step into a new and exciting stage of their lives, even if Ian was somewhat torn by his burning desire to make something of himself in music.

"Kevin and I picked Ian and Debbie up at the train station when they got back from their honeymoon in Paris," says Carole. "They seemed happy, as if they had had a good time."

The couple began married life at Doreen's parent's house in Stamford Street, Old Trafford. This made the journey into work a short and simple affair as well as allowing a close proximity to the city's nightlife. The pair stayed for several months before they found a home of their own in Chadderton and then, after that point, Ian maintained a close contact with his family and visited often.

Doreen's parents, Leslie and Edith, were easy going; Leslie liked to laugh and joke and Edith would do anything for anybody. Their house in Stamford Street was quite large while Ian's parent's home, although appearing reasonably spacious, actually had only two bedrooms upstairs, so when Ian and Carole were both living there, Ian had to sleep in the front room downstairs.

Although Carole is of the opinion that Debbie was "calling the shots in their relationship", no-one within Ian's family were aware of any arguments between the couple. However, Doreen thought that Debbie lacked a sense of humour. "Debbie was a bit prudish," she says. "Ian's granddad would always be happy, laughing and joking, but she'd be staid. He'd do daft things – like picking a comb up in the street and saying 'Look what I've found, you can have that' but she wouldn't see the funny side. You'd be a bit frightened of saying something if you were having a joke."

After their stay at Old Trafford, Ian and Debbie moved to a small terraced house in Chadderton, near Oldham, a mere skip away from Ian's parents' house in New Moston. In order to facilitate the move, two offers of kindness from Ian's family were gratefully received. Firstly, Ian's Auntie Nell lent the couple the required deposit of £300[1] to help them buy the Chadderton property; secondly, Ian's father Kevin and grandfather Leslie took it upon themselves to help renovate the house, decorating, stripping floorboards, and doing general repairs.

"On the day of the removal they had a job getting the mattress up the

---

[1] Doreen remembers that Debbie insisted it was paid back after Ian's death.

stairs because the stairs were so narrow," Doreen remembers. Carole recalls going there with her friend Karen to wait in while something was delivered – the couple were both working. "They'd done it all very modern compared to what was the done thing then – obviously in the Seventies it was all thick shag pile carpets and brown and beiges. The stripped floor was painted black which was a bit way-out really then. It was all ultra-modern."

Ian and Debbie were both working in the same building – Sunley House – at this point, though in different departments, Ian for the Manpower Services Commission – principally a job creation scheme – and Debbie for the Department of the Environment.

The daily bus ride into town from their new Chadderton abode was somewhat arduous. Also, Debbie disliked the dark, tight network of Chadderton streets, the unwelcoming nature of the dingy pubs in that area, in addition to the remoteness of Oldham. As a result, they did not stay at this house for too long.

For the time being, though, they lived the normal life of a newly-married couple, its routine enlivened only by music. Nevertheless, there was room for dreams, however distant. Ian Curtis still wanted to become a rock star. That stated, beyond incessant scribbling of would-be lyrics in note-books, he hadn't quite worked out a way of forming and becoming part of a band.

CHAPTER 4

Here Are The Young Men

"There was a man there in a rubber suit. You don't see many rubber suits." – Terry Mason

Peter Hook, who was born on February 13, 1956 and who will henceforth be known as Hooky, became friendly with Bernard Dickin (aka Sumner/Albrecht), who was born on January 4, 1956 and who will henceforth be known as Barney, at Salford Grammar School. Although not in the same stream together, they became acquainted with one another between classes and also befriended a third Salford Grammar School boy, Terry Mason.

All three boys had spent their childhoods in the gloom of industrial Salford. Hooky, despite a brief and unlikely spell in the Caribbean, lived in a two-up two-down in Ordsall, close to Manchester docks, while Barney grew up in Lower Broughton, close to the River Irwell. Both would later admit that memories of happy childhoods spent in dreary Salford would significantly flavour the music of Joy Division.

It seems that both Hooky and Barney were able to negotiate their schooldays and surroundings without falling prey to bullies and intimidation. "We weren't wusses," says Hooky. "Far from it. But we were both clever enough to befriend the right people and stay out of the real trouble. We weren't idiots, frankly and there were quite a few of them about. I think myself and Barney were just two kids on the same level."

After leaving school, Barney, Hooky and Terry remained friends. At 16 they all bought Lambretta scooters which provided a shared interest to enforce their bonding. They managed to pay for these by doing various jobs, Hooky and Terry cleaning offices from 5.30 until 7.30 in the evening and Barney working in a local supermarket. Together they would also investigate latter-day glam and garage bands that flourished in the mid-Seventies. One of their haunts was The Roxy Room at Pip's disco, situated beneath The Corn Exchange behind Manchester Cathedral. Terry was able to get the trio in free because his dad knew the bouncer on the door.

One of few places in Manchester where a flamboyant dress sense was positively encouraged, Pip's became an early meeting place for many of those who would form the Manchester punk scene.

In the summer of 1976, Terry convinced Barney and Hooky to go along with him to the Sex Pistols gigs at Manchester's Lesser Free Trade Hall. Barney brought along his regular girlfriend since schooldays, Sue Barlow, whom he later married. Although some believe that the importance of the Lesser Free Trade Hall Pistols gigs have been somewhat overstated, they were almost certainly a trigger for the musical ambitions of many in attendance.

Pete Shelley and Howard Devoto famously shelled out the necessary £32 to hire the hall on Friday June 4, 1976, and, to more poignant effect, on Tuesday July 20, where they would make their debut appearance as Buzzcocks. The first gig, missed by Ian Curtis and wife Debbie, saw Pistols manager Malcolm McLaren, clad in black rubber, accosting pedestrians on Peter Street like some downbeat and desperate spiritual street hawker. Even when he succeeded, many of the wary Pistols gig goers were immediately swamped by the music of the support band, a progressive rock act called Solstice.

Sex Pistol Glen Matlock: "There were two gigs… yes, I remember one of the Free Trade Hall nights was the very first time we played 'Anarchy In The UK' on stage. That was the night that Tony Wilson saw us and immediately booked us for his television show, *So It Goes*. We didn't know it at the time but how amazing it was, to have had all those people at that show. I thought Buzzcocks were wonderful. Much better than The Clash, who were just like a bad version of ourselves. Buzzcocks had a great attitude. They were quite cute, in a way. Very provincial but they had incredible songs. Love songs that sounded like nothing else on earth. They were on the second time we played, as well as Slaughter & The Dogs."

Ian and Debbie attended the second gig, unknowingly filing in alongside not only Barney, Hooky and Terry Mason, but many of the oncoming Mancunian rock illuminati.

Terry remembers sitting next to Malcolm McLaren: "We wouldn't have known who he was but then – he was all rubber suited up and there's us – looking back on it – naivety isn't quite the right word, we weren't particularly naïve but we'd never come into contact with lots of the people that were there. There's a man there in a rubber suit. You don't see many rubber suits."

Famously, on the morning after the second gig, Hooky went out and purchased two items: a bass guitar for £35 – quite a hefty sum for a quasi-punk in 1976 – and an accompanying book, *The Palmer Hughes Book of Rock 'n 'Roll*, which came complete with a set of stickers that could be fixed on the guitar neck; useful and, what's more, great fun even if they did dilute the image a little. Barney already had a guitar and an amp and was learning basic chords by then. Terry Mason was equally determined to learn an instrument.

The members of the budding band were all living at home, and all had mundane day jobs. If nothing else their immersion in music, whether reading the music press or holding loose practice sessions in bedrooms and kitchens offered a relief from daily tedium. Mostly their slowly evolving rehearsals took place at Barney's gran's house, which was closer to Manchester city centre. "We were both shit," says Hooky with time-honoured succinctness. "I never thought I would grasp the basics. Barney kept showing me the chords."

A series of sessions with entertainingly cacophonous results was an ongoing feature of their partnership. "Well, it sometimes makes me wonder… when I see very young bands today, just how much more adept they are than we were… and for a long time after that," admits Hooky.

Pete Shelley remembers that after the second Pistols' gig Barney, Hooky and Terry informed him of their musical ambitions. "They came up and the general gist was, 'We're thinking of starting a band, how do you do it, what do you need, how do we go about it?' There was one time when we all got in a car and went off with John Maher[1] to check out a drum kit that somebody was selling. I think Terry was supposed to be the drummer at first."

In the wake of the Pistols, and with Buzzcocks, Slaughter & The Dogs and The Drones now starting to perform regularly, the developing Manchester punk scene was suddenly heavy with potential front-men. In retrospect, it seems almost bizarre to note that Ian Curtis, Steven Morrissey, and Mick Hucknall were all fluttering tentatively around this tiny and insular scene.

---

[1] Buzzcocks drummer.

Although the London fanzine *Sniffin' Glue* had famously proclaimed, "Here's a chord... here's another... now form a band!" it didn't quite work like that. The Sex Pistols, it was noted, had been evolving – if only as a rhythm section – for several years. The Damned were practiced and studied musos. Joe Strummer had spent several years on the London pub circuit. Pete Shelley had fronted the Leigh based Jets Of Air. The Drones had been cabaret teen pop hopefuls Rockslide. The thrash of instant punk was, in truth, a ludicrous and artless cacophony. You had to learn to play. You had to knuckle down and put in the hours. Hooky has admitted, on numerous occasions, that he really didn't think they would ever break through that solid barrier which separates the novice from the one whose fingers begin to move with a fluency born of hours spent practising. However, to the pair's joint astonishment, their musicianship did continue to gel and improve.

The Sex Pistols would play in Manchester, at a different venue, on two further occasions towards the end of 1976. With their 'Anarchy' tour in tatters due to tabloid outcry, their concert schedule simply disintegrated into a mess of council-forced cancellations. Twenty scheduled dates were immediately whittled down to just three, though the good burghers of Manchester, it seemed, were immune to the paranoia that gripped their counterparts elsewhere in the UK. In December 1976, the Pistols played The Electric Circus twice in ten days, and on the first of these dates, December 9, Ian Curtis made the journey to the Collyhurst venue. As Ian had taken to scrawling the word 'HATE' across the rear of his jacket, it might have been seen as an act of provocation in an era when even the wearing of drainpipes jeans was ludicrously regarded as such.

This was to be a dramatic night that would be imprinted in the memory of all who attended. As Ian entered the club, he would have vanished into a pitch-black mess of debris and chaos, and this evening was even more edgy than usual. The hippie types, as yet unconvinced about punk rock's surging momentum, scowled in the corners. The more outgoing punks, meanwhile, wore clothes which, unlike the punks of London, were largely homemade, at least in their efforts to provoke a punk statement: shirts nicked from dad's wardrobe and scrawled over with biro slogans. But it was clumsy, ungainly artless apparel. Within The Electric Circus, at least, Ian Curtis' latterly famous 'HATE' scrawl would have seemed perfectly at home.

As Hooky noted: "Ian was really wired when I first met him... at The Sex Pistols gig at The Electric Circus. It was probably the perfect introduction. He seemed out of it but so did everyone, I guess."

A blinding flash of light exploded from the stage and came into vision:

the stunning, leering ugliness of Johnny Rotten, larger than life, warped by flu, eyes flying from a speeding mind, staring eyes, accusing snarl. He was the pure physical embodiment of 'grab it and run', with attitude in buckets, and that rabid, unworldly leer. Something special was undoubtedly taking place; an intoxicating, illuminating exhilarating, inspiring experience. You could catch that attitude and cling to it, and carry it home. It was a complete night of punk too, with short swift sets from The Clash, Buzzcocks and Johnny Thunders' Heartbreakers preceding the Pistols. In later years, many would try to recreate that atmosphere. All would fail.

Hooky: "From that night, every time we went to The Circus, Ian would seem to be there. He told us that he had some kind of band but I think he was just messing around, as were we really. But we didn't have many options, to be honest. We were worried that we would never get on that bandwagon, frankly. Buzzcocks, Drones and Slaughter & The Dogs all seemed to be miles ahead of us. They all had their own identifiable sounds. They seemed to know what they were doing and we were just messing around."

Terry Mason appeared to share their vision and became a vital aspect of the initial dynamic of the band: "After The Sex Pistols played there The Electric Circus started running two regular gigs a week with London bands coming up and we'd meet Ian and his mate Iain [Gray] there. It wasn't a gentleman's club but it was like being in on something early on. You'd recognise the people who are there. It's like going to the football – when it used to be standing up – you'd recognise the people around you and then after a few years you'd grunt and nod at them from time to time. We were sort of on grunting and nodding terms with Ian and his mate. We were very quiet and Ian used to go a bit daft. Dancing and jumping about when bands were on. He just used to bounce more than anyone else."

The music-based relationship between Ian and his friend Iain Gray had matured beyond a vague dream by this point. An amiable, intelligent character, Gray had attained a modest prowess on the guitar and he and Ian had embarked on embryonic rehearsals that would have mirrored the early stirrings of Barney, Hooky and Terry. While the vision was certainly intact, however, the wherewithal was lacking, leading to a state of hopeless and dreamy isolation which was extremely common at the time. The encouraging push of The Sex Pistols had inspired many would-be musicians to scamper to second hand music shops, and fumble in bedrooms over rudimentary chords.

As 1977 dawned, the atmosphere at The Electric Circus appeared to soften. Manchester was becoming Britain's second punk city with The

Electric Circus and The Ranch Bar remaining the central meeting points. Ian was just one of a number of intrigued 'wannabees' regularly attending both venues.

Steve Burke (Shy), who was working behind the bar at The Electric Circus, remembers Ian from those days. "We used to see Ian all the time but I wasn't as familiar with him as I was with Barney, Hooky and Terry. I remember them when they used to go down to Pip's Disco, to The Roxy Room in Pip's, which used to play a lot of the better glam stuff... Bowie, Iggy, Velvets. A lot of the Manchester punks had initially been part of that glam scene. That's how they got to know each other. But I don't recall Ian from there. Actually, I found him a little bit more difficult to approach, I don't know why. It could have been because one of the first times that I bumped into him at The Electric Circus, he accidentally knocked his pint all over me. It wasn't his fault, but it was a bit clumsy. He was diving about all over the place with a pint in his hand. I think he apologised. There was no problem. But he seemed a little bit on edge, to me. I'm not sure I remember Debbie. I do recall another guy with him [Iain Gray]. He was certainly becoming a well-known face around town although he wasn't one of the Salford or Moss Side lads. So he was seen as being a bit of an outsider, but amiable enough."

Ian's sister Carole didn't figure Ian as a punk at this time. "When Ian was into his punk phase we were into discos," she says, "though I would never class him as a punk rocker. I don't remember seeing him in a jacket with 'HATE' on it. He might have stuck it on and then pulled it off when he went to work. He had a donkey jacket and a leather one. I could imagine him doing it, putting a sticker on – he did do things for effect. He was too stylish for the punk look though. He was ultra-fashionable – if it was a woman you'd say chic and up to date but with Ian it was a step ahead from what other people were wearing."

At this time Ian and Debbie were still commuting together from Oldham to their jobs on different floors of the Sunley Building in Manchester's Piccadilly, the tower building shooting up beside the Hotel Piccadilly and a high rise for the time.

One of the advantages of working in Manchester's Piccadilly was that it offered Ian Curtis a chance to drift along to some of the more intriguing music 'hang-outs' in the city. Virgin Records, a natural lunchtime destination for any aspiring musician, was located in Lever Street, just across Piccadilly Gardens. Ian also spoke about his fondness for the Spin Inn Disc Shop, whose stock consisted mainly of northern soul records, situated on Cross Street. It was the specialist nature of the shop that appealed to him.

Perhaps more significant were the lunchtimes spent drifting into Piccadilly Plaza, the hideous and largely unpopulated concrete monstrosity situated beneath the prestigious Piccadilly Hotel. This was a soulless cavern-like shell, lined mostly by empty shop fronts, with crisp packets and cigarette ends underfoot and a vague smell of urine.

Ian had good reason to drift through that shell, however, for in contrast to its deadbeat appearance, it housed unlikely areas of glamour. The studios of Piccadilly Radio lay a short distance up the escalator on the first floor of the Sunley Building and, although as a commercial radio station it hardly represented the city's growing punk awareness, it did monopolise the city's airwaves and every pop star visiting Manchester could be seen drifting in for the obligatory interview.

More importantly, at least for Ian, would be the unlikely presence of the northern offices of RCA Records, an establishment manned at all times by the ebullient Derek Brandwood, head of promotion. Speaking in 2001, Brandwood noted: "I lived in a weird world where I would commute into this atmosphere of rock biz glamour. And the thing was that RCA really was a glamorous label even if it employed American promotional methods that didn't necessarily work over here. But I would commute to work, driving in from a totally ordinary existence and then, suddenly, I would be a close friend of the most extraordinary array of people. RCA had Iggy Pop, David Bowie, Dolly Parton."

Brandwood recalls Ian Curtis stopping by the office. "He was a likeable lad who would drop in every now and again. I can't remember if he said he was starting a band. I probably gave him some promotional material. It was actually quite tedious in that office and Ian would have made a change from Piccadilly Radio DJs."

Meanwhile, the nascent band featuring Hooky and Barney continued to limp on in a vaguely forward motion. The bedroom rehearsal practices petered out into a three-piece shrug, with an old school friend called Martin Gresty attempting to add vocals.

"The band seemed to be more a state of mind for a while," says Terry Mason. "Barney had an amp, Hooky had a bass guitar, I had a guitar and couldn't figure out what I was doing. We had to find a drummer and also a singer. You had your mates who you thought looked right – in this case there was a guy called Danny Lee who could out-Billy Idol Billy Idol. He could do his lip, he had the hair but he couldn't be arsed. We weren't even sure that he could sing but seeing as no-one had any songs it didn't really make that much difference. Then the idea was one of Barney's mates would have a go. A lad called Wroey who lived near Barney's gran. He came to punk a lot later on but did it a lot better than us. We were never quite right as punks. Even during the early days, when no one knew particularly what to wear. Basically you knew you had to throw away the flares. Anyway, then we realised that no one we knew was ever going to be a singer. So that's when Barney put the advert in Virgin."

The Virgin noticeboard proved instrumental in attracting a further array of potential front-men. Terry Mason: "There was one I remember – this guy, he was mentally disturbed. And yet again we're at this situation where we were completely moving away from our safety zone – what we knew and understood. We were quite insular. We were having to see people we didn't know and see if we wanted to be in a band with them. This one that me and Barney went to see – he was great on the phone. He said he wrote songs. We went round and, of course, we were expecting someone to look fairly similar to us – you know shortish hair, whatever. This guy looked like one of the early reject moulds for Mick Hucknall. He had red hair that stuck up like that and he appeared to be wearing a cushion – this top that had a head-hole and arm-holes in. I think it may have been orange. Or was it two-tone? The facing bit was more in velour and the back was in satin. We're there thinking, 'What we going to do? Let's see what he's got'. He then proceeds to pull out a three-string balalaika that he's built himself. And he starts to play these songs and we're in his house and we don't know what to do. We had to sit through this guy's mental illness and then we said we can't give him anything just yet – we've got to see who else answers the ad. Then, fortunately, Ian answered. Otherwise it would have been a very bad band."

For the untested Curtis, auditioning for any kind of band must have seemed a daunting prospect. As it turned out, his audition was nothing like what he might have expected, for Barney had an idea to organise a bonding session to see if Ian would fit comfortably into the band's embryonic dynamic. Quite how this would demonstrate his abilities as a front-man is a difficult to ascertain, but it certainly broke the ice.

Terry Mason: "The audition wasn't an audition. We sort of vaguely knew him and we'd been scared by the balalaika man – you know we didn't want any more of that. The audition was we wanted to see if we liked him. We took him out to Ashfield Valley [in Rochdale] and we went wandering about in all the mud and crap. Yes, walking out in the country, jumping over bits of streams and that. Ian had come quite well dressed. I had boots with holes in. I ended up with plastic bags wrapped round my feet. We were running about in the woods, and, of course, Barney being completely prepared came in wellingtons. He didn't bother to tell anyone else you'd probably need all this, and he's there just laughing at us. Ian certainly got his feet wet that day. And that was the audition."

With Ian on board, the trio started to rehearse regularly in Salford. Iain Gray just fell into the background. "We never really knew him," says Hooky. "I don't know how serious it all was... but we were moving so fast we barely took notice."

Terry Mason: "At that point – I mean it was a bonus when we found Ian could sing. And he had all these index cards with bits of songs on bits of paper. But it was more – well, he looks about right, we get on with him. Oh, the other thing was he had a PA. Of course it's not what you think of when you think PA. He had these two WEM column speakers and this tiny PA amp. He had equipment! He was serious! That was an even better sign. The first rehearsals probably would have been at the Swan. It's a pile of rubble nowadays. It was near where I used to live in Weaste, a rough arse Salford pub. I sorted out the Swan because my cousin was the chairman of the Salford branch of the Manchester City supporters club, which had its meetings in the Swan, and I said we needed a room to rehearse. Even though they paid a tenner or whatever to use it for their meetings they just let us use it for free and it was great. I think Barney used to pick Ian up on his bike and drop him off at the station. Or if Ian was in work he'd make his own way... no he wouldn't – he was useless at that, he'd probably need to get a lift off Barney or Hooky."

The band didn't actually use the same room as the City supporters but chose instead to use a bigger room that was not as plush – more like a junk room. The next step for the band was to find a suitable drummer.

Terry Mason: "We met all sorts – some were nice people. There were some who banged a knife and fork on a plate and thought that was drumming. You had to know a bit more than that – otherwise I'd still be in the band. We had this situation with drummers so I decided to trade in Iain Gray's amp – just to rub salt into Iain's wounds, when Ian joined us I bought Iain's equipment – and I got a drum kit. It was a very cool looking drum kit – covered in black leatherette, rather than being a silver sparkle one. Then I realised that drumming was quite difficult. So I thought I'd get some lessons and in the meantime we're still looking for drummers and we found Anthony Tabac."

Tony Tabac was a likeable, intelligent and laid-back character who initially seemed well suited to the band. It was only later, after playing an initial six gigs, that it became clear that he wasn't fitting snugly into the dynamic of the band. Terry, though valiantly trying to learn both guitar and drums with the idea of becoming part of the group, was coming around to the idea that musicianship was perhaps not his forte. Nevertheless, they settled down into a regular rehearsal routine, mainly at the Swan. In the absence of any talent for either guitar or drums, Terry Mason tentatively assumed the role of manager, arranging and organising things for the band.

Meanwhile, the Manchester punk scene had suddenly gained some small credence in the national music press. Local gig reviews by Paul Morley had started to appear in *NME,* and by Ian Wood in *Sounds.* A new venue, The Band On The Wall on Swan Street – a jazz club and pub which had a curiously London ambience – provided the perfect platform where both the bigger bands like Buzzcocks and the Drones, and a number of developing outfits, could gain experience.

On March 3, 1977, Ian and Debbie went to Manchester Apollo to catch Iggy Pop's infamous Idiot tour, just one of a lavish peppering of key events which took place in the city around this period. This particular Iggy tour included the not inconsiderable added attraction of David Bowie playing keyboards, a high level inclusion that caused slight panic among promoters who instructed their ticket sales staff to inform customers that it would "not be a David Bowie performance, you know". Not that Iggy Pop needed introducing to the swelling punk audience of the city.

It was another electrifying, stimulating and utterly inspiring evening, with the crowd all too well aware that they were witnessing exactly the right performer at exactly the right time… and seemingly in exactly the right city.[1]

For Ian, now so close to making his own onstage debut, the sight of Iggy Pop, completely consumed by his own level of stagemanship, must have been truly inspiring, partly through the sheer physicality of his performance and partly through his almost unique ability to lift the music simply by being there.

Typically, for an extreme night at Manchester Apollo in 1977, the ludicrous battle between security guards instructed to keep the crowd seated and an audience who, understandably, had no intention of remaining seated, raged on for most of the concert. When Iggy Pop signalled for a final surge the bouncers retreated, allowing the crowd to swell to the front, ecstatic with their minor victory.

---

[1] This is not to be confused, as it so often is, with a similar – albeit Bowie-less – performance at the same venue, later in the year; this time captured for posterity by the cameras of Tony Wilson's second series of *So It Goes.*

Ian left The Apollo in a state of exhilaration. In witnessing the performance, Ian Curtis had taken a step closer to realising his own dream.

Throughout the spring of 1977 Terry and Ian met in Manchester regularly during the daytime. Terry: "We'd meet up at lunchtime when he was working in town and read the music papers. The pair of us by that point were eagerly waiting for the music papers coming out – *Sounds* and *NME* – and devoured the lot and we were just running over it with each other. We used to say things like: 'Wouldn't it be great to go to the CBGB club or whatever.'"[1]

Determined to try and make something happen the pair would also ring up record companies. "Because we didn't have a phone we used to go to Kendall's," says Terry. "They had a nice phone that was inside the building so it was quiet. It wasn't like you were ringing up Virgin Records and they could hear all the traffic in the background. So we'd be filling the machine full of 10ps to try and get tapes in and see if anyone was about."

In this age of blanket mobile phone use it is easy to forget that they are a relatively recent phenomenon. Terry didn't have the luxury of a phone at home either and remembers: "Then, even using the phone for business… where I worked you weren't allowed to make a business phone call before 1pm unless you got your manager's permission. And if someone rang you at work everyone in the room would be staring and throwing you daggers."

This lack of a phone became the vital factor that later prevented Terry acting as the group's manager.

In May 1977, to Deborah's delight, and possibly Ian's too, the couple managed to move to Barton Street in Macclesfield, via another short stint with Ian's grandparents in Stamford Street.

This was a double-fronted, terraced house with a communal yard. It was situated on a corner and consequently narrowed towards the rear end, giving the house an oddly triangular appearance from parts of the inside, particularly in Ian's 'blue' room (on the left of the front door alongside the ginnel) and, to a lesser extent, the kitchen at the rear.

By day, Debbie and Ian would jointly commute to Manchester and, during the evenings that Ian wasn't locked in the dusty practice room in Salford, he would evidently brood at home, smoking, scribbling lyrics and listening to records by bands that were considerably further down the line.

---

[1] CBGBs in New York was originally intended to feature country, bluegrass and blues but it became famous as the springboard for Blondie, The Ramones, Talking Heads, Television and others.

The move to Barton Street was unfortunately timed. The trauma that accompanies any house move is arduous at the best of times but this move coincided with the build-up to the band's first gig, naturally enough at The Electric Circus where they had secured a prestigious support spot to Buzzcocks along with Penetration and John Cooper Clarke. Such a debut would ensure instant exposure to the Manchester rock fraternity.

From the outset, Ian Curtis had recognised the value of hanging out, as much as possible, with Buzzcocks and their manager Richard Boon. As it happened, Boon and Shelley lived on the same road – Lower Broughton in Salford. Indeed, the name Stiff Kittens, which Ian's band was originally called, seems to have originated from an incident that involved the Buzzcocks.

Recalls Pete Shelley of Buzzcocks: "We played the Ranch Bar. The Ranch was the place that was happening in as much as… well, it wasn't a full on gay bar… this was an under age drinking den really. In order to play there we had to go and see Foo Foo Lamarr[1]. So we made an appointment and saw him at his sauna. He was in towels and we arranged to do a gig at the Ranch Bar. Anyway, as we were bringing the gear down the stairs – they were steep the stairs down to the basement bar – and the premise's cat had had kittens and somebody stood on one. We all thought it was dead, a goner – hence stiff kittens. It didn't die… no kittens were harmed in the making of… but it had its moment of looking like it was."

Buzzcocks, be it Pete Shelley or Richard Boon, subsequently suggested 'Stiff Kittens' as a name for this new band out of Salford. It may not have held enough mystique to remain their name for long, but it did create an initial stir around Manchester.

Terry Mason: "What we had was two parallel courses at this point. There was the band, project Stiff Kittens or whatever, who used to talk to Pete Shelley. We were Shelley's mates. Hooky was learning bass out of a book and Barney was a bit smug because he'd had a guitar for years and could play a bit. I still had the idea to play guitar. We thought we were a band because we were talking to Shelley. [At the same time] Ian used to spend more time talking to Richard Boon. Meeting up with Shelley… we found out where he lived, it was not that far from Barney's gran's… we went round and that, again, was the biggest shock we'd ever had. First of all we're now talking to someone who is quite openly gay. We're from Salford, late Sixties, Seventies. Salford didn't do gay. Well they did but it

---

[1] Manchester club owner and drag celebrity.

was someone called Lawrence. Everyone called them Lol and you had to watch yourself around them."

During the nervous build-up to the debut gig, Stiff Kittens became Warsaw, though the name change wasn't easy. Ian Curtis had never warmed to the idea of Stiff Kittens, believing it to be the kind of name that a copycat punk band would use. Even at this early stage, it seems, Ian was looking beyond the obvious trappings of a punk 'movement' that was beginning to attract sheep-like tendencies. In Manchester, despite producing many excellent and exciting shows, The Drones were certainly falling into this trap by writing lyrics such as, "… I wanna see the Queen at the end of a beam… I wanna see the Pope at the end of a rope…" It was all becoming a little cartoon-like. This was understandable in view of how the desire to shock was close to the punk ethos but the band that Ian Curtis was about to lead had ideas based around a more intelligent but equally controversial alternative.

Hooky, reminiscing during the time of the 1988 re-packaging of Joy Division product, recalled: "Ian really wanted something darker than Stiff Kittens, which none of us really liked. I think 'Program' was another possibility and we almost became 'Gdansk' at one point."

From that standpoint, it's easy to understand the transition to Warsaw, adopted partly in reverence to the gloomy David Bowie *Low* track, 'Warszawa'.

The change didn't occur until after the Stiff Kittens moniker had attached itself to the bottom of a bill that rose through Penetration, regular visitors to Manchester down from Durham, John Cooper Clarke and, finally Buzzcocks, although their performances would be capped by what was by now becoming a regular climactic appearance by John The Postman, surging through 'Louie Louie' to close the evening. One of the poster runs for the evening failed to mention either Stiff Kittens or Warsaw and, in its place, added the Birmingham band, The Prefects.

Anyone who has been in or around a band at their inception can understand the trepidation, if not sheer terror, felt by the untried musicians, that petrifying leap from the practice room to a stage. To compound their anxiety, Warsaw really did find themselves performing in front of most of the Manchester movers and shakers, largely because this show would prove to be one of the integral Electric Circus 'punk Sundays', a weekly rendezvous where scenesters had the opportunity to judge the cream of punk related bands from Britain and America – The Clash on their White Riot Tour, The Jam, Stranglers, Ramones/Talking Heads, Vibrators – all parading before them.

The presence of Stiff Kittens/Warsaw was, naturally enough, a fairly low-key affair. Being at the bottom of the bill, under whatever name, was to perform early doors, before most of the audience had arrived. Nonetheless, the sparse audience included various members of The Drones, standing by the bar and casting nervous glances towards the stage, Paul Morley from *NME*, Ian Wood from *Sounds*, and many of the instantly recognisable faces of the scene.

Mick Middles watched the entire gig under the impression that it was The Prefects. "I don't know why we were duped in such a way," he says. "I think we had actually already seen The Prefects at that point anyway. At the end of the set I told Steve Shy that I really like The Prefects whereupon he informed me, 'That was a band from Manchester and they are called Warsaw'. The difference was that we hadn't really recognised Ian as the guy who used to hang around the Circus. Now he was in a band, he seemed different."

Paul Morley, who stood next to the *Shy Talk* and *Ghast UP* fanzine contingent throughout the performance, noted in his *NME* review "… there is a quirky cockiness about the lads that made me think, for some reason of The Faces, twinkling evil charm."

This was an extremely perceptive comment and it's difficult to understand how Morley could have reached this conclusion from just one performance. In latter years, the laddish camaraderie of Warsaw/Joy Division and New Order would attain huge infamy and, rather like The Faces, their gang-like mentality would certainly flavour their better performances.

"I knew Ian reasonably well," says Morley. "I guess Ian knew me as well because by then I was writing for *NME* and he was a big fan of *NME*. I was the local writer for *NME* so in a funny sort of way from early on I was somebody that Ian knew of. When he met me he knew who I was because I'd already started writing for *NME* and I'd written about them before I met him. For early Warsaw I wasn't necessarily that overwhelmed by them. I thought they were unformed a little bit, not quite finished. I think he knew that as well, that they weren't great, they weren't magnificent, they were just an ordinary local band. I think in a funny sort of way he quite respected that – in the way that good people in music do, they like to be challenged a little bit. And if they understand and appreciate that it's for a good reason. I mean I wasn't nasty, I just said 'Here's an interesting band, bit like this, bit like that, could be great.'"

Despite gaining positive reviews in both *NME* and *Sounds* on the back of one edgy performance, Warsaw continued to improve through a modest series of gigs during the summer of 1977 with Tony Tabac still occupying the drum seat. Two days later they played at Rafters, supporting Johnny Thunders' Heartbreakers in front of a disappointingly small audience.

Terry Mason remembers bumping into the former New York Doll and his band in a fish and chip shop before the gig. "After we'd had what passed as a sound check we went out to get something to eat. To our surprise there's Johnny Thunders & The Heartbreakers in the queue as well. For one of those bizarre moments it brought it home that you were really in a band. They'd been doing it for five years. It seems silly but there we were in the same chippy as two of the legendary New York Dolls and they'd just done a sound check as well."

At their first gig Warsaw had asked Penetration what they knew about other gig opportunities. As a result they got the chance to play a few days later, on June 2 – the day of the Queen's Silver Jubilee – at Newcastle Town Hall annex with Penetration, and The Adverts from London. Of course there was no money on offer for Warsaw. It was a bank holiday and there was no way they could afford to rent a van, particularly as it would have had to be rented for the whole weekend. Terry and Hooky knew a lad named Danny MacQueenie from school and he agreed to drive them up to Newcastle at no cost in his 7-ton Luton furniture van that he used for work. Two of them were able to sit in the front but the others had to endure the whole journey in a huge, boomy, unlit van, bracing themselves around corners, sitting on sacks, not knowing where they were with Ian peering periodically out through small holes in the steel walls. At one point Ian exclaimed: "I think we're lost I'm sure we've just gone past Scotch Corner three times."

Terry: "When we finally arrived we turned up in a van bigger than any of the other bands or even the PA hire van and we jumped out and between the lot of us there was only just one small amp to bring out of it." The group had no need to bring any instruments or kit since, to save time, all the groups were sharing gear that day.

Another Rafters gig followed on from this, as well as a couple of memorable shows at Manchester's Squat Club. Of particular interest was a gig at the Squat where they appeared second on a bill topped by The Fall with John The Postman's Puerile and The Worst below them.

The Squat was an old Victorian school hall situated off Oxford Road (near the current Contact Theatre), named because an anarchic fringe of Manchester Polytechnic students had squatted there to draw attention to the lack of student accommodation. Once a hall of learning, it had now become the perfect punk venue. The Fall were the leading downbeat intellectuals of the time. By contrast, John The Postman had expanded his one man act into a full scale band with a humorous edge while The Worst, managed by Steve Shy, really were a band of little ability but massive attitude. In the middle of all this came Warsaw. It was an edgy, nervous performance with Barney's guitar registering far too loudly and Ian Curtis' vocals uncomfortably low in the mix. Nobody took any serious interest. It was a frustrating evening.

Buzzcock Steve Diggle recalls early sightings of Ian and Warsaw: "I can't remember the first time I met Ian, to be honest. It would have been just after the time with Stiff Kittens. I think Pete and Richard knew them before me, though I am not sure why. I do remember seeing Warsaw at The Electric Circus. It was very raw, very much a young band trying to find their way. I think it would be right to suggest that, at that point, they weren't quite sure which way they would be moving in terms of music. That's perfectly natural. They sounded a bit like a rougher version of The Banshees, who were one band who were never as bad as they made out in terms of musicianship. That was often the case with bands at that point. They pretended to be more inept than they actually were. That thing about learning two chords and then climbing onstage, well, that was OK but then you still had to do it once you had got on that stage. We had all been playing a little longer than was claimed at the time. But Warsaw did seem very raw."

Lest we forget, Ian Curtis was still employed in what might be regarded as a professional capacity during the first stirrings of Joy Division. He and Debbie had not been long in the house in Macclesfield before Ian obtained a transfer from his job at Manpower Services in central Manchester. His new position was as 'Assistant Disablement Resettlement Officer' based, most conveniently, at the Employment Exchange in Macclesfield. This job would give Ian no little satisfaction as he was able to help those who had struggled with work due to illness or disablement, offering advice about benefits to which disabled people were entitled to claim or steering them back or towards some kind of suitable employment. Ironically, given how Ian would subsequently suffer from epilepsy, he worked with people who suffered from this particular condition and every month, as part of his job, visited the David Lewis Centre in Alderley Edge. To this day the Centre cares for both adults and children suffering from severe epilepsy and other associated neurological problems. They provide assessment, care and treatment to enable such individuals to develop to their maximum potential.

Although Ian found his new job rewarding, and later may have even considered returning to it, his experiences at the David Lewis Centre left a bad picture in his mind regarding epilepsy. He saw some of the worst possible cases and it touched his tender heart. The impression it left in his mind would unquestionably lead to a degree of pessimism, even hopelessness, with regard to his own epileptic diagnosis in the not too far distant future.

After about six gigs with Warsaw Tony Tabac's enthusiasm had started to wane. "Anthony Tabac drummed at the May gig at The Electric Circus," recalls Terry. "I think he did Johnny Thunders at Rafters. And he certainly did the Penetration gig at Newcastle, and probably a gig at the Squat. His last gig was Rafters on June 30. He was middle-class and awfully nice. We could never figure out if it was his sister or his girlfriend that was always round him. He just wasn't reliable. I think he was concentrating on his other business. So then we had to find another drummer."

The band's growing reputation meant that a number of potential drummers had started to gather with intent. One of them, perhaps the most vociferous, was Steve Brotherdale, a fast-talker on the scene who was not lacking in self-belief. There are suggestions that Brotherdale even attempted to prise Ian Curtis away from Joy Division to become the lead singer with his 'other' band, Panik, ironically managed by Rob Gretton.

Mick Middles recalls meeting Brotherdale at The Band On The Wall. "He was making phone calls from the foyer, talking deals and rock biz, talking big. No one really took any offence but it didn't seem too real."

Later he would become known as Steve B'Dale and take up the drum position with Manchester glam band V2. Although he proved quite successful in this role, Brotherdale's bombastic character never seemed suited to the dynamic of Warsaw. However, he did hold the drum seat during Warsaw's first venture into a recording studio.

On July 18, 1977, the band – with Brotherdale on drums – booked into Pennine Sound Studios in Oldham for one night. Although only a grubby four-track studio, it was nonetheless perfectly adequate for the first recordings by a rudimentary band.

Five songs were completed, all of which would appear on various bootleg releases during the forthcoming decades, including the highly prized 'Dal Cuore Della Citta'/'From The Centre Of The City'. The other songs – 'Inside The Line', 'Gutz', 'The Kill' and 'At A Later Date' – were all a bit too close to The Stranglers, complete with over-dominant bass line.

To the band it felt like a release, of sorts, and Ian Curtis, spiked with an ambition that far outweighed the promise of that tape, thrust copies in the direction of fanzine scribblers in The Electric Circus. Steve Shy and Martin Martyn both seemed singularly unimpressed, as did Paul Morley, who was simultaneously beginning to realise that a life spent in the managerial hot seat with The Drones was perhaps a little misguided and wouldn't endear him to the powers-that-be at *NME* where his real ambition lay.

Whatever the reaction to these earliest recordings, they proved to be the swansong for drummer Steve Brotherdale. Terry Mason was far from impressed with him. "Steve Brotherdale... Steve bigmouth," he says. "I'm sure he had some redeeming features somewhere but they weren't obvious. He annoyed me intensely. It was that he'd sort of been in bands before and all of a sudden he was a punk. He wasn't of the same sort of mentality as us lot. He saw this as another band to be in. He wasn't one of us. He wasn't right. He was completely false. But yet again punk was hitting this momentum where all these people who'd come in late on it looked far better at it than we did – the people who'd been there. Years later people appeared with hair like [a Mohican] and pins and all that shit. We were into that secret early on."

Brotherdale's occupation of the drum seat was never secure as far as the rest of the band were concerned and he soon fell foul of Barney and Hooky's barbed Salfordian wit. Next up was Steve Morris, a far more promising candidate.

Terry Mason: "After Brotherdale left Steve Morris came in. Steve somehow contacted Ian. Steve was never really in the little gang. [He] was quite different from all of us again. He was basically... rich. His parents had a company that he worked for. They did fitted kitchens. Bespoke of course, none of your MFI rubbish."

Steve Morris, born in Macclesfield on October 28, 1957, had, like Ian, attended King's School. They also shared a similar accent although arguably Steve's was the broader of the two. Despite Steve's comparative affluence, there was nothing snobbish about him. "Steve was a right yokel," adds Terry. "He could have had a smock and a straw in his teeth."

After a nervous audition, held at the Abraham Moss Centre in Crumpsall, North Manchester, it was clear that Steve was obviously blessed with capabilities well beyond all previous drummers they'd tried. He was also well-educated, as Terry noted: "Steve seemed to have read stuff that we'd never read. We were very under-educated. It seems ridiculous because we went to a grammar school but we managed to do that and not come away with an awful lot of education. We had barely read anything."

The band continued gigging locally with Steve Morris in the drum seat and among those struck by the change was Vini Reilly, then starting out with Ed Banger & The Nosebleeds and who would later gain recognition with Durutti Column. Reilly had not been particularly impressed by the early band. "My first thought was that Barney was a bad guitar player," he says.

"The thing was I didn't like the tone he had on his guitar. I thought 'Why's he using that tone. It's all wrong and it doesn't work. It's neither one thing nor another, a really spiky and silly tone.' What did hit me was that Steve the [new] drummer was very, very unusual. The drum patterns that he was using were really bizarre and I'd not heard patterns like that before. That intrigued me. Ian was quite laid back at that gig[1] I seem to remember. He didn't really go for it but I thought he was definitely interesting and I knew he was the Ian I'd met in '75 so I was intrigued to see what he was actually like.

"It was very, very untogether and a bit of a barrage. I thought they hadn't rehearsed. I was looking at the equipment they were using and I was obsessed with the fact that the tone on the guitar was wrong. As I said Ian wasn't going for it, he was quite repressed at that gig. But, even though he was repressed – I could hardly hear what he was saying as the PA system was so bad so his vocals were quite muffled but he kept coming out with these lines that were just not lines that lead singers sang. They usually sang about, you know, clichés and everything that Ian sang was not a cliché it was just different. So the two things that were really different were Ian and Steve the drummer."

Vini nonetheless gained respect for Barney's playing later on, and changed his mind about his guitar tone. "If it had any other tone then it wouldn't have worked. It was a spiky, silly tone. He was really thrashing the guitar, Barney, but there was no power there. I thought they hadn't got a powerful enough amp or the guitar's not got powerful enough pick-ups. It just wasn't right. I think that's how, accidentally, Barney's tone in Joy Division evolved.

"As it is with most guitarists – it's just accidental. Coincidences and stuff. On *Unknown Pleasures* it was the only tone that would work."

Meanwhile, 'out there' in punk Manchester, the thin scattering of local bands was starting to become repetitive. No matter how many ambitious teenagers were struggling over their chords and triplets, the scene had really only thrown up three serious contenders, Buzzcocks, Slaughter & The Dogs and The Drones, and once you'd seen them all three or four times there wasn't much else left to see.

The Electric Circus, a slightly dangerous, paranoia inducing building when full, was always ill-fated and subject to closure from the authorities. When that happened, when it was initially forced to close at the beginning

---

[1] Reilly is probably referring to The Electric Circus show on October 3.

of October 1977, the punks took it as a sign of oppression, that they were not being allowed to party. Having something in common to fight for naturally acted as a bonding element, and in fact inspired a hitherto unseen feeling of camaraderie. It certainly led to a situation where the final weekend at The Electric Circus became one of the essential gigs of 1977 for any band within the Manchester area.

Everything about 1977 had combined to make The Electric Circus something way more than a crumbling ex-bingo hall in a deadbeat area of town. By the autumn months, the venue had been raised to another level entirely, where an atmosphere of sheer exhilaration co-existed with delicious unease. The sense that somehow this was special, the lovely depravity, the appalling stomach churning beer, the lack of health and safety measures, the filthiest toilets in Manchester (the only other contender was the Mayflower). It was all this and everything else, and it all came together in a climactic fulfilment in the final weekend of October 2 and 3, 1977.

Ian Curtis arrived at the frenzied scene on the Saturday, and was evidently determined to force Warsaw onto the stage that day but eventually settled for an appearance on day two.

Mick Middles saw Paul Morley emerge from the club to greet the queue with the words: "Everyone who is anybody is already in. Why are you not in there?" He laughed and, pulling rank as an obvious guest lister, waltzed back through the crowd and up the steps.

Not so Ian Curtis. Not for him the triumphant arrival of a genuine artist. Not a star… barely an artist, he shunned the very notion of 'specialness', and stood meekly in the queue. "I think we are on today," he shrugged, simultaneously buying a copy of the Sheffield fanzine, *Gun Rubber* from a red-panted, white-haired Bowie-punk called Martyn Ware who would one day front Heaven 17.

Rumours were rife among the crowd and in the dressing room. Virgin Records would be recording the event for posterity, no doubt as a kind of parallel album to the London live punk compilation, *Live At The Roxy*. It would be rough and ready, without a doubt – and it was – but would hopefully capture some sense of atmosphere. In effect it did, largely because of Paul Morley's evocative sleeve notes. By the time the record would eventually surface, in April 1978, Warsaw – who would then be called Joy Division – would have been allotted just one track, 'At A Later Date', memorable largely because Ian Curtis would scream, "Do you all remember Rudolf Hess?" at the start of the song.

The recording was significant insofar as it demonstrated just how far the band had travelled during the intervening six months. On the last night of

The Electric Circus, Warsaw were spirited though incoherent. Once beyond The Fall and Buzzcocks, Mick Middles felt that theirs would prove one of the most memorable sets of the entire weekend.

Terry Mason felt otherwise. "No one gave a shit," he says. "It was only after Joy Division became so famous that gigs like this become memorable."

Tony Wilson remembered seeing Warsaw, though, and noticing something "different" about Ian: "The two memories I took from that was that it was an absolute caterwauling of sound. It was completely punk in that it had completely no technique whatsoever. There was just an absolute barrage of fucking noise. It wasn't stupid punk or false punk it was real punk. It was completely anarchic and just a fucking mess. Glorious loud noisy mess. But, I can remember thinking that the lead singer had something very strange and very special about him. I remember thinking he was a bit weird and interesting. The band sounded shit but he looked special."

Photographer Kevin Cummins, alongside Paul Morley a member of the pseudo-band The Negatives, who played two sets during the weekend, recalls a strange atmosphere inside the venue. "The thing about The Electric Circus crowd was that the room was split, almost into two or three bits. You had the upstairs balcony, where people used to go and have sex and take drugs. You had the downstairs bit at the bar, where three hundred people would run around. Then you had the front bit, for the bands, where all the people who had just read *The Mirror* and *The People* who would write these absurd over the top punk articles… and they would have read these articles and believed them and believed that the thing to do was to go and gob at bands. So, most of us, the actual people in the Manchester scene, would go and stand at the back. Just past the DJ booth, and we would stand around talking for most of the time and then, if anyone came on who we liked, we might wander up to the front.

"On the last weekend at The Electric Circus, where Joy Division made their debut on vinyl on that live EP, the only people at the front were all the people who wouldn't normally have gone to gigs. Some of them were people who were trying to make a name for themselves but were never really involved, and the music press people who came from London for the weekend. They all went down the front. But most of us stood at the back for it. We – The Negatives – went on and played both nights… I've a got a tape of that. We had a different vocalist on each night. We had this mate of Paul's (Morley) on vocals for the first night and Pete Shelley on vocals for the second night. All the bands were playing for the Pat Seed Scanner Fund, which was the big Manchester thing at the time. And that was important because we all felt that it was about time that Manchester punks proved that they could do some good and not be just a bunch of arseholes. Unfortunately, that all backfired because the two guys who ran the club fucked off with all the money. I remember taking a picture of Alan from The Worst and Pete Shelley presenting a cheque for £750, which had been raised on that night then, the next thing I know, the old bill are around at my house, telling me that the cheque had bounced and they started asking me what I knew about the two guys who ran The Electric Circus.

"But I think that Warsaw came out of that rather well. Perhaps better than any other band... apart, perhaps from The Fall, who were far more advanced. They were still naïve but there was something about Ian that stood out. Of course, the place was full of record company A&R men and none of them noticed Ian's talent, did they? Typical, really."

CHAPTER 5

Leaders Of Men

"I really think Ian thought of the name... Anything that had any relationship to Germany was interesting to Ian." – Mark Reeder

The gig at the Electric Circus was swiftly followed by one with Slaughter & The Dogs and V2 at Salford Technical College on October 7. This particular show is significant not only for the trouble that occurred but because it was probably the first time Martin Hannett saw a performance by the group. There was some argument about who should go on prior to Slaughter, Terry Mason recalling that they tossed a coin for it and that Warsaw lost.

The trouble blew up when a gang of local lads, known to Warsaw from neighbouring pubs and the Ranch Bar, objected to the presence of Slaughter & The Dogs fans who had travelled from Wythenshawe to offer their support. Bottles and bricks were thrown at every window around the gym and coffee area, and when hostilities ceased no windows remained unbroken. Enraged by the violence, the social secretary blamed Warsaw, simply for being there, although it was arguably no more their fault than the other groups, particularly since they chose the sensible option of lying low in another room as the windows came crashing in.

Mick Middles recalls standing by one of the windows with a few friends when a sudden noise was followed by splintered shards of glass shattering all around them. "Somebody shouted 'It's the Teds... It's the Teds...',

Manchester at the time having suddenly become infested with a mysterious neo-Teddy Boy faction which appeared to exist solely to wipe out the evil punk fad," he says. "People scattered in all directions."

For Middles and at least one of his mates, refuge turned out to be a convenient photo booth in one of the corridors, where they remained until the flurry of activity died down. He does not recall seeing Warsaw or even knowing that they were on the bill, but had attended for Slaughter & The Dogs, arguably the most exciting live act in Manchester at the time.

Paul Morley was also present and Terry remembered that after their set Warsaw won a bottle of wine in a competition and offered to share it with him. To the astonishment of the group, Morley drank the wine and then took a couple of bites out of the wine glass.

There is some uncertainty as to why Martin Hannett and his girlfriend Susanne O'Hara were present that night. Terry Mason thinks they came as representatives of Music Force, the agency that had booked the gig, but Tosh Ryan and Lawrence Beedle are sure that the agency had collapsed by then due to "membership inertia". Nonetheless, Martin definitely paid the groups at the end of the night, and it seems likely that he continued to promote local bands independently after the demise of the agency since this had been one of his roles within the organisation.

Music Force was a musicians co-operative founded on socialist principles set up initially by Victor Brox, Bruce Mitchell and Tosh Ryan in 1972, specifically to help out-of-work musicians find live gigs after the spread of discotheques in the early Seventies had tended to make them redundant. Shortly thereafter Martin Hannett was co-opted onto the committee at the behest of Bruce. Lawrence Beedle also became a key figure booking bands since he was the social secretary at Manchester Polytechnic, the agency's main venue.

Before long, Music Force diversified into other areas, including PA, van hire and the dark art of bill-posting. Martin Hannett found himself employed in a number of roles, including trying to tempt bands of some repute into the city for bare minimum payment and, more intriguingly, procuring musical and PA equipment for student unions in the city.

Through this, Hannett developed an understanding of electronic gadgetry that would, in time, famously extend beyond the 'manufacturers instructions'. Thus did Hannett develop his true genius: a unique ability to simply toss the instruction booklet to one side and push a device somewhere to the left of its limitations. It was a talent that began early in Hannett's career as he came to the conclusion that he owned an ear that was not, strictly speaking, of a 'conventional' nature.

Hannett began building his reputation at Manchester's Indigo Studios on Tuesday, December 28, 1976. Adopting the name Martin Zero – possibly derived from a gig promotions name connected to Music Force that he called 'Ground Zero' – he became the producer of one of punk's greatest moments, the record that firmly established the DIY ethos of the independent record label.

Buzzcocks manager Richard Boon recognised in his clients a certain verve and fire that appeared unique. Their unlikely mix of influences, from Captain Beefheart to The New York Dolls, certainly separated them from the full-tilt mayhem of bands that formed on an almost nightly basis in the slipstream of the Pistols. Boon contacted Martin Hannett, for whom the opportunity to work with their strange array of twisted speed-freak love songs seemed perfect.

They made an EP together and called it *Spiral Scratch*, and it was the first genuine indication that Martin Hannett had a pair of ears that reached beyond convention and were capable of producing moments of genius.

"We had decided to make an EP on our own label," recalls Buzzcocks guitarist Steve Diggle. "I think it was Howard (Devoto's) idea initially but I can't be sure. We didn't really have any choice. The fact was that nobody in London gave a shit about Manchester. In truth, Sad Café were signed and I think the London record companies thought that that was it. That was Manchester. Nothing else could be happening. The only reason why we decided on an EP was because we could put it out in a picture sleeve, like the old EPs of the Sixties, like *The Beatles' Hits* or something. Not very punk, really. Later on we were credited with creating this whole new independent way of thinking… but it was just how it happened.

"Anyway, we chose four tracks from our thin repertoire. It wasn't difficult to choose. My track was 'Breakdown'… I don't know, Howard and Pete came up with 'Boredom', 'Friends Of Mine and 'Time's Up'. It all just fell together, to be honest. We all trooped down to Indigo Studios in Manchester to work with a really, really odd guy who, at the time, was called Martin Zero. It was a really strange choice for us because he had been involved with Sad Café and the old Manchester scene. He was a hippie, as well. That was a strange choice for a punk band although, looking back, all producers and engineers were hippies really. Same with The Sex Pistols people. I suppose they were just older musicians who had gravitated into studios. Still, it was an odd choice for us. Very odd as it turned out. We didn't really know anything about Martin other than that he worked for *New Manchester Review*, which was a listing magazine at the time. He was just a guy who told us that he was a producer. Well we didn't know any other producers and obviously we needed one. So we took him on."

Tosh Ryan remembers Martin as being: "… literary. He wrote some great things in the magazine we [Music Force] had – the *Hot Flash* magazine. I remember there was a singer/guitar player called Kevin Ayers and he ran off with Richard Branson's wife to Tenerife way back in the Seventies. Martin wrote this article and it was headed up 'Record mogul's wife splits with Ayres, Branson left in pickle'! Absolutely brilliant. He edited the magazine for quite a while. There's this great photograph of the editor on an inside page which was Martin and he was sat, cross-legged, on the psychiatrist's couch that we had in the office and it looked as if he was just levitating, just floating like some beatific God. Stunning."

The label Rabid Records was founded in 1977 by Martin, Tosh Ryan and Lawrence Beedle with money from Music Force's flyposting operation, though the idea of running a record label had always been in their backs of their minds. "We had an intention to run a record label," says Ryan. "Right from the start it was part of its constitution, its manifesto. That was the specific area that Martin was interested in. Martin always wanted to make records and he said right from the start that we should have a recording studio and buy recording kit. I disagreed with him in lots of ways for ages. It's always in retrospect I think that Martin was right. All the stuff he did with John Cooper Clarke – I condemned it. I thought we were wasting a lot of money. We were spending fortunes."

Lawrence Beedle recalls that Martin wanted to be like Phil Spector. "I had an illusion about a little record company like they had in America that issues singles – like the way Chess Records or Atlantic Records started out," he says. "Tosh was good at publicity, talking on the phone, he had a lot of contacts and I could do the admin and Martin could do the studio. And we had a bit of success. At that point Rabid was run from St. Paul's Rd [Tosh's house] but Martin was closing down Music Force. The first set of records actually got delivered to 178 Waterloo Terrace – a lovely Georgian building still there."

Rabid's first release was the single 'Cranked Up Really High' by Slaughter & The Dogs in May 1977, produced by Hannett. It's logical to assume, therefore, that Martin was present at the gig at Salford Tech that October night more because of his interest in Slaughter & The Dogs than Warsaw. Perhaps it was fate. Martin's dream of becoming a producer was materialising.

Never one to limit himself to any particular style of music, one of Hannett's earliest forays into sound production, had him working with a

Stoke-on-Trent band called Afro Express who had hired his services to produce an album that would, in time, sell in large quantities in Nigeria. Through this experience Martin found out how records were pressed, how labels were created and how the forces of distribution could be used to promote success. Rabid Records therefore encapsulated many elements that would soon inform the embryonic Factory Records. C.P. Lee, in his book *Shake Rattle And Rain,* states that without Music Force there would have been no Rabid and without that, "there would have been no Factory Records, without Factory there would have been no Haçienda, and no 1988 Summer of Love."

October 1977 was an eventful month for Warsaw. Salford Tech was followed the very next night by their first headline gig at Manchester Polytechnic where Lawrence Beedle had been the social secretary. Tosh Ryan remembers that someone called Timothy Llewellyn had become the social secretary after Lawrence vacated the role and that Tim also had a room and phone upstairs in the offices of Rabid, which had moved away from town to a house in Cotton Lane in Withington. It seems that Tim was acting as a booking agent. Given that he was also on friendly terms with Martin and Susanna O'Hara, this would explain why Martin was still involved with this side of things and had doled out the gig money the previous night. Terry remembers that this gig at the Poly was also their first show with a proper PA.

On October 19 the group played at Pipers, a venue more recognisably known as the Cyprus Tavern on Manchester's Princess Street but renamed Pipers one evening a week when they had a regular disco/band night, much as the Russell Club was called Factory on Fridays.

After a relatively busy October the rest of the year was on the quiet side. In an attempt to generate some gigs the band placed themselves with a local 'Search For A Star' talent quest being run by an agency in Leigh which supplied acts to pubs and CIU working men's clubs. In order to obtain bookings the band were obliged to appear before a panel of judges from the agency – there was no audience – on a talent night at The Stocks in Walkden.

It was a very strange night, with Warsaw appearing between pub singers and comedians. Because of the bad press that punk was receiving at the time the agency stressed that the group had to tell anyone who asked that they were 'a bit like Deep Purple', this despite the fact that Deep Purple had ground to a somewhat inglorious halt the previous year. The band duly did the allotted time on stage, packed up and went home thinking nothing more would come of it. To their surprise they eventually got a call from the agency offering them a New Year's Eve slot at the Spinning Apple in Liverpool.

"We'd never heard of it," says Terry Mason, "and I don't think anyone has ever heard of it since."

Whether the agency thought the band had any talent or whether they were simply short of a band to offer the Liverpool venue is a matter of conjecture but in the event the audience included plenty of enthusiastic punk fans and the group were paid £100, the most money they had ever seen.

When Warsaw arrived they were told they had to do two sets either side of midnight. Since their repertoire was somewhat limited they augmented the set with a few interesting covers. "They did 'Anarchy In The UK', 'Louie Louie' and some dodgy Velvet Underground numbers," says Terry. "The high spot of the night was when midnight approached everyone did a conga out into the street and kicked every car that was parked there, in rhythm with the sixth beat. 'It's a Liverpool tradition!' they told us."

The week before this rousing end-of-year send-off, on Boxing Day, the group had paid their second visit to Pennine Sound Studios to record what would become their first release under the name Joy Division. A cheaper rate was quoted for the day after Christmas and in keeping with his spirit of enterprise and endeavour, Ian had managed to raise the finance for this project. Nevertheless, Terry remembers it was a cold and miserable day and they all had to get up early when everyone else was on holiday. Terry's mum made chicken sandwiches on barmcakes for everyone from the leftovers of Christmas Day lunch, without which they would have gone hungry since in those days it was impossible to find food in Oldham on a Boxing Day or a Sunday.

Paul Morley had already written about Warsaw when he did a piece on Manchester music, and he was actually approached by them to act as producer. "They went off to record *Ideal For Living* and I was going to produce it," he recalls. "In a drunken moment one night I said, 'I'll produce it' and they said, 'Great'. But I had a hangover and never turned up. They were all meeting in St. Ann's Square before driving off to somewhere in Rochdale. Thankfully I didn't turn up – I was too drunk to get out of bed. A weird bit of history nearly got made there. It was very gung ho. They were going off and they were ever so excited, two days I think they got."

Four tracks were recorded at this four-track facility. This might be regarded as quite an achievement for such a short time in a studio but they were pretty much recorded live. Production-wise there was not that much going on apart from a bit of reverb here and there. Perhaps Morley did the right thing by staying in bed. He didn't think that much of the EP anyway: "It sounded really awful and muffled and dirty. It didn't have any sound at all, you know." The tracks completed were: 'Warsaw', 'No Love Lost', 'Leaders Of Men' and 'Failures'.

All agreed that the name Warsaw was beginning to seem rather dull, which may have been one reason why A&R men hadn't even begun to show an interest. It was also too close to the name of another band of the era.

"They changed that name after there was a group around at the same time called 'Warsaw Pakt'," says Mark Reeder. "This group recorded an album at night and it was in the shops the next day and it was rubbish. It was like one of these pseudo punk rock records by a load of pub rockers. I think they were a bit embarrassed to be associated with a group that had a similar sounding name. So to immediately distance themselves from this record they changed their name."

Around this time Ian was reading a book by Ka-Tzetnik 1355633, the Nazi-assigned number of an Auschwitz survivor who had adopted it as a pen name. Some say the author was Yehiel Dinur, other's Karol Cetynski but, translated from Hebrew, the author's sister is the central character and the story is based largely on her diary. It tells of the plight of a 17-year-old Jewess taken to the brothel (or "Doll House") of a concentration camp where women were sterilised and used by Nazi officers as sex slaves. In the course of their duties they were obliged to smile and appear happy or risk death, hence the derivation of the term 'Joy Division'.

"I really think Ian thought of the name," says Mark Reeder. "I've actually never asked Bernard this but I don't think Bernard thought of it although he did read the book that Ian had. Maybe Bernard had given Ian his book about the Joy Division, as I know Bernard had this book at home. Anything that had any relationship to Germany was interesting to Ian. When I first went to Germany he was interested to know what it was like 'cos he'd never been. I told him it wasn't much different to here but cleaner. He was interested in the Third Reich but I don't want people to believe that he was some kind of closet fascist because he wasn't. That's the sort of thing it invokes in people's minds when you talk about it. The whole secret history aspect of Nazi Germany, which was hidden from school curriculum history, was one of the things that fascinated Ian – discovering such things like the poor camp girls who were made to serve as whores for the Nazis. [That] wasn't in school textbooks. It's possible his interest in this subject might have been awoken by *The Night Porter*, which was a highly controversial film touching remotely on this subject. He had mentioned this film once in conversation, so I believe he might have seen it."

The group made their first appearance under their new name at Pip's Disco on January 25, 1978. Pip's was one of the few Manchester night clubs that appeared willing to allow punks free rein, largely because it was really several discos within a large complex, one of which – the Roxy Room – had a fairly enlightened musical policy. Here, during the mid-Seventies, it was possible to pose the night away to the sounds of Lou Reed, Iggy Pop, the Velvets, Bowie, Roxy Music, T Rex, The New York Dolls and a select scattering of compatible garage bands like MC5 and The Seeds. Barney, Hooky and Terry Mason, discerning fans all, had spent numerous evenings in the Roxy Room at Pip's, as had most of those who formed Manchester's punk inner circle in 1976 and '77.

Of course, the clothes worn by many of the latter-day glam addicts was, if anything, even more extreme than the new punks, so the bouncers – who were just as ferocious as any elsewhere in the city, as Ian Curtis would discover – were rendered incapable of noticing the sudden influx of punks. Not being fashion conscious, they simply couldn't tell the difference.

Pip's was therefore the natural venue to house the transition from glam to punk, though as a rock venue it never really worked. It always seemed a touch too eccentric, too electronic. Although it would find itself reborn in the new wave era at the start of the Eighties, at the time of Joy Division's first gig it was a clumsy, awkward room, where the audience didn't quite know how to react and the bands always seemed strangely uncomfortable in their surroundings.

Terry Mason's memories of Pip's are coloured by his having witnessed an altercation between Ian and the bouncers. "We did the first one as Joy Division at Pip's. Ian got thrown out 'cos he was bladdered and being an arsehole. We had to plead with the bouncers to let him back in 'cos... 'He's actually the singer with the band'. This was all before the epilepsy either came on or became apparent. At that point he was still Jack the lad like the rest of us... me and him were Jack the stupid lads. We were on Special Brew and blackcurrant... we used to have loads of them. I was a boring drunk. Ian would just be bouncing all over the show and throwing himself about."

While this may have seemed normal behaviour in the Electric Circus, it wasn't at Pip's. "Pip's wasn't a punk place," adds Terry. "The venue was having sort of punk gigs or 'gigettes' – 'cos they were so small – but it was still Friday night dancing round your handbag mentality with the bouncers there. The audience was your proto-punks that were still about then – we probably had Mick Hucknall in the audience or someone like that. You didn't know who they were at the time though."

Joy Division's set at Pip's built towards an intensity that was pulsating but ragged. The bass-line reverberation crumbled through the entire sound while Steve Morris physically punched it to a higher level with 'They Walked In Lines' snagging on the attention spans of the few who had started to encircle this increasingly fascinating group.

Mick Middles recalls that John The Postman, always among the more perceptive of observers on the scene, had started to notice there was something special about the band. "He would talk about Warsaw/Joy Division with an unexpected degree of reverence," he said. "He said things like, 'Walking into Joy Division gigs was like attending church.'"

That night, in these strange surroundings, Ian Curtis seemed distinctly jittery, perhaps desperate, following his altercation with the bouncer. He attracted more unwarranted attention with a clumsy attempt to sweep a broken glass to the side of the stage, a simple act that served only to heighten the tension.

The miniscule set crumbled to an edgy halt, the band glanced at each other, and nervous ripples of applause were spiced by taunts. Hooky, never one to suffer stage-side fools, leapt into the crowd where there was a brief flurry of fists. An unhappy gig or a tiny triumph? History has recorded the latter although the band left that night feeling curiously depressed. There had been a vague hope that Tony Wilson, the local TV presenter, might have been present but his instantly recognisable features were nowhere to be seen at Pip's.

Perhaps more importantly, a slight division had occurred within the audience. The glam following at Pip's, led by a posse of Bowie-ites who were moving very cautiously towards punk, preferred a touch of showbiz flash and banter, while the more serious punks, to whom flash and banter was anathema, favoured the low key approach of Joy Division. On glam side of this localised divide and rooted in the unease of the evening was an 18-year-old misfit called Steven Morrissey, a prolific letter writer to fanzines, whose dissing of both Joy Division and New Order would famously echo down the years.

By the spring of 1978, Rafters had emerged as the leading small-scale venue in Manchester city centre. Rather bizarrely, The Electric Circus had re-opened following its infamous closure, but it never managed to regain its former glory. For a short while therefore, Rafters, with its city centre position on Oxford Road, became the place to see and be seen.

It was far from ideal. A long, thin, subterranean shoebox that had served time as a folk club in the mid-Seventies, it now took on the ambience of a scampi-in-a-basket disco. Nevertheless, it would host its fair share of classic punk gigs. Howard Devoto's fast emerging Magazine performed to a cramped, steamy audience, and equally intense were gigs by Elvis Costello, Buzzcocks, XTC and Johnny Thunders & The Heartbreakers. When it was packed, the only sensible method of actually seeing the band on stage would be literally to hang from the rafters that stretched the length of the venue. A great deal of the footage that appeared in the second series of Tony Wilson's *So It Goes* was from a series of gigs at Rafters; the first time also that many of the Manchester music people would notice Wilson, usually accompanied by Lindsay Reade, in their midst.

During this period Wilson became friendly with one of the Rafters DJs, Rob Gretton, who had been involved in the circle that surrounded Slaughter & The Dogs and Rabid Records. Gretton's Slaughter-dedicated fanzine *Manchester Rains* was openly on sale at Rafters, taking its place alongside the later issues of *Shy Talk*, *Ghast Up* and the Paul Morley single sheet 'zine, *Girl Trouble*. It became a Rafters institution to purchase each other's fanzine and read them in the club's various alcoves. To a large extent, The Electric Circus and Ranch Bar elite had resettled inside this comparatively safe and plush interior.

There was a certain degree of frustration within the ranks of Joy Division during the early months of 1978. Ian Curtis and Terry Mason might have continued in their attempts to catch the attention of the largely uninterested London record companies, but the band were making little headway within their own city.

Terry Mason: "Me and Ian were tracking what was going on, both in Manchester and nationally. However, it did seem to be going wrong. At the start of '78, the gigs really died. It seemed that we had become the most unpopular band in the city and The Fall seemed to be playing in the city every two weeks. On top of this, there was a bit of shit flying around that we were Nazis."

The line between being a band whose lyricism displayed a fascination for Nazi history and a band who were openly regarded as 'Nazis', was on the thin side during the atmosphere of paranoia in 1978, when British underground music was viewed as the front line against the horrific resurgence of the far right National Front. Only the tiniest of rumours was needed to attach a negative vibe to a band that had named themselves Joy Division and used Nazi imagery in their lyrics and artwork.

Terry Mason recalls that Rock Against Racism, the emerging organisation that at the time was running anti-National Front gigs across the country, wouldn't even talk to Joy Division at that point. "They did, later, when we became hip again, but they were nervous of having an association with us and you can understand why," he says. "But the hard truth was that we had slipped from about fourth to twentieth in the pecking order in a city that didn't have that many bands. It was difficult for me because I was starting to become isolated. I started to find it hard to bring anything to the band."

Ian Curtis had remained in contact with Buzzcocks manager Richard Boon. It was a significant period for his band who, finally (just), dented the Top 40 in February with 'What Do I Get?' and, at the beginning of March, released their debut album, *Another Music In A Different Kitchen*. The album, produced by Martin Rushent, gained deservedly excellent reviews in the music press. Despite this, and surprisingly, it was The Drones who were the first of the Manchester punk bands to boast the status of actually having an album released, although their *Further Temptations* had proven a somewhat lacklustre affair.

Nevertheless, all this prevailing activity served only hasten the anxiety within Joy Division. With *An Ideal For Living* recorded and awaiting some kind of release (as a paper-fold in a plastic sleeve) and with Virgin's 10-inch LP *Live At The Electric Circus* due out in April – carrying with it Joy Division's vinyl debut, a raucous rendition of 'At A Later Date' – there did, at least, seem to be some kind of forward movement.

Terry Mason: "The thing about *An Ideal For Living* was that, back at Pennine we had done a deal where they would present us with the seven-inch records with our own label, Enigma. The problem was that we didn't know anything about distribution at all, not a clue. We were also waiting for Barney to come up with the sleeve. He was working for Cosgrove Hall animators at the time. Meanwhile we were stuck with a lot of these records in white sleeves. Eventually we would do a deal with Tosh Ryan at Rabid, I think… but for a while we were just handing a few across the counter at Virgin and things like that."

Mark Reeder worked at Virgin Records and remembers Terry coming in with them: "We were the only shop in Manchester that sold punk rock records," he says.

When *An Ideal For Living* eventually did surface in an official guise, it was clothed in the notorious Hitler Youth drummer-boy sleeve, just the kind of thing to stoke the paranoia of supporters of Rock Against Racism.

"It does seem a stupid thing to do," says Terry Mason in hindsight, "to put it in that sleeve. But… in all honesty, we didn't really think about it at the time. In fact, we thought it was arty because the hip film at the time was *The Tin Drum*. That was something everyone was talking about. I am sure that was why we did that."

An independently-released 7-inch EP wasn't likely to change Joy Division's fortunes, however, and gigs remained hard to come by. Despite repeated appearances by The Drones, The Fall and even The Worst in the city centre, in the two months that had followed Joy Division's debut at Pip's, they had managed to secure just one gig and hardly a prestigious one at that.

On March 14, the band made their first appearance at Bowden Vale Youth Club, deep in the leafy suburbs on the fringe of Altrincham. This unlikely venue had been courageous enough to present regular gig nights featuring such local acts as The Freshies, The Distractions and Fast Cars, all bands that had failed to gain any following in the city centre. For the fast improving Joy Division, the situation was close to unbearable though Ian or Terry Mason continued to contact the three or four journalists who serviced the city, providing Joy Division info and gig invites.

Next on the agenda was a travelling showcase event organised by two leading London independent record labels, Stiff and Chiswick, but when it arrived in Manchester, offering local bands a chance to perform in front of their respective A & R men, most city onlookers regarded it with considerable disdain. The prevailing opinion was that the Stiff Test/Chiswick Challenge was little more than a talent contest, a crass, unworthy project that would serve only to degrade those bands who co-operated. Indeed, many felt it was simply rubbing salt into the wounds for the London labels to arrogantly expect provincial bands to perform at their bequest, like dogs in a circus.

Local journalist Bob Dickinson who, like Rob Gretton was a Rafters DJ, was working the decks on the night of this infamous gig. "They just went round the country publicly auditioning local bands and the one that they thought was the best won the prize of having a record released by them," he recalls. "It was a very, very long night and I was just standing there cueing records in between bands. All the bands were dreadful, they were really boring. They all seemed to be pub/rock bands. The place was really full and the night was getting later and later – at that time gigs did go on until two in the morning. Nowadays they are on stage at 8pm or 7.30pm or something. At that time people didn't care how long it went on. At the end of the night there was supposed to be this band on called Joy Division but I kept on hearing during the course of the night that they were going to get thrown off the bill because there'd been some argument because they'd turned up late."

Among the bands on the bill was The Negatives, who perhaps most typified the prevailing Manchester attitude towards the event. Very much an ironic joke, they still featured Paul Morley, Kevin Cummins, Dave Bentley and Steve Shy among their fluctuating line-up. According to Manchester legend, a row broke out between the pseudo band factions of The Negatives and Joy Division – in particular, Ian Curtis – who were evidently taking the entire affair very seriously indeed.

Paul Morley recalls the event as 'dreadful'. "Everyone went along to audition [and] we'd got this stupid joke band The Negatives. I never thought of it as a row. Joy Division were very wound up about getting on and because of all these bands they were getting pushed back later and later, way beyond midnight and they were getting very tense and very passionate about it and thought they were going to lose their chance and they thought it was people like me that were stopping them. That was the night Rob (Gretton) saw them."

Kevin Cummins is less dismissive of The Negatives. "They didn't really exist," he says. "It was just me and Paul (Morley) sitting up all night, talking bollocks and pretending to have ideas for being in a band and how you would do it; just going down that whole trip, really, having song titles. [We were] sitting there with the Stockport *Yellow Pages*, sending out a list of fictional gigs at working men's clubs around the north, The Grey Parrot in Northwich, Our Lady & The Apostles Social Club, legendary new wave venues every one. *Sounds* printed the entire tour list. We thought that was hilarious, as you do at that age and we thought it would be quite funny to advertise that we were going to play and then not turn up. And then we thought, 'Why don't we just do it?' I think we thought we were Henry Cow and we would turn up and make a bit of a noise and people wouldn't know whether to take it seriously or not."

The confusion was understandable. The cleverer journalists of the day – Morley, Ian Penman, Jon Savage – seemed content to endorse any kind of well-dressed, cacophonous racket. Could The Negatives, therefore, be taken seriously? Certainly within the more pretentious areas of the music press… yes. The idea of breaking music down into fragments, of ridiculing the traditional rock format, would have appealed to Ian Curtis, who had already taken a liking to the anarchic Throbbing Gristle, who broke down every conceivable barrier. And yet, Ian Curtis was about to represent the traditional elements of rock music, albeit in a ridiculous contest where they would be pitched against, among others, an entertaining fake. In later years,

Paul Morley would express embarrassment at the notion of The Negatives being higher on the bill than Joy Division.

Kevin Cummins has a clear recollection of the altercation between Ian and Paul Morley. "We decided that we would have guest vocalists for every gig, because no one had done that, which is why we had Pete Shelley singing on one night," he says. "Conceptually it was quite good although some people just didn't get it. In fact, even some people in the band didn't get it. It was never ever meant to be serious in any way. But when we came to the Stiff Test/Chiswick Challenge night, Paul wanted to do it and I didn't. And Paul hated... absolutely *hated* Warsaw... or early Joy Division.[1]

"Paul got really drunk and tried to have a fight with Hooky and Ian, which wasn't advisable, really, certainly not with Hooky. This was at Rafters and this was why they just kept getting pushed down the bill because Paul was being more vociferous, really, with people who had come up from London. Those A&R people knew Paul's name but didn't know anyone who was in Joy Division. So they thought that we must be more serious than them. We didn't give a toss. We weren't interested. People like Jon Savage, who were obviously in on the joke, would review us and would just say, 'This is great because... blah blah'. Thing was it was for people in London to read and take it seriously. We all just chose instruments we couldn't play, deliberately. Because I liked to think I could play bass guitar a little bit, even if it was upside down, I wasn't allowed to play it.'

In contrast, Joy Division seemed steadfast in their determination to make an impact on the night: "Joy Division were so serious," says Cummins. "In fact, they were more than that. They were very aggressive at the time, in the way that lots of bands are when they are not really gigging and they have got to try and push themselves. They reminded me of Slaughter & The Dogs, in a way. They would turn up and claim to be the support band, whether they were or not and they would play at Rafters or wherever. That was OK. It was how you got on. But because we weren't serious, we would stand back and take the piss out of that attitude and they would get more and more wound up. On that night, at Rafters, they just wanted to be signed up. By anyone. It didn't matter. I think Terry Mason was manager at that point."

---

[1] In reality Morley seems actually to have been largely indifferent. As he said earlier: "For early Warsaw I wasn't necessarily that overwhelmed by them. I thought they were unformed a little bit, not quite finished. I think Ian knew that as well, that they weren't great, they weren't magnificent, they were just an ordinary local band."

Terry Mason: "Well, we wanted something to happen. We were determined to make something of it. The fact that The Negatives had day jobs that were quite interesting actually pissed us off at the time. We saw Paul Morley and Kevin Cummins farting about onstage and being arty. It just made us very angry, especially Ian who was very committed to getting somewhere. He hated seeing these people just fucking about. There were about 13 bands on and we were really pissed off because we should have been welcomed with open arms and given a reasonable spot. At one point we were even told 'Sorry lads, there is no time for you'. That was really infuriating for everyone."

The notion that there was some kind of back-stage disagreement also made an impression on Bob Dickinson: "There was some back-stage arguing and no-one was quite sure whether they were going to go on but – I think it was about half past one in the morning – they eventually got on stage and they played for about 20 minutes, I think. I'd never seen them in their previous incarnation as Warsaw. They came on stage and they were wearing what I thought was biker gear – leather trousers and biker boots.

"He (Hooky) definitely had leather boots on and, I think, leather trousers. They had short hair so they didn't look like Hell's Angels. I thought they were a heavy metal band at first – when they first came on I thought we were going to get some good old head-banging music. But I just found as soon as they came on that they were absolutely electrifying, especially Ian Curtis who was a really compelling person to watch – even though it was such a short set. I found them… the phrase that immediately sprang to mind was negative, negative energy. I thought it was very appropriate for the time. They were totally unlike any of the bands on that night. They didn't care at all what people thought of them. All those other bands on that night were desperate to be recorded by Stiff or Chiswick and they were trying to please the audience and to entertain."

Sitting spellbound in the audience was Rob Gretton who had already tried his hand managing with The Panik, a Manchester glam outfit overly reliant on the influence of The New York Dolls. Gretton had produced a fanzine for Slaughter & The Dogs and in the day time worked in Manchester Town Hall surveyors department. Keen to get into the music business, he produced a single for The Panik which was released by Rainy City Records, but he was searching for something else, something special and that night he decided he had found it in Joy Division.

"They sounded European and the music was like their first EP," says Bob Dickinson, "[It was] that sort of material and it sounded doom-laden and negative but really compelling. It was something that sucked you in. It was confusing. I didn't know what to make of it but I definitely thought they were different from anything else on that night and the only one that I wanted to watch all the way through and I was excited by it. The only other thing I remember about that night was afterwards. I was standing on the dance floor and the audience was on their way out. It was empty and covered with that glittery look of all the rubbish and detritus that a crowd leaves behind them on a dance floor, the glass and plastic and rubbish and cigarette ends and there were people sweeping up this rubbish and there were bouncers telling you to clear off 'cos we're locking up in five minutes and all that sort of thing. And Rob Gretton is coming towards me across this dance floor and he's completely – well, I suppose he's drunk, but he's delighted, he was so happy, absolutely over the moon with Joy Division. He was in heaven. He was asking me what I thought about them and he was saying, 'I'm going to manage that group, they are the big break I've been looking for – they are what I've been wanting all along.' And he was just ecstatic about them."

Lawrence Beedle also remembers Rob's enthusiasm: "Rob took myself and Martin to meet Joy Division and he wanted to get involved with this band and he wanted them to sign to Rabid. Martin was quite keen and I thought we could sell some records. [Then] Tosh saw the Nazi iconography and said 'No way.'"

Nevertheless, *An Ideal For Living* was subsequently distributed by Rabid Records after Gretton became involved with the band. Beedle: "Rob turns up one day, and I agreed to sell the records for him through our network… if we brought a record out, we could sell a couple of thousand straight off. So he came round to Cotton Lane with about 1,000 of them in boxes and we distributed it. Rough Trade sold some and others would take a box. We had a deal with a local record distributor, Wind Up Records, who liked us. It was through their back leasing company that Martin got his blue Volvo. We originally met them because there was a record shop in Wythenshawe Civic Centre called NSS (a chain of newsagents) and to get the record in there you had to go through Wind Up Records as they would supply all the records to the NSS chain."

It was after Joy Division's set at Rafters that night that there occurred the infamous incident between Ian Curtis and Tony Wilson, which took place next to the pool table at the bottom of the steps to the venue. In the film *24 Hour Party People* Lindsay Reade was portrayed as playing pool with Tony Wilson's friend Alan Erasmus during the altercation. Tony Wilson: "I saw the belligerent side of Ian that night. He said, 'You're a fucking cunt, you haven't put us on television', to which I didn't reply but I said to myself, 'You're next on the list, you stupid twat.'"

"Whatever Ian said to Tony Wilson, it certainly wasn't very polite," says Terry Mason. "Ian was pissed and angry. We had been drinking Carlsberg Special all night and we had been really messed around. You couldn't blame Tony Wilson for becoming all agreeable. He did what every sensible person would do when a drunken nutter comes and swears at you from five inches from your face. Ian wanted to know why Wilson hadn't put them on television. Tony just agreed, quite rightly. I think the incident must have done the band some good, actually. It was a way of salvaging something from the night. No one from Stiff or Chiswick ever approached us."

CHAPTER 6

The Beat Of The Show

"Nobody could have been aware, at that point, just how good Joy Division were about to become. I have no idea if they knew it themselves but I sense they did… they weren't just another punk band pulled in from the streets." – Derek Brandwood

By the spring of 1978 there was a distinct likelihood that Ian Curtis' visits to the RCA office in Piccadilly Plaza would bring about the release of an album by Joy Division. The momentum was certainly building and although the Stiff Test at Rafters hadn't produced anything tangible, the band was beginning to attract a small but growing local following. What's more, the chaotic musicianship that characterised the Warsaw era was now receding and in its place were recognisable song structures and increased musical confidence. In addition, Ian Curtis' lyrics were beginning to show signs of a rare, if not unique, vision, his phrasing carrying a curious emotive heart, even though they were still spiced with references to Nazi Germany.

Ian was also emerging as the most 'driven' member of the band – alongside Terry Mason – and it was this drive that initially impressed Derek Brandwood at RCA's northern office.

Brandwood was a silver haired dream-talker, an amiable, eternal enthusiast and music visionary who, time and time again, showed a tendency to recognise major talent in embryonic form. Sadly his considerable achievements in this field were never fully rewarded, for many artists who benefited from his drive and passion during their formative years then moved on to success with bigger management outfits, often in London. In later years, Brandwood would recognise and nurture both Lisa Stansfield and Russell Watson, his encouragement, enthusiasm and sheer hard work laying the foundations for their respective careers.

In 1978, Brandwood's role at RCA wasn't clearly defined, though part of his job was to escort stars to interviews. "I would commute to work, driving in from a totally ordinary existence and then, suddenly, I would be a close friend of the most extraordinary array of people," he says. "RCA had Iggy Pop, David Bowie, Dolly Parton... I would be working with all these people. I would drive all over the north with Harry Nilsson in my car trying to get interviews. And no one wanted to know. Even the record company didn't like him... and I would tell everyone that this man is a genius. As he was. Probably the best singer I have ever encountered. Well, maybe Ian was up there. That always struck me as strange. I seemed to have an ability to recognise great singers... Harry Nilsson, Paul Young [from Sad Café and Mike & The Mechanics], Lisa, Russell and Ian."

In 1978, Brandwood was beginning to tire of his role as RCA northern rep. Mostly his job consisted of plugging, that is furnishing northern radio stations with RCA product, as well as arranging interviews and physically transporting the artists from radio station to radio station. What he really wanted was something more organic, his own label, maybe. "I had no A&R powers at RCA at all," he stated in 1999. "But I was more than well aware of all the things that had been happening in Manchester for a good eighteen months. It was absolutely typical of the music industry, really. There I was, working in a city that was just bursting with talent and potential and all the young A&R men would rarely be venturing out of London. And I was being forced to plug this substandard stuff that they had signed. It was so frustrating but like talking to a brick wall. The funny thing was that, as it happened, I didn't even have to go to a local gig. A major talent from Manchester of the time, of any time, would just come walking straight into my office and basically ask us to sign his band. That is basically what happened. Was I aware of Ian Curtis when he wandered into the office on that day? I had seen Warsaw at The Electric Circus, I think. But I can't recall whether we had talked about them... or as Joy Division at that time. You see, Martin Hannett was in the office all the time... and Paul Young would venture in on an afternoon and it would just be a lot of chat.

"I had taken on Richard Searling – the famous Northern Soul DJ - as assistant and, the thing is, I must admit that I was looking for something beyond a local band. Beyond punk, if you like. Sad Café were very close."

Of Ian Curtis, he later noted: "It is true to say that Ian Curtis was besotted with David Bowie and Iggy Pop. It is also true that Ian Curtis seemed immensely star-struck when he wandered into our office. I don't know why. Joy Division was already on the move by this point although, perhaps, few people could yet see it. Ian told me that he didn't really want to be on an independent label. It was obvious that he wanted to be with a major label. I was a bit concerned about his apparent shyness. I mean, it must have taken guts for him to wander into that office but, once in there, he was silent and difficult to budge… in fact he was just difficult. Not in a nasty way, don't get me wrong, but in a kind of… a kind of awkward way. As if he didn't quite know what to do and he wanted us to snap him up. It could have been that he was still naïve enough to think that anyone who works for any record label would have the power and the desire to just sign them on sight. A lot of people thought that and it could well have been the case. I don't know."

Terry Mason: "The RCA thing was entirely Ian. I had nothing to do with that and, I suppose, that weakened my position a bit as well. It was just a matter of practicality. RCA was situated beneath where Ian worked. I was working at the CIS Building across town and I couldn't feasibly get across at lunch-time. So Ian would talk to Brandwood. It was surprising, to all of us, that something appeared to be happening, but we had absolutely nothing else going for us."

Meanwhile Richard Searling had pursued a link with John Anderson, head of Grapevine Records, a man who had shown no interest in becoming linked with any music outside of soul and R'n'B, and the American Bernie Binnick, one time executive with Swan Records in Philadelphia who'd released The Beatles' 'She Loves You' in the US in 1963, after Capitol rejected it as uncommercial. More recently Binnick had been producing soul records designed specifically for export from his Miami base.

What happened next would probably have become one of the great quirks of rock history had it led anywhere other than up a particularly frustrating musical cul-de-sac. Searling had an idea for a local band to record a northern soul record. It could have been any band, frankly, but Ian Curtis happened to have arrived in the office and so the series of events were set in motion.

Derek Brandwood: "I remember that it took me back a bit, at the time, the way the pieces seemed to drop into place. There was part of me, right at the beginning, that sensed that this wasn't going to work. But Richard was an honest guy with a love for music… and I think you would say the same for everyone involved. What's more, the chance came before anyone heard of Joy Division. All that was necessary was to pull the two parts together."

Richard Searling: "It was very simple. John Anderson wanted to make a lively new recording of the soul record, 'Keep On Keepin' On'. It wasn't a particularly revolutionary idea. The N.F. Porter version was fantastic but you could see how a sharp, young English band could add a vital spark to it."

Anderson and Searling had already set up a label base with the specific intention of bringing new soul into Britain and floating it through the powerful club circuit. When considering who in Manchester could record this, Searling and Brandwood immediately thought of the gutsy young man who had so ingratiated himself with their lunchtime schedules.

Meanwhile, the young band seemed unsure of how to progress. They were typically vulnerable, leaving important decisions to pub get-togethers that inevitably followed an intense practice session. There would surely have been some confusion, therefore, as the request for a meeting reached their ears. The people from RCA, the people whom Ian knew, were apparently about to offer some kind of a deal.

Were Joy Division about to be signed to RCA? Not Quite. But it seemed close enough… almost.

When the notion to record 'Keep On Keepin' On' was initially put to the band, during a meeting between them and Searling and Anderson, Hooky darkened the proceedings with a sense of understandable apprehension. This was tempered, however, when Searling outlined the full extent of a deal that, of an instant, extended from the recording of a one-off single, and a cover version at that, to the recording of a full album. Searling, Anderson and Binnick, whoever they were, would fund the recording and place it before the eyes of major record companies. While this carrot was dangled, Ian Curtis was trapped between elation stemming from the possibility that the band might achieve a deal and a reverse emotion brought about by the realisation that, despite the shock of good fortune, RCA was not actually signing the band.

Brandwood: "We felt, and we expressed this to the band, that we were putting in an investment that was considerable when you take into account our lack of resources. We could instigate and oversee the recordings and move the band on."

Although housed in a building that had all the architectural allure of a Seventies technical college on the outskirts of Watford, Arrow Studios boasted much the same state-of-the-art technology as Stockport's more famous Strawberry Studios and even boasted the same engineers and, at one point, manager.

But there was little fire in Arrow Studios on May 3, 4 and 5 of 1978. While the whole point of the exercise was to produce a record brimming with soul, in reality Joy Division found little in the way of inspiration there.

Derek Brandwood: "I will never forget walking down to that studio after, I think about three days, and finding the band huddled in one corner, full of sulks and John Anderson and Bob Auger sat still at the mixing desk, bemoaning the fact that the band couldn't play and that he could have wrapped the session up with any bunch of jobbing musicians. This seemed odd to me as Joy Division were very much into the act of recording their own material that wasn't soul in any traditional sense. In fact, given the industrial overtones, it was quite the opposite. I think it was just two sides coming together out of convenience. It was never going to work. That much was obvious."

There is a certain irony in that the three musicians who would one day become New Order refused to use synthesizers which seems little short of hilarious in retrospect. There was no hilarity at Arrow though. Richard Searling, Anderson and Auger presided over the recording of 11 dull and clumsy tracks, a number of which would later surface on Joy Division's carefully constructed box set, *Heart And Soul*, released in 1997.[1]

Terry Mason: "To be honest, they probably would have been better signing one of the R&B bands, like Gags or Any Trouble, who were in Manchester at the time, rather than Joy Division. At least they would have provided the musicianship. But although it was the soul idea that started it all off, the people involved started to sense the spirit of the band and think that there might be something in this punk thing after all."

Deborah Curtis has noted that Ian was alarmed that he was expected to perform as a soul singer. It was simply a bizarre clash of culture that led to a breakdown of communications between Anderson and the band, in partic-ular between Anderson and Ian Curtis. The American music ethic was far removed from the lack of formal skills that distinguished English post-punk, while the English arm of RCA, hovering like a dark, damp cloud over these proceedings, remained largely unsullied by the vibrancy of embryonic acts like Joy Division. The division at Arrow between the stoic professionalism

[1] As soon as Joy Division's Factory career got off the ground, the RCA tape circulated with a ferocity that, although localised, was seized on with all the fervour of Dylan and The Band's *Basement Tapes*. It was only the lack of emotive resonance on the recording that would prevent it from attaining a status beyond curiosity. In the event, it was so hugely overshad-owed by later and rerecorded material that it tended to languish as a one-play curiosity, its unfinished nature all too naked for all but the most fanatical of ears.

of Anderson and a very nervous band was no doubt exacerbated by the suggestion that their vocalist should sing like James Brown.

Derek Brandwood: "Nobody could have been aware, at that point, just how good Joy Division were about to become. I have no idea if they knew it themselves but I sense they did. I sense they knew that they were better than that; that they weren't just another punk band pulled in from the streets. But that didn't really show in those sessions, so perhaps you can't blame Auger and Anderson. They just thought they were working with substandard musicians. I might be wrong in that. It's just that, looking back on it, maybe Joy Division were simply frustrated. Maybe the ideas they were starting to work on were actually well in advance of the capabilities they showed in the studio."

Cowed by subservience to an adept recording team, and cowed by the technology itself perhaps, Joy Division's only possible course was to retreat within their own capabilities. They had little choice.

The level of incomprehension was further raised by the emergence of recording and publishing contracts. Beyond Terry Mason, Joy Division was gapingly managerless, and contractually inexperienced. With contracts to peruse, the band would decamp – to the pub, undoubtedly – where each clause would serve to tease out and amplify frustrations within their own dynamic. The recording contract was lifted directly from a standard RCA draft. Although begging professional guidance, it wasn't exactly a legal precipice. By contrast, the all-important publishing contract was loaded with Americanese. In confusion, the band approached Buzzcocks manager Richard Boon, no doubt hoping for simple, uncomplicated assistance.

Terry Mason: "I really don't think anyone really looked at that contract. I recall that Steve cast an eye over it but, to be honest, Steve would have signed anything just to get out of the house. He was living with his parents and he wanted to be out recording... anything. Ian was different because he was married, of course. But it was still that simple. He just wanted to do it and here was a chance. What other option did they have?"

Simple, uncomplicated, it wasn't. Down at Arrow, Joy Division's raw, stone cold sound reverberated around the studio to negative effect. The resonance that flowed from *An Ideal For Living* – and would flow more copiously in the improved 12-inch format that would arrive in the summer of '78 – seemed lost amid a tangle of ideas that failed to separate Hooky's lead heavy bass with Steve Morris's rolling percussion. Worse, however, was the Curtis voice which sat above the mix in a semi-punkish shout. In stark comparison to the more celebrated later moments of the band, the Curtis vocals seemed adrift, dislodged and reedy.

Anderson could taste the coldness and in desperation he surreptitiously added some synth into the mix. His reason, to fatten the sound, was wholly understandable, but it fell awkwardly on Joy Division's ears. Ian Curtis, in particular, loathed his detached contribution, and reacted with a frustration that drifted towards anger. At a subsequent band meeting Joy Division mercilessly trashed the Anderson approach. Within six months, however, they would be seeking to expand their own music in a similar fashion.

Derek Brandwood: "I can only recall that a decision was made to use the album as a demo to try and attract some kind of serious interest. In a sense, we all knew this was a waste. Four songs would have been enough and we should have just picked four and gone for that. As it was, approaching people with a full sub-standard album was simply never going to work. I can't believe that we didn't see this at the time, as it now seems achingly obvious. You just don't give record companies that much. You have to give them something to work. Not that it really mattered. I knew that Joy Division were lost to us. I can't remember if I really thought that they were going to really go places. I can't claim that. But I saw a huge change in Ian. When he first came into the office he was full of awe and excited by the possibilities. After the recording he was completely detached from us, as if he had decided that it just hadn't worked and he was determined to look somewhere else. I just knew he had gone."

Terry Mason: "I think that, in general, the band were pretty happy with the tapes. Well, they were happy that they had had that experience. Ian was just happy that they had done something else after *An Ideal For Living*. It seemed like a progression. Ian could say, 'Oh, I have recorded an album'. The whole band could say that. So things were visibly happening even if, at that point, the only thing that showed we were still in existence were gigs."

Meanwhile, as the RCA episode began with promise then started to turn ugly, Rob Gretton was nurturing the idea of offering his – until then, meagre – managerial talents to the band. He had encountered Bernard Sumner, apparently by chance in a telephone box, and convinced him that his services might prove valuable. Sumner, however, evidently forgot to mention this to his colleagues, which caused some confusion among the ranks.

Hooky: "Rob had been at the Stiff Test/Chiswick Challenge talent night... [and] we kind of knew him before, but he was a shadowy figure, to say the least. But, obviously we knew about him from Slaughter & The Dogs and all of that. Actually, we must have been well aware of his DJ-ing too because my girlfriend had given him a copy of the record the week before we played. We had been down there, sussing Rafters out. Sussing Rob out, too, if I recall correctly. Mostly we just wanted him to play our record, possibly because we thought that, if people became used to it, they would be more responsive to us on the night. Some naïve shit like that. I don't know. But Rob obviously liked what he saw... in fact he saw our best set that night and he asked Barney if he could manage us. But Barney never told us, he completely forgot. It wasn't a Mark E. Smith bit of manipulation or any of that. Barney wouldn't have thought like that. He just said yes and then fucking forgot all about mentioning it to the rest of us. So there was this really weird moment where we were in rehearsal and this grey haired man in glasses came in and sat down. We were playing away and I thought, 'Who's this dick?'."

According to Hooky, Ian was visibly freaked by the intrusion. "He was always the most sensitive in that respect. He'd be singing away and then, suddenly, he would pull back. It wasn't a big deal, just a bit off-putting when you are not expecting anyone to come in. The thing was that Rob either had incredible confidence or he just thought that we were expecting him. As it turned out, it was the latter. Not only was that the case, he also believed that we had all agreed to his managing us. That came as a bit of a shock, I can tell you.

"So we played through our set and he stayed there, nodding his head and when we stopped it was a really awkward moment. Just silence, then Barney said, 'Oh aye lads, I forgot to tell you...' Barney's not changed, still as daft as ever.

"I think we kind of gathered around, kind of sensing each other out. Ian was a bit agitated at first and you could certainly understand why. So what did we do? Well, naturally, we went to the pub. Rob started talking about Man City, no doubt. And music. And probably women. That was about the extent of it. We thought, well this isn't so bad. It was just a gang of lads. Ian softened completely... well, at least I think he did. There was always, perhaps, a slight edge between Ian and Rob. Maybe... yes, perhaps something."

Rob Gretton was from the Newell Green area of Wythenshawe, noted for the Newell Green public house, where people blessed with all sorts of talents mingled in equal measure with local villains. Newell Green, the pub and area and beyond, Baguley and Wythenshawe – once Europe's largest overspill – still sits on the edge of plush Cheshire, next to the escape route to the airport and Wilmslow's cloying luxury.

In this very pub, at various times, it was possible to rub shoulders with Durutti Column's Vini Reilly, Sad Café, Mike & The Mechanics and

Toggery Five singer Paul Young, Cult guitarist Billy Duffy, Martin Hannett, Eddie Garrity, latterly Ed Banger, ACR'S Donald Johnson, and, if extremely lucky, Johnny Marr, whose family had been 'moved-out' from inner city Ardwick.

Rob Gretton was an intelligent Catholic boy, a former pupil of St Bede's, the premier Catholic Grammar School, deep in Moss Side, a geographical fact that surely enforced his deep love of Manchester City, which was also based in the locality at that time. Gretton would travel home and away, neatly garbed in the crombie/Levi's sta-prest, brogue 'Royals' mode of the day. There was nothing remotely unusual in a lifestyle that would see him attempting to chat-up the feather-cut girls at the Motown discos at Longley Lane Cricket Club in Baguley or, as reported by Mike Eastwood on the Joy Division Central website, sneaking under age into one of two pubs, the Firbank or the Red Rose.

Tales of Gretton's football supporting exploits are multitudinous, probably prone to nostalgic exaggeration and have liberally peppered previous Joy Division books. Most famously – and true – was the tale of his fleeing from the hate-fuelled hoards at Nottingham, where, heavily outnumbered, the City 'Gents' found themselves hurtling through a local housing estate before leaping into the cover of a convenient front garden. In there, down among the roses, Gretton turned around to be greeted by the smiling face of a fellow City supporter named Mike Pickering. In later years Pickering's extraordinary career would combine the roles of a particularly surreal booker and DJ at The Haçienda before forming three bands, Quando Quango, T-coy and, rather more famously, M People.

Perhaps the finest prevailing image of Rob – as portrayed so perceptively by Paddy Constantine in *24 Hour Party People* – was of a man who fully endorsed the kick-back qualities of cannabis. It has been noted, on many occasions, that Rob's features were forever encircled in a cloud of blue smoke, in particular on the terraces of Maine Road where he would counter lacklustre performances by his team of choice with cynical detachment. It was this detachment that so flavoured his celebrated managerial style. Not to everyone's taste perhaps, and occasionally to the detriment of both Joy Division and New Order, he would often construct an impenetrable shield of defensive apathy.

Despite their initial reaction of slight bafflement, the band seemed to take to Gretton. They enjoyed his sardonic edge and utter lack of pretension, even Ian, the most sceptical. Unlike the guys beyond Brandwood at RCA, Gretton was a street fighter in attitude. He was also not given to the kind of Machiavellian tampering that had seemingly become the norm with band managers, even at street level. With Gretton the spade remained spade-ish. You would always know where you stood. More than that perhaps, in interview or in terms of simple camaraderie, it quickly became almost impossible to distinguish Rob Gretton from the rest of the band. More than a manager, Gretton had joined the gang – and the first thing the gang wanted was to be relieved of the contractual situation in which they found themselves thanks to Brandwood *et al.*

Terry Mason: "All of a sudden I was shunted sideways. It was a terrible situation for me. Rob seemed to have all the cards. He had a little bit of managerial experience, though not much. But he did have a phone, which was a big plus. There was also the thing that his girlfriend, Lesley, worked at a solicitors. Not a music solicitors but, nevertheless, it was certainly handy. Of course I was incensed. I said I would get an injunction without actually knowing what an injunction was."

Gretton, however, made it quite clear that he was willing to meet the band's contractual problem head-on. "That was my first task as manager," he said. "I knew that if I could get the band out of that situation then I would be in. I would be the manager. It was that simple."

And with admirable ferocity, he achieved this. In an infamous telephone call to John Anderson, Rob Gretton outlined the fact that, if this release were to proceed on RCA or anywhere else, the band would require £10,000 and 15 per cent of future royalties[1]. By present-day standards the amount seems miniscule, but to Anderson who had, alongside Searling and Auger, funded the project from his own bank account, the request seemed little short of outrageous.

Only Gretton and Anderson can say how that telephone call was terminated. However, it is safe to assume that both receivers were slammed down to effectively put a full stop at the end of the relationship between band and putative backers. Rob Gretton would later admit that, during these proceedings, he felt rather like a small time Malcolm McLaren, though it was hardly *The Great Rock'n'Roll Swindle*. However, as Gretton was not involved in the initial entanglement, he quite rightly felt that he had nothing to lose. What's more, as he had already consulted a lawyer, Gretton's baggy sleeve was cleverly concealing a playable ace.

A solicitor's letter duly arrived on Anderson's desk informing him that, as the publishing contract was American by nature, it wasn't enforceable by

[1] As outlined in C.P. Lee's excellent tome on Manchester's musical history, *Shake Rattle And Rain*.

British law. In effect, the contract was almost null and void. It still required an agreement by which the band would have to pay £1,000 to purchase their own tapes. Even this small amount caused disagreement and the amount was eventually lowered to £850, leaving the investors feeling faintly mugged. For Gretton, however, it was a triumph that would cement his reputation, at least within the Joy Division circle. As a 'blooding', it was a perfect start. Refreshed, victorious, he could now begin the art of rock band management. For Gretton knew, full well, just how rapidly this band was evolving.

Terry Mason: "There was a certain amount of money needed, and Rob managed to get this by re-releasing *An Ideal For Living* on the 12-inch Anonymous Records format, in that dreadful scaffolding sleeve."

The Band On The Wall, on Manchester's Swan Street, was not unlike a London pub venue. Once the domain of thieves, villains and charlatans, it is often claimed that in pre-war times murderers could be hired in the pub, although not from behind the bar one senses, for a modest fee and a couple of pints of bitter. This probably wasn't the case in 1978, although the sundry reprobates who gathered to catch Manchester's embryonic punk acts often had a rather unholy appearance. By this time, having been transformed into a jazz club by local saxophonist Steve Morris, it was a simple matter for the Band On The Wall to change from a pub rock to a punk venue as well as playing host to the low-brow high-spirited antics of the Manchester Musicians Collective.

Among their ranks were Mick Hucknall's soon-to-be infamous Frantic Elevators, and the venue housed ground-breaking gigs by Buzzcocks, The Fall, John The Postman and, on four occasions, Joy Division.

The 'Collective' evenings were the most entertaining, although not always for the most aesthetically sound of reasons. Peopled by vociferous members of rival bands, they offered a rolling bill of young hopefuls, a vital first step to a stage and, more often than not resulting in a cacophonous racket produced by shy bass players, overtly aggressive guitarists who often entered into solos from which they couldn't neatly emerge and slap happy drummers.

But there was talent among this constant howl, and Ian Curtis attended the Band On The Wall on a number of occasions prior to Joy Division's spirited debut. In witnessing the sell-out Buzzcocks show back in 1977 (May 2), he had seen one of the classic Buzzcocks moments, with Pete Shelley singing mysteriously into two inflated condoms, later to be reunited with Howard Devoto onstage who famously claimed to be 'just dusting off my hat'.

Ian Curtis was also spotted sitting on the benches at the rear of the club chatting to Mancunian *Sounds* journalist Ian Wood. Wood, a local tax inspector, did not conform to the shabby industrial chic adopted by many of his peers at the time. Bearded, soberly attired, quietly spoken and helpful, his middle-class tones contrasted sharply with all who moved around him and had his editors at *Sounds* been aware of his courageous detachment from the scene he covered, they might not have treated him so fondly. Ian Curtis didn't know Ian Wood. However, his curiosity was aroused as Wood sat at the rear, furiously scribbling notes. This alone was something of a faux pas in an age when rock journalists barely even bothered to watch the bands they covered, let alone be seen actually taking notes.

"Curtis kept on asking me just what I was doing," reminisced Wood in 1980, who in 1979 had switched allegiance to *NME*. "It was as if he was fascinated by the process. I told him that it was just rough copy, that I would type it up when I got home at night and post it the next day. I think he couldn't understand why a man who works at the tax office would be working for *Sounds*. He really couldn't work that out. He thought all rock journalists looked like Paul Morley, young and part of the scene. I was 25, positively ancient. But he saw me at the Lesser Free Trade Hall, I think, and had been intrigued. I didn't know if Warsaw or Joy Division were any good at that point, but I did like the way he was taking it all so seriously. That's my point. I may not have been the average rock journalist… but he wasn't the average rock singer either. He was different, strangely focused."

The fact that two other journalists did catch back-to-back Band On The Wall performances by Joy Division is almost entirely down to the bullish tactics of Rob Gretton. Both writers, Paul Morley for *NME* and Mick Middles at *Sounds*, experienced the force of Gretton's unbridled enthusiasm immediately prior to the respective gigs. Morley's enthusiasm seemed the more positive:

NME 3/6/78

MANCHESTER
Joy Division were once Warsaw, a punk group with literary pretentions. Warsaw Pakt forced them to change names.

They disappeared for a while at the end of last year, and have re-emerged with their new name, an EP and their pretensions even more to the fore.

Their record attempts to communicate in an almost tangible way all the abstraction of Buzzcocks' "Spiral Scratch". It is called "An Ideal For Living", and is on the Enigma label. It proclaims on the sleeve that "this is not a concept EP, it is an enigma."

84

Despite all this, the record is structurally good, though soundwise poor, a reason it may not be widely released.

They're a dry, doomy group who depend promisingly on the possibilities of repetition, sudden stripping away, with deceptive dynamics, whilst they use sound in a more orthodox hard rock manner than, say, either The Fall or Magazine.

They have an ambiguous appeal, and with patience they could develop strongly and make some testing, worthwhile metallic music.

Paul Morley

It's interesting to note Paul Morley's comparison to Buzzcocks, particularly as Joy Division had yet to work with the man who would famously help to define their sound, *Spiral Scratch* producer Martin Hannett. There were some in Manchester, however, who remained sceptical. From the Buzzcock's ranks, Steve Diggle was less enthusiastic.

"In truth, I don't think Ian's stage presence really hit me in those early gigs," he says. "If anything, he seemed a bit unsure on-stage. That was definitely the case in the early gigs and, to some extent I think he carried that insecurity with him. Maybe that was what people picked up on. I am not sure. I think it possibly was, because an audience can sometimes sense when a performer is a little ill at ease and it can then go two ways. Either they deride him or her and the whole thing fails, or they feel an empathy. It was certainly the latter with Ian, which is one of the reasons why the Joy Division thing has lasted. I wasn't a fan in the early gigs… well, I never was, but later I would come to understand the appeal. But at the time that Paul Morley started writing really good things about them, I couldn't see it. They still seemed a bit old fashioned to me."

Jeremy Kerr was, and indeed still is, a member of ACR (A Certain Ratio) a Factory band who frequently played alongside Joy Division. His first memory of seeing Ian Curtis was performing at the Band On The Wall a few months before his first gig with ACR at the same venue in November 1978.

"There were two or three bands on," he says. "Joy Division did 'Sister Ray' at the end. It was during the intensity of that that Ian started throwing the mike stands around the stage and trashed the drum kit (threw it over). It was like The Who – you know, Keith Moon and all that. I thought that was the best thing about the gig. Also I liked that track 'Sister Ray'."

In the late summer of 1978 Terry Mason and Hooky, together with two other friends, took a holiday around the south of France and Spain. "This seemed to put the focus on the difference between Ian's life and ours," says

Terry. "We were young and having fun and not thinking beyond that. But Ian, of course, couldn't be a part of that. There were other reasons that he couldn't go on that trip. Ian had bad eczema which meant that he couldn't go out in the sun but this holiday really brought home the fact that we were much younger in attitude than Ian. He was very much a married man. We had two-and-a-half weeks of acting daft in France and Spain."

Ian Curtis on stage; dancing at the heart of the sound.
(Pierre Rene-Worms)

Doreen Curtis, Ian's mother, at his christening, at St. John's Church in Old Trafford, 1956.

Ian, aged five, at the railway museum in Manchester.

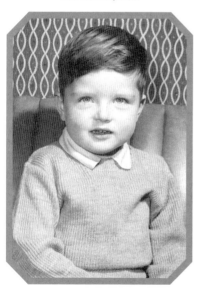

Pre-school age Ian, at the Stamford Street house.

Ian, the gallant knight with his sword and shield.

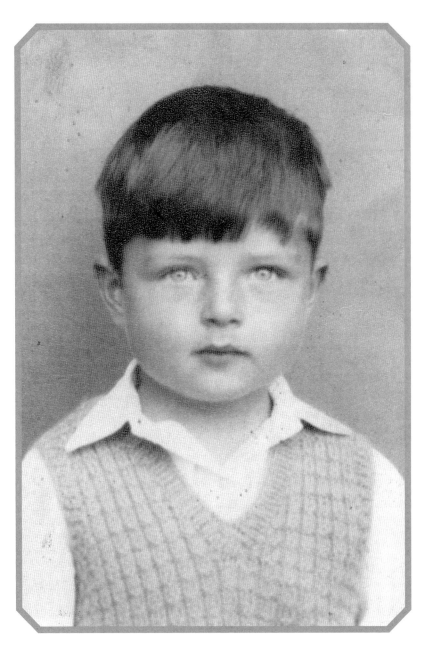

Ian aged around five.

Ian and his sister Carole at a Christmas party held for the families of the Transport Police in 1964. Ian liked to get up on stage even then.

Ian's drawing, inspired by his love of The Lone Ranger Davy Crockett – 'The King of the Wild Frontier'.

Ian on a family holiday in Canvey Island. Left to right: Kevin Curtis, his wife Doreen, a local friend, Ian and Carole.

At home with the family, celebrating Christmas in the mid-Sixties,
seated left to right: Ian, Carole, grandpa Les, grandma Edith (Ian's maternal grandparents)
and standing, aunt Barbara and Doreen.

Aunt Barbara's wedding to Brian Lloyd in 1970.
Ian is on the far right, next to his sister Carole.

THE KING'S SCHOOL, MACCLESFIELD

Report for the Term ending...... 11th July 1970

Name...... Curtis I.K.   Number of times absent—Days —   Half-days —

Form...... U4B   No. of Boys...... 37   Average Age...... 14-3   Place in Form...... 6

SUBJECTS	Grade or Place in Form or Set	Number of Boys in Form or Set	MASTER'S REPORT
Divinity	2		He has worked very well throughout the year and deserves this high position. DFH.
English	4		A very good year's work. JER
History	8		A very creditable year's work. G.C.R.
Geography	9		A year of satisfactory work and effort, with a good examination mark. AM.
French	2		A very capable year's work indeed. R.W.
Mathematics	20		He has worked well, and made satisfactory progress. MAT
Physics	18 =		He has worked steadily throughout the year. RWB.
Chemistry	5		A good year's work. DEB.
Biology	23.		A satisfactory year. PK
~~General Science~~			
Add'l. Maths.			
Music			
Art ~~German~~ ~~Greek~~	AB		Reasonable effort and fair progress — with adequate scope for further improvement. SRJ
Latin Woodwork Metalwork	2/20	2a	Intelligent and efficient always. L.W.

Form Master's Report   An intelligent and capable boy who has worked very creditably. R.W.

Headmaster's Report   Very pleasing progress. AttGooper

The next Term will begin on...... 4th September ......at 9 a.m.

A NOTE ON GRADING IS GIVEN OVERLEAF

Ian's 1970 school report from King's School, Macclesfield.

Ian, Doreen Curtis, Kevin's sister Auntie Nell, Kevin Curtis, Carole (holding one of Nell's dogs), Ian's maternal grandparents Les and Edith, and Nell's husband Uncle Ray on the occasion of Nell and Ray's silver wedding anniversary

Carole and Ian in a photo booth at Manchester's Piccadilly Station, 1978.

Ian with Carole and mother Doreen on holiday in Austria in 1971.

Ian marries Debbie Woodruff at St Thomas's Church, Henbury,
on August 23, 1975.

CHAPTER 7

This Is the Way, Step Inside

"Psychologically Ian probably was quite close to someone like Kurt Cobain that was genuinely interested in the meaning and the magic of the music, not the stardom." – Paul Morley

Ian Curtis and Factory Records would become inextricably linked not only for the remaining years of his life but for eternity. Whatever else Factory might have done to promote and preserve Manchester's independent music scene at the tail end of the Seventies and beginning of the Eighties, its key achievement in the eyes of most music people was signing and nurturing Joy Division. The group and the label fed off each other, in time creating a dual entity that was both separate and united, a statement of parallel intent, a cultural kinship, a marriage in monochrome.

Away from his role as a TV presenter, which brought with it a degree of localised fame, Tony Wilson was harbouring the vague notion of what he termed "a different kind of record label". With this in mind, he'd paid close attention to the relative successes of two other local labels, Richard Boon's New Hormones and Tosh Ryan's Rabid Records.

His plans took on a more concrete form when, on his stag night, exactly 12 months after his first date with Lindsay Reade – at a Slaughter & The Dogs gig in Stockport – he took his actor friend, Alan Erasmus, and Alberto Y Los Trios singer C.P. Lee along to catch a band called Flashback, performing at a Failsworth pub. The band, which would later change their name to Fast Breeder, were soon to become managed by the enthusiastic Erasmus, though their subsequent implosion took him by surprise and left him with just two musicians, drummer Chris Joyce and guitarist Dave Rowbotham remaining.

The idea of building a band from this insubstantial base was duly talked up by Wilson and Erasmus and the latter soon introduced ex-Ed Banger & The Nosebleeds' guitarist Vini Reilly to Joyce and Rowbotham. This rather awkward looking trio was soon bolstered by the arrival of Ex-Alberto's bassist, Tony Bowers. Excitement and trepidation hardly filled the air as news of this unlikely unit started to filter out. The new band had the look – and to some extent, the sound – of an ailing pub rock outfit – not exactly the stuff of revolution. However, while they may not have had a direction or held that much in the way of promise, they were fortunate in having the indomitably enthusiastic Wilson cheering their corner and were soon christened Durutti Column, a moniker lifted from a situationist comic strip.

Wilson and Erasmus next hatched the notion of finding a new venue to bring the swell of post-punk bands back into the city on a regular basis, in particular a place where Durutti Column could be seen and heard. The Russell Club, in Hulme, seemed to fit the bill.

While The Electric Circus provided the perfect post-apocalyptic setting for the thrash of punk and Rafters neatly captured the warmer glow of its softer and more marketable cousin new wave, there can be no doubt that this small, chunky club in Hulme would be the perfect venue for the stark industrial side of post-punk.

Alan Erasmus had known Don Tonay, the proprietor of the Russell club, for years, mainly through a shebeen[1] that Tonay ran on Monton Street in Moss Side called Monton House. This 24-hour club revolved to the sound of ska and reggae music, with gambling upstairs, and served all-night West Indian food. Erasmus' father, who preferred jazz and didn't drink, came to England from Jamaica in 1945 and stayed after meeting his white mother. The family grew up in Wythenshawe and Alan remembers that there were virtually no black people there then. Much of the appeal of Monton House to Alan (and other legal drinking clubs such as The Reno and The Nile above it) was simply that black people had a presence as well as a voice in the music that was played.

Tosh Ryan remembers that The Russell Club, aka The PSV (Public Service Vehicle) Club, began life as a cinema called the Bijou on Russell Street. The council needed to knock the building down, probably to make

---

[1] An illegal drinking establishment.

way for a dual carriageway or other new road link, and were obliged to compensate the owner, Don Tonay, who then moved The Russell to a brick building on Royce Road in Hulme.

The new venue was awkwardly situated within the giant shadows cast by the Hulme Crescents – vast, curved, flat-block schemes built on the rubble of slum clearance and intended initially to instigate an architectural inner-city utopia. The vision failed, of course, and famously so. Long before the dawn of punk, the Hulme Crescents had been rather unfairly labelled Valium City. However, despite the obvious social problems of the crescents, the area was alive with a vivacious youthful energy, thanks to the vast number of students and post-students living there, and was a perfect spot for the Russell Club, which resembled the Golden Garter in Wythenshawe, a square brick cabaret club, somewhat the antithesis of the chromed discos of the city centre with a certain anti-glam ambience.

At a meeting at the Cavalcade, Erasmus remarked to Don Tonay that his club was always dead on Friday nights, and Tonay agreed to allow him and Wilson to promote a few pilot gigs there on that night. The arrangement was that the pair would take the door money and the club would take the bar. The new wave of groups would provide a diversion from the ska and reggae music often heard there.[1] When Erasmus noticed a sign on Manchester's Deansgate proclaiming 'Factory Clearance', he suggested Factory as a reasonable name for their Friday promotions.

The first Factory night, held on May 19, 1978, featured Durutti Column and Rabid act Jilted John, who would soon enjoy an eponymous Top 10 hit record, produced by Martin Hannett, with a chorus of "Gordon is a moron". Lindsay Reade recalls: "I remember seeing Alan's and Tony's face as they watched people arrive through the door that night. They seemed to be sharing a private joke and when I followed their gaze and saw an extremely beautiful young woman I became convinced that Tony was having an affair! I later discovered their excitement was simply because so many people had turned up. It didn't surprise me because it seemed there was a buzz around Manchester music then and a need for another venue apart from Rafters."

Erasmus remembers sitting on beer barrels at the close of this first night and counting the money. This was rapidly spent on Durutti Column's rehearsal rooms and posters for the club.

★　★　★

[1] Years earlier Tosh Ryan had organised gigs with Martin Hannett for Burning Spear and Inner Circle at the Russell Club, in return for 10% of the takings.

Don Tonay later decided to hand the running of each night at the Russell club over to local promoter Alan Wise, who had already been promoting gigs at Rafters with Nigel Baguley. Tonay would be paid rent with the door and bar take to be shared by the promoters. "The Factory Club made money on the door and lost on the bars, which is not what night clubs are supposed to do," recalls Wise. "We had no idea how to run the bar and a bar manager we had was pinching the stuff and taking it out to the Jamaican clubs, and watering the beer down. When we caught him at it he said it was no good for people as strong as it was – they would get drunk! It was just people coming into a club who liked the music such as Joy Division. We put that group on dozens of times and the crowd began to grow and they had something. Whether or not you were a fan of that type of music – which I wasn't particularly – you had to admit they had a talent and a style that the others didn't have. Somewhere amongst there was a talent."

Wilson and Erasmus were soon joined by Peter Saville, a Manchester Polytechnic art student who had befriended Wilson, and produced artwork and designed posters. "[Saville] gave the club an image, which was important to it," says Wise. "Tony had the good sense to know it had to look good. Then Tony got interested in the record business. I had no interest in it. I didn't realise that was where it made the money. I was pretty stupid 'cos I didn't know how it worked. My main interest was in the barmaid called Anna."

If black had been the dominant colour of punk, then grey would rise to the fore during the post punk aftermath. Almost all the emerging bands of the industrial north – The Fall, Joy Division, Durutti Column from Manchester, Cabaret Voltaire, Human League from Sheffield, Gang of Four, The Mekons from Leeds, Echo & The Bunnymen, The Teardrop Explodes, from Liverpool – were swathed in a uniform greyness. More importantly, this was also the colour of the second-hand overcoats worn by their followers, while monochrome became the shade of choice favoured by photographers.

On the third Factory night, Mick Middles was invited to the club by both Rob Gretton, who promised it would be the perfect venue for his new band, Joy Division, and Tony Wilson, who correctly stated that the evening, with Cabaret Voltaire and Durutti Column both performing, would be perfect for a *Sounds* review. Middles, a rookie at the time, relayed this information to a surprisingly intrigued *Sounds* office. The feeling in London was that this new swell of northern bands did, at last, appear to be one step ahead of the new wave acts that permeated the London scene. With Paul Morley also receiving a similarly unexpected but positive response at *NME*, it really did seem that some kind of spotlight had started to move cautiously to the UK's northern cities.

It certainly appeared that Wilson, Erasmus and Wise had stumbled upon something that might catch the public's imagination. The subsequent live review in *Sounds* was upbeat, though Middles would later admit that he didn't have the experience to realise the shortcomings of the under-rehearsed Durutti Column. He did, however, notice a low-key rivalry between Rob Gretton, who kept promising a great show at the venue from Joy Division, and Erasmus, who was equally enthusiastic about Durutti.

Whatever the rivalry, it was immediately obvious that, in The Factory Club, Manchester had found a great new venue, perfectly sized to house the new post-punk scene.

Joy Division played their first Factory gig on the fourth of its Friday nights, June 9, with Pete Shelley's group The Tiller Boys – comprising Shelley, Eric Random and Francis Cookson – which was described in the ad in *The Manchester Evening News* as "definitely another kitchen".[1] Terry Mason remembers that Joy Division supported Alan Vega's Suicide at a very early Factory night but is unsure of the date. Eric Random remembers Pete Hook driving round Manchester trying to collect bits of equipment and lead wires before the gig.

Despite Rob Gretton's persistence and Joy Division's continuing development for the better, the band remained several steps behind Durutti Column, at least within the vague framework of the still non-existent record label.

Terry Mason: "It was decided that maybe Joy Division would be useful to the furtherance of Durutti Column, who were then still the full band. We did a couple of gigs with them at this point. These included The Fan Club in Leeds [October 24], which was the gig where Rob suggested that I should mix the sound, mainly because he couldn't be arsed doing it himself, I think. That gig was typical. It was a right dive… as most of our gigs were and was situated in the red light area. That is where we met with Harry who was running Peak Sound and Light out of Hazel Grove. It just seemed to be the perfect next step. Suddenly, although Factory didn't really exist as such, not beyond the club anyway, it seemed as if we had an in-house PA company. So it felt like we were moving forward. We also had Tony Wilson hanging around, so that made us all feel important as well. I think Ian liked

---

[1] The Tiller Boys supported Joy Division again on October 20, 1978 and also released a record on the New Hormones label in 1979.

that aspect… having Tony on board even if, in truth, we were only there to make Durutti Column look better."

Ian continued to remain slightly distanced from the rest of the band. He usually travelled to gigs with Steve Morris while Hooky and Barney travelled with Terry Mason, this trio maintaining a solid friendship. "I was still very much part of the initial gang, more so than Ian or Steve really," says Terry, who recalls that after the Leeds Fan Club gig both Joy Division and Durutti Column went out to eat together. "What's more, in a rare fit of generosity, Tony Wilson paid for it. That was a real big deal for us," he says. "Normally we would be left to go out and grab a kebab or something. Even though, looking back, it was all a bag'o'shite really, we thought it was fantastic to have a sit down meal paid for by someone else. It was happening in our heads… we were on the move. Tony was there… he had decided to put Joy Division on the telly. Our own PA. It felt like a real band at last."

"For sure when a man pays for a meal it is an important stage of interest – with groups as much as with girls," says Lindsay Reade. "I remember that night. The audience didn't seem all that interested in the band but their morale was lifted hugely by Tony's enthusiasm."

Vini Reilly too recalls the period when Durutti Column and Joy Division existed in the same close environment. "I remember one of the Factory gigs we were sound-checking and Joy Division were waiting to do their soundcheck… they were all standing in the middle of the room. It was taking forever. Durutti Column at that point were a five-piece band. Tony Bowers, Dave Rowbotham, Chris Joyce on drums and there was an actor called Colin. I walked towards where Joy Division were waiting, sat on their instruments and flight cases and stuff just to apologise that my band were taking so long to soundcheck. I was pissed off with my band and I was embarrassed. I thought it was very rude because it meant Joy Division's soundcheck was going to be very short. So I went and apologised and Ian stepped forward and just touched me and said 'Don't worry, it's cool.'"

This appears to confirm the notion that Durutti Column was perceived as being the leading act. "That's what my band's perception of it was," says Reilly, "but I actually thought it was just bullshit and so did Ian. Neither of us was into any of that stuff."

It is an accepted feature of rock etiquette that the senior band on any gig will do their soundcheck first and take as long as they like doing so, even if this cuts into the time remaining for the support act. The members of Joy Division certainly didn't presume they had reached the level where they'd soundcheck first (and take as long as they wanted). Whatever the circumstances, however, Ian didn't buy into this protocol. "I have asked many people who knew Ian if they thought he would have been comfortable as a rock star," says Lindsay Reade. "All but one of them have said no."

Paul Morley agrees. "Psychologically Ian probably was quite close to someone like Kurt Cobain that was genuinely interested in the meaning and the magic of the music, not the stardom," he says. "I don't think he could have become a Bono because I think he was more uncompromising and more committed to darker dangerous things… and would have pushed the music out into a darker area. I don't think it would have been as commercial as New Order, personally."

True to his word, Tony Wilson finally convinced the powers-that-be at Granada Television to allow Joy Division a short one song slot on *Granada Reports* on September 20, 1978. At first glance, this seems like a fairly modest debut on a regional news/magazine show and similar slots had previously been afforded to all manner of bands from Manchester and Liverpool, from Ed Banger & The Nosebleeds to The Fall, Teardrop Explodes and Alberto Y Los Trios Paranoias. However, while most of these appearances would soon be forgotten, the Joy Division film, with the band surging through 'Shadowplay' with a pink-shirted Ian Curtis dancing robotically on TV for the first time, would echo down the years and become a familiar addition to countless latter-day music documentaries. Its importance is magnified because so little film footage of the group exists.

It was a curious little film. Negative images of the roads of Hulme, lifted from a *World In Action* programme, were spliced and added as background footage. It wasn't terribly sophisticated but, in that naïve state, seemed to perfectly suit a band that was clearly finding their way. It's intriguing to note that while Curtis dances to the camera, his fellow band members appear sullen, locked into face-down anonymity.

In August, 1978, Tony Wilson received a phone call from his friend Roger Eagle, who at this time in his life was working as a promoter in Liverpool. Although Eagle would never become a part of Factory, it was probably this call that sets the wheels in motion for Factory's enduring legacy, its record label.

Roger Eagle, who died in 1999, was a key figure in the musical history of Manchester and Liverpool. Despite working extensively in the rather dubious areas of club management and gig promotion over a period spanning more than three decades, nobody seems to ever have had a bad word for a man whose infectious enthusiasm and seemingly unparalleled musical knowledge served to touch and inspire all who moved within his circle.

Oxford-born Eagle became the DJ at Manchester's legendary Twisted Wheel Club in the late Sixties. During his lengthy spell at 'The Wheel', Eagle displayed a rare talent for promoting and befriending the finest acts of the era's blues underground – John Lee Hooker, John Mayall, T-Bone Walker among them – repeatedly drawing them back to the city. Almost unwittingly, he completely changed the concept of the club DJ, bringing his own personality and knowledge to the decks and helping to instil ferocious enthusiasm and understanding of R'n'B among the club goers of Manchester. In this respect he laid down the initial groundwork for Northern Soul and, beyond that, for DJ culture in general.

Moving to Liverpool in the mid-Seventies, he promoted gigs at The Stadium and, displaying a rare talent for being in exactly the right place at the right time, co-owned and ran Liverpool's Eric's Club in 1977, providing the breeding ground for the core of the Liverpool punk scene that would spawn The Teardrop Explodes, Echo & The Bunnymen, Wah! Heat, Frankie Goes To Hollywood and The Lightning Seeds. He took under his wing a young DJ called Mick Hucknell who was also the leader of the ramshackle bluesy punksters, The Frantic Elevators. Hucknall schooled himself among Eagle's richly endowed record collection, and released a single on the Eagle run Eric's Records.

Eagle's call to Tony Wilson in the summer of 1978 was to propose the formation of a new record label that would combine the emerging musical talents of Manchester and Liverpool; a label to serve as a credible alternative to the all powerful record business in London. Wilson was enthusiastic. The idea seemed to be built on solid ground. Plenty of talent was obviously materialising in the two cities and presenting itself before them. With Eagle talking about a wealth of new talent from Liverpool, discussion turned to a launch product, which would bring the two cities together.

Eagle's idea harked back to the days of the great budget priced compilations of the progressive era – Island's *We Can All Join In* and *EL Pea*, CBS's double album *Fill Your Head With Rock*. All were record label 'sampler' discs, released at a budget price with the intention of promoting a label's full roster to a new audience via selected tracks from their individual albums. Eagle suggested having one side for each city.

Wilson was thinking it all over with Alan Erasmus on a Saturday night when he decided to drop a tab of acid. They were sitting in the living room of Durutti drummer Chris Joyce at the time, and as the effects of the acid began to take hold Wilson was flicking through Joyce's extensive record collection. He chanced upon a copy of Santana's *Abraxas* which had been imported from Thailand and, in the eastern tradition, had been printed on paper, rather than card and sealed in a layer of thin plastic. Staring intently at this curiously stylish packaging, the acid intensifying his imagination, Wilson envisaged the idea for 'The Factory Sample'.

The next day, driving to Liverpool, Wilson came up with the idea of a plastic bag and a sheet of folded paper that would house not an album, but a pair of seven-inch records. He thought his idea was aesthetically beautiful and would make a statement about his label's cultural intent. Eagle, however, was set on an album and simply couldn't agree, so Wilson drove back to Manchester determined to pursue his idea alone. Liverpool would not provide half of the Factory roster. His label would be a Manchester label.

Industrious to a fault, it wasn't long before Wilson had all the elements in place. A label born from The Factory Club would naturally be called Factory Records and initially feature the stars of that venue, Durutti Column – of course – and the fast emerging Joy Division, as well as the Sheffield industrial avant-garde act, Cabaret Voltaire.

In the meantime, Martin Hannett's star had risen considerably in the wake of his work on *Spiral Scratch* by Buzzcocks. His production of Slaughter & The Dogs' 'Cranked Up Really High' had been suitably raw, though perhaps the group's approach lacked opportunities for recording innovation. More attention grabbing was his work with a young Sheffield actor named Graham Fellows who, under the name Jilted John, gave Rabid Records a surprise number three hit that September.

Hope and ambition hovered in the air. Suddenly all things seemed possible. The cogs in the wheel that would turn Factory Records were slotting neatly together; Wilson, the visionary entrepreneur, Hannett the visionary record producer, and Peter Saville, the visionary designer.

Back in Macclesfield, meanwhile, Ian Curtis remained blissfully unaware of the cogs that had started to turn. Indeed, such was his domestic situation – Debbie was by now pregnant with Natalie – that he remained somewhat aloof from the developments taking place at ground level.

"It was just increasingly obvious at this point how different Ian's life was to ours," says Terry Mason. "These people were still my mates and we still went out drinking and doing all the things that young lads do. The only problem with Ian was that on his nights off from the band he couldn't often relax with us in that way, simply because he was married. Naturally, he couldn't become as immersed in things in the way we could.

"Just after our holiday [with Hooky] in France we came back and the band played at The Royal Standard in Bradford [on September 10, 1978]. We all had a curry on that night, which was considered very exotic. Mind you, there weren't that many options in Bradford at that point.

"We could bum about and have a complete laugh... do whatever we wanted. But Ian was tied down and in a more mature existence. It wasn't a concern... well, not to us but I am sure Ian found the situation frustrating. He couldn't join in our little games. You never knew quite where the evening would lead."

Ian was only too aware of his responsibilities as a father-to-be. On the domestic front there was a new addition to the Curtis family even before this impending birth, a border collie he and Debbie called Candy after a song by one of Ian's favourite bands, Velvet Underground's 'Candy Says'. Ian wasn't the only member of Joy Division to make a commitment, however, as Barney also took the plunge into marriage – to Sue Barlow – in October 1978. This was probably a factor in the closeness that developed between Ian and Barney as time went on.

Despite the differences between Ian's life and that of the others, it was becoming obvious, in rehearsals and live performance, that Ian had began to assume a natural position as leader of the group. "No one would actually say it, but it was Ian," says Terry Mason. "It had got to be Ian's band and it was his vision, really, that had started to drive things.

"The songwriting often began with, if you want the posh word for it, 'jamming'. The real phrase is 'fucking about'. That was how Joy Division operated, fucking about in various practice rooms. Not quite knowing what they were doing. There was a naiveté to it. No doubt about that. Ian would sit there with reams of paper, just listening. He would pull lines out and try them, see if they would fit in. No one really knew how to go about writing songs. They didn't have a clue and maybe that is what made them work. Somehow it did work. But the more this process moved along, the more it became Ian's band. His vision, whatever it was, became the guiding force. That's just a natural process. The power of the lead singer because in all honesty, he is the one the press all really want to talk to. He became the mouthpiece."

On October 11, 1978, Joy Division recorded 'Digital' and 'Glass' at Cargo Studios, situated on a hill leading out of Rochdale. John Brierley's well-equipped studio would later morph into the comparatively plush Suite 16, christened by Tony Wilson (a pun on 'Sweet 16') and co-owned by Hooky. Back in 1978 it had assumed a mid-range position in the hierarchy of local recording facilities. Affordably two steps below the lush confines of Stockport's Strawberry and yet stacked with the devices necessary to keep the inquisitive producer happy, it was the perfect demo studio for the major companies and the BBC; perfect also, for a new independent label. As such it would become a stalwart Factory studio.

The finance for the recording (and the subsequent release) came from money left to Tony Wilson by his mother who died in 1975. "I remember a conversation Tony and I had in our bedroom," says Lindsay Reade. "He was wondering if his mother would object to a good portion of his inheritance being spent on what was – to all extents and purposes – something of an artistic frippery. We were lucky in that we didn't need to dip into that fund to survive and I said that, unlike the dead, money did not belong in a dead stone vault. I thought, therefore, that his mum would approve. I don't think either of us seriously expected the money to return however."

It was Martin Hannett's unenviable task to bring together the four acts that would be on *The Factory Sample*, the introduction to the world of Factory Records.

For Joy Division, it would mark the coming together of band and their natural producer. For Ian Curtis, and indeed for any singer, the in-studio dynamic between producer and artists would be vital, especially in view of Curtis' ongoing unease about the process of recording.

The title 'Digital', while having no apparent relevance to the familiar song lyric – "I feel it closing in, Day in, day out" – was probably, and appropriately, named after Hannett's inroads into the digital domain at this point in his career. Martin took delivery of the new AMS Digital Delay two weeks before Joy Division went into Cargo. "It was digital, it was heaven sent," Martin told writer Jon Savage when asked about the new machine.

Tosh Ryan remembers how Martin was obsessed with digital technology. "[He was] researching digital technology way, way before it even became thought about in general terms, in broad consumer terms," he recalls. "He said to me once, 'I need £700 to buy a CD player'. I said, 'What the hell is a CD player?' He said, 'I need it and I need it now'. I remember buying it – it was one of the first generation of CD players. When we got it Martin showed me a CD and I thought, 'That looks weird. Can you show me what's on the other side? You know… can you play the B side.' He was showing it to me and he said in the future you'd be able to get information on here. He said you'd be able to get movies on them, music, pictures, text. I didn't believe him. I thought he was talking bollocks. He was ahead in his thinking. He was advanced."

Without the slightest regard for thrift, Martin Hannett would bang his fists on the table and demand money from Rabid.

Ryan: "We had arguments all the time. He'd say things like, 'Don't fuck with my budgets right'. He said to us, 'We need to buy this thing called a Digital Delay line'. I remember Laurence writing the cheque for £1,200. I thought what the hell is that? There's reference to it in *24 Hour Party People*.

We had to go out onto the moors to meet this guy, Stuart Nevison. Martin went out there with the cheque for £1,200. You can buy them for £80 now, a good one. He built it for us. We commissioned Stuart to make it. Martin needed it. 'I've got to fucking have it,' he said. He was working with Clarke and Jilted John then. The AMS enables you to put a delay on a sound so that you can alter the tone, the pitch, where it goes. It was built into the recording rack rather than having it on a particular instrument."

Martin Hannett thus became the first producer to change the way the drums sounded by using this brand new machine. Steven Morris' rock-based drum sound became a sharp crisp disco beat when fed through the delay. Few would deny that the effects Martin created on this record are simply stunning, a giant leap forward for Joy Division, especially when these two tracks are compared with those of *An Ideal For Living*, even though there was only being a matter of months between the two sessions. Hannett produced an echoed effect on Ian's voice that was as compelling as Ian's onstage performance, and which helped create an intimacy between singer and listener.

Terry Mason was a close observer at these early sessions. "We had seen Martin at gigs but he was completely different in the studio environment," he says. "This was his domain and he was a tyrant in the studio. This was immediately obvious at Cargo. Basically, he didn't want anyone about. He didn't want musicians in the studio. He felt that they got in the way of his creative process. He had a problem with them because they would talk all the time and annoy the fuck out of him. The thing was that, at Cargo, there was nowhere to get out of the way. There was no space and, even if the band went out to the pub, that meant they would come back bladdered and would talk even louder, which would annoy him even more. Basically, Martin didn't like musicians.

"Martin was probably a better musician than any of the band, although I don't recall how good he was in Greasy Bear. He would be really strict from the start in one way and yet he could also be very loose and allow them to do their own thing before seizing control."

Without doubt, it was an attraction of opposites. Joy Division were down–to–earth, fired by laddish camaraderie. Hannett, by contrast, did not even seem to have been raised on this Earth. His hippyish demeanour astonished the band, and they were further dumfounded when he locked the studio door and slapped drugs on the table. As Bernard Sumner would later note, in *Sounds*: "Martin was into wild experimentation. There was no notion of making a pop record. He was the hippie on smack, there's no other way of putting it. And we were a band on speed. It was always that way with Martin."

The relationship had its lighter moments in the endless interplay between Hannett, who often refused to even speak to the band, and manager Rob Gretton, himself no shrinking violet when it came to dealing with life's eccentricities. At least here could be found some kind of common ground. "Get those fucking cunts out of the way so I can make a fucking record," was one infamous and not untypical Hannett remark.

Joy Division performed for the second time at the Factory club on October 20, 1978, but still hadn't found their true platform. Just three live reviews into an unsteady relationship with the music press, they were still feeling their way.

That night Rob Gretton skulked by the bar; sardonic and anxious, his white 'Mallan' streak highlighting his temples as he cast glances about him with an air of genial resignation. This was the night he handed copies of the 12-inch version of *An Ideal For Living* to anyone who might be able to lend a hand, journalists, local promoters and photographers.

"Goes some way to righting the fucking wrong done by the 7-inch," he sighed although, even then, everyone sensed Rob's unease in regard to the recording. He realised all too well that the band, *his* band, had left that place behind; that just to revisit those songs, even in the full attack of the twelve-inch version, was to ignore the seismic advances made by the band in the intervening six months. Things were gathering pace, and this was no time to be looking over your shoulder at past indiscretions.

"You can interview the band tomorrow," he told *Sounds* reporter Mick Middles, and it seemed more of a command than a request. Middles' editor at *Sounds* had been singularly unimpressed when the opportunity of interviewing Joy Division had been suggested earlier in the week. To the London-based music press the emergence of another Manchester band was still not greeted with overwhelming enthusiasm, despite their general interest in the post-punk north.

That night, backstage, Ian Curtis seemed a bundle of nerves; twitchy, troubled, chain-smoking, chain *talking*, pacing the floor, kicking the wall, spinning yet polite… *ever so* polite. Ian Curtis always seemed so polite.

There was always something intriguing about him. One glance at Ian Curtis, be it in a bus queue or backstage at The Russell Club, was sufficient to realise that he had a curious cultural edge, an expanding record collection, that he was the singer in a band. It shone through despite the fact that he was dressed in the manner of a civil servant on lunch break; very anti-rock'n'roll yet curiously subversive at the same time.

As it turned out, Joy Division's spirited, throbbing set that night showed little hint at embryonic greatness. It was the same set they had played at the Band On The Wall. It was bigger on the Factory stage, louder, more arresting perhaps, but still lacking that certain spark.

John the Postman, dancing badly by the stage front, disagreed. Clutching his freebie 12-inch, he unleashed an unlikely and unexpected torrent of praise on behalf of the band. Mick Middles, for one, couldn't ever recall the perceptive postman being so animated before. Perhaps they would be worth an interview after all?

It was a gift of Manchester, back then, that amid the dingy and the disagreeable, the fantastic habitually loomed. In terms of music, this was perhaps true of all cities, where promising bands and scenes would emerge from decrepit rehearsal rooms and band meetings and interviews that took place in particularly unappealing drinking dens.

One of them was The Gaythorn, unappetising, dour and austere, a hovel really, situated just a hop across the road from the site of a sailing emporium that would soon be transformed into The Haçienda, and was the venue for Joy Division's first encounter with the national music press. It was not to be a particularly perceptive interview, as the journalist Mick Middles would freely admit. The true reason he ventured down there on a Sunday evening owed more to the persuasive powers of Rob Gretton than any genuine prescience about the musical possibilities of the band.

"Ian Curtis seemed to smile a lot," recalls Middles. "It was a nervous and inquisitive smile. The smile of a man not quite at ease with the situation but, nevertheless, excited by the possibilities."

In his book *From Joy Division To New Order*, Middles would write: "Ian Curtis seemed the most open; the most jovial, even. Certainly the only band member who seemed to actually enjoy the process of being interviewed."

Ian spoke about his writing: "I have got this little book here. Full of lyrics, it is. I just pull it out and see if I can fit something in. I have loads of lyrics in reserve… all waiting in there. I'll use them when the right tune comes along. Sometimes it's a line from one song mixed with a line from another. Sometimes the original lyric gets completely changed… it just gets used as a guide lyric and leads to something else. You never know. But I have to have this reserve… this 'lyric bank'. Some of the songs are two, three years old. 'Leaders Of Men', for example. I don't write about anything in particular. It's all subconscious stuff. Scribble… sometimes feelings or things that pop into your head. Does that sound pretentious?"

At one point during the interview, and much to the journalist's surprise, Curtis turned his back on the band and beckoned Middles into a tight, conspiratorial huddle. This was entirely due to one off-hand remark the writer had made about the art shock troupe Throbbing Gristle that appealed, it seemed, to Ian Curtis.

"*They* don't understand," whispered Curtis, the flick of his wrist indicating the four others sprawled vicariously around the room. "They don't like Throbbing Gristle."

"Oh fuckin' 'ell... he's found a soul-mate," sneered guitarist Bernard Sumner, strongly suggesting that Throbbing Gristle were regarded by three quarters of the band as one step too far into the murk of avant-garde.

"So are we gonna be talkin' arty bollocks for the rest of the interview," enquired the mischievous bass player, Peter Hook, feigning an air of exasperation. He cut a curious dash, Hooky. With his Wrangler's stuffed into ungainly motorcycle boots, both of which were firmly implanted on the split red vinyl that coated a loose stool

Except, of course, he wasn't quite 'Hooky', not yet. What's more, Joy Division were only just Joy Division and even they hadn't quite come to terms with what that might mean. They were still just some band from somewhere, a name lost on the antipathy of music press editors, barely able to suppress their yawning indifference for anything that might be bubbling to thought-provoking effect in Manchester.

The Ian Curtis that emerged from this interview was not a darkly clad boy with a sullen brow, poring over scribbled lyrics, or grasping a heightened intensity onstage, wild and abandoned before the nervous glances of Bernard and Hooky. This was a different Ian Curtis, a beaming, anticipatory face, high on the thoughts of consuming the food that had been placed before him. That it was but a lowly meat pie seemed of little consequence at the time.

Yet Ian's glee seemed barely containable. Thrusting his right hand forward, he firmly grasped the tomato sauce bottle that Rob had placed dutifully before his pie. A darkened globular crust crowded the neck; not disgusting enough, it seemed, to dilute Ian's glee. Turning the bottle rapidly upside down and slamming his left palm into bottle's base, he caused a tsunami of ketchup to gush forth and unduly swamp his dinner.

It was a cartoon moment, a freeze frame, a still. Hooky's head dipped and smacked against his palm. Bernard and Steve fell to a schoolboy huddle of chuckles, leaving Rob's sardonic growl to state the obvious.

"You would do that when there is a journalist present, wouldn't you? What about our aura of cool? What did I tell you about that? He'll write all about this now... it will become the *ketchup* interview."

CHAPTER 8

Isolation

"He felt like an alien, like it was something to be embarrassed about." – Mark Reeder

Although the four members of Joy Division could still act like kids when the mood took them, it was becoming increasingly obvious to them all that Ian Curtis, by now their recognised leader, wasn't a kid any more. Whether Ian liked it or not, there was no getting away from the fact that his status as a married man with a child on the way set him apart from Hooky, Barney and Steve. Also, he lived some distance away in Macclesfield. Until 1978, when Ian was still job commuting into Manpower at Piccadilly, he'd get a lift to band rehearsals at The Swan from Barney, who would pick him up on his bike after work and drop him off later at the station for his journey home.

Steve's recruitment to the band had an added advantage in that he also lived in Macclesfield and was therefore able to give Ian a lift in his car. After leaving the Swan the lads had a couple of band practises in Ian's home town, in a pub in Macclesfield that was famous, according to Terry, for having a mad landlord. "There was a guy there who had ostriches," he recalls. "He'd do an ostrich egg for the regulars. There was a bit of a bust up between Hooky and Barney at this pub. Barney was having go at Hooky's contribution – 'All you do is play bah bah bah on the bass' – this was a bit insulting as, since Hooky had come up on his motorbike, it was left to him to take Barney's equipment back to his house."

Subsequent forays into practise rooms found Joy Division at the Alexander (or little Alex, as it was known, by Alexandra Park) and The Salford Arms. Terry: "We were there because we found out it had a rehearsal room that was £12 a night and we went downstairs and watched TV. We were just hoping that they'd keep the TV on Granada so we could watch *Happy Days*. This was the first broadcast and we were so desperate to see it – that's us serious northern po-faced bastards. We had a drink and watched it and then went upstairs and had a rehearsal. We only used that rehearsal room once."

Later in 1978 the band came upon the most evocative of all their rehearsal spaces, T.J. Davidson's on Little Peter Street. It was here that Kevin Cummins took a series of memorable monochrome Ian Curtis photographs and the famous 'Love Will Tear Us Apart' video was made, both of which have become synonymous with the enduring image of Joy Division[1]. Situated on Little Peter Street, T.J. Davidson's was little more than a dusty and unused warehouse complex; a series of dour rooms from the industrial age. Tony – T.J. – Davidson was another Wythenshawe bred entrepreneur, who would sit like Buddha in a central office, collecting the rehearsal rent and building a small roster for his label, TJM Records, from the wealth of bands who used the facility.

T.J. Davidson's was on the same street that would later boast The Boardwalk, and was used by many up-and-coming bands, grateful for a rehearsal space close to the city centre. For anyone with an interest in the Manchester music scene, it was simply a godsend, a place where you might encounter Buzzcocks, The Distractions, Mick Hucknall's Frantic Elevators, Linder's Ludus and Joy Division, among many others.

For romantics who liked to imagine Manchester music emerging from the grimy residue of its lost industrial heritage, it just seemed perfect, although this might have been lost on the young Joy Division.

Terry: "The room that everyone seems to know of – the brown room, which is the one where 'Love Will Tear Us Apart' was filmed – was on the front of the building. We got moved out of there – I think it was costing too much – so we moved to the back of the building. It was a long room and it was a bit further away from the toilets. It was as if there was a radiator and radiator shelves along the length of the room. All around was coke cans. I'd gone in with a can and put it down and forgot which one was mine. I

---

[1] The group used T.J.'s until autumn 1979 but were actually using another space – the Rialto in Salford when 'Love Will Tear Us Apart' was filmed there. They only returned for the filming.

grabbed hold of one thinking it was mine and got a mouthful of piss and a couple of fag ends. They were just too lazy to walk 20 or 30 feet to the toilet."

Nor was this an isolated incident. When Joy Division played Eric's on July 15, 1978 it was the first time they had secured the services of Oz PA, who would go on to work with them regularly. "That night was the first time we got a rider," remembers Terry Mason. "Roger Eagle gave us a couple of cases of Carlsberg in bottles. The support band kept nicking them so we got some and emptied the lager out and Barney and Hooky pissed in a couple of them and put the lids back on carefully. Then Rob [Gretton] comes in the dressing room and, being his generous self, when he sees Oz PA – Eddy and Oz – come in, seeing that they've been working for us, offers them a couple. Eddy took a mouthful of straight piss basically."

Ian's family lived close to Manchester and he liked to visit his parents at weekends. His father would drop him at Piccadilly for the train ride to Macclesfield. If not, T.J.s was quite handy, being just a few minutes walk from Oxford Road station.

Proprietor Tony Davidson[1] recalls that Ian was far and away the most talkative of all within Joy Division's circle. "Obviously I knew Rob from way back. But Rob knew me, as well. Ian didn't," he says. "He wasn't from the streets in the sense that I was. He was different from the other band members. Ian wasn't over-friendly, as many bands were, probably because they thought I could help their careers. Ian wasn't like the guys in Victim, who I brought over from Northern Ireland and were just bemused by me because I drove a flash car and wore good clothes. But Ian was fascinated. I don't think he could quite work out what it was that I did. Not many people could, actually. But Ian was the most curious of the lot. I liked him. He seemed honest."

Mick Middles witnessed a private run through of the Joy Division set, performed within the darkness of T.J. Davidson's but can't recall much in the way of detail. "The band were polite, tentative, eyes flashing. Gretton was affable to the point of chummy," he says. "Thumping drum intro. I recall Hooky swinging a low bass and Barney, guitar clutched tight to his chest. Ian, stock still and central. A dark, shadowy sound. Darker perhaps, than I would ever recall them again. I was thinking of Siouxsie & The Banshees. It was too loud, too forced, too eager. Eight songs, perhaps nine, clattering away, can't remember what they were. I recall noticing a few extraordinary

---

[1] Interviewed at the 'In The City' music seminar in Manchester, 1993

dips and peaks. Ian was intense but then they all seemed to be really embarrassed in between each song and afterwards. I suppose it's easier to perform to a crowd than to one person."

By the end of 1978 there was no mistaking the fact of Debbie's pregnancy and, in consequence, Ian's imminent fatherhood, a circumstance somewhat at odds with his youth and impending rock star status. The profile of the band was growing at the same rapid rate as his unborn child; still somewhat under the surface, not yet quite born, but increasingly obvious as, of course, was Debbie's bump. Ostensibly all was going well, but there can be no question that Ian was beginning to come under escalating pressure from several different angles.

There were a few gigs in and around the North West that November, even a few down south; one in Bristol and the group also supported The Rezillos and The Undertones at Canterbury and Brunel University. Immediately after two home town gigs at the renamed New Electric Circus and The Factory, the band all went off to York on December 22, driving to the old walled city straight after finishing work. Terry can recall how tiring this was: "Most of the early gigs we'd drive back. Huddersfield, Liverpool, Leeds. A lot of the London ones we would drive back and get changed into suits and go to work having got home at six in the morning. You forget what it was like. When you see all these manufactured bands nowadays and all that – the fact that we'd get out of work early, load up a van, drive down to London, do a gig, come back like zombies and then go straight to work."

Immediately after Christmas, on December 27, Joy Division played the first of many London gigs at The Hope & Anchor in Islington. The venue itself was no palace, but this was offset by the importance of their London debut and what it might portend. In reality it was a dark basement in a small pub, and in 1978 Islington was far from the happening place it would become in the Nineties. The turn out for this inaugural gig was disappointing to say the least, which indicated the group's growing fan base had not yet extended this far south. Getting the gear down through a trap door was a hassle and to cap it all Barney had to be dragged from his bed, suffering with flu. The mood in the car on the return journey was miserable. Ian must have known in some way that he was sick and in need of a bed as well as Barney because a fight erupted for the sleeping bag that Barney was using. It was during this tussle that Ian had his first recognisable major epileptic seizure, thrashing about and hitting the windows. Steve drove to the nearest hospital in Luton, where Ian was given Phenobarbitone tablets and a referral letter for his doctor.

Quite why Ian should suddenly suffer from epilepsy at such a relatively late age – he was 22 at the time – remains something of a mystery. As a child he had always enjoyed good health, while sister Carole appeared to be the unhealthier sibling of the two. Neither Doreen nor Carole ever saw Ian have a fit. Doreen: "He definitely never had any fits when he was growing up. The only thing he had – he had a cyst on his tummy button. When we first came to New Moston he saw Dr. Parry and I went with him to North Manchester to have it taken off. That's about the only time I've known him be ill. I saw no sign. When the boys rang me and said he'd been taken ill I was amazed. They had to turn back after the London gig and took him to hospital. They hadn't found out what it was."

About a month later, on January 23, 1979, Ian Curtis was clinically diagnosed as epileptic after seeing a specialist at Macclesfield Hospital.

The human brain is made up of millions of nerve cells that affect every facet of our behaviour, movement and feelings. To make these things happen, the brain sends and receives messages along millions of nerve cells called neurones. The nerve cells do this by passing electrical signals to each other. A seizure happens when, for many different reasons, some kind of electrical disturbance suddenly interrupts these signals. Epileptic seizures are all caused by interrupted signals, and so start in the brain. The word 'seizure' describes a sudden event where there is a change in a person's behaviour, feelings, and awareness of where they are. Ian spoke about 'awaking' from a fit – clearly his consciousness was lost, as during sleep. Epilepsy is diagnosed when there is a tendency to have repeated seizures.

There seemed to be no obvious cause behind the onset of Ian's seizures. His mother thinks that Ian might have taken a blow to the head at some point in his teens, that he had become involved in an argument with some lads and one of them apparently kick boxed Ian's head. She has also suggested that the stress of getting married may have contributed, or the flashing stage lights under which Joy Division performed – or indeed a combination of all these things.

Carole believes Ian's lifestyle might have been a factor. "There was a hut… they must have had a disco or something there and that's where Debbie recalls that at age 15 he'd gone a bit funny and fallen over but I think he was just drunk. Kids being kids he was probably experimenting with this that and the other. I remember someone coming up to me and saying, 'Do you know your Ian's taking drugs?' and thinking my dad'll kill him if he finds out."

Increasingly, Ian's fits became associated with the gigs. The lights on stage seemed to be a trigger, which is why a band decision was taken to abandon strobe lights from this point onwards. There is the possibility that the effort Ian put into his performance was also a factor, along with the lifestyle that is visited upon the working rock musician: lack of sleep, irregular meals and a surfeit of alcohol – all of which are part and parcel of life on the road – are known to reduce the seizure threshold and increase the likelihood of a fit.

Whatever the cause, Ian could certainly be described as having a 'low seizure threshold' – someone who is more likely to start having seizures when there is no apparent obvious reason. Indeed, there is no known cause for as many as 70% of all people who develop a seizure disorder.

Mark Reeder believes that stress was the biggest single factor in causing Ian's epilepsy, and therefore could have been triggered at any point in Ian's life. "I think Ian had epilepsy before the band," he says. "I think it was the stress of the whole situation he was getting himself in that brought it on. It just builds up and then it's like a hiccup in your head. The stress of his responsibility to his family and the pressure from home, coupled with maybe song writing pressure to excel and then stage-fright, apprehension–type stress before gigging and then later the stress of dealing with a deep down inner-feeling of wanting to get out of his relationship with Debbie. It was all causing him turmoil. It all accumulates. He might have even had fits when he was a kid when he was put in very stressful situations. He could even have had fits and people didn't know about it. Perhaps they were rare and no one had seen them happen, or he might not really have been aware of what was actually happening to him – like he just felt a strange feeling – or he kept it secret as he did many things in his private world. Epilepsy was considered a handicap or something otherworldly back then. Of course, when it started happening in front of others, he just couldn't hide it any longer."

Mark Reeder speaks from experience since he has suffered epileptic fits himself. He believes they were caused by stress. "And because I was going weeks without sleep," he adds. "I was running a bar in Berlin and doing the record label and all the things associated with a label – going to clubs. I was burnt out. The stress brought on these fits. I didn't realise it until after I'd had about three. I went to the doctors. I'd noticed that the side of my mouth and my tongue had gone black. I wondered what it could be. The doctor asked if I'd had any blackouts and I said I had. I was on the way to work one day and the next thing I knew three hours had gone by and I was lying against the door at home and I was thinking to myself, 'What are you doing on the floor?' I had no kind of real awareness that anything had happened at that point. It was only when it happened the third time and I noticed what was going on. I knew I was about to black-out. At first I thought it was something to do with my blood pressure. But it wasn't the same feeling as fainting. The doctor did a scan and stuff and said I'd had an epileptic fit. He said the fact that you've had a couple of fits doesn't necessarily mean that you will have epilepsy for the rest of your life – it could be just because you are under such stress."

Mark's experience caused him to look into both the treatment and perception of epilepsy. "Epilepsy is looked at in a totally different way now than it was in 1977," he says. "When you were epileptic in the Seventies you were a mutant. You were handicapped. Today it's looked at in a different light. In the mid-Nineties there was a different perception of what it could be and how it's caused and what to do about it. They said that before they wanted to give me medication of any kind I should try and decrease my stress level by cutting the work down – stop the bar or stop the label, you can't do both. So I stopped running the bar. Then they said if I still had fits after that they would review things. Once I stopped the bar the epilepsy went. I've only ever had one fit since – a year and a half ago. I was under really, really bad stress then. My record label partner left the company and it resulted in costly lawsuits."

Ian crossed a line the night of this first fit. Whereas previously he'd worked at assisting the disabled, now he was in need of assistance himself. Ironically, in the months leading up to his first fit Ian had been visiting the David Lewis Centre to observe and study epilepsy. Unfortunately images of patients wearing helmets and knee pads served only to exacerbate the despair and embarrassment he felt about becoming epileptic himself.

"Ian was always embarrassed about being epileptic," says Mark Reeder. "He felt like an alien, like it was something to be embarrassed about. When we were in the van coming back from Berlin to Britain he had a fit while I was sat next to him. At first I wasn't really aware but Hooky went, 'Look, he's having a fit'. I said, 'What shall we do?' He said, 'Oh nothing, just leave him, he'll come out of it'. It was the first time I ever saw anyone having a fit next to me. I saw someone in the street once when I was a kid. I expected him to be flailing around but he wasn't like that at all. Then, after about 20 minutes, he'd come out of it and it was like 'Give us a fag'."

Seizures vary in strength, with the most serious referred to as 'grand mal' – where consciousness is lost – and the milder known as 'petit mal', which have a shorter duration. Both conditions are caused by an electrical instability in the brain.

Alan Wise was another in Ian's circle with some experience of epilepsy and could relate to Ian's condition more easily than others at the Russell

Club. "I got physically ill in the club with attacks of 'petit mal'," he says. "Ian had a couple of attacks of 'grand mal' and he came to the office to talk about it. My opinion was that the people around Ian had no concept of his illness. They didn't know what it was or how to cure it. Also with the drugs that he took and the state that he got into with the music and the chanting – which was quite hypnotic and repetitive – it was really an epileptic state he was getting into but it could bring on a real epileptic state."

Wise actually advised Ian to abandon Joy Division, to no avail. "I spoke to him once and told him, 'Look you shouldn't go on stage, you're not well, you're risking your health'. I said the epilepsy has a very strong downside, the depression afterwards. The people around him seemed to think that he could recover from an epileptic fit in 10 minutes and feel all right. But epilepsy is a mood-changer. He was very poorly advised. I just think he shouldn't have gone on to perform in front of an audience after an epileptic attack. It's a sort of working-class thing… 'Come on then, get on with it.' He had two epileptic attacks at the club. [Going on stage was] either very brave of him or very foolish."

Dr. David Holmes, now a senior lecturer in psychology, also knew Ian since they were both in bands at that time. He thinks that epilepsy could be an indication of over-activity in the brain. "Epilepsy is a common symptom of hidden neurological damage," he says. "People with neurological problems are not that common and often form the upper crust of intellectual individuals. They have disabilities, they have problems, they have twitches, they have some difficulties getting on with people but often, as with manic individuals, have a flash of brilliance in some area that allows them to think more quickly, act more quickly or in some way excel. It's rare to find one of these individuals who is not like that – unless they have more profound brain damage or something. Many high fliers and brilliant performers I know have got neurological twitches, possibly a sign of brain over-activity as with epilepsy. From a quiet sensitive state they can abruptly launch into conversation when others have lost the momentum but are often frustrated by wanting to achieve more and not getting pleasure from what they are doing, which makes them strive beyond the norm."

This concurs with an age old belief that emperors and saints were supposed to be afflicted with epilepsy, and in ancient times it was called the holy sickness. Alexander the Great was a sufferer.

Initial drug treatment of epilepsy is generally used on a trial and error basis.

Anti-epileptic drugs act on the brain and different types of drugs are used, with doctors having little choice but to experiment with various types of available anti-epileptic drugs. One drug could be effective with certain patients while others might react quite differently. Ian's first prescription of Phenobarbitone is still used in the treatment of epilepsy today but some of the drugs he was put on later – such as Valproate and Carbamazepine – are nowadays used for the treatment of mental disorders. Typical side effects might be tiredness, drowsiness and a slowing of mental performance. Alcohol generally doesn't mix well with these drugs. But alcohol was part of the territory.

"We just got shit faced all the time," admits Terry Mason. "There wasn't usually a rider though and so we had to get drunk on our own money. No one was overly flush with money. But we were young lads on a night out somewhere and Ian never had to drive so he could have a drink. Basically it was lager we were on. It was more a situation of cutting back rather than quitting when Ian became epileptic. "

Medication obviously changes the mood pattern of the brain, and certain individuals around Ian noticed he was behaving differently. Vini Reilly thought it was a factor in causing Ian to become depressed. "As soon as they put him on medication for the epilepsy that's when he started to change," he says.

Clearly as time, and subsequent fits, went on the medication took more of a hold on Ian. Reilly believes that Ian gradually began to lose his sense of reality: "If you're depressed and you don't take medication your feet are on the ground and you feel depressed and it's awful. However bad it is you can experience the depression. You can control your actions in response to the pain you've got. You can say, 'I'll do this now, I'll go to bed or whatever'. When you're on medication you lose that control. You're not in a fit state to make a decision. The ground is taken from under your feet and you're left floating in mid air and you can be blown about in one direction or another and that's what happened with Ian. He was not grounded, he had no sense of reality and he lost a sense of who he really was. He didn't have a clue what was going on. He didn't know which way round he was – it stood him on his head and turned him inside out. The medication destroyed him completely. It took away all his powers and all his ability to control his own destiny."

Reilly had experience of being on medication himself. "That's what the medication that I was on and that Ian was on does to you," he says. "It takes away your own control. That's how it works. It works for some people but it would never have worked for me and it would never have worked for Ian. We both talked about that and understood that."

It would be quite normal for anyone discovering that they have become epileptic to suffer from some kind of anxiety and depression as they learn to cope and adapt to it in their social environment. For Ian, given his responsibilities with a budding band and baby on the way, the situation was doubly distressing.

At the close of 1978, those involved in the Manchester music scene could look back on a year of mixed blessings. While interest in Joy Division was certainly gathering pace, especially in the music press, the year's big Mancunian triumph remained Buzzcocks who in December enjoyed a fourth hit single, 'Promises', which climbed to number 20, and continued their association with *Top Of The Pops* and Radio One.

In the city itself, The Factory Club had become pivotal to the underground scene as the venue for a series of eclectic and inspirational gigs, including a spectacular night on October 28 when The Pop Group, an influential band from Bristol, were supported by Ludus, a new group fronted by Manchester artist Linder. Joy Division, who had performed at the club two days earlier, seemed particularly fascinated by The Pop Group, who were evolving at a similar pace and would later be heard discussing the gig during an interview conducted by ex-Rafters DJ Bob Dickinson, by this time writing for the *New Manchester Review*.

For Ian Curtis, further aesthetic inspiration would arrive in December with the release of an album that would become a firm favourite of his, *D.O.A. The Third And Final Report Of Throbbing Gristle*. It was an extraordinary record, which included one track comprised entirely of computer data and another based on a series of telephone death threats. However, it was another track that utterly captivated Ian, a dour statement of hopelessness and alienation called 'Weeping'.

CHAPTER 9

Monochrome

"When you shoot a band, any band, you always seem to pick out the outsider in the group. Look at every shot… the outsider was Ian… again, not just with my shots. With Anton… Paul Slattery. The results were strangely similar." – Kevin Cummins

As 1978 gave way to 1979, Ian Curtis found himself on the brink of a downward spiral, with every aspect of his life pulling in opposite directions and demands on his time ever increasing. Impending fatherhood meant that the need for a regular income was more acute than ever, so he had little choice but to carry on working full-time despite his growing commitment to Joy Division. Debbie was nearing the end of her term and, quite naturally, wanted to have her husband at home. Between January and March Ian had several increasingly violent fits at home. Ian's mother recalls him telling her that one of his fits occurred while out walking his dog Candy in South Park. Evidently the dog waited patiently by his side until he regained consciousness.

In recent years there has emerged a widespread belief that 1979 was the peak year of the post-punk boom, the year when the bands with torn t-shirts and a healthy disrespect for their elders mastered their craft and began to deliver music worthy of their initial promise. But whatever developments might have excited the taste-makers in London, you could be forgiven for failing to notice this impending richness in Manchester, let alone

Macclesfield. Although local acts were performing at The Factory Club, the Mayflower and a thin scattering of opportunist venues in the city, artistic development seemed less of a priority than reckless hullabaloo.

There was one notable exception. Although it wouldn't be released until March, The Fall's debut album, *Live At The Witch Trials*, was revolving on many Manchester turntables in January. Ian Curtis, for one, would have been all too well aware of the tremendous leap The Fall had made since their debut single emerged in June '78. Joy Division, by their own admission, had already eclipsed their excellent two song contribution to *The Factory Sample* and must have felt a powerful urge to come up with something to equal Mark E. Smith's idiosyncratic artifice.

Envious or not, Joy Division's fortunes took a divisive turn for the better at the start of January when they emerged as the focal point of a substantial article in *NME*, effectively a post-punk update of Paul Morley's huge 1977 piece on the Manchester scene in general.

Morley had already written about Warsaw and Joy Division before he met the group and became intrigued not so much by the music – that would come later – but by the personalities involved. "We met in a pub just at the bottom of Piccadilly station," he recalls. "Kevin Cummins was there as well. Ian was incredibly shy, they all were. He didn't say much at all and it was really hard work. And then I guess I was really shy too. Rob was there. I didn't get any sense of – that thing that's now come out more and more – that they were quite crude and practical jokers. I never really saw any of that. They were just very, very soft and sensitive, very shy, almost passive, and the interview was really hard work. As a journalist you start to think it's your fault. You're panicking – you're not getting any good quotes from them."

The difficulty, in squaring the eloquence of Ian's Curtis' lyrics and musical intelligence with the reserved lad who seemed naturally ill at ease in interview would continue to fascinate Morley, who later concluded: "He put all his quotes in his songs, put it that way. You went to interview him and he'd written his songs and even the early ones with Warsaw or 'Digital'… they were incredibly articulate, literary songs. So it was always really weird when you met him and he could barely speak. You'd go: 'Where does it come from?' and he'd say: 'Dunno, just wanna be good'.

"I wanted more than that and I wanted him to be Lou Reed or Iggy Pop and have his great quotes – but he didn't sell himself that way. He was literally selling himself through that and that was what was keeping him alive in a way I guess – because he was so fucked up in his life, these songs were so important, like his protection for a while."

Morley had somehow persuaded *NME* editor Neil Spencer to put Ian on the cover when his story was run. "In the end they put a little picture of him on," he recalls, "and they shared the cover. It was the first cover of the New Year, 1979. It was a little picture that Kevin took of Ian, with snow behind him. It should have been the cover really and it's proved to be the case."

Kevin Cummins also has vivid memories of the background to Morley's article, which explained Joy Division's standing within the scheme of things in Manchester at that time. In retrospect, it seems strange to note that in reality Joy Division had barely risen above the raft of local bands that performed regularly at the Band On The Wall.

"Paul had suggested that we might cover three Manchester bands for the *NME*, as a one-piece article about the Manchester scene," says Cummins. "His favourite three bands at the time were Spherical Objects, who were Steve Solamar's band ,The Passage, who included Dick Witts and Tony Freil, and then Joy Division.

"They were the three bands he perceived as being the most interesting in Manchester. Paul told me that he thought it was really important to get a lot of really good pictures of Steve Solamar because he wanted to try and convince *NME* that that should go on the cover. I was dubious. I thought there was no way on earth that Spherical Objects would go on the cover of *NME*. But we did the Spherical interview. We did Dick Witts and The Passage. We spent a day with each of them and then we did the Joy Division piece… and the band wanted to do it on a Saturday. I was annoyed because City were playing and it meant that I would miss the match but they insisted."

Displeased that he would miss the football game, Kevin collected his cameras and went out to meet up with Joy Division at Manchester Cathedral. "We did those pics where Joy Division were standing in the snow at the cathedral and then with the band stood around the art and furniture in the shop. And then we went to Hulme. We spent all afternoon doing the pictures, really. And the band were great. They were really into doing as many different things as possible and trying not to look like a band. Because we had done a bit of a weird shot of Steve Solamar and then this picture of Dick Witts which showed Dick watching telly and he was on the telly… because he was doing some arts shows on the TV at the time. We told Joy Division about these shots and they agreed that they really didn't want to look like a band. So we took them into this shop on Chapel Walks, which sold art and furniture. The guy who owned it, Jonathan Silver, was a mate of David Hockney's. He just let us wander about and do what we wanted. That was very important because, mostly, if you go in a shop, especially with a band, the manager or salespeople start to hover about and that intimidates the band and ruins the chances of getting a good shot. It worked superbly because they were so… so un-rock star pictures."

Indeed, with their short, neatly combed hair, sombre clothes and solemn demeanour, Joy Division looked more like a quartet of Mormons visiting from Utah than a traditional rock band. This became a crucial factor in the way they were perceived by hawkish music writers anxious to pour scorn on what *NME* would shortly term 'rockism', a catch-all pejorative that denoted the kind of image and behaviour personified by groups with long hair and flared jeans who performed heavy metal or art rock and were well past their prime. Joy Division didn't look like they owned a blues record between them.

This photo session produced the famous 'cigarette and raincoat' shot of Ian, which surfaced in April 2005 as the cover of *Mojo*, but it was the interview that followed, in the Brunswick pub near Manchester's Piccadilly station, that intrigued Paul Morley. There was just something different, perhaps even not quite right, about this Ian Curtis fellow.

Kevin Cummins: "After spending all afternoon with them and noticing how compliant they were, we quite liked that and then we sat in the pub and talked bollocks for a couple of hours and… this was the moment when Paul truly changed his mind about Joy Division. He suddenly realised that he liked this lot. He found something really interesting about them that he hadn't noticed before. He told me that he thought he was going to make Joy Division the focus of the piece rather than Spherical Objects. It sounds crazy now, but that's how close it was. Joy Division emerged from that piece looking like an important force. You could sense it in the pub. Paul was warming to Ian. Ian was strange because he had this intelligence but it wasn't immediately obvious when you met him. He didn't have that immediate charisma. You had to talk to him for a while. I think Paul tapped in to that… by accident, probably."

Cummins is of the opinion that the article, which proved such an important breakthrough for the band and served to awaken the rest of the music press to their importance, came about largely through luck. "It was obviously a bit of a lame week at *NME*," he says. "It was just after Christmas and they didn't know quite what to do. They didn't tell us that they were going to do this, but they did a weird split cover with The Raincoats on… maybe some band from somewhere else in Britain and then a picture of Ian. It was a messy cover with three photos, as if to stress that this stuff was happening all around the country."

There can be no doubt that from this moment, thanks to the *NME* cover – shared or not – Joy Division began to be taken seriously. "It suddenly

seemed so obvious," continues Cummins. "They were really good to photograph. Ian was tremendously photogenic, actually. In that strange way
when someone doesn't necessarily catch your eye when you see them in the
street, but take a shot of him and he would stand out. That's what seemed so
obvious to us. I mean he was curious to photograph. You had to get him to
put his carrier bags down and all of that. He wasn't a natural in that sense.
But, as we have seen over the years, he had an unusual quality on camera."

Intrigued by Ian's photogenic qualities Cummins went on to take the
photographs of him inside T.J. Davidson's rehearsal studio that gave the band
their enduring monochrome image.

Again, chance played a part in this – largely because the music press at the
time favoured black and white photography. "Nobody was publishing in
colour," says Cummins. "So the simple thing was, to save money, you just
shot everything in black and white. I was buying my own film. It was not
like there was any record company to give you a stack of money. So I was
very parsimonious with it. At the time, if I got one picture in *NME* I would
probably get about £7.50. And a roll of film plus processing would cost you
close to that amount, by the time you had made a print. These days, when
you are working with a band, it can be quite exciting to just overshoot and
see what comes out. But then, I wanted every frame to count, so I would
never overshoot because I would be really conscious of the fact that, if I did
two rolls of film, it would cost me twice as much and I wouldn't be making
any money. I didn't think that, twenty five years on, I would still be selling
them… perhaps I should have. But for every Joy Division there was a stack
of negs that would never ever get used again. I sometimes did stuff for the
New Manchester Review as well. I think the first session…the famous Joy
Division session at Tony Davidson's studios… the first seven or eight frames
of that shoot was some rugby player who used to play for Sale, who I was
doing for the *New Manchester Review*. The other reason was that Manchester
at that time was a dark city. Even then we were only just cleaning up a lot
of the public buildings. The light was very flat and, if you shot outside in
Manchester between November and March it would look like *A Taste Of
Honey*. Because of that, and because every picture of Joy Division was taken
for a music paper, they would always be thought of in terms of black'n'white."

This is undoubtedly true. Joy Division were Mancunian monochrome on
a level shared only with The Fall. However, early shots of The Fall depicted
a band in the anti-fashion Salford dress code of anoraks and market stall
jumpers. Joy Division, on the other hand, always appeared smartly clad with
perhaps a touch of the soul-boy shining through the earnestness of their tai-
loring. Joy Division effortlessly found a niche in their visual sharpness that

seemed to prefigure the musical sharpness that was just over the horizon. The trousers came before the drum beat, all perfectly shot amid the northern gloom.

Kevin Cummins is convinced that, again, pure chance played a part in the evocative shots taken at Tony Davidson's rehearsal rooms. "Had the walls not been painted black, then people today would have a completely different perception of Joy Division and a different perception of Ian Curtis," he says. "It certainly wasn't just me. Other shots were taken there as well… it saved time. Get the shots taken fast at the rehearsal rooms. I don't think anyone gave it a moment's thought, to be honest. But it was that blackness of the wall… it certainly seemed to suit Ian."

Terry Mason is quick to point out that the walls were in fact brown.

"A particular turd brown favoured by Manchester council," he adds, "cheap, probably stolen paint."

There was a certain paradox emerging here, with both Ian and the band. Gloomy, grainy monochrome shots might have been thought suitable to accompany the music, but this certainly never squared with the light-hearted, laddish nature of the band. This was even more apparent with regard to shots of Ian on his own. This amiable, often smiling character was almost always captured in gloom.

Kevin Cummins: "I do have a picture of him smiling… and it does seem a bit strange. But what I used to do was wait until the band had stopped joking between themselves and snap them just after. There is one shot of the band stood underneath that bridge in Hulme and the three of them are laughing behind Ian's back. That was Bernard who, obviously with Ian being really serious as the lead singer, decided to take the piss behind his back. He (Ian) couldn't see that going on and I just took one shot of it and didn't want to take anymore because it didn't seem rock'n'roll. Well, it didn't really seem fair on Ian. Looking back, I suppose it would have been quite perceptive. When you shoot a band, any band, you always seem to pick out the outsider in the group. Look at every shot… the outsider was Ian… again, not just with my shots. With Anton… Paul Slattery. The results were strangely similar."

The image of Ian Curtis as the eternal outsider, remote yet coolly observant, contrasts with his genuinely friendly nature but still reflects qualities that were present in his character. Ian wasn't aloof and, despite being a natural leader, never considered himself superior to anyone around him. He loved his family, never forgot a birthday, yet his own sister, while always remaining close to her brother, describes him as "different". Asked to explain exactly how he was different, she could not find the words.

One day in 2005 Carole Curtis was at her home leafing through a book of pictures when she came across Ian's photograph staring out from T.J. Davidson's rehearsal rooms. Still looking at the picture of Ian, Carole noticed that there was an English dictionary lying nearby and she asked Ian to give her a word from the dictionary that would describe the way in which he was different. She got ready to open the dictionary at random and the first word her finger pointed to was going to be it. She had a final word for Ian: "Give me a word that will describe you. Do it properly". She then opened the dictionary. The first word she saw underlined by her thumbnail was "communicate". As she looked to the right of it she felt a shiver when the words continued "with the dead". "Communicate with the dead" was the definition for another word to the left of the sentence – "Medium". *The* word, though, was *communicate*.

Lindsay Reade can recall Tony Wilson noticing that Ian was "different" the first time he ever saw him at the Electric Circus. "The band sounded shit but he looked strange and special," said Wilson, whom Reade believes was unusually perceptive when it came to recognising special qualities in people. He could also see just where this uncanny difference in Ian resided; not even in his unusual dance but in his eyes.

As well as sharing an *NME* front cover in January 1979, the band enjoyed a further breakthrough when on the last day of the month, they travelled to London to record their first John Peel session at the BBC's Maida Vale studios. The celebrated Peel Sessions required a different discipline to normal studio work insofar as they were recorded "almost live". After several run-throughs of each song, the takes are tweaked with the producer requesting each and every musician to perform "add-ons". For some bands – The Fall in particular – the format always seemed perfect and even sur-passes many of their official releases. This wasn't the case with Joy Division who needed the guidance of Martin Hannett in which to flourish.

At Maida Vale that evening producer Bob Sargeant and engineer Nick Gomm took four songs – 'Exercise One', 'Insight', 'Transmission' and 'She's Lost Control' – and stripped them back to a basic, sparse sound. There seems little doubt that their intention was to re-create the resonance Hannett had created on *The Factory Sample* and in this respect they were remarkably suc-cessful. More importantly, however, was the way in which the engineers succeeded in making the evening's other guests, Generation X, sound hope-lessly outdated.[1]

---

[1] As noted in Dave Thompson's *True Faith: An Armchair Guide to Joy Division and New Order*.

As for John Peel, although he went on to famously support The Fall, on his 1987 retrospective *Peeling Back The Years,* he noted: "I always think of them [Joy Division] in a rather romantic way, as being introspective and rather Russian… listening to them always makes me feel slightly central European."

In retrospect, *The Factory Sample* can be seen as the beginning of an unchallenged association between Joy Division and Factory, a relationship that was further cemented when their manager, Rob Gretton, became an integral part of the burgeoning label. By March 1979 Gretton had come to the conclusion that the "indie" dream was something he might transform into a long-term career, especially if he could bring about a situation wherein he and the band were in control of their destiny. He was not unaware that in a position like this he could create business advantages for one and all.

At the time, however, the future wasn't so cut and dried, not least because on a day-to-day basis Joy Division were still a gigging band obliged by circumstances to survive without the cushion of a record deal. It was a peculiar trait of the period that vast oceans of music press coverage were often showered on bands in states of relative infancy. Although it was never intended as such, a surfeit of gushing praise brought extra pressure to maintain and even build on the resulting momentum. The earnestness of the music press belied its quixotic nature; the downward slope for bands on the first rungs of the ladder was never more than one negative review away. It was a precarious position wherein the domino effect of rave reviews could slam into reverse, regardless of whether or not an act had improved or regressed.

It was a dilemma that lay more with career development than artistic progress. The out-with-the-old-and-in-with-the-new philosophy of *NME* and their ilk demanded that a young band had always to be in a state of growth and Gretton was fully aware of this. Money – a commodity generally ignored by music critics who believed business to be alien to artistry – was the key to the problem, of course. It probably wasn't the highest priority for a gang of nineteen year olds bouncing up and down the M6 in a Transit van either, but the more worldly Gretton knew perfectly well that success or failure depended more on a sizeable record company advance than on all the rave reviews put together.

Factory was by no means the only contender. In the spring of 1979 there was the distinct possibility that Joy Division might sign with Buzzcocks producer Martin Rushent's Genetic label or, indeed, its parent company, Radar Records.

Radar had surfaced as the fashionable home to Elvis Costello and Nick

Lowe, thereby establishing for itself a genuine knack of producing chart hits while retaining the credibility that was essential to appeal to the music press. They had also signed Bristol's The Pop Group whose debut 12-inch single, 'She Is Beyond Good And Evil', immediately became a favourite of Joy Division. Released in March 1979, it saw a band of limited musical potential stretch a funk backbeat to the edge of psychedelia. The trick would be later perfected by Factory's A Certain Ratio and would heavily influence Joy Division's subsequent rehearsals.

Martin Rushent had been carving out a name for himself with Buzzcocks by successfully welding a modern approach to the framework of fairly simplistic pop songs. He was also successful in dusting away the pub rock cobwebs of The Stranglers and adding a necessary vitality to the rawness of Generation X.

More experienced than Martin Hannett if considerably more conservative in the studio, Rushent nevertheless managed to produce stylish contemporary music that would also slot into radio play format. Hannett himself was an admirer of Rushent's work in fact, and to any record company executive Rushent would be the perfect producer to tame the untethered aspects of Joy Division. The question was whether or not the band would appreciate his intervention.[1]

With all this mind, on March 4 Joy Division marched into London's Eden Studio's to record a latterly infamous five-song demo for Genetic, not least because a sizeable record company advance was on the cards if the tracks passed muster. A reputedly head-spinning, ego-boosting £40,000 was floating in the air, a sum way beyond Factory's pockets – though Tony Wilson thought that interest in Joy Division from Genetic/Radar/Warner Bros was a good thing. That, after all, was an achievement in itself. "The whole idea of being an independent record label in 1978/9 was to get your band or your mate's band signed to a major label," says Wilson, "because that's what everyone wanted. There was a tiny period when we may have felt differently but I can remember interviewing Tosh Ryan – this was before Factory, and probably around spring 1978, after he signed Jilted John to EMI and Gordon The Moron, and he signed John Cooper Clarke to CBS. I interviewed him in a Granada cutting room and asked him why he'd signed the bands to majors and Tosh laughed and, quite rightly, said 'You're

---

[1] As it turned out, Rushent would use the new influx of affordable technology, from the Linn Drum – a programmable drum machine that used samples – to syn-drum pads to create an early Eighties 'new romantic' sound that would rapidly date – and would never have suited Joy Division.

living in the past'. [He was referring to] the idealistic past of summer of 1977 when everyone thought we could do it ourselves."

The five songs recorded as demos for Genetic were 'Insight', 'Glass', 'Transmission', 'Ice Age' and 'Digital'. Under Rushent's watchful eye they were sheathed in a bright, shining vivacity hitherto unheard in Joy Division, but what they failed to achieve was the unparalleled intimacy that Martin Hannett would subsequently bring out in the voice of Ian Curtis. This is most evident on 'Transmission', certainly a lively recording but one which lacks any Curtis warmth.

Regardless of this flaw it a superb demo, proof indeed that this was a band on the move. The demos skirted the rounds in Manchester – all local journalists certainly heard the tracks – and most expected the band to move from the interim Factory to a more stable base at Genetic. It was a pivotal moment in the progress of the band: to stay with Hannett or go with Rushent?

Rob Gretton was working out the economics. *The Factory Sample*, released somewhat bizarrely on Christmas Eve – clearly not a commercial move – had nonetheless been received very well. Indeed, when all were sold and the plus and minus columns totted up, the record made about £500 profit. Rob knew that singles made only pin money and that albums were where the real money was made, and with this mind he made a proposition to Wilson one night in The Band On The Wall. He suggested the band record their first album with Factory and then go on to Warner Bros.

It is because of this – because Joy Division was the first group of any stature that chose to stay independent – that Tony credits Rob Gretton with creating the independent record movement. Wilson: "This kid from Wythenshawe proceeded to sketch out a deal… which I agreed to on the spot – because why not? This turns out to be the most generous record deal ever done for musicians in history. His other thought was, 'Tony's a fucking idiot and I'll get a fantastic deal out of him', which he did that very day."

"To a lot of people it may have seemed a really courageous decision for the band not to go with Genetic," says Terry Mason. "I mean, no one had seen any money at all… and it was like, well, go on and record an album but you still can't have any money. But it wasn't quite like that. In fact, to be fair, it was very astute of Rob to stay with Factory. In his words, he didn't want to have to go to London and, as he put it, talk to cunts. As it turned out he could stay and talk to the cunt in Manchester! The Genetic deal wasn't that big, really, the bands who had been signing at the time, like Buzzcocks, would get considerably more than that… plus you don't actually get

£40,000 in your hand. It has to stretch an awful long way. I really think it was common sense on Rob's behalf and the band understood that."

Rob knew, of course, how the band had improved since the previous year's attempt to complete an album at Arrow Studios. Both in terms of all round musicianship and Ian's songwriting, they were powering to an exciting new level. Despite the worrying reality of Ian's continuing bad health, half a dozen gigs during February and March saw their confidence level rise considerably.

Two gigs in London, the first a return to the Hope and Anchor and the second, three days later on March 4, at the famous Marquee Club on Wardour Street supporting The Cure, preceded a return to the acutely unfashionable Bowden Vale Youth Club on March 14.

Over time this latter gig attained sufficient infamy to feature in Mark Paytress' book, *I Was There*[1], which focuses solely on classic gigs from the rock'n'roll era to the present day. Terry Mason doesn't recall it as being anything special, however, which suggests its notoriety was at least in part due to a set of evocative photographs taken by local news photographer Martin O'Neill. His depiction of Ian Curtis with his head clasped in his own arms, with the band in typical heads-down concentration, would become as iconic as the Cummins shots from T.J. Davidson's. O'Neill's image, perversely enhanced by a background of vivid flock wallpaper, evoked a powerful sense of time and place. In 2005 his pictures from that night became the focus of an exhibition at Hale Library.

"I do vividly remember the gig, well, things about the gig, if not the actual set," he says. "The problem was, of course, I was concentrating on taking pictures, so the music didn't really get to me. But I was actually onstage snapping away. And it was a really small stage. Hooky wasn't happy with me being there. In fact he told me to fuck off at one point. I didn't really blame him as there wasn't a great deal of room. However, the main thing that did strike me was Ian... almost literally. I didn't know anything about Joy Division at that point. They were one of a few bands that played there and it was my local venue, really. There was The Freshies, The Distractions, Fast Cars I think... and somebody mentioned V2, though I don't recall them.

"But there I was, just taking a snap and Ian came to the fore and suddenly started to dance in this extraordinary manner. I mean I just thought 'What the fuck are you doing, man? Mind me fucking camera, won't you!' I had never seen anything like it in my life."

[1] Cassell, 2005.

Many in Manchester would later claim to have been present at the Bowden Vale gigs and most of them questioned the wisdom of such a fast-rising band performing at this unglamorous venue. But there was method to Gretton's apparent madness. He believed that a series of gigs, regardless of the venue, would prepare the band for the recording of the essential first album.

Drummer Paul Hanley, later to become a stalwart in The Fall, was there to see his brother Steve performing with support band Staff 9, and also has vivid memories of the evening. "I was very young and not very familiar with Joy Division, though Steve had the *Ideal For Living* EP," he says. "My brother Steve and Craig Scanlon seemed quite friendly with them though, probably from sharing a tomato shaped ketchup dispenser at the café next door to Tony Davidson's rehearsal studios. There were two things, which really stuck in my mind about the gig. One, inevitably, was Ian Curtis' dancing, which, cliché though it is, really was a sight to behold. It didn't seem linked to normal dancing… [not] based on enjoyment of music or getting into the rhythm at all. He just looked like some unseen force was making him do it. The other thing I can remember about them is that Barney had what looked like a home-made synth[1], which lay, completely untouched, on the floor throughout the gig. Apart from one occasion where he made it make a noise not unlike a police siren, he never went near it. Whether this was a deliberate statement of intent, a pointer to the fact that synthesizers would take up their rightful place in the band as soon as he could figure out where to put them, or just that he couldn't be arsed playing it because he'd forgotten the stand, I suppose we'll never know."

Hanley wasn't aware that Joy Division appeared any more serious than other bands on the Manchester circuit. "[They and The Fall] were often criticised for being miserable, but it's worth noting how desperately serious most people in bands were at that time," he points out. "This was long before lad culture held sway in guitar bands. Both bands had a highly developed sense of humour, but gigs then were a serious business, as you'll know if you ever went to see The Passage. Joy Division never seemed miserable to me, just very, very focused. Being in a band then, especially in Manchester, I suspect, wasn't really about having a laugh. Certainly in The Fall the idea that you played a gig for your own enjoyment was a complete non-starter, and very probably still is. I remember being struck by their solid determination… especially Ian. He was a man who knew exactly what he wanted."

[1] Terry Mason believes the 'synth' was, in fact, a Woolworth's bontempii reed organ – basically a cheap harmonium.

CHAPTER 10

Unknown Pleasures

"Of course, there was his situation with him about to become a father but, to be frank, he did his bit, we did our bits and that was that. It always feels strange when people try and read so much into every lyric…" – Peter Hook

While the fates of Joy Division and Factory Records were now inextricably linked to what seemed like everyone's approval, the downside was that the members of the group had effectively kissed goodbye to £40,000, a sum that that in 1979 would comfortably buy at least two houses.

Ian Curtis' mother and sister both believe that Ian really didn't care about money, that it would never have been a motivating factor to him. Nevertheless, it is unlikely that Debbie Curtis, now entering the final stages of pregnancy at home in Macclesfield, was unconcerned about her husband's income, and Ian, a traditionalist at heart, would certainly have wanted to be a good provider. Indeed, the decision to record for Factory, rather than Genetic or even continue with RCA, probably seemed foolhardy to Debbie.

Of course, had the group signed with Genetic, the money wouldn't necessarily have been shared out there and then – it would likely have been kept back to keep wages and rehearsal rooms running – but, nonetheless, it is a sobering thought that Ian Curtis' share – assuming it to be one fifth – would have been £8,000, which is a great deal more than he actually saw in his own short lifetime.

"Everyone likes to be independent but everyone likes having money," says Terry Mason. "Because of his situation money did actually matter to Ian."

Mason confirms that there was tension between Ian and Rob Gretton, if not the occasional row, around the issue of money, but believes that Ian's struggle was more within himself. "Ian needed money but didn't want to give up this idealism that we'd seemed to build around ourselves," he says. "No one would like to say, 'Oh no… I really would like to make lots of money'. At that point it was our freedom – you know, we've got the best deal in the world. But then it was only the best deal if we'd got paid. Earning it was fantastic. Seeing it go into the bank was another matter. I think it was more an internal thing with Ian. He wanted all this but at the same time he wanted to be one thing but in a way he knew he needed the other thing. He wanted the freedom that Tony was telling him was the most precious thing in the world, yet at the same time Tony was picking up God knows what a week from Granada – and telling us 'It's fantastic what you've got there'. Ian went up to the heady heights of earning £50 a week while lesser bands were earning more money."

In April 1979, Ian joined the rest of Joy Division at Strawberry Studios for the recording of *Unknown Pleasures*. The rarefied atmosphere of a modern recording studio was a world apart from his domestic situation at Macclesfield, but the consolation was that the band's hectic gig schedule would cease for the duration of April, allowing Ian more opportunity to return to Macclesfield and his pregnant wife.

Nevertheless, as front-man, lyricist and, to a large extent, melody writer, a great deal of responsibility was placed on his shoulders. No one could be in any doubt that this would be Joy Division's one and perhaps only chance to make a serious impact on a national level. Solid gigging in February and March had helped the band build on the Paul Morley *NME* article and develop a sizeable reputation, at least in the all-important music press. It was a reputation that could easily dissipate, should an album arrive that failed to live up to this heightened state of expectation.

Strawberry Studios, on Waterloo Road at the top end of Stockport's Underbank, was unlike any other studio in the north of England. It was built by Kennedy Street Enterprises as the house-studio for a circle of talented musicians who had survived since the Merseybeat heyday of local bands, Wayne Fontana & The Mindbenders prominent amongst them. The core of these musicians, Eric Stewart, Kevin Godley, Lol Creme and Graham Gouldman, would record at Strawberry as Hotlegs before accepting the guidance of Jonathan King and re-emerging as 10cc. It was a significant development, with 10cc developing a reputation for producing adventurous, innovative pop music while using hugely innovative recording techniques. The mixing desk at Strawberry had been famously used for the ground-breaking over-dubbing of 10cc's biggest hit, 'I'm Not In Love'. According to their co-manager and Strawberry owner, Rick Dixon, that famous recording necessitated he and various studio engineers standing around the control room holding vertical screwdrivers, around which ran the recording tape. It was an idiosyncratic piece of recording that would have been worthy of Martin Hannett himself. Indeed, in time, Hannett's own eccentricity would rank alongside any of the myths that were embedded into the fabric of the Strawberry folklore.

Hannett, now about to add to the Strawberry legacy with his work on *Unknown Pleasures*, adopted the studios as his spiritual home, a play station for his talents with a mind-bending mess of electronic possibilities which even came complete with his unofficial 'office' across the road – the Waterloo pub, with its colourful collection of locals.

It has been suggested that the Waterloo became *almost* as important as the studio itself, with Hannett convinced that the breaks between recording were every bit as important as the work at the mixing desk. It is certainly true that the pub became a convenient means for him to escape for a while, not to mention a handy place for him to send musicians who were unwelcome in the control room. It was a place to drink and think, to settle musical scores, battle out the egos, soften the rough edges of dodgy bands before guiding them back into the studio. Hannett's craziness did have its occasional moments of commonsense.

Lindsay Reade spent a great deal of time at Strawberry Studios during the recording of *Unknown Pleasures*. "The perception of Martin always being in the pub is not how I remember it at all," she recalls. "He worked very late into the night, after pub hours. I don't really remember Martin drinking that much in those days, although he obviously smoked a lot of dope and I have no doubt that there were many substances. But, again, like Martin's so called craziness, it wasn't quite like that. Martin was a craftsman. He was very, very methodical and he knew what he was doing. Sometimes this could be a bit boring… because, obviously you would be eager to hear the song more in its entirety. But Martin was immensely patient. He would do things over and over again until he got it just as he wanted it. It was a really good and relaxed atmosphere though. I loved being there, to be honest. It wasn't tense at all."

Martin Hannett's background was in progressive rock, blues (Pete

Farrow) and punk (Slaughter & The Dogs, Buzzcocks) in which he had sought a 'live' feel in attempts to 'catch the moment'. Since his work on *A Factory Sample* however – and since his introduction to the AMS Digital Delay – he had been wandering in a completely different sonic area. The 'live' sound, the youthful, vibrant and chaotic clashing of instruments, was something he now sought to avoid. In effect, his attack on the standard band dynamic could be traced back to *Spiral Scratch* and the manner in which he created an atmosphere that initially served to disappoint and anger the band. The very same was said of *Unknown Pleasures*. Three members of Joy Division would, in numerous interviews, claim to have been similarly disappointed with a record that, to their ears, simply lacked the power of their live performance. Only Ian Curtis – and, Rob Gretton, actually – seemed attuned to Hannett's brilliance in incorporating a European ambience into the music, thus giving it an unlikely longevity. Which is why, as we write this book at the close of 2005, *Unknown Pleasures* echoes so forcefully within the music of countless bands from the new millennium.

With the benefit of hindsight, locating Hannett's brilliance seems easy, obvious; not so easy however, for a band entering the scary glamour of Strawberry Studios, their one big chance seemingly in the hands of this 'loose cannon'. Terry Mason has already spoken of Hannett's paradoxical character; one minute he would be instilling a benevolent despotism on musicians in the studio while, in the next, allowing them ample space to express themselves.

Lindsay Reade saw Martin simply as the man at the helm rather than oppressive tyrant. "The band were so meek in those days and it's hard to picture them like that now," she says. "But they did give the impression that they were really enjoying themselves, that they were completely happy in that environment. Mind you, for a lot of the time, the band wouldn't be in the studio at all. They would be downstairs playing pool, watching TV or whatever. Martin would call them up, of course, if he needed them but, for the most part, they seemed content to let Martin take control of the reins. Somebody had to. Alongside Martin was the engineer, Chris Nagle. He seemed very young at the time and eager to help and learn from Martin. All in all it was a very positive environment."

Nevertheless, with Hannett around, anything could happen and what he demanded would have seemed totally alien to any band that had emerged from punk, specifically a total sound separation. This wasn't confined to separating each instrument and voice, however; famously, in the case of Steve Morris' drum kit, the producer isolated each individual drum sound, forcing Morris into the unnatural situation of playing one sound at a time. For any drummer who had evolved as part of a band, co-ordination would have always been the key. Morris would later tell writer Simon Reynolds: "I would end up with my legs black and blue because I'd be tapping on them quietly to do the other bits of the kit that he wasn't recording."

Hannett's conception was to avoid any trace of 'bleed-through' from drum to drum, instrument to instrument. It was a technique that would kill all traces of live dynamic while, at the same time, creating a ghostly ambience. It was also a courageous route to take. Rather than play safe by capturing that verve and spirit of Joy Division's live set, Hannett adopted a completely opposite strategy. In later years, this trait worked against him insofar as eccentricity became his norm and, as a result, lost its power.

With *Unknown Pleasures* Hannett strived to *contain* the explosion. You can hear this, most obviously, on the famous disco-drum lead-in to 'She's Lost Control', where the stark, sharp, focused sound becomes a thing of beauty in itself and creates the perfect backdrop to the other powerful instrument of beauty within this band, the voice of Ian Curtis, hauntingly powerful and smothered in reverb.

In fact, the twin dominating instruments of the album would be the voice and the snare drum and it is in that interplay that much of the record seems so strikingly singular. At the time, the only obvious comparison would be Iggy Pop's *The Idiot*, which also famously fused a Eurobeat to a rock sensitivity. Some 26 years later, that prominent snare sound, with lengthy reverb, still occasionally catches the listener unawares. It's a subtle trick enhanced by the lovely softened plump of the bass drum.

Paul Morley: "A lot of bands know they want to be different, they know what they like, they know that Tony Visconti has given David Bowie this sound and Kraftwerk sound like that – but have absolutely no idea how to get it. Delays and echoes and reverbs and the complication of the mixing desk. But it was something Martin Hannett did – he took each instrument and he gave it its character. He turned Steve into an extraordinary drummer, Hooky suddenly had a place where that lead guitar bass made sense. So absolutely he lifted them way beyond their immediate surroundings and gave them something incredibly special. In hindsight it seems even more important that he did that. Because the songs were incredibly imaginative and lyrically they were incredibly inventive without being framed and having a sound that was completely unique. They could have just sounded ordinary. Ordinary punk or even heavy metal. I know for a fact – I think Hooky and Barney to this day don't like the sound of *Unknown Pleasures* because it's too fizzy and it's too electronic, I think they wanted a much more dynamic thing, you know almost Black Sabbath. That's what actually made it an absolute classic because it didn't sound like anything else. I think Martin definitely gave them that."

Barney later stated that he was shocked when he heard *Unknown Pleasures* mixed because it wasn't the way the band had envisioned it sounding. They had wanted a hard, rocking sound and Martin had used various ethereal sound effects, including miking up the elevator shaft with the lift going up and down, and the sound of broken bottles.

You tend not to notice greatness when it stands next to you in the super-market or at the bar. Perhaps this is why Morley had initially undervalued Hannett: "There was something about Martin, because he was a local guy and he came from M/C you didn't really think he knew what he was doing. Because he was just a bod, you know. And a bit of a strange one as well. [He was] the first person I ever saw smoke dope. Didn't really know what he was doing and he talked in a really strange way but you felt he knew something. And he did it. He did an extraordinary job and all great albums in history, whether it's The Beatles or U2, Bowie, Pink Floyd, they all have a great pro-ducer that's making it happen. So it was absolutely fantastic that Joy Division had him – and he'd had experience because he'd done Slaughter & The Dogs and whatever and because he'd done *Spiral Scratch* – he'd done something interesting already so he really *did* know what he was doing. We just thought that local bands didn't know what they were doing and cer-tainly local producers didn't – this is what started to melt that whole idea that it had to come from London and it had to be a name producer. This was the first proof we'd had that things do emerge, they can become original from unexpected sources and surroundings. And I do think that about what Martin did – what he did to Stephen to make him drum like that and sep-arate the kit and doing all sorts of strange, psychedelic things – they were all unbelievably important."

Martin Hannett died in 1991 and cannot therefore confirm at which point he realised the sheer elegance of Ian's voice and the unique way it could be balanced against his eerie vision of Joy Division's musicianship. One senses this must have been during the recording of 'Digital', back in Cargo in Rochdale, and it would be interesting to learn whether Hannett heard something in Ian's voice that was missed by everyone else, even the members of the band. Perhaps Curtis himself was unaware of it? It hadn't, after all, been apparent during the Arrow sessions.

"I have been asked a million times about Ian's state of mind during the recording of *Unknown Pleasures* and it is difficult to remember, difficult because he didn't seem any different to the rest of us," Peter Hook told journalists in 1988 while promoting Factory's Joy Division compilation album, *Substance*. Sitting on an amp in Suite 16 Studio, Rochdale, which he co-owned, Hook continued: "Of course, there was his situation with him about to become a father but, to be frank, he did his bit, we did our bits and that was that. It always feels strange when people try and read so much into every lyric… well, we don't know any more than anybody else, if you want the truth of it. We were all so excited to have arrived at a studio armed with great songs and a real sense that we could do something that was genuinely different. Most people believe we achieved that but, of course, it was a bit lost to us at the time because we didn't really like it."

Hooky did confirm that there was an understanding between Martin and Ian that the band was not privy to. "We didn't take much notice of it," he said. "We thought it was a simple case of Martin trying to ease Ian's nerves and Ian was quite nervous in the studio. They went to the pub a couple of times, I think. Then again, of course, it could have been simply because Martin wanted a fucking drink. Perhaps a bit of both. But it was apparent that Martin was building some kind of intimacy there… we didn't really notice it at the time and we didn't really like the recording, but that might have been part of it. Certainly Ian started to relax after that."

Linsday Reade also noticed the bond between the producer and singer. "I think there was a special closeness between Ian and Martin, born out later perhaps by Martin's sorrow after Ian died," she says. "But it wasn't something you'd particularly notice at the time – I think it was kind of private between themselves."

It seems likely that Hannett recognised and embraced the iconic star quality of Curtis and vice versa. Hannett's nurturing of the Curtis voice and song would be testament to his genius. As Vini Reilly, would later say: "I don't use the word genius very often… it's an overused and lazy word. But with Martin I have absolutely no hesitation in using the word genius. And I have worked with him very closely. I saw into exactly how he operated. And there was no one else on earth like him. No other producer came close to Martin. Genius indeed… yes."

The intimacy of *Unknown Pleasures* – and more so, on the follow-up album, *Closer* – was a distillation of the producer's vision and the voice with which he was working. Hannett's great Joy Division gambit was to suggest an intimacy between the listener and the voice they were hearing, if not the actual singer. The separation of the instruments drew the listener towards a voice with unusual resonance, giving the impression that the singer was singing to them alone. In later years, this technique would often be compared to recordings by two other tragic figures, Nick

Drake and Jeff Buckley, the former of whom died long before Joy Division emerged. Even beyond the tragedy of both of their lives and that of Ian Curtis, the comparisons do hold water, Drake in particular. Although he never tasted anything approaching major success during his lifetime, the haunting quality of Drake's voice on what are essentially lo-fi recordings continues to attract listeners, so much so that this slightly mysterious artist is vastly more appreciated in the 21st Century than he ever was when he was alive.

Hannett's decision to compress the energy levels of the rhythm section and bolster this with Bernard's distorted minor note guitar line placed the focus squarely on Curtis' vocals. One can understand why musicians who desired only to blast through the mix would be unsettled by Hannett's work. It is unusual that Hook's bass is reduced to a thin line and then pushed to the top of the mix, especially given the bass guitarist's leather-clad macho stance and style of playing, with his instrument almost touching the floor. Hannett was effectively amplifying the insecurities, deliberately morphing Joy Division's thick sound into something wholly unnatural. It would lose power naturally but gain a subtle resonance.

Not all of the album is so subtle, however. Hannett's use of effects could often seem extreme. On 'I Remember Nothing', for example, he inserts the metallic clank of an old lift door to supreme effect, as well as smashing glass, a Hannett signature sound. This can be a dangerous game although it's interesting to note that nobody ever accused Martin Hannett of studio-gimmickry.

Bernard Sumner's memories – as told to *Mojo* and in numerous interviews elsewhere – always seemed to place the emphasis more firmly on Hannett's curious mind games, and less on the technical aspects. "I have said a few times that Martin's idea was to create a scene within that studio," he has said. "He never wanted to make a fucking pop record. He wanted to experiment. To get as many drugs as possible in the place, lock the doors and don't let anyone get out. That is the fucking truth of it. We were on speed throughout our entire recording. That's how it was."

In truth, that's how it was with many albums recorded at the time, particularly at the hands of a hedonistic producer. Few, if any however, would attain the beauty of *Unknown Pleasures*.

While Joy Division focused on their music, Ian Curtis could be forgiven for being distracted. During the short period allotted for the recording and mixing of *Unknown Pleasures*, Deborah Curtis was about to give birth, with April 6 as the due day. In the event, as so often occurs with first babies, the child was late and inducement took place on April 16, Easter Monday. During the intervening ten day period, Ian was just a phone call from being whisked away from the action at Strawberry, easily reachable in the event that he could comply with Deborah's wish for him to be present at the birth.

Distracted as he might have been, Rob Gretton, for one, felt Ian's focus on the music did not waver. "Ian had actually started to change in rehearsals," he says. "It was different onstage, obviously because of the element of performance, but even on-stage, now you come to think of it, there was a kind of subtle change. But in Strawberry he really did come to the fore. It was great to see because it was a challenge for Martin. Suddenly Ian was forcibly pushing his ideas across. And the band would listen, too, simply because it started to make sense. He was almost conducting the band. I am sure the lads would back me up on that."

There seems little doubt that Ian found his true power during the recording of *Unknown Pleasures*. Curtis' presence remains the key aspect of the album's endearing allure. It is his voice and lyricism that served to transform a collection of fine, delicately recorded songs into something that would be admired for decades to come, an album upon which critical appraisal would intensify as time went on; unlike the debuts by their immediate peers, Public Image, Cabaret Voltaire, Psychedelic Furs, even Echo & The Bunnymen and Teardrop Explodes, whose debut albums gradually lost the overt critical acclaim accorded to them in the heat of the moment. By contrast, *Unknown Pleasures* would continually bubble to the surface of those myriad and slightly ridiculous 'Top 100 Albums Of All Time' magazine listings, regularly taking its place alongside the lines of *Blonde On Blonde* and *Revolver*. Such a hallowed future would have seemed wholly absurd to the four band members at the time. Nevertheless, something special was certainly taking place.

"It's a unique situation, really and I think many people feel the same way," says Mick Middles. "During the latter half of 1979, *Unknown Pleasures* was never off my record deck and then, for almost three decades, I never heard it. To listen to it intently in 2005 therefore proved a weird experience. Of course, production values have changed and we are all now used to hearing popular music in a completely different way... so, in a sense, *Unknown Pleasures* has actually changed. For a start, I couldn't believe the number of effects that Martin had used. I am certain I never really noticed them the first time around. Back then, I thought it sparse and eerie... but now, although it sounds clipped and precise, there seems to be whole lot more going on."

Curtis stakes his claim early on the record. Indeed, the first line of track one, 'Disorder' sees him deliver the evocative line, "I've been waiting for a guide to come and take me by the hand…" Immediately the listener seems to be embarking on a journey with Curtis… hand in hand, perhaps, walking to the centre of the song. However, there is a curiously hurried quality in Curtis' delivery, edgy, detached, almost a poetic wander towards the final climactic flurry – a Joy Division trademark – and the creak of desperation.

In contrast, 'Day Of The Lords' is laconic, almost funereal in places. To some, the moment when that reverb-soaked voice emerges from low in the mix to ask, poignantly, to say the least, "Where will it end?", signals the birth of gothic rock. Curtis, seemingly lost in this mix, gains authority as the song marches on and towards the end, despite the Hannetesque jingly effect, he attains a faint trace of Jim Morrison, and not for the last time.

'Candidate' signifies the 'new Joy Division', a new power, with unique interplay between voice and guitar, poetic delivery – notoriously difficult to pull off – and a final conflict between voice and wild echo. 'Insight' begins with more Hannett trickery as the band is immediately pushed back by an extraordinary disco snare, contemporary in its day albeit it rather dated now, with Ian's voice rising levelly with the bass line, another Joy Division trademark which was destined to become relentlessly copied, not least by darkly clad American bands with balding, tattooed, gargantuan bass players. Joy Division's influence here, would warp through the decades and attain a cartoon element.

It may come as a shock to those brought up in the CD age, if not the age of iPod and Podcast, but LPs in 1979 had two sides, each with a distinct beginning and end. This restriction shaped the pace, sequencing and production of an album and was a vital aspect of its overall character. *Unknown Pleasures* proved to be beautifully symmetrical; two neat, perfectly balanced sides of one album, which would be further enhanced by Peter Saville's enigmatic sleeve. It would be absolutely impossible to achieve the full iconic effect of *Unknown Pleasures* within the cheap plastic packaging of a CD, let alone the post artefact world of iPod.

Thus, the first half of *Unknown Pleasures* simply had to conclude with 'New Dawn Fades', another immensely poignant track, given the course in which this story moves. The trudging guitar rose through the scale before allowing Ian Curtis total and utter command in what is his best performance on the album. Like Mark E. Smith, Ian had the knack of catching the imagination with one line from a pack of lyrics and, in 'New Dawn Fades', the delicately sung "A loaded gun won't set you free…. so *you* say," would echo down the years. The concluding "so *you* say" hints that the writer believed it could, perhaps, set you free.

The second side of the original vinyl album of *Unknown Pleasures* – which still sells well, apparently – opens with its most famous song, 'She's Lost Control', although many fans became confused by the ambiguous artwork and tended to regard it as the album's opening song.[1] The simplistic disco drum intro is among the finest moments in rock history and has survived as, after the guitar build-up to 'Love Will Tear Us Apart', the second most accessible intro to the music of Joy Division for future generations of fans. "Confusion in her eyes it says it all, she's lost control…" Whoever the girl was, is possibly not the point, although apparently it was inspired by an epileptic girl that Ian knew and was trying to help in his job as Disablement Resettlement Officer at the Employment Exchange. Although perhaps the least personal moment of the album, the song attaches itself to the lives of its listeners; a pop song with a leaden subject, perfect and blessed with a famously sky high bass line.

'Shadowplay' is the natural partner to 'She's Lost Control'. For those familiar with the Granada footage of roads beneath the shadows of Hulme, it's virtually impossible to disconnect the lyric from that stark vision of cruising along in a car, driving (to gigs?) in Manchester city centre. Even the powerful line, "We could only stare in disbelief as the crowds all left" couldn't dilute this vision. Glorious machinegun drum flurry, too.

'Wilderness' is arguably the least effective moment on the album. Quite a funky mix, though, and the slightly muddled beginning settles neatly towards the song's conclusion. For once, however, the voice fails to dominate, despite the immortal scream of "Tears in their eyes". Some Joy Division aficionados will surely take exception to this and cite 'Wilderness' as one of the most tender of Curtis' lyrical moments. It's a valid point although, for once, Hannett could have softened the musical attack and achieved a greater sense of balance.

'Interzone' strongly recalls Iggy & The Stooges. If Warsaw had still existed, this would have been their flagship song, a garage-band slash that cuts against the prevailing tenderness of the Curtis-led album. That stated, it neatly wrong-foots the casual listener and dramatically leads to the concluding 'I Remember Nothing', a big. gargantuan song with Ian forced into a wail. Six minutes of unleashed paranoia, which finally softens to a com-

---

[1] This is irrelevant nowadays as the age of iPod and Podcast has provided the fan with the power to choose their own running order.

fortable conclusion and, once again, leaves the listener thinking fondly of the finer moments of Jim Morrison; a testament, indeed, to the resonance and power of Ian Curtis.

Paul Morley: "*Unknown Pleasures* is my favourite of the two Joy Division albums. I remember hearing it – I got a tape from Rob – I used to get tapes from local bands – you kind of knew they were a local band. But I remember that one. That to me was why the sleeve was so important too because Peter Saville gave me the sleeve that made you realise that it was special – which also was unusual for a local band. Suddenly they had a sleeve that was like better than anything by Bowie or better than anything by Roxy Music and these were really important things, cos you thought that a local band didn't. The fact they had a sleeve like *Ideal For Living* – the awful Nazi drummer boy – that's kind of more what you thought – and suddenly they had this extraordinary, powerful, iconic image. Very mysterious you know. And the whole idea of 'Outside' and 'Inside'. The idea of a fantastic journey into a place that you realised what a great thing a vinyl album was and I think that's becoming more and more true. The thing we've lost now, that vinyl journey into a place and out of a place. And because *Unknown Pleasures* was so atmospheric – for whatever reason – drugs, madness or just sheer intensity of life – it really was a vinyl classic because of that. A two-sided journey. I remember hearing it for the first time and just being absolutely stunned because it sounded so massive, international. It sounded proper. And the previous attempts to do it hadn't quite sounded right – you know, sounded a bit tinny or a bit muddy. Suddenly there was this incredible sleeve – the heartbeat – and the whole idea that they were so bad at interviews, that this replaced their interviews in a way Peter Saville's iconography replaced them ever having to do interviews."

CHAPTER 11

Just For One Moment I Thought I'd Found My Way

"Hooky wanted to twat him. He would have done, too… and I would have let him. It was something of a set-up and the lads are a bit upset about it… I'm not, doesn't bother me at all. In fact, I think it's all a laugh, frankly." – Rob Gretton

Natalie Curtis was born on April 16, 1979, which was Easter Monday, a national holiday, and like many first-born babies, she arrived late and had to be induced. Ian's joy at becoming a father and love for his daughter was tempered by the knowledge that his epilepsy might compromise the child's safety and therefore make him redundant when it came to handling her. Like most first-time mothers, Debbie was in the full throes of mother love and fully preoccupied with taking care of her infant, and this may have further alienated Ian, both from the bonding process and from his wife. Furthermore there was no let up in Ian's work commitments, Joy Division being obliged to play a gig in London at the Acklam Hall on the following day, April 17, at which they were supported by John Dowie and where Hooky had his guitar nicked. The pressure was on and London gigs were considered too important to cancel.

Six weeks later, on May 24, the day after a gig at Bowden Vale, Ian was at home when he had his most serious epileptic episode to date. Debbie phoned Ian's mother that night after he was admitted to hospital, informing her that she'd called an ambulance when, after four consecutive fits, she was unable to wake him.

There can be little doubt that Ian was seriously depressed by his worsening epileptic condition and this, coupled with the various types of medication he was taking, must have had a negative effect on his mood and increased the distance between Debbie and himself. Indeed, Debbie herself has described the personality change in Ian, stating that he had "all but stopped talking to me".[1]

The divide between the private Ian and the public's perception of him, as portrayed in the music press, was increasing. With a little help from the photographers, notably Kevin Cummins, Ian and Joy Division were able to create iconic images of themselves with a seemingly natural ease. They could simply do no wrong in this respect. Wearing raincoats muffled up against the elements evoked a fashionably dour group set against backdrops of grim streets in Salford and Macclesfield, but in reality they were worn for reasons of sheer practicality. "How clever," an Australian journalist once noted on seeing Joy Division heavily over-coated against the Stockport snow. How clever? It was freezing out there. Similarly, the famously raincoated Ian Curtis snapped with a cigarette could have been brilliantly choreographed… but wasn't, of course. It was simply the luminous aspect of Ian Curtis; an innate ability to shine through a lens.

This natural ease was more than a mere look or vision. Almost without knowing it and, despite the protests of the actual musicians who wrote it, they had just recorded the album that most perfectly evoked the spirit of 1979. When *Sounds* reviewed the album, they stole a headline from the great Public Image song of the time, *Death Disco*. These two words would have been equally appropriate as a title for the Joy Division album, though perhaps not quite so apposite as *Unknown Pleasures*.

A great album needs iconic packaging and Peter Saville's task, daunting in retrospect, was to capture the shocking simplicity of the music in one immediately striking design that leapt out from the record racks. As it turned out, it wasn't Ian Curtis, nor Peter Saville, who discovered the Fourier Analysis that so enigmatically graced the cover of Joy Division's debut. The image was apparently discovered by Bernard Sumner as he flicked through a copy of *The Cambridge Encyclopaedia Of Astronomy* by Simon Motton and spotted diagram 6.7. This curiously compelling image depicted one hundred consecutive pulses from the first radio pulsar but at

---

[1] In *Touching From A Distance*, Faber & Faber, 1995.

the same time might be perceived as a cross section of a vinyl album or something vaguely nautical. Nevertheless, as the image was given to Saville, complete with instructions about how to place it on the sleeve, there was still a great deal of *designing* to be done. Saville eventually reversed the instruction to produce a black inner sleeve housed by a white exterior.

"I contradicted the band's instructions and made it black on the outside and white on the inside which I felt gave it more presence," he told *Mojo* in 2005.

"I had this idea of graining," he continued, "because we had an expanse of flat black on the outside and texture would give it a more tactile quality."

Knowing that it would be called *Unknown Pleasures*, he believed an enigmatic black object would more perfectly evoke the title than an expanse of white.

This simple, effective, iconic image would eventually attain a classic status all of its own and, increasingly through the years, emerge enigmatic and proud on thousands upon thousands of t-shirts, badges and posters. With its curious and slightly disturbing power, it became a perfect visual accompaniment to the music.

Oddly enough, the striking outer-sleeve design wasn't immediately welcomed by the members of the band. Mick Middles can recall an episode when, in exchange for a copy of the album, Rob Gretton instructed him to pick up the finished artwork from an address in Didsbury and deliver it to the manager at The Factory Club later that evening.

"I don't really know if Rob was playing some kind of game with this," he says. "I have no idea why he didn't pick up the artwork himself... perhaps he simply didn't have transport. But I certainly wasn't going to turn down the opportunity of getting hold of a white label of the album. It was a moment I will never forget. It was upstairs at The Factory Club, near the counter where they served that goat curry. Ian McCullouch was there, from the Bunnymen, possibly Paul Morley, and Kevin Cummins certainly. Rob was just handing out the albums and instructing us to review them. I don't think he realised that it wasn't actually up to us. None of us had that power. But then came the strangest moment of all. I handed the artwork across, having enjoyed a sneak preview on the car journey. At this precise moment, even though it had been Bernard who handed Saville the initial image, neither Rob Gretton nor Ian Curtis, nor Tony Wilson... nor any of the band had even seen Saville's field of black. I swear that Rob's initial reaction was little short of a scowl... a creased face that seemed to scream, 'How am I going to sell *this* to the lads? They are going to hate it.' That's how I read the situation, anyway."

Rob thought the image should be larger, that it would stretch across the *whole* cover and not lost, as it is, so thickly framed in black. "It should have been fucking white," he murmured, his eyes rolling up to the ceiling. "A white sleeve, because we wanted to appear upbeat, basically because we are sick of bastards like you stating that we are miserable… and it should have been fucking large."

He had a point. Although Saville was clever enough to allow the image to lose itself on that sea of black – and, in 2005, would tell writer Colin Sharpe that he considered it his finest work – the immediate reaction to the image on that sleeve was that it seemed rather lost, rather pathetic. What would the music press make of it?

Joy Division's relationship with the music press had been edgy since the days of Warsaw. Hooky liked to play interviews with an air of detached belligerence, even if his generally endearing nature usually shone through in the end. Barney was always the most difficult, suspicious perhaps, often awkward and opinionated and this awkwardness would increase in sync with his general confidence. Steve would be ever-friendly and musicianly, perfectly capable of chatting freely about anything from Kraftwerk to Fairport Convention without displaying any trace of reserve. Only Ian seemed genuinely intrigued by the method of the interview. As Paul Morley had discovered, Ian's intelligence wasn't immediately obvious, but tended to seep out as an interview progressed. To add to the strain of things, Rob liked to hover above an interview, at times peppering it with opinions that more often than not clashed with those expressed by the band. This was refreshingly honest and perhaps proof that whatever was happening with this band, it was unfolding naturally, without the overt managerial guidance that had characterised too many puppet-like bands through the ages.

This touchy relationship with the press was further exposed in July at the low-budget 'Stuff the Superstars Festival', a one-day affair organised by *City Fun* magazine at The Mayflower Club in Gorton, Manchester. The writer in question was Dave McCullough of *Sounds* who, after being plucked from his position as editor of the perceptive *Alternative Ulster* fanzine, had become the paper's 'left-field' correspondent. McCullough, a huge champion of Manchester's The Fall, arrived at the Joy Division cause fairly late. However, prior to his infamous interview, he had grown hugely committed to Joy Division, even if his knowledge of the band had, by his own admission, not been as great as one might have expected from a professional music writer. That stated, he certainly did not approach the interview with the intention of exposing any weaknesses in Joy Division. On the contrary, he was concerned that his writing might not fully capture the flavour of this most fascinating band. He was a fan… until, that is, he arrived in Stockport to interview them.

In truth, and despite McCullough's considerable journalistic talent, it was a piece of writing as dark and drab as the Stockport buildings he ridiculed en-route to the interview. This didn't exactly endear him to his northern readers. Unusually for the normally perceptive McCullough, he dropped a clanger during the bizarre intro, which painted the town in a curiously archaic image.

He wrote: *"There is a carnival of sorts throughout the town, and the effect of seeing mums, dads, granddads and kids decked out in flowers and straw-hats, beaming benignly at the silly pomp of marching brass bands and bouncing, scantily-clad Lancastrian lasses, is a surreal, living, Lowry landscape."*

A surreal, living Lowry landscape? Worse still… Stockport, as even a London-based music scribe should have known, is very much a *Cheshire* town. Nevertheless, McCullough's interview proved to be one of the most fascinating of Joy Division's short career, even if the writer couldn't seemingly be bothered to check out the band names.

Here is a snippet. *"Everything started off calmly enough. I spoke with singer Curtis and the guitarist (yes, 'the guitarist'! I didn't discover the names of the other three members of the band, such was the impersonality of their communication) who told me the band formed in May '77 some time after they'd seen the Pistols, the catalyst of their inception.*

Has the sound changed since then?

Ian: "It's changed quite a lot, yeah… it's still changing now. We wrote those songs on the album a long time ago… the sound of the album isn't dated, but style-wise it has."

How long did you spend on the album?

Ian: "Four and a half days at Strawberry. We worked, say, from two o'clock in the afternoon to four in the morning getting it done."

Were you surprised by the favourable reactions it received?

Ian: "Yeah, I'm a total pessimist, I suppose. I mean our first single got bad… I mean UNFAVOURABLE, but, I thought, very well written, reviews. One compared it to John Lennon, another to Stockhausen… the comparison between the two was quite good!" (general guffaws)

Guitarist: "Thing is, we don't go that much on reviews."

If that latter remark is the case, I can only say each member spent an EXTRA-ORDINARY amount of time during the next three hours talking about the, ahem, Rock Press.

Similarly I ask them about the mechanics of their music and with formulated stiffness, like rehearsed dummies under the eye of manager/overseer Rob Gretton, clearly not at his brightest on the day, they trotted-out statements about democracy and miraculous spontaneity in song writing.

"We don't want to give people straight answers. We'd rather they question things for themselves." Ho hum.

The irony was, of course, that even by, as they thought, remaining inscrutable and, ahem, Obscure, the band provided us with gargantuan evidence of their pseudness and, more to the point, their cerebral shortcomings. Ian remained contentedly silent as I became increasingly irritated by the absurd masquerade that was taking place. Manager Gretton (obviously assured of his own cleverness) and the bearded bassist in particular gave the impression that they suffered from serious mental deficiencies as they groped about in the dimness of their 'attitudes', smugly spouting non-sequiturs that wouldn't sound too polished on a very bad episode of Crossroads, *and generally giving the impression that they'd spent much too long watching BBC2.*

I suggest for instance that the Nazi imagery of their first single confused a lot of people. No reaction. Much later I ask Ian how the band's name came about, knowing by chance that Joy Division was the term used by the SS to describe the Jewish women they saved from the gas-chambers for their own pleasure. Ian tells me that it's just a name.

I become angry.

Soon it is the bearded bassist who takes control of all the verbal rallies, with a bludgeoning, clumsy style, revealing raging neurotic symptoms as he tells me everything in inverse, ironic confessions.

"So you're saying the lyrics are pessimistic, then, are you?" he bawls, as Slattery and self, knowing I hadn't so much as mentioned the word 'pessimistic' throughout the conversation, can't help but start laughing.

"Aw, fuck off..." the bearded one tells me. I switch the tape off and get up to leave. "Sorry, d'you want a drink?..."

I thought afterwards how pathetic that sounded: when it came to the crunch, what they wanted more than anything else, more even than presenting me with an honest account of themselves (even if the contrived anti-image is really them) was a couple of pages of publicity in Sounds. *So much for the vague psychology, so much for the steaming hot guitars, the chaps wanted A MENTION!"*

During the week prior to the interview, Dave McCullough had telephoned Mick Middles to enquire about the band and their attitude towards the music press. Although Middles can't recall the exact conversation, he feels he may have warned McCullough about Hooky's apparent belligerence and would have certainly have mentioned the contrast between this attitude and Ian Curtis' apparent fascination with the music press.

As it turned out, McCullough's infamous article, which angered the band considerably, actually paralleled many similar encounters. Later on that same day, the relationship between the band and the *Sounds* team seemed only to worsen.

Rob Gretton, sitting in The Rock Tavern pub in Gorton, puffing profusely on a 'cigarette', was heard to offer the opinion: "He's a cunt, that Dave McCullough."

This might seem a touch harsh in print, but Gretton's delivery was laced with typical humour. McCullough wouldn't take offence… which was just as well as he was standing well within earshot.

"Let's just say that the interview wasn't exactly a success," Gretton stated, and moaned that *Sounds* had seen fit to assign a "…London-based wanker to interview the band."

"Hooky wanted to twat him," he continued. "He would have done, too… and I would have let him. It was something of a set-up and the lads are a bit upset about it… I'm not, doesn't bother me at all. In fact, I think it's all a laugh, frankly."

This wasn't captured on tape and we can't be sure of the exact words, but Gretton brushed the incident aside with his usual sardonic aplomb.

Six feet away, standing squarely at the bar, flanked by photographers Paul Slattery and Kevin Cummins, encircled by members of The Distractions and Fall manager Kay Carroll, Dave McCullough was bemoaning the lack of grace displayed by Joy Division. He had a point. Every burgeoning rock act in the country wanted Dave McCullough to travel to their home town, Slattery in tow, to capture them amid parochial tomfoolery. Not surprisingly, the only member of Joy Division who seemed willing to converse with McCullough during the day was Ian Curtis. The cynic might suggest that this was simply because Curtis was concerned about the damage that an incensed Dave McCullough, probably the most influential non-*NME* writer of the time, could do to the band's image. This wouldn't be the first or, indeed, the last time that Ian openly displayed his dislike of the band's general aloof attitude. They wanted to be portrayed as a distant, arrogant group of musicians, supremely self-confident. Rob Gretton certainly revelled in this professional 'stand-offishness' and openly encouraged it with Joy Division and, later, with New Order. It was good fun and seemed to square with Factory's stylish sense of distance not just from the rock press but from virtually everything else that related to the traditional music industry.

Ian Curtis, however, always appeared keen to display a desire to *communicate*, be it in person, to a gathering of fans or to journalists. Throughout his short career, Ian, regardless of the attitude of the rest of the band, showed journalists both respect and politeness. This might not have been a particularly 'sexy' image, and it has certainly become lost in the intervening years, but it is difficult to find a single music writer who disliked Ian Curtis, something that cannot be said about the rest of the band.

The 'Stuff the Superstars' event might, in retrospect, sound like a rather glamorous affair. It wasn't. The Mayflower was the most austere and unwelcoming hell-hole venue in Manchester; appalling toilets, undrinkable beer, dirty plastic glasses, an inconceivably muddied sound and, at all times, an icy cold ambience.

Terry Mason described it as the "world's smelliest venue" and remembers that Barney left his jumper there.

Dave McCullough reported on Joy Division's set with these words: *"… and later that evening I saw them live. The songs are even hotter and more vigorous than on the album, but on reflection suffer from a stunning lack of anything approaching contrasting humour. The black, over seriousness denies any real, life-like communication and you are left with what is by its very nature a contrived, engineered set of songs.*

"Later in the evening the guitarist was seen searching around the Mayflower for his 'woolie', which he'd lost. It was a funny, contrasting scene, but somehow I don't think it'll ever make its way into a Joy Division song. It's maybe too close to reality for that.

"It was such thoughts that drifted through my head as we rattled back down the blank highway the following evening. Conclusions began to form. You can't equate Joy Division's earnest technique (grim dress, grim image) with the hard, real, financial, 'Factory' Records zeal in which they are plainly shackled. The ardour is always tempered by the money and no amount of under milling obscurity will convince me that Joy Division's stark, murky militancy is real.

"For, at the moment, the music is too supercilious (like the people) to ring true. It too often seems intended to make the listener feel inadequate. On the other hand bands like the Gang Of Four have made good business out of the same mind-game. Maybe these days you like being made feel inadequate… Maybe Joy Division don't print their names on their records cos they're frightened of something. It could be themselves."

It's possible that Dave McCullough sensed a mild unease within the Joy Division camp which certainly wasn't apparent from the band's onstage form. Few of those who witnessed the 'Stuff the Superstars' appearance could be left in any doubt about the growing presence of Ian Curtis on stage; the ferociously driven focal point of the most exciting band in Britain. This was now a band fast approaching the peak of their game and critics from across the music press were simply squabbling over superlatives. But such success brings with it a whole new bundle of pressure of expectation. Curtis had stepped into stardom, a fact bemoaned by Deborah Curtis who felt now felt that her husband, the pop star, had become "public property". It is understandable that she should have felt estranged, as key decisions concerning Ian's future were now taken solely within the context of the band without regard to Deborah and their baby daughter.

The situation was hardly uncommon. Beatle John Lennon's wife Cynthia gave birth to their son Julian on April 8, 1963, just as 'From Me To You' was ascending the charts and lighting the fuse that would explode in Beatlemania. After three years hard graft in Hamburg and Liverpool, Lennon was hardly likely to abandon the escalating success of his group in favour of a nine-to-five job that brought in a steady income to pay for nappies and ensured he was home at nights to help change them. Indeed, it's a situation shared by everyone married to a burgeoning pop star, particularly a front-man (or woman). An aspect of the character is snatched away for public consumption, be it in the day-to-day activities of a band on the road or in interview. It is virtually impossible to successfully fulfil both roles.

The night before the Mayflower gig, on July 27, the band played a concert at the Imperial Hotel in Blackpool. The gig was promoted by Section 25. Larry Cassidy, the lead singer, recalls: "There was us, Joy Division, The Last Torpedos from Liverpool, OMD and another local band called Final Solution. I think we were on last. Paul Wiggin[1] and I had seen Joy Division at Eric's and we really liked them. Everyone got £30 – each band. It was quite a big room – a ballroom. There was no bar or anything so we could let in kids. It was in aid of a charity – International Year of the Child. We made badges and everything. We made a few quid and we sent it to them – not a lot. Rob Gretton said he quite liked what we were doing – and would we like to make a record. So we fixed up at Cargo – went there one day and did 'Girls Don't Count'. Rob and Ian produced it and the engineer was there – the guy that owned Cargo at the time. Ian liked us. It wasn't like coming up and slapping you on the back and saying 'You're great' or anything like that."

According to Terry Mason the wives and girlfriends of the band – Sue, Debbie, and Gillian, Stephen's girl – were unwilling to let their men loose for a wild night in Blackpool and were therefore all present at the gig and keeping an eye on them – much to their annoyance.

He also remembers a black Hillman Avenger in the car park of the hotel on which someone had sprayed the bonnet with the squiggly lines from

---

[1] The guitar player in Section 25.

Unknown Pleasures, and – from the sublime to the ridiculous – that they all stopped to eat Kentucky Fried Chicken on their way out of Blackpool.

On August 2, Joy Division returned to London to headline at the YMCA on Tottenham Court Road, in front of a sizeable crowd, including many from the all influential music press. Indeed, for hip young Londoners, this gig was deemed wholly unmissable.

Legend tells of a below par and tentative Echo & The Bunnymen nervously opening this show, Echo at this stage in their career being a drum machine, the one member of the pre-Pete Defrietas band not armed with a ready stream of Scouse wit. Teardrop Explodes, another Liverpool band evolving at considerable pace, were also on the bill.

While Joy Division were thundering to new and exciting levels, Echo & The Bunnymen were proving no less intriguing. Armed with a handful of distinctive songs, in Ian McCullouch they had a golden voiced pretty boy singer who, in terms of sound and vision, could have posed a genuine challenge to Curtis. McCullouch had plenty of presence and his porcupine appearance would emerge with considerable natural charisma during the following twelve months.

Ian Curtis, however, was a different prospect altogether. In common with Iggy Pop – and as most accurately displayed on the Factory video *Here Are The Young Men*[1] – Curtis had developed his skill of physically winding the music to new levels of intensity. To put it succinctly, when Ian danced, Joy Division were instantly a better band. It might begin with a flick of the wrists, a couple of gentle sways, a nod of the head, a backwards shimmy, standing on tip-toes, a sway to the left. No dance instructor would recognise such moves. But co-ordination and a frenzied rhythm combined to produce one of the most compelling sights in the history of British rock, a natural perfection, channelling the emotive power, spilling out onstage. This YMCA gig has often been cited as one of the band's most mesmeric, not least by Rob Gretton, whose enthusiasm for his own band almost exploded at the sight of the opening 'Dead Souls', a ferocious number on any given occasion but here, before the rowdiness of the London audience, offering unprecedented levels of intensity. Joy Division was indeed a happening band and there was no doubt that Ian Curtis was its true star.

As if to emphasise this fact, an *NME* front cover at the time depicted a self-assured and now familiar Ian Curtis relaxing into this role alongside a comparatively uncomfortable looking Bernard Sumner. Familiarity is the

---

[1] Released September 1982.

trick of fame, and Ian Curtis now looked as if he had finally found his true home.

Three weeks later, on August 27, Joy Division headlined one of the most bizarre events in the history of British rock. The Leigh Festival was, in terms of seizing the moment and attracting a crowd worthy of its extraordinary bill, an unprecedented disaster.

It took place in a field directly adjacent to the site of the most famous festival ever to grace the north west of England, 1972's extraordinary Bickershaw Festival, in which a most unlikely defunct mining village played host to the likes of, amongst others, The Grateful Dead, Dr John, Captain Beefheart, The Kinks and Country Joe McDonald. At the end of that particular affair, festival organiser and future TV presenter Jeremy Beadle was heard to bemoan the "… 'Gigantism' that will kill rock festivals."

It wasn't 'gigantism' that dogged the Leigh Festival but quite the reverse. If any rock event could claim to be the precise antithesis of the commercial scale of Glastonbury then Leigh would effectively fulfil that role. Within Factory circles, it would become known as 'the festival of the giant turd', simply because that was apparently the object that so entranced Ian Curtis during the course of the event. However, it remains possible to sense a metaphorical significance within Ian's sighting of that turd. It did seem an apt discovery.

Arriving at Leigh Festival was in itself unsettling in much the same way that away supporters can be unsettled on arrival at a non-league football ground where the locals might be hostile if, indeed, there are any locals at all. Leigh Festival was signposted by a strapped-up rip of cardboard daubed with juvenile writing informing punters: "Festival site… this way!"

This make-shift sign was the handy work of Lewis Knight, an entrepreneur who owned a string of furniture shops in the area as well as the land on which the festival was sited. "It was a slag heap, miles from anywhere," says Terry Mason. "It was only when I came to drive away that I found out that the truck I'd rented had no lights. I drove home with the hazards on instead."

One of the organisers of the event, Chris Hewitt, recalls: "It was a three-day event and the organisation had started long before Factory or Zoo came on board. In fact, I am pretty sure it was my idea to contact Tony Wilson… I thought it would guarantee a lot of publicity. It's funny because on all the websites now, we see all these Peter Saville posters advertising the Leigh Festival. But I don't ever remember seeing any Peter Saville posters anywhere. The only publicity I remember was that Lewis Knight had some small box trailers like you tow behind a car that he would leave parked around Leigh as free advertising. They normally said 'Lewis Knight's Discount Three Piece Suite Centre' on the side so he changed the poster signs to big sheets of paper saying 'Pop Festival'. He also hired some goons with walkie-talkies to stop a Woodstock-type breach of the non-existent fence – obviously they just walked up and down the boundaries of the industrial waste grassland and challenged probably one person trying to get in over 72 hours.

"The Factory poster only lists the Monday as it wasn't really a Factory or Zoo Event. Factory meets Zoo was just one third of a three-day event organised by local Leigh people, and myself. Look at the picture of OMD playing and there are just over two people in the crowd – I don't reckon there was ever more than about thirty or forty there and Mick Middles and Jon Savage had hyped it up in the press, probably because they were in the pockets of Factory. There was a joke amongst the bands that 'it's your turn to be the audience now whilst we play'."

The full story of the Leigh Festival disaster belongs elsewhere but for Ian Curtis, performing to a scant gathering in the open air next to a defunct colliery, it was arguably the most ludicrous gig he had undertaken since Bowden Vale youth club.

Backstage on the final day, Curtis was nose deep in a book. Distractions singer Mike Finney enquired as to the nature of this tome, and it turned out to be Jean Paul Sartre's *The Age Of Reason*, the first volume of Sartre's acclaimed trilogy, *Les Chenims de la Liberte* (*The Roads To Freedom*).[1]

This was extremely hip reading matter of the time and as liberal arts philosophy goes, quite an accessible and enjoyable read. Unknowingly, Curtis had started a trend here insofar as his habit of carrying esoteric reading matter around in a plastic bag – initially a Manchester joke of the time – would soon be copied by a number of supporting bands. Arthur Kadmon of Ludus would never be seen without his 'hip bag', more often than not containing the works of Camus, Mailer or Fowles. Mark E. Smith even lampooned the trend in the song 'Carry Bag Man'.

Ian's reading habits acquired a certain local infamy and speculative reports of his literary nourishment began to find their way into *City Fun* magazine. At Leigh Festival he told Mike Finney that he had also enjoyed

---

[1] A vivid depiction of the Paris of 1938; a city of nightclubs and galleries, communities of students, communists and homosexuals; a world of intellect and degradation. Against this squalid background, the hero Mathieu Delarue plots to force an abortion on his reluctant mistress.

Dostoyevsky's *Crime And Punishment* and was particularly fond of the first paragraph which resurfaced in Howard Devoto's 'Song From Under The Floorboards'. Other apparent favourites included Albert Camus, J.G. Ballard, Jack Kerouac and William Burroughs.

The link between The Distractions, who performed early on the Leigh bill, and Joy Division is worthy of a mention. Although only fleetingly a Factory band, with one albeit great single, 'Time Goes By So Slow', the connection between the two bands was forged on a series of dates during which the lightness of their pop songs perfectly balanced Joy Division's dark introversion. Inspired by these gigs, Paul Morley once claimed: "If Joy Division are the perfect rock band for the Eighties, The Distractions are the perfect pop band". Intriguingly, while the remainder of Joy Division shied away from the hip core who surrounded The Distractions (who have been largely written out of their considerable central role in the Manchester scene), Ian Curtis warmed to Mike Finney, whose cheery bonhomie may have seemed a welcome refuge.

"Ian was always extremely open and agreeable with me," says Finney. "When we played with Joy Division he absolutely went out of his way to seek me out and talk about the two bands. It seemed natural at first, because that's how I always knew him. Then, slowly, I started to realise that perhaps he wasn't like that with everyone. I also noticed that the rest of Joy Division, while always being perfectly OK with us, were also a little bit wary because we were very much a live band. I am not saying for one minute that we were on the same planet as them in terms of sheer talent… we weren't. We were a dance, pop soul band who liked to get up on stage and lighten up the crowd. He once… it could have been at Leigh… I am not sure… but he once went on and on about 'Time Goes By So Slow'. He wanted to know when it was written. Had it been written immediately after a break up? Was it written in a state of despair, I suppose that, looking back, you could look too deeply into that. My theory is that he was just discovering that song-writing could be cathartic. I don't know if that was ever the point with Joy Division but I did sense that that was what he was thinking. I knew nothing about his private life. I don't remember meeting Deborah and, frankly, The Distractions were a sexual and emotional minefield at the time. I think Ian wanted to know how we dealt with all that. I don't know, frankly. But there was a kind of link between us."

As to the problems of Leigh, Ian Curtis knew a disaster when he was about to play in one. Tales of giant turds aside, he was the one member of Joy Division who was concerned when he scanned the audience from the area behind the stage which, incidentally, stood on top of a half-sunken pub cellar. His "What the fuck?" look at Rob Gretton was met by the kind of shrug that Gretton, and only Rob Gretton could suitably affect. Meanwhile, a trickle of people entered the arena and sat cross-legged, awaiting the action.

Those who arrived in cars were actually instructed to park at the rear of the field. While this might have seemed like simple commonsense at the time, it did little to fuel the performance fervour of the bands. There is an image of Freddie Mercury at Live Aid of which most people are aware. Taken from behind the Queen singer, it captures the moment when he punches the air in triumph, no doubt in the knowledge that his band has blown every one else on the bill clean away, while the vast Wembley crowd stretched away to Wembley's rear circle. Well, Leigh Festival was nothing like that. From behind the stage, amid various tufts of grass, a few knots of sundry post punks and sullen raincoated youths were scattered hither and thither, with half a dozen cars – it was even possible to name the owners of the vehicles – parked to their rear. As a vision of a spectacular festival, this lagged somewhere behind a parochial village fete.

Behind the stage, the nervousness that preceded a performance before a thin scattering further dampened the atmosphere. Members of A Certain Ratio huddled, team-like around Tony Wilson, a green-wellied figure in a white suit, urging his troops on, as if a football manager.

In terms of the performances, Wilson had little to worry about. Although it was a catastrophic commercial failure, Leigh was an artistic success, with superb sets throughout the day. Highlights included a spirited A Certain Ratio who seemed to stress the differences between themselves and Joy Division.

"Just don't compare me to Ian Curtis," said Ratio singer, Simon Topping and he certainly had a point. ACR had moved swiftly and naturally away from any such musical comparison. "We don't even like Joy Division," they added, almost in unison and not unreasonably. One of the most obvious problems was that Topping, resplendent in savage short back'n' sides, did resemble Ian Curtis onstage, not in action and certainly not in voice but in his immediate physical presence and the clothes he wore which, despite Wilson's ambition to garb then in hot funk desert shorts, bore a strong resemblance.

There was little resemblance backstage, with Topping vociferous and laddish while Curtis chose to drift quietly in the shadows, aloof from Ratio and aloof also from the powerful and profoundly Liverpudlian banter emanating from the Echo & The Bunnymen camp. Elsewhere backstage, most members of most bands chose to amuse themselves by leering at a particularly attractive technician who had unwisely chosen to wear a skirt when her job entailed climbing up the scaffolding.

There were few dull moments. OMD appeared edgy and somewhat adrift, but nonetheless armed with glorious melodies. Echo & The Bunnymen had discovered the potential within the voice of their enigmatic singer and Teardrop Explodes were quite simply 'going for it'.

But without any question of a doubt the event belonged to a tense and striking Joy Division, with Ian Curtis framed by the spotlight on a rapidly darkening night, riding beautifully on the band's rolling fractious intensity, wrapping himself around the mic, hurling his voice into the Lancastrian air.

'Transmission', their finest song of that moment, capped the performance and strayed into the subconscious of many onlookers for many years to come,

Tony Wilson hugged Ian Curtis as the band eventually filed from the stage.

CHAPTER 12

Taking Different Roads

"Maybe it would be good and fair to Ian if people knew how much love there was between us and what a simple romance it was. We just met and we fell in love and we were very attracted to each other and fell immensely for each other and cared for each other and it could not be prevented. Ian needed me in his life. Love takes people by surprise and it is so chemical when suddenly two people click together." – Annik Honoré

Annik Honoré[1] has maintained an almost complete silence about her relationship with Ian Curtis for these past 25 years. When Lindsay Reade re-established contact with her at the start of the research for this book, it seemed unlikely that she would break her silence. Her response was understandably guarded. She was clearly a private person albeit warm, friendly and kind but really she wanted to leave things at that.

In a letter to Lindsay, she wrote: "I was thinking that I am outside the official story of Ian's life and do not mind staying like this. I am shy and discreet and have accepted I was not appreciated by Joy Division's following. Everybody seems to have accepted Debbie's version and taken it as true and honest and I have come to terms with it. I have come to learn that there is no such thing as the truth or else there are several truths. It all depends from whose point of view you see it and everything is so subjective."

---

[1] Pronounced Honourey

Shortly after this she sent what she hoped would be a definitive e-mail on the subject of her relationship with Ian: "Ian and I were certainly very close emotionally and felt a lot for each other. I think I just came at the right time when he was in need of comfort, affection, tenderness and that my presence was soothing to him. He was very gentle and very soft and very caring. I think the fact that I was a foreigner was part of the attraction and also the fact that I was very kind and maybe more kind of refined than girls he had met before. Our relationship was very platonic and very pure and romantic but also quite abstract. He felt quite diminished by his disease and quite frightened of how it would evolve. He never said much about Debbie and the little he said was that they had grown apart and that their relationship was over and was even before we met. I must say that at 22 I could not imagine being married, let alone having a child. He told me how much he loved his little daughter and how lovely she was but again it appeared all very unreal. He seemed afraid to hurt her and not being able to look properly after her."

There was much more in this e-mail but it seemed to be pretty much all Annik wanted to say on the subject. Prior to this contact, she had given a copy of Ian's letters to a screenwriter named Michael Stock and had answered his questions because he seemed genuinely interested and wanted to have a more clear understanding of who she was and what had occurred between her and Ian. Because he was a complete stranger, it took Annik some time to agree but she was assured he had the support of the band and he came recommended by Michel Duval (who ran Factory Benelux born in Brussels in 1979 and Les Disques de Crepuscule with Annik after Ian's death). Michael Stock wrote a screenplay for a film about Ian's life but seemingly it never got off the ground.

Subsequently, another movie screenplay – entitled *Control* – was mooted and producer Todd Eckhert wrote to Mark Reeder with a plea that he needed to contact Annik and asked if Mark could help him. Mark thought that if a film was going to be made about Ian, then it ought to contain an accurate portrayal of Annik and not just the impression of her that Debbie Curtis might have imagined. Mark hadn't spoken to Annik for over 21 years and was quite stunned when Todd called him on the phone and, as they were talking, at that very moment he received an e-mail from Annik. He responded by suggesting to her that this was her chance to tell her side of the story. Her initial reluctance wavered when he impressed upon her his belief that talking about it would help her to put the affair behind her and hopefully put her mind at rest.

As a result Annik was persuaded to meet with the director and screenplay writer of the movie, even though she was not, in principle, particularly in favour of the film being made and would have preferred her relationship with Ian to remain a private matter. "I really do not understand why people want to do a movie about Ian's life," she says. "It is different with a book but why have someone to play his part and only guess and imitate who he really was? He wanted peace. His life was not a film."

Later, having read two different drafts of the screenplay Annik would say: "I do not care about any movie. All I hope is that my name is not in it because as I clearly said to Todd I do not relate to any of the dialogue so I don't see why it should be in my name. All I can see is people wanting to make a movie, just a movie and they seem to feel very righteous that they know it all."

Mark Reeder, who would go on to have a relationship with Annik after Ian's death, begs to differ. "I think it's important the story is set straight for her and her kids too. This is as much her story as it is Ian's, Debbie's and the band's and Factory's. She is certainly not a groupie, nor is she the kind of person to wilfully want to destroy someone's marriage or an on-going relationship, as she is actually much too diplomatic. She was always under the impression that Ian's marriage was virtually over, as this is obviously what Ian had led her to believe. It would be really nice to finally clarify her position in this poignant story. She is a very, very sensitive, lovely person."

Annik Honoré was born on October 12, 1957, in southern Belgium where she grew up. She was a tomboy when she was young, an outdoor girl who spent much of her free time playing with her dog in a forest near to her home. English was her favourite subject at school and after secondary school she went to a language college for two years, learning English and Spanish. After leaving without sitting her exams, she decided she'd had enough of the countryside and at the age of 20 came to live with a friend in Brussels, where for a few months she worked in an office which wasn't to her liking. She spent most of her free time listening to rock and pop music, her tastes coinciding with the kind of artists that were championed by *New Musical Express*, and travelled to Paris, London and Amsterdam to see concerts, including Patti Smith, Siouxsie & The Banshees, The Clash, Generation X, Iggy Pop and David Bowie. Because of her huge enthusiasm for music, she became involved with a Belgian magazine/fanzine called *En Attendant*.

Since none of the artists she liked ever seemed to play in Brussels Annik decided to relocate to England. She had already visited the country once, spending six weeks of a summer holiday in London attending a college near Sloane Square to improve her English. At the time she'd rented a room in a house in Delvino Road in Parsons Green and so in 1979 she got back in touch with her old landlady. There were two rooms that she rented to students, one small one and a larger one with a bathroom. The larger one wasn't available but Annik took the small one on the understanding that after the holidays, when the larger one became free, it would be hers. This is where she lived for a year and where Ian Curtis came and slept over once or twice. When she first arrived in London she didn't have a job and didn't know where to start looking for one, though she thought initially she might sell jeans on a market stall. The landlady, Miss Freeland, told her about someone she knew at the Belgian Embassy whom Annik might ask about a job. She arranged an interview and it turned out they needed a French speaker. She met the Chancellor, took tests in English, French and Dutch and was duly employed there, beginning in September 1979. She was 21.

Annik first saw Ian on the night of August 13, 1979 at the Nashville Rooms in West London. Because she liked the album *Unknown Pleasures* so much, she had travelled especially from Belgium to see Joy Division play there. They made a very strong impression on her and she decided to request an interview with Joy Division for the *En Attendant* fanzine.

"I loved *Unknown Pleasures*," she says. "The very first time I heard it, it really moved me. It was very powerful. I had never heard anything like it. Joy Division had style and were simple at the same time. The music and the voice were so intense, they just hit me. Ian's voice was deep and sombre and the lyrics seemed meaningful. There was an urge to it. I knew I had to see them and that I would not be disappointed."

Annik, together with a friend named Isabelle, approached the sound engineer at the Nashville Rooms and asked if it would be possible to speak with the group. She then spoke to Rob Gretton who was quite happy for an interview for *En Attendant* to take place, especially since the fanzine was published abroad. Annik met the band briefly and as they were due to play in London again in two weeks' time – on August 24 at Walthamstow Youth Club – the interview was arranged for then. This gig was the second at this particular venue, the first having taken place on March 30. Both gigs came about after the band met Dave Pils and Jasmine at the fateful Hope & Anchor show. Jasmine was the youth club organiser and she arranged the gigs. Because they were unable to afford hotels, the group stayed frequently with Jasmine and Pils, who lived in Walthamstow, when they were in London, as they did on this occasion. Dave Pils also became part of the Joy Division road crew, at least for the London gigs at this point.

The interview with Annik and the band lasted four hours and she still has a two-hour tape in her possession. The atmosphere on tape seems very friendly, funny and cheerful. Ian and Steve's strong regional accents stand out and, to a lesser-trained ear, their voices sound quite similar. Ian's voice is the more high-pitched, which is odd, considering the depth of his singing voice. Someone says "Mee gee-taahhr" for "my guitar". They are clearly enjoying the attentions of this beautiful foreigner, who was asking rather unusual questions for a rock interview, and it began with a discussion about Siouxsie & The Banshees. Annik was a huge fan and actually went to around 100 of their gigs. Rob's comforting and amusing drawl rambles away. There is no mistaking him. Ian asks Annik what she thinks of films. Barney asks if she has a favourite. She mentions Woody Allen. "Do you like horror films?" she asks the group. "Some are just laughable," replies Steve. Ian says something about the film *Eraserhead* – that it got him thinking. Rob makes a joke about the chicken in this film (when all the blood comes out of it) and compares it to a visit to a chip shop.

Later on Annik asks: "Do you believe in love?" Someone breaks into a song: "I believe in…" (Buzzcocks). Annik wonders what the boys think of make-up. Although Ian admits to having worn it when he was younger, he says he likes girls who can look attractive without any. At one point in the interview, after Rob has been light-heartedly discussing the ethics of religion, a kettle is heard to be merrily whistling away and Jasmine makes tea. (Annik remembered what a lovely girl she was.) A few moments later there is another comforting sound as Bowie's album *Low* is put on the turntable. This was Ian and Annik's favourite album. Everyone sounds happy and ebullient in the way that only the young can be, when life holds so much promise, when disappointment is just a word and death is so far away as to be unimaginable.

Later Annik would remark about this interview: "We talked about marriage, children, love, death and health without having any idea that two months later we would go out together. It was then that I found out more about him being epileptic, although I thought he was after seeing him on stage, being married to Debbie for five years, Natalie. All the 'problems' or 'difficulties' were approached without knowing they would become such obsessions in our lives, such barriers."

According to Terry Mason, after this interview the whole band slept on the floor, on sisal matting, all in the same room.

The relationship between Annik and Ian developed slowly after this first meeting. They became friends gradually, meeting one another at various London gigs and certain regional shows. Their next meeting was at the Leeds Sci-Fi Festival on September 8, and by this time Annik was living in London.

Her enthusiasm for music in general and for Joy Division in particular was huge and, with a fellow enthusiast called Michel Duval, she began making tentative arrangements for the group to play their first gig abroad, at a venue called Plan K, which was about to open in Brussels.

And a spark had been lit between her and Ian. Annik: "There was some electricity in the air every time we would see each other, every time we looked at each other."

It is a measure of Joy Division's speedy rise to prominence that gigs were now beginning to flow thick and fast, leading towards a full-scale commitment during October when they would support Buzzcocks on a full-length British tour.

On August 31, the band performed at London's Electric Ballroom, a venue whose size reflected the fact that they were becoming established on the London circuit, this being the kind of venue that would host shows by bands like Siouxsie & The Banshees. Terry recalls that because of Joy Division's increased status the promoter at this gig provided something they had not really seen before – a rider! Because they were from 'up North' it included cans of Mackeson stout, a drink favoured by the elderly. To everyone's surprise, Barney was quite partial to it.

There was an eclectic bill that night featuring sets from Scritti Politti, Monochrome Set and A Certain Ratio, thereby placing four of the most intriguing bands of an intriguing era on the same bill. It was also the occasion of Joy Division's largest singular audience to date, with reportedly 1,200 stuffed into the famous Camden Town venue. The restlessness of that particularly vociferous crowd during the support acts also offered a strong hint of Joy Division's impending advancement. As Ian danced at the front of the stage, the mood changed from edgy restlessness to a bouncing and adoring mass.

The next day, September 1, saw the band recording two songs for BBC2's *Something Else* television programme, which was broadcast on September 15; 'Transmission' followed by a frenzied rendition of 'She's Lost Control'. This was filmed on Oxford Road in Manchester and the group had to be there by midday which meant an early start after a very late gig in London. The group were all somewhat the worse for wear, not least because of the new found luxury of a rider, which was unlikely to be conducive to Ian's health.

Something Else was one of the first of the so-called 'Yoof TV' shows, a mix of music and chat, fun enough to enliven a Tuesday evening though dogged by the technical shortcomings of the day. Television at the end of the

Seventies had an infuriating inability to effectually present a 'live' performance by a rock act in anything approaching a flattering setting.

As with so many similar recordings, and most local television encounters with rock music, each instrument would be separated to create an overall diluted effect[1]. As such, when Joy Division fans across the country who had been entranced by the band's mesmeric live sets settled down to watch their favourite band on television – more often than not overseen by curious and unimpressed parents – they witnessed little more than a band battling against the tide.

Joy Division was on with The Jam (performing 'Going Underground') for this half hour programme. As the camera swung to catch Tony Wilson enthusiastically exploding with superlatives about them, it also caught a confused Steve Harley from Cockney Rebel, who, in an unbecoming and unexpected lack of grace, could only utter, "These kids can't play their instruments."

Even if true, Harley missed the point by a country mile. And Steve Harley of all people – a former rock journalist. Surely he should have known better than that?[2] Not that his comment appeared to phase the band who approached the show with a display of almost wide-eyed innocence. Nevertheless, true to form, Hooky would later state that he thought Harley was an "… arrogant old twat". Almost a compliment, really.

The alternative event of the year in 1979 was Futurama at Queen's Hall, Leeds – in a big old indoor market hall – which followed on September 8. To many who attended, however, Futurama was a full-on nightmare of hideous proportions. The entire population of post-punk Britain, it seemed, was crammed into a giant bean can and draped across a singularly uninviting floor. It was Leigh Festival in reverse. Back then, all space and light; at Futurama, black and crammed, twelve angry drinkers deep at every bar, sallow speed-freak faces clutching beer cans and hollow sexist whooping as Altered Images, fronted by Clare Grogan, took to the stage. Many understandably questioned the use of the phrase 'sci-fi' in the context of this event, for this was a positively Dickensian scene. Nevertheless, it was refresh-

---

[1] This was no different from each instrument being miked up separately for live shows. The challenge was that TV recording engineers had been trained to produce a 'clean' sound and would have built up a 'traditional' sound mix, i.e. vocals and guitar up front.

[2] Ironically, Harley was a one-time idol of Ian Curtis, who had previously cited Cockney Rebel's 'Judy Teen' as one of his favourite songs. Nor was Ian alone in this. Hooky, Terry and Barney had all tried to see Cockney Rebel at Salford University but had been refused admission as it was a Student Only gig, this refusal perhaps helping shape the band's negative attitude towards college gigs.

ing to see bands like A Certain Ratio performing before a huge and swaying crowd, even if the days of spitting at bands had not entirely receded. It was one of ACR's finest gigs, if memory serves. They injected a ferocious funk into the dead shell that was Queen's Hall.

Jeremy Kerr from A Certain Ratio recalls the event and the era with special fondness: "It was one of the great things about that time. The fact that there were genuinely a great many interesting bands but also that there were people in place who would allow us to play in some of the most extra-ordinary places. We will always be grateful for that period, for being given the chance to play to so many people. 1979 was an excellent time all round. I am not sure we all appreciated how lucky we were."

At Futurama, Joy Division performed with supreme confidence that immediately distanced themselves from the remainder of the bands on a huge two-day bill which featured just about every act of the post-punk genre, be it Scritti Politti, Cabaret Voltaire, Gang Of Four, The Pop Group and the surly, defiant Public Image Ltd. For sheer attitude alone, Pil would claim the gold medal, but few fans who left that vast and soulless venue were in any doubt about the leading act of the day… it was Joy Division and by a big margin.

"We were second on the bill to Pil," says Terry. "John Lydon had us cleared from the back stage area because they were so big yet when the reviews came out we were the stars of the show."

Although the Festival is remembered by all who attended as a fairly grim experience, there was an intangible *presence* about Joy Division and, in par-ticular, Ian Curtis at this point in their career. His charisma simply grabbed the attention, and while the edginess of his performance may have been in part due to his apparently worsening condition, it certainly racked up the tension. Many who stared at him in wonderment were lost in twin states of curiosity and admiration.

Joy Division's set on this occasion – 'I Remember Nothing', 'Wilderness', 'Transmission', 'Colony', 'Disorder', 'Insight', 'Shadowplay', 'She's Lost Control', 'Atrocity Exhibition' and 'Dead Souls' – would surface on numerous bootlegs which, for the most part, captured a band in fero-cious form in front of a massive festival-sized crowd.

Following Futurama, on September 22, there was a return gig at the Nashville Rooms in London's Earls Court, and for Barney, Hooky, and Steve, who were all still in full-time employment, this meant a half day off work followed by a return to work the following morning. At this point the group were still using the van that had been purchased by Hooky and taken on the European holiday in 1978, and it had carried the gear to all Joy Division gigs since. He and Terry generally shared the driving between them, and although it wasn't pretty or fast, it still carried them wherever they needed to go.

"The weekend before I'd been helping Hooky and his brother Chris put a new clutch in the van," recalls Terry. "We were coming home from the Nashville Room gig on the M1, the van was probably struggling to do 55, something like that, cos it was knackered and just as the M69 joins the M1 or where it joins the M6 we noticed this truck was coming on by the slip road and the thing just hit us – smack into the back of the van. Fortunately the van had shit tyres. If it had tyres that had any grip we would have turned over, as it was we slid from one barrier to the next (the central reservation barrier to the one at the side). The back doors flew open and the equipment started flying out of the back. The rest of the band were coming behind in Steve's car and Steve's seeing his drum kit came flying out of the van and almost hit his car."

Hooky was driving at this point with Terry beside him in the front. A roadie called Twinny usually travelled in the van with them but fortunately for him he wasn't present that night. "Twinny would have gone in the back of the van with the equipment cos he could sleep anywhere," says Terry. "If he had been there he would have gone out of the back and been dead."

As a result of the accident Steve needed to acquire a new drum kit. "Hooky lost a bass cab out there," says Terry. "It was the first stuff that we had so Steve's drum kit wasn't in flight cases – which we had later on – they were just in fibre cases so going from nought to sixty miles an hour on concrete didn't do them any good. He had these sort of elliptical drums. It turned out the truck driver had just fallen asleep. The tractor units of artics rock a bit and it must have rocked him to sleep. He kept saying there was no need to worry about calling the police and there was nothing much wrong with the van. We'd almost been killed, there was equipment all over the road, and this truck driver didn't think we needed to bring in the police."

The van was written off, Steve's drums and Hooky's bass cab were firewood, but no one was hurt – not even a claim for whiplash!

After this accident the band decided to purchase flight cases for their equipment. Terry Mason recalls this being another excuse for them to exercise their endearing sense of fun, specifically on the slight incline of Little Peter Street, outside TJ Davidson's rehearsal rooms. "Once you've got flight cases the first thing you realise is how much fun they actually are," says Terry. "They're made to be safe and built to protect the things inside so they made good toboggans on the street. Ian hated foam rubber so it was weird that he got in one. There were these little kids who used to hang round TJ's and we'd put them in, close the lid and roll them down the road that TJ's was on. There mustn't have been many cars about then."

CHAPTER 13

A Different Kind Of Tension

"… an audience can sometimes sense when a performer is a little ill at ease and it can then go two ways. Either they deride him… and the whole thing fails, or they feel an empathy. It was certainly the latter with Ian." – Steve Diggle

On September 28, a triumphant Joy Division returned to play their 'home' gig, at Manchester's Factory Club. It was an unmissable night, even if the band's following had now swelled way beyond the club's limited capacity.

A dense forest of fans greeted them that evening. Just three days later they would be opening the Buzzcocks tour at Liverpool University, and this gig proved a perfect booster for both their confidence and their tour budget. On the night it was encouraging to witness a relaxed Ian Curtis fronting a tight, confident band, seemingly poised to surge serenely into the heart of a potentially arduous Buzzcocks tour. Following the set, in the austere back-stage area, with Rob Gretton seemingly ebullient, an amiable Curtis was smiling into the night. Hovering uneasily beside him was Buzzcocks manager Richard Boon and his partner Sue Cooper.

All wasn't well within the Buzzcocks camp. Boon was unnerved by the lack of interest that had greeted the release of the band's third album, *A Different Kind Of Tension*. It wasn't so much that it was a poor album but that there was little doubt that it arrived with the uneasy feeling that the Buzzcocks' moment was about to pass. Understandably, Boon wanted to attract as much positive attention as possible from the music press. He needed to court sympathetic journalists.

Mick Middles, a lifelong Buzzcocks supporter, recalls the genuine tension surrounding the group. "It seemed that I was one of those positive forces for the band, which was certainly true. Richard wanted me to review one of the early gigs on the Different Kind Of Tension tour. It was suggested that Richard and Sue should drive me to the Leeds University gig on October 3, where I would be instructed to review only Buzzcocks and not Joy Division. This seemed little short of bizarre. Contacting *Sounds* the next day, I was to discover that separate journalists from the same paper would be covering Joy Division and it had been at the insistence of the Buzzcocks' United Artists press officer that they shouldn't be allowed to review Buzzcocks. It was an extraordinary, perhaps unprecedented situation. It seemed obvious that they were scared of Joy Division.

"On the day of the Leeds gig, the atmosphere in Boon's car seemed slightly edgy, particularly when I happened to mention a call from Rob Gretton also inviting me to the very same gig. 'But I am only reviewing Buzzcocks,' I announced, which relieved the tension a bit.

"As it turned out, I needn't have worried. Buzzcocks turned in a ferocious set, although I noted that other publications did seem to downgrade their performance. Nevertheless, chatting with Ian Curtis during the tension fuelled period between the two band's sets appeared to create further mistrust."

Middles recalls a lovely moment, however, when he was abandoned in the dressing room and, dogged by shyness, unable to latch onto the banter from either band. "Just one person noticed that I was uncomfortable in that situation," he recalls. "It was Ian Curtis. He saw me, walked over to the fridge, pulled out a can of Red Stripe, wandered over and handed it to me. I thought it a wonderful gesture. Nobody else there really cared.

"The cynic might suggest that Curtis was merely oiling the press, but that wasn't the case. I was just a minor provincial writer. There were many far more important people in that room and Ian knew that. But I think he recognised his own shyness in others, and how debilitating it can be."

The Different Kind Of Tension tour was one of the most memorable in recent rock history. On the one hand, there was a powerful support band on the ascendancy while on the other, there was a bill-topper struggling for consistency. More intriguingly perhaps, the two bands attracted different sets of fans, with Buzzcocks still drawing a large section of young *Smash Hits* reading teens and Joy Division the older *NME* crowd of more serious demeanour. The bands were light and dark, polar opposites.

Buzzcocks' Pete Shelley disagrees. "I always saw the similarities," he says. "I mean the fact that they were different to us was something to be applauded. If they'd been cookie cut-outs, it wouldn't have worked. At the time it was just taken as being different ways of expression."

The band members themselves were less aware of any tension than their respective managements, but if there was any tension between them it was off-set by a Mancunian camaraderie, a series of juvenile japes on the parts of both bands.

"It was incredibly annoying because we were a much better band than we had been a year earlier, when everyone was writing such fantastic things about us," says Buzzcocks guitarist Steve Diggle. "That's the way it is. Obviously, after so many years doing this, I can see that now, but it annoyed us at the time. We all thought *A Different Kind Of Tension* was a really strong album but it wasn't really a singles album, which is what everybody wanted from us. So this was the crux of the problem. People had decided that we were a lightweight singles band, and derided us when we tried to do something a little more serious. At the same time they were praising Joy Division for not being a lightweight singles band. So it was a no-win situation for us.

"All this would have been fine, but they were getting fantastic live reviews from that tour and yet, night after night, we were blowing them away. I am not putting them down… really I'm not. But that was the reality. We were simply further down the line than them and it showed. I thought Joy Division were fantastic and we helped them a great deal on that tour. Particularly Ian, who wasn't really that confident of his performance. I mean, he was a natural but perhaps didn't quite know it. But we did help him… an awful lot, actually.

"I truth, I don't think Ian's stage presence really hit me in those gigs. If anything, he seemed a bit unsure on stage. That was definitely the case in the early gigs and, to some extent I think he carried that insecurity with him. Maybe that was what people picked up on. I am not sure. I think it possibly was, because an audience can sometimes sense when a performer is a little ill at ease and it can then go two ways. Either they deride him or her and the whole thing fails, or they feel an empathy. It was certainly the latter with Ian, which is one of the reasons why the Joy Division thing has lasted."

By the start of the Buzzcocks tour everyone in Joy Division had finally given up their day jobs and was receiving wages of £35 a week from the band's account. By August of that year they would have used up much of their holidays from work in doing the gigs prior to the tour. They all had to give up regular work completely to make this tour possible.

Barney only stopped working the week before the tour began, though Ian had stopped a bit before that. Gigs like London's Electric Ballroom would have netted in the region of £2,000 with perhaps between £500 and £750 from Futurama in Leeds, both of which helped to swell the band's coffers. At the start of the tour the band, Rob Gretton, Terry and Twinny were all paid the same wage. Ian had been put on wages before the start of the tour.

As the opening shows on the tour were relatively local to Manchester the band travelled back home from the early northern gigs at Liverpool and Leeds. Terry: "Being on tour is a fantastic experience, especially as a support band. No pressure on you. Not worried about whether it's a full house or not. At that point we weren't constantly having to go off and have radio interviews because Radio Liverpool or whatever wouldn't want to speak to us cos we weren't Buzzcocks. So it was great, work was finished by nine o'clock and you could get on with the business of drinking and womanising. In the early part of the tour the band would get really pissed off because they had to go home. But then came Scotland, beginning with Glasgow.

"This was the first night of the tour that we all (both bands and crew) stayed over and all in the same hotel. We all got completely lathered, totally shit faced. Back at the hotel, Sarge, the Buzzcocks' minder, offered to drink a pint of piss for a tenner. No one had that sort of money to spare, so like kids we asked Rob if the band would pay for it – me, Barney, Ian and Hooky all pissed into it."

"The police were called to a couple of the gigs," recalls Pete Shelley, "to the hotels anyway. At Glasgow everyone was in the bar. I went up to bed but in the morning the police were there checking everyone's bags because the bar had been raided – the shutters had been prized open and all the bottles of spirits had been taken from behind the bar."

Terry recalls that breakfast trays were thrown about and plant pots turned over as well. "Glasgow CID went into Ron Clarke's (Buzzcocks lighting man) room, grabbed him by the bollocks and pointed out that it was no laughing matter breaking into bars in the Holiday Inn in their town."

The tour would be quite debilitating with late nights, drinking and long journeys driving from one place to another. On October 7 the tour came to Aberdeen in northern Scotland. After the gig at the Capitol Theatre, Hooky was driving Steve's car back to the hotel and was stopped by the police and breathalysed. Since the reading was negative the beer on the rider obviously wasn't as alcoholic as they had previously thought. The next day Joy Division travelled to Dundee for the last night of the first part of the tour and decided to have an 'end of term party'. Twinny had got into the habit of staying up longest, getting drunker than anyone else and occasionally a bit obnoxious. It was assumed this night would see him go somewhat overboard.

Terry: "I think it was Aberdeen where he did the game of saying to people in the room, 'I bet you £5 I've got two pairs of hands'. Someone would always fall for it. Then he would drop his pants and you'd find out that he'd been to a tattooist and he's got hands coming out onto his buttocks saying 'Let me out of here'. We decided we'd set Twinny up. He was sharing a room with me that night. We'd noticed that there was a cot on the landing of the hotel. So we took his bed out of the room, hid it and put the cot where his bed was. Then, as always, we took all the light bulbs out so he couldn't see where he was going. We also set up 'haunted house' – we made strings of empty coke cans so that when he came in we'd pull them and it would sound like a ghostly chain rattling. We stayed up waiting for him to come back. Twinny opened the door and, knowing roughly where his bed is, falls into the side of the cot, and then the cans start. People outside in the corridor were pulling the strings. He was that arseholed he didn't bother looking for his bed, I think he just curled up on the floor."

Exhausted but elated, Joy Division had a couple of days rest before setting off for their first European gig at Plan K in Brussels. This show was the first they would play at Plan K and could be seen as the forerunner – as the Russell club was for Factory – of Crepuscule Records. Annik Honoré was the contact in London to find the groups that would come over and discuss the money they would receive and other arrangements. Her colleague Michel Duval was in Brussels organising the tickets, posters and advertising. Strangely Plan K's address was 21 Rue de Manchester, which was actually a five-storey building that had once been a sugar refinery.

Terry: "We'd been told that we were playing an oil refinery, not an ex-sugar refinery. So we thought it would be easy to find – which it wasn't. When we arrived we discovered that we've been booked into a hostel, not a hotel. There were only two rooms, one which Rob and Ian had – because Ian had to have his sleep – and the rest of us had to share together, like the seven dwarfs. Everyone scrambled for the bed they wanted and Ian came into our room. There was a giant smokers ashtray on a pedestal in the room. There were so many people in the room they must have thought there'd be so many people smoking. This room didn't have a window out to the world but it had a window out to the corridor, for some reason. Of course it wasn't en suite, so Ian decides he needs a piss and because of the attitude brought on from T.J.'s – laziness basically – he decides to piss in this big ashtray. Someone from the hostel was walking by and we've not closed the curtains fully and he sees Ian pissing in an ashtray in the middle of the room. So this big black man comes banging on the door, shouting at us in French or Flemish and Ian says to him: 'You tell me what to do and I will do it!' We're just pissing ourselves laughing – Ian's been caught being very naughty.

"The next day we go to the gig and Ian was really made up that William Burroughs was on, reading, and Ian's a big fan. He wanted to tell Burroughs what a great person he thought he was. Ian went over and I think he somehow hoped that Burroughs might know something about him, about his lyrics, but he just blanked him really, as if he was anybody from the crowd.

"Cabaret Voltaire were supporting us. Ian liked watching them but what we noticed when they were on was that they owned their own strobe and the lighting guy had one on for them. We had to make sure that when we were on this guy didn't try to use it – and he did try to use it, we had to stop him. The building had quite big rooms, everything had been painted white, there were probably about 200 or 300 people in there. The group went down well. Plus there were more arty farty types there, with Burroughs being there as well.

"We had unlimited beer on the rider along with plenty of soft drinks – orange juice, tomato juice and some coke. Before we left the gig we put a couple of cases of Duval in the back of the van and the band put a load of soft drinks into the back of the car. I was driving the van and I'd just stopped at the traffic lights and two of them – Ian and Barney or Hooky and Barney – ran out and threw the tomato juice and orange juice all over the windscreen of the van. So I've got a sticky, horrible mess, can't see out of the window on the wrong side of the road at the wrong time of night without a fucking clue how to find the hostel. Not only that but when we got back the hire company were less than amused by the sticky mess on the front of the van and we got charged for it."

Soon after returning to the UK the band began the second half of the Buzzcocks tour which involved a punishing schedule beginning in Wales at Bangor University on October 19. Alongside the two bands was 'Dudno', a superfan of the Buzzcocks insofar as he went to every gig, sleeping rough in his car along the way. Joy Division became his number two band and he was happy to run errands for them if required. His parents owned a hotel in Llandudno where Joy Division stayed overnight, though the Buzzcocks stayed in Bangor.

On the one of few breaks in the Buzzcocks tour schedule, Joy Division played an Electric Ballroom gig in London on October 26 which, although taking up a much needed rest day, brought in vital income to help fund the tour – probably about £1,500. It was at this aptly titled venue that Annik and Ian shared their first kiss, on the backstage staircase. By this time they were already deeply attracted to one another. She wrote to Carole: "I could feel something was happening… that emotions were starting to flow. How nervous and shy Ian was when he would see me, how nice and delicate as well. I always tried hard to stay calm and not say a word that would reveal what I was feeling but then he came to me, took me by the hand and I didn't resist."

Many years later as she was clearing out her attic, Annik found a scrap of paper with a set list that she had lovingly written out, with this date in October and the venue as the Electric Ballroom. She noted: "Ian sat by my side nervous."

She also found a headed sheet of paper from the promoter for the gig, Straight Music Ltd, giving the playing times for that night: 8.15-9.00 A Certain Ratio; 9.15-10.00 The Distractions; 10.30-11.30 Joy Division. Underneath Annik had written: "He took me by the hand took me in his arms in the backyard of the Electric Ballroom. He was beautiful and shy. We spent the night together. 1st kiss Ian annik. 2 lovers forever."

But their developing relationship wasn't as straightforward as this implies. Concerned that Ian was married, Annik had actually tried to nip their friendship in the bud, as she revealed in a long letter she sent to Ian's sister Carole in 1980, shortly after Ian's death. This letter pinpointed dates and meetings and in it she described her torment right at the outset: "The guilt was there since the beginning. I felt guilty about loving a married man but it couldn't prevent our love to exist. So for a month it was on and off, whenever I would feel too guilty it would be over for a few days but then it would start again. Too hard to resist. And he would always say that it was over at home, that they didn't love each other anymore, they had gone separate ways and were distant. I still didn't know if it was true or not. All I know is true is that we love(d) each other immensely. Still, when the Buzzcocks tour was finished, I left Ian. I knew it would be very hard to see each other and I still felt too guilty going out with a father."

Annik Honoré and Ian Curtis were never lovers in the strict meaning of the term. "What nobody knows (or hardly anyone) is that Ian and I never made love, or at least not in sexual terms," she says. "Our relationship was made of love and tenderness and care but we slept together like two kids even if fully in love. I know it is strange to understand, especially now when

I in the meantime have realised how wonderful sexual love is and how important it is in a couple but it never took place between Ian and I. He was far too sick and maybe I was far too shy. We kissed a lot, we cuddled, held each other and felt very close but it was to do with share of hearts and souls more than bodies. Ian was my first real love. And Mark came a year after Ian's death because he knew Ian and could understand me so well. Mark was my very first lover in the true sense of the word."

On October 27 and 28 the Buzzcocks tour came to Manchester for two home town gigs at the Apollo with a big party scheduled after the opening night's show. According to Terry there were major sulks from the band as wives were present. Their presence wasn't encouraged – perhaps not so much, as Terry has suggested, because the boys couldn't get on with the business of being in a band but because it rather put a damper on the fun and games they liked to get up to.

Distractions singer Mike Finney, who had been a close friend of both bands for a number of years, recalls that Buzzcocks drummer John Maher was celebrating his birthday on the 27th. Maher, a fast car fanatic who in later years would become a big name in international drag racing, had just taken delivery of a brand new, open-topped sports car. Finney: "Ian Curtis, lost in an apparently typical bout of mischief-making, hurled Maher's birthday cake from the Apollo window, the tumble of crème and sponge crashing horribly into the new car's leather upholstery." When asked about this incident, Maher replied: "There was a lot of that stuff going on. It was always in a good spirit though. I think that the tensions existed within each band rather than between each band."

The following night, October 30, they played at the De Montfort Hall, Leicester, where, unusually, Joy Division and their road crew were staying in the same hotel where boredom set in with bizarre consequences. "Hooky and Steve had gone to bed and it ended up that my room became 'party room'," says Terry. "Me, Dave Pils, Twinny, Ian and Barney decided to play pitch & toss which is throwing coins against the wall – nearest to the wall wins – but in this case the furthest away loses. Barney liked things unpleasant for other people so he decided it was for forfeits. There were four forfeits written on small pieces of paper folded up and put into the 'Ashtray of Doom' from where you had to pick them out if you lost.

"The first round commenced. The players were Ian, Barney and Dave Pils. Dave Pils lost the first round, goes to the 'Ashtray of Doom' and gets 'spitting in the face for a minute'. Under the rules it was allowable for the receiver of the spit to wear a towel around his head and neck so the spit was only in the face. Dave towelled himself up, looking like some bizarre nun and our two spitters spent the first 25 seconds of their minute in really loud hoiking and then the first spit hit straight into his eye.

"Next round, Ian lost, went over to 'Ashtray of Doom' and got 'spitting in the face' as well. So now it was incessant spit, spit, spit – they knew that making the great noises didn't produce the best results.

"For the next round, Barney lost. He went to the 'Ashtray of Doom' and got 'Shitting out of the Window'. Barney dropped his pants, waddled towards the sash window, arse out of it and shat. We were quite into shitting and shit at that time. We used to read the runes in them.

"I'd had enough and said the next round had to be the last. They went ahead and Dave Pils lost. He pulled out 'Shit in the Hand'. The ruling was quite strict in that not only did you have to let one turd drop into one hand but the clock didn't start until another turd was in the other hand and then it was 10 seconds.

"Obviously if you're going to have someone shitting on you, you don't want to be overly dressed in case of any splashback or spillage. So Dave stripped off to his underpants and sat in the bathroom, cross-legged. He was a very skinny, small lad and he was there like some bizarre Ghandi with his arms out either side and his palms upwards waiting for his deliveries. The challenge then was that Barney had just had a shit out of the window so there might not be a lot left and there could be a bit of a wait.

"Ian waddled over, squatted and produced, fortunately, a button. That was lucky. Then Dave had to wait until a turd landed in the other hand before the clock started. Fortunately, Barney also produced a button. After 10 seconds Dave scurried off and started scrubbing his hands for all he was worth. The rest of us just fell about laughing."

Annik must have been present at the Buzzcocks/Joy Division gig at Oxford New Theatre on October 30 since she still has in her possession Ian's set list, written in his familiar capitals, from that night: 'Walked In Lines', 'Only Mistake', 'Leaders Of Men', 'Insight', 'Ice Age', 'Love Tare Us Apart' [sic] and 'I Remember Nothing'. Joy Division's sets while on tour with Buzzcocks were considerably shorter than when they performed headlining shows.

As the tour progressed, Steve Diggle noticed that beyond the camaraderie and banter a darker problem was beginning to emerge with regard to Ian. "It was the strangest of tours in so many ways," he says. "It started off edgy but quite friendly but, I don't know, seven or eight gigs in and we started to notice that the Ian 'situation' wasn't good at all and was something that certainly seemed to be worsening. He was having a lot of fits… whether on stage or otherwise."

Pete Shelley also recalls the worsening situation: "It was almost like he was having a fit on stage, but in one place though. It wasn't like he was flailing around. He was very contained within it. It was almost like he was trying to find the word or the feeling. I think that was his way of centring himself, grounding himself. He definitely caught people's attention. He wasn't leaping around outwardly. There was an intensity in his being there. I'm not a theatre person but it upstaged everything else that was going on."

This intensity, theatrical or otherwise, was certainly becoming more obvious as the gigs went by.

Steve Diggle: "That was something that we hadn't really been aware of at the start of the tour but it became increasingly obvious just how ill he was, literally night after night the situation worsened. I am not suggesting, for one moment, that the people around Joy Division should have done more. I think they were actually too close to him to really notice the extent of it. I honestly think that was the case. And that was the irony. Despite all the tensions between the two bands, Ian actually seemed closer to us, particularly me for some reason. He spoke of being scared of where the next fit was coming from. It was terrifying really, but then he would seem to be fine again. It was difficult to tell when he was on stage… it was difficult to tell what state he was in. The band – Joy Division – were really intense and serious… concentrating on their set, which is how it should be but I think that's why Ian liked to speak to us. I had a sense that he needed to get away from the band."

Diggle recalls that the tensions and banter seemed to fade as the tour wore on and a sense of perspective was gained. "Perhaps it was the intensity of the work load," he says. "But Ian obviously wasn't well. That's not in dispute, is it?"

He also remembers an occasion when an ambulance was called to take Ian to hospital to recover from fits. "On one gig we found ourselves doing extra encores just to allow time for the ambulance to get away. That was something that never came over in the press. It was very clever, really, because nobody seemed to see that going on. The press turned up every night and never got an inkling."

Terry remembers this occurring on the night of November 2 at the Winter Gardens in Bournemouth: "Ian threw a massive fit, so much so that we had to call an ambulance, and, in order to allow time for the ambulance to get in and out, I asked Buzzcocks to spin out their encore."

Pete Shelley: "I remember when we played in Bournemouth he'd just had a fit when we were on stage. We'd almost finished and word came to us and so we played some extra songs so that the ambulance would have time to pick him up."

Terry also recalls groupie trouble after the gig on the November 4, at the Colston Hall in Bristol: "Ian and Barney were dragged off by two slappers. When Ian returned he was a bit sheepish. One slapper said to the other, 'He's a fucking waste of time' (referring to Ian). We broke into Barney's room and threw in a banger which went into the sink where he'd been washing his shirt and it burnt large holes in it."

Barney's revenge came as they all prepared to leave for the gig next day, November 5 at Hemel Hempstead Pavillion. Terry: "Barney always said 'You'll be sorry. Barney always gets his own back'. His revenge was swift letting the tyres down on Steve's car, the same car in which he had to travel, and then just sat in the car while Steve and Hooky changed it."

Luckily that morning the group had time for a late start and a leisurely drive to East Anglia for a gig at West Runton Pavilion on November 7.

The climax of the Buzzcocks tour was two nights at London's Rainbow Theatre in Finsbury Park on November 9 and 10. Terry: "We'd been warned how Buzzcocks played japes on support bands on the last night of the tour, and we were ready for it. In the end all they did was take the battery out of the Syndrum – but Steve only used it for 'She's Lost Control' and I'm not even sure it was in the set that night. Expecting the worst, Joy Division had prepared their retaliation; mice, maggots, shaving cream, and eggs were bought and brought into the Rainbow. At the changeover the band set about their tasks, pints of maggots placed at strategic points on top of amps, on drums, monitors and some on the lighting desk in the auditorium. Buzzcocks went onto the stage to see their crew scampering about brushing maggots off stuff. Out in the auditorium Buzzcocks lighting man Ron Clarke sees maggots crawling over his desk, he freaks and turns the desk upside down shaking them out. Here they are at a grand final show of a UK tour, performing the first song and it's all a bit of a circus.

"The show continues without any more incidents but it's only when Buzzcocks wanted to get back to their hotel that they discover that the japes haven't finished. Whilst the Buzzcocks' set was on, Joy Division have gone out and opened the small ventilator windows on the tour buses and put six mice in each. They've also sprayed the windows and door handles with shaving foam. The drivers of the buses try to clear off the foam with windscreen wipers which makes it worse. Then Steve's car drives round and they throw eggs at the buses and the people trying to get in them. After two circuits of the block the car is stopped by the police who ask Dave Pils why he was throwing eggs. When the buses arrive at the White House Hotel (both bands were staying at the same hotel as an end of tour treat), Sarge says, 'Let me get rid of these' and throws the six mice out of his van against the wall of the hotel, much to the shock of the hotel's other guests, many of whom had been across town that night watching Abba."

Although battling with her emotions Annik had decided to end her relationship with Ian. She wrote to Carole: "I was afraid of the feelings I had for Ian, I knew if we would stay a bit longer together I would never want to leave him anymore, never want him to go back to Macclesfield and love is something I didn't feel strong enough to face… I still regarded myself as a teenager although I was 22 years old. Anyway it was over, so I thought, but could not stop thinking of him. And also Ian rang me to see how I was and always found a reason to ring me. I was silly enough to think he would be my best friend."

On December 8 Joy Division played a Saturday 'matinee' show, at Eric's in Liverpool. This was a special session in the afternoon at reduced prices for the younger fans, sadly something unheard of nowadays. This was followed by a repeat concert in the evening in which the main band would go on early (having gone on last in the afternoon) and the support band would finish the show (usually to a substantially diminished crowd). Annik was present and again had retained Ian's set list from this night: 'Passover', 'Wilderness', 'Disorder', 'Love Will Tear Us Apart', 'Insight', 'Shadowplay', 'Transmission', 'Day Of The Lords', '24 Hours', 'Colony', 'These Days', 'Incubation', 'Lost Control' and 'Atrocity Exhibition'. On the back of this Annik had written her own review of the gig: Most moving, wonderful, magic, magnificent group in the whole world playing that night. I'm in love with them. Joy Division.

She continued in her letter to Carole: "When we met again in Liverpool we felt very uneasy and just looked at each other without knowing exactly what to do. I remember how sad he looked in the restaurant when I said 'You are my best friend'. He took me back to the station and we kissed each other on the cheek. How childish."

They would not see each other again until 1980.

CHAPTER 14

Atmosphere

"There was absolutely no sense of stardom about Ian at all." – Alan Hempsell

Ian Curtis skims across the stage. His movements, at once awkward and rhythmic, appear to force the tempo. His arms are flailing, his eyes rigid. Suddenly he snaps out of his trance and launches into a scorching vocal; almost a shout, almost a command.

"Dance, dance, dance to the radio..." he sings, proffering one of the truly iconic sights of the post-punk era. It's a perfect and lasting vision of a unique artist: Ian Curtis, trembling and alone, singing 'Transmission'.

Recorded on the cusp of July and August, 1979, the eagerly awaited 'Transmission', already a firm favourite with his audience, was released as a Factory single in November. In many ways, it was a song that Ian Curtis had to 'live in' for a while; feeling his way around it in performances, experiencing the way it allowed him to explode onstage with a captivating rebel yell of "Dance, dance, dance... to the radio...." Ian brought a unique rhythm to that line, pulling it from the heart of the song and hurling it out with a manic sense of defiance.

Both 'Transmission' and its steely B-side, 'Novelty', were created in the sessions for the original RCA demos and were seen as throwbacks to the pre-Martin Hannett era. Thus, for a while, 'Transmission' was seen as somewhat dated; a victim of the band's fast moving changes of artistic pace, an artefact from old practice room sessions, suited only to the *old* band.

It was Ian's suggestion that Joy Division resurrect it, and try to breathe new life into it. It was probably its potential as a live song, the element of 'performance' it gave to the singer, that made Ian feel it was worthy of a second chance. There was something in that simplistic lyric that still appealed to him, something in the chorus which gave added thrust to its general pace, with furious guitar riffs cutting directly against the main flow of the lyric.

The band had attempted to pin down the definitive recording at Manchester's Central Sound in July 1979. Also recorded at that session, which surfaced mysteriously on bootlegs, were a thinly clad version of a surging new song, 'Dead Souls', as well as 'Novelty' and two separate versions of 'Something Must Break'. Curiously, the vocals on all these tracks were buried well in the mix, causing Rob Gretton to doubt that any of them would ever be suitable for release as singles.

Scampering back to the by now more familiar Strawberry proved the key. The new 'Transmission' was little short of spellbinding, separating the true emotive qualities of Curtis' voice from the heart of the music. Also, as noted somewhat ironically by Dave Thompson in his excellent statistical book *True Faith: An Armchair Guide To New Order, Joy Division…*: "… any song that frequently mentions the word 'radio', is guaranteed to be lavishly peppered across the airwaves…"

Ian Curtis' lyric was an intensely personal examination of living a life in existential darkness; a sightless existence, a lonely place where relationships are formed only through sound. His concept of loneliness is perhaps best reflected in the line, "Touching from a distance, further all the time," the first phrase of which would be used by Deborah Curtis as the title for her memoirs.

What is intriguing about the Strawberry recording was Hannett's sense of reserve. He somehow manages to restrain the song's true emotive power, brilliantly pulling back an elastic tension before unleashing Curtis into a gloriously freefall chorus of "Dance, dance, dance to the radio…."

It was certainly a triumph for Hannett. Returning to an old song, hitherto deemed commonplace, and recreating it as a rallying call of anthemic proportions across post-punk underground Britain was surely a highlight of his extraordinary career. The same might be said of Ian Curtis, of course, who was now attaining a truly captivating presence on record.

With expectations running high all round, and with the full backing of virtually every music press writer in the country, the release of 'Transmission' promised *serious* chart action for Joy Division. It had everything, surely? Power, emotive resonance, hooks, mystique! It was to be catalogue number

FAC 13 for the label had, in the words of Tony Wilson: "An almost Babylonian obsession with numbering their stuff." Hence 'Love Will Tear Us Apart' was FAC 23, whereas the two albums were multiples of five.

They were to be disappointed. 'Transmission', one of the defining singles for a generation fleetingly referred to as "the cult with no name" (young men in grey overcoats with chiselled features and serious haircuts mainly, frowning into their beer), never even made the slightest dent in the charts. In retrospect, as echoes of Joy Division are heard in the work of so many bands still riding high in the charts, it seems extraordinary to note this abject failure. Who was to blame?

Tony Wilson: "That was the track that made me go, 'Oh fucking hell this is a hit single'. I drove off to London to try and get a plugger. I did get a plugger arranged, got the name and number of the best plugger in town. I played him the song, he loved it and agreed to handle it for two grand. Came back to Manchester and Martin Hannett said, 'We don't treat music as a commodity; so we don't use pluggers.' Rob and Alan didn't disagree."

This idealistic approach has, over the years, made the Factory catalogue immensely collectable – but at the time there was much gnashing of teeth. There can be little doubt that in terms of generating record sales, the decision not to put FAC 13 ('Transmission') and FAC 23 ('Love Will Tear Us Apart') on Joy Division's concurrent albums lost them a great deal of album sales. Perhaps it was a shade naïve of him but Wilson thought that 'Transmission' would sell with or without marketing and the clout a plugger could bring to the equation. As he says today: "It's all about songs. If Ian hadn't written a dozen great songs we wouldn't be doing this[1]. There'd be no industry. Interesting story, interesting sideline, blah, blah, blah, but if there weren't the great songs it wouldn't be happening."

In the event, Wilson optimistically went ahead with a huge pressing by Factory's standards. "[We did] 10,000 of these fabulous little 7-inch singles with their exploding nebula, textured card sleeves," he says. Unfortunately, only 1,000 were sold immediately and Wilson ruefully recalls seeing the stockpile of 9,000 records at the pressing plant. "I remember that Daniel (Miller, founder of Mute Records) had a single called 'Warm Leatherette' by The Normal in the next wire mesh pallet beside ours at the pressing plant. I noticed each month how his pile went down much more quickly than ours."

Although he was a party to the decision not to use a plugger, Rob Gretton called a band meeting at which he questioned for the first time the

---

[1] Referring to this book and films about Ian's life.

wisdom of keeping an increasingly popular band within the auspices of a small, independent label. According to Gretton, reflecting on the period in 1995, Ian Curtis was the sole member of the band who was unconcerned about the failure of 'Transmission' to achieve any commercial success. Given the other issues that were impacting on his life – fatherhood, epilepsy and Annik – Curtis was maturing at a fast pace, and it's more than likely that he was beginning to question the shallowness of fame. 'Novelty', the B-side of 'Transmission', posed the question: "What are you gonna do when the novelty is gone?", a line which has always suggested a writer increasingly examining his role at the heart of things, and maybe even his desire to remain in there.

Ian Curtis' thoughts on pop stardom do appear to have shifted somewhat during the course of 1979. His respect for Throbbing Gristle's anti-commercial attitude certainly hadn't abated and, perhaps not surprisingly, it was Ian who would forge the first noticeable link between them and Joy Division. In this regard he was instrumental in placing the band's next – and perhaps greatest – single, the extraordinary double A-sided 'Atmosphere'/ 'Dead Souls', not with Factory but on the enigmatic Sordide Sentimentale, the distinctive label that had just released Throbbing Gristle's disturbing double A-side, 'We Hate You Little Girls' and 'Five Knuckle Shuffle'. Genesis P-Orridge explains: "Ian really liked it – the way the cover looked. So it was through that that Joy Division did the release with Sordide Sentimentale."

The Throbbing Gristle release was an elaborately packaged set, containing these two genuinely unsettling songs: 'We Hate You Little Girls' questioned the accepted notion that everybody loves little girls, while 'Five Knuckle Shuffle' –about masturbation, presumably – was a morbid bass noise over which Genesis P-Orridge repeated the line "You are gonna get fcd up/you are gonna be fed up" over and over again. Most people did. It was typical of Throbbing Gristle to produce a disc that made the art of listening unduly arduous, but to anyone attuned to the TG philosophy, this intentional monotony was little short of captivating, both as a soundtrack to their wonderful manipulation of the media and as an aspect of their entire, unsettling aesthetic package. Throbbing Gristle made people think.

Ian's enthusiasm for Throbbing Gristle was further enhanced when he befriended Alan Hempsall, the charismatic front-man with off-kilter funksters and Factory label mates, Crispy Ambulance. He recalls: "We owed a lot to Bernard and Rob, but Ian was very nice as well. There was absolutely no sense of stardom about Ian at all. It was always just like a bunch of lads having a laugh with our mates, which is what it became. We did a number of supports. They were very important to us because we started in Factory and then, when Michelle Duval came in expressing an interest, we would suddenly be on Factory/Benelux. I think that was because Tony really didn't like us at all, but we didn't mind. We still felt like one of the family and Ian felt like a friend. He didn't have to treat us kindly, in fact few rock stars are so gracious, as anyone who gets close to them will understand, but I think it's important to note that Ian was always very personable. I am sure he had an ego. We all have to have an ego to get onstage and particularly as a singer, but there was none of that with me. Nothing. Just a helpful guy"

Hempsall was a fellow Throbbing Gristle fanatic and equally fond of swapping Genesis P-Orridge stories. "I remember Ian talking to me at The Factory Club about Throbbing Gristle's Sordide Sentimentale single. Ian was massive into Throbbing Gristle and I know he did used to ring Genesis P-Orridge a lot. He told me about that and seemed quite proud of the relationship. However, that wasn't such a big deal in a sense. TG encouraged people to ring. I started ringing as well. There was an element of TG that was all about breaking down the boundaries between audience and performers but not in a sycophantic way. That was all part of it. I know that Ian admired all that, the way Throbbing Gristle had become more than just a band... well, they never were a band as such, were they? I think it's probably true to say that Ian envied the looseness of Throbbing Gristle. I am not sure he was comfortable within the framework of a conventional band."

Genesis P-Orridge touches on this aspect of their work in an astonishing chapter in Simon Ford's brilliant TG book, *Wreckers Of Civilisation*. The very point of TG was to break down the conventional format of a band, allowing the dynamic to splinter in many directions. Given the heavy workload of Joy Division, Ian may well have envied the freedom and courageous stance of Throbbing Gristle. Whether he could have accepted the liberal extremism of a shockingly aesthetic unit such as TG, is doubtful, however. Compared to Genesis P-Orridge, who pushed, and still pushes[1] his life to aesthetic extremes, Ian would seem to be thoroughly conventional, at least on the surface.

Alan Hempsall: "Anyway, Ian was going on and on about 'Five Knuckle Shuffle' and I just wanted to know where to get hold of a copy. It was just like two fans talking. I don't think the rest of Joy Division were so into Gristle, it was certainly mainly Ian. He was into a lot of reading, as well... very much into his Bill Burroughs, was Ian. I remember him telling me that

[1] He is now a woman!

Genesis P-Orridge had put forward the idea of Joy Division doing a similar kind of single for Sordide Sentimentale. I knew that Rob was into it. I have no idea about the others but I do know one thing… I could never have imagined how brilliant that record would turn out. One of those records, like 'Anarchy In The UK', you never forget the first time you heard it. Listening to 'Atmosphere', *still,* the hairs on the back of the neck begin to stand up."

Indeed, the first bleak seconds of 'Atmosphere' convey an unparalleled intimacy through the close-up timbre of Ian's voice. Lyrics that are awash in ambiguity – "Walk in silence… don't walk away, in silence…" – suggest the head-in-hands desperation as a lover leaves for the last time; hollow moments of realisation, of a life lost, a killed passion, the final embers of dream. Ian's voice might be the loneliest in the world as it hovers above Hannett's simplistic mix, a flickering candle of truth, of grim realisation. Pop music was never meant to be like this: the fire of youth vanquished and an emotive power so effortlessly believable flowing through the lyrics. And then, slicing through the pitch black like a shard of glass, there's the blinding white light of sound that cuts straight to the heart.

The darkness of' 'Atmosphere' rippled out across post punk Britain, a clash of light and dark which filtered slowly into the consciousness of others, not least The Cure's 1989 masterpiece, *Disintegration*, which offers a reflection of 'Atmosphere' in varying degrees of grey on practically every sweet song. *Faith*, The Cure's morose 1981 epic, would arguably side even closer.

'Atmosphere' is really in a genre all of its own, settling eternally into the more solemn fringes of goth rather than the cartoon version which gathers in knots of teenage angst in new Millenium shopping malls. 'Atmosphere' would travel to less obvious shores, too. Pick up any copy of the 'outsider music' magazine *The Wire* and discover a thousand sub-genres with their roots dangling in that very same moment. It was a moment that came largely from Ian Curtis, too. All the other elements, the Hannett technique, the savage swathe of that synth, the velvety sheen, *all* those elements simply exist to bring you closer to Ian Curtis. He was and remains a most shockingly believable singer, touching the very places you choose to ignore.

'Atmosphere' was originally titled 'Chance' and previously aired in a Piccadilly Radio session where its John Cale-esque hollowness was easily eclipsed by the new recording. It was unquestionably the finest piece of music to emerge from Rochdale's Cargo Studios and probably the finest piece of music to emerge from Rochdale. It would almost certainly have provided Joy Division with their initial hit record – if, indeed, hit record be the point – had it been ushered into the world via a more traditional format. As it was, the somewhat secretive arrival of 'Atmosphere', elegantly cloaked in the gatefold sleeve, seemed perfectly fitting, as did the panegyric text by Jean-Pierre Turmel and the lush painting by Jean-Francois Jamoul and Anton Corbijn photograph. Could there have been a more gloriously mysterious method of announcing the band's arrival on the European stage? Even if Factory didn't reap immediate proceeds, they were intelligent enough to adopt an unusually holistic view.

Of course, 'Atmosphere' wasn't alone. As Rob Gretton stated elsewhere, it was married to 'Dead Souls' and this would remain his favourite Joy Division song, not least because it so effectively highlighted the growing resonance of the Curtis voice. 'Dead Souls' would, in later years, become overshadowed by 'Atmosphere' and yet, at the moment of release, it demonstrated just how far band and producer had travelled.

Just 1,578 copies of 'Atmosphere' were pressed, many of them mailed to freebie-grasping journos and friends. Of course, the entire Sordide Sentimentale affair was a marketing disaster from day one, effectively restricting the band's new emotive power to all but their core following. In the short term this did them no favours at all but in the long term it guaranteed that the record would become exceedingly collectable and the whole affair added immensely to the myth of Joy Division in years to come.

Lindsay Reade remembers how the rarity of this record automatically increased its value on the spot, unlike 'Transmission': "There seemed to be hundreds of the 'Transmission' 'exploding nebula' singles knocking about – they were virtually being given away," she says. "Hence, 'anti-marketing' might be viewed as quite an effective marketing strategy."

On November 26, with 'Atmosphere'/'Dead Souls' quietly awaiting release – it would eventually surface in March 1980 – Joy Division returned to the BBC's Maida Vale Studios to record their second John Peel session, which was broadcast on December 10. This offered a chance for the band to 'loosen off' and ease their way into four songs that would, presumably, form the basis of their second album. Meanwhile, *Unknown Pleasures* was continuing to sell in healthy amounts.

The four chosen songs had all been allowed to develop naturally during the Buzzcocks tour. Indeed, one of the advantages of incessant touring was the opportunity to rehearse new material and, more than that, test them out on eager audiences. As such, many Joy Division devotees were already familiar with the quartet of glorious songs they unleashed for Peel: 'Sound Of Music', 'Twenty Four Hours', 'Love Will Tear Us Apart' and 'Colony'. Despite the comparatively watery sound, the session reflected a distinct change in direction for the band, especially on 'Love Will Tear Us Apart'. Its force would take some time to develop but at Maida Vale Ian Curtis laid down an angst-laden vocal which sat temptingly over a delicious – soon-to-be-classic – rising keyboard melody and thumping, exotic bass.

To outsiders, the future of Joy Division seemed blindingly bright. To Ian Curtis, coiled inside his own increasingly personal lyrics, it appeared rather more uncertain.

On December 18, 1979, Joy Division set off on their second European trip, this time to Paris. Les Bains Douches (meaning literally 'the bath showers') was a stylish swimming baths in Paris that had re-opened as a nightclub. It is believed that this was the opening night[1]. Some of the smaller plunge pools still contained water and people could be seen playing noughts and crosses with giant sticks in one of them. Joy Division were the main act. There would have been a support but no one can remember who they were, least of all Terry Mason whose main concern was buying sufficient duty-free booze to keep everyone happy not just on this trip but also over Christmas. Ian was evidently getting a taste for vodka. "None of us really liked drinking, we just liked being drunk," he says. "Vodka was a popular spirit because mixed with orange juice it didn't taste of anything other than orange juice."

In France and elsewhere, the band had no money, almost to a man. Ian Curtis, with a wife and child, was more aware of it than anyone as £35 a week didn't go very far, even in those days. For this reason the group took on various jobs to earn a bit of extra pin money, including menial work gluing album sleeves for other Factory acts. One such extra-curricular activity occurred in Alan Erasmus' first floor flat in Palatine Road, Didsbury, which had fast evolved into the headquarters of the up-and-coming Factory Records. Vini Reilly had recorded his first album, *The Return Of The Durutti Column*, with Factory's now in-house producer, Martin Hannett, and the record sleeve design was very simple – a sheet of sandpaper. This had to be glued onto a white cover and the joke was that when you put it in with your other LPs it ruined your other record covers. Joy Division went along for a day's gluing session and were provided with a porn video to keep them amused during the monotonous chore.

[1] Les Bains Douches became one of the top clubs in France and is still running today. In the late eighties, a branch of Bains Douches was opened in Los Angeles.

Tony Wilson remembered that when he walked in at the end of his working day, probably when he had finished *Granada Reports* around 7pm, he saw Ian standing behind the desk sticking the sleeves together while the others were all sitting on a sofa watching the video. Tony thought it funny that there was this white glue all over the place and had an idea it would make a good scene for a film. His impression was that since his need was the greatest Ian was doing all the work so that he could earn all the money. Terry Mason was there all day too, however, and he saw the situation rather differently. "We all did sandpapering," he recalls. "Barney was more taken by the porn. But Ian was easily swayed by Barney into not doing any work and watching it as well. I think if there was a check of whose hands were the reddest it'd be me, Hooky and Twinny. It was a bastard of a job. I'm not sure if Barney nicked the video. Probably didn't do him any good cos none of us had video players. The VCR was Alan's latest toy. He'd got one of those Granada ancient top-loaders – it was dead loud and cranky. Its remote was on the end of a wire that was less then a metre long so you still had to sit near the TV with it. But at the time it was real high tech."

Terry said they had been led to believe they were doing piece work but in reality they all got paid the same – £5. For some reason, they didn't receive their payment until April 1980. Perhaps it was postponed until some money came in from the release of the Durutti Column album in late 1979, or it might have been simply because, as Terry says: "Tony never had the cash on him." Tony handed it over to them after the gig at the Moonlight in London. He'd got hold of some cash that night.

After *The Return Of The Durutti Column* was released, Vini remembers Ian chatting to him at a gig where they played together. "Ian came up to me and just said that he really loved the album and thought it was very unusual and really beautiful. He used language that young guys in a band don't use. The way he spoke and the way he expressed things was very realistic and truthful. Lots of guys would say 'Oh that's really soppy', or they'd be uptight about using words like beautiful. But Ian actually used the word beautiful. I thought this was a very unusual guy. There was a real understanding. There were no barriers at all. He was someone I could speak to. I didn't have to put an act on for him or be macho. It was very nice and open."

The last Joy Division gig of 1979 was the Factory party on New Year's Eve, in a warehouse over a smaller city centre Woolworth's in Manchester's Oldham Street. Not to be confused with the big Woolworth's facing Piccadilly Gardens (which was burnt down), this smaller branch had closed down (perhaps because they didn't need two so near to each other) and later opened as an Argos store. Tickets were by invitation only. It was Tony

Wilson's idea to stage this party, though any hopes he had of running a pay bar were dashed because there was no liquor license, hence the bar was free. The members of Joy Division gratefully accepted per diem money as if they were on the road but after receiving their £5 each they went straight to Yates and hit the 'All Ins' – drinks made from a measure of sweet Australian wine, hot water, lemon and sugar, now called blobs. They were pretty drunk by the time they got back to party but if it hadn't been for this party they would have had nowhere to go on New Year's Eve.

Vini Reilly can recall a warehouse event to which few people were invited, which was most likely this same party. "I think it was Tony's idea," he says. "It was some kind of a party thrash and there were instruments and amplifiers lying around. Tony really wanted me and Hooky to play bass and someone else to play drums. He wanted some kind of jam session. I went to Hooky and said to him 'Shall we jam?' Hooky turned round very scornfully and said "What's jam?" He was really off with me. Ian immediately stepped in and said something quite reassuring to me and just chilled me out – because he could see I was quite insulted really. Hooky was being a bit awkward with me. Ian was very nice to me. The jam didn't happen anyway."

Terry remembers: "Ian was trying to snog someone – a girlfriend of either ACR or The Distractions – even though Debbie was in the same building, if not room. The guy in question got pissed off, and Rob sent me in to sort it out. I was smoking a cigar 'cos it's new year. This kid takes a swing at Ian, I move in and get punched on the end of the cigar and it was just like in a cartoon – I look like a cartoon character with shreds of cigar spread across my face like a starfish. Next thing I know I'm throwing up in Piccadilly Gardens and resolve not to drink until Easter."

Terry actually kept his resolve and, despite arduous touring with the group in the New Year, nothing alcoholic passed his lips until the following Easter. This perhaps gives some indication of the state of intoxication all the band were in that night but it was a familiar picture everywhere in Manchester on New Year's Eve. Sadly, this particular New Year's Eve was to be Ian's last.

CHAPTER 15

Destinations Always Change

"He was a very kind man, very polite, very soft spoken. That's why I didn't recognise him at all in that movie [24 Hour Party People] where he was speaking crudely and roughly and saying 'fucking' words." – Annik

Annik Honoré and her mother spent Christmas 1979 on holiday in Tunisia, staying for three weeks. Annik hoped that the distance placed between her and Ian might help strengthen her resolve not to let their feelings for one another develop any further, but she couldn't help her enthusiasm for the band and this was drawing her closer rather that away from her new love. Trying to forget Ian was, in her own words, "useless and a waste of time". And clearly he was not willing to let her go.

Annik's letter to Carole continued: "He rang me again when I got back to London and told me about the European tour. It would have been easier maybe if he had not been in Joy Division but they were/are my favourite band and I just wanted to go to Holland to see them play and also in Belgium. It is the way I am – when I like/love something, I would travel for miles to see it – so I had to go to Europe to see them play. And of course, it all started again over there on January 11 in Amsterdam. He came to me again. Explaining how stupid it was to run away from each other when it was impossible not to love each other, that it didn't matter if he was married or not. And since that night we were lovers for ever. Six wonderful days in Europe. Six days together all the time."

Warsaw – Peter Hook on bass, Ian Curtis on vocals, Steve Brotherdale on drums and Bernard Sumner on guitar - knocking on the door of Manchester punk, June 30, 1977, at Rafters. *(Kevin Cummins/Idols)*

Steve Brotherdale: early occupier of drumming hot seat. *(Kevin Cummins/Idols)*

Hooky, "a bassist who could eat Jean Jacques Burnel for breakfast", according to *Sounds. (Kevin Cummins/Idols)*

Peter Saville, Tony Wilson and Alan Erasmus pose outside The Russell Club for a *Sounds* feature, June 15, 1978. *(Kevin Cummins/Idols)*

Future Joy Division manager Rob Gretton, pictured here in his days as a Rafters DJ, mixing reggae, soul and punk. *(Kevin Cummins/Idols)*

Kevin Cummins: "They were really good to photograph. Ian was tremendously photogenic, actually." Joy Division in Hulme, January 6, 1979. *(Kevin Cummins/Idols)*

Ian in Central Sound Studios,
January 6, 1979. *(Kevin Cummins/Idols)*

Bowden Vale Youth Club, March 14, 1979. Martin O'Neill: "Ian came to the fore and suddenly started to dance in this extraordinary manner. I mean I just thought 'What the fuck are you doing, man? Mind me fucking camera, won't you!' I had never seen anything like it in my life." *(Martin O'Neill Photography)*

Ian with his daughter Natalie, 1979.

Joy Division producer Martin Hannett, a genius of the mixing desk.
(Kevin Cummins/Idols)

Ian on stage at The Factory Club,
July 13, 1979. *(Kevin Cummins/Idols)*

Ian at the Stuff the Superstars Festival
at the Mayflower Club, Gorton,
July 28, 1979. *(Paul Slattery)*

Joy Division photographed in Stockport after an 'edgy' encounter with
the music press, July 28, 1979. *(Paul Slattery)*

JD in London to play at the YMCA
on August 2, 1979. *(LFI)*

Annik's use of the word 'lovers' ought not to be misconstrued as literal. She said many years later: "I was afraid to make love with Ian because it had never happened to me before whereas he had, especially being married, and it seemed like we were not on equal terms. Then again it never seemed to be a problem as we had a very full relationship in terms of feelings and devotion and holding each other and staring into each other's eyes felt so strong."

In retrospect, Annik considers that the time they spent together on Joy Division's 1980 European tour – a matter of days, really – was the time that she and Ian really began to get to know one another.

Before the group set off for Europe they returned to Pennine Studios, Oldham on January 7 and 8. It was their hope to find a new single and because they'd only recently recorded 'Sound Of Music' and 'Love Will Tear Us Apart' for the John Peel session, they set about re-recording them to a greater level of intensity, together with another song called 'These Days'. There was little doubt in the band's collective mind that 'Love Will Tear Us Apart' was the dominant track and a dead cert for the next single. That stated, the Pennine recording of the song lacked the necessary resonance and was treated as little more than an exploratory demo. This version would surface next to 'These Days' on the B-side of the 12-inch 'Love Will Tear Us Apart' and later on *Still*.

Although all four members of the band were completely impoverished on New Year's Eve, some fairly meagre funds were made available to them for the forthcoming European tour. Terry: "On the run up to [the European tour] you picked up £5, the statutory per diem money. You could get quite a lot. Wages were being paid as well." Ian's pay was increased to £50 a week from Christmas 1979, largely because of his extra responsibilities with a wife and child, and also, as Terry adds: "And, well, he was the genius behind the band". The others were still receiving £35 which would remain in place until May 4, 1980, when it was increased to £50[1].

On January 10 the group and crew caught the overnight ferry from Hull which left at around 9pm and arrived in Rotterdam at 6am the following day. There were two vehicles: a rented minibus for the band with the crew driving a three-ton truck that the group had paid to be fitted with a tachograph. This regulated how many hours the truck was in motion and freed the drivers from having to fill out a log[2]. The PA and

---

[1] Terry Mason noted these figures in his diary at the time.
[2] It was not permitted to drive more than 10 hours in any one day.

truck was owned by Harry DeMac whose company PSL – Peak Sound & Light – was based in Hazel Grove. Tony Wilson had first contracted Harry's PA services for Joy Division's Leeds Roots Club gig on July 27, 1978, and PSL had gone on to provide most of the PAs at the Russell Club. Rob Gretton now decided Joy Division deserved a decent PA on this European tour as until now their PAs were makeshift affairs involving Ian's columns, speakers and PA amp or speakers borrowed from Gillian Gilbert's sister who was in a band. This arrangement began even before Stephen Morris and Gillian became partners.

On board ship, Terry was probably the only one who actually retired to his cabin. "I was pissed off, I'd just been sacked," he says. He'd been told on the boat by Harry DeMac that the band didn't want him to do the mixing any more (although he did, in fact, carry on throughout the European tour).

The rest of the band and crew stayed up drinking duty free booze, so much so that Harry was in no state to drive the truck at 6am in the morning (he'd been drinking whisky, whereas the others were mainly on lager). After clearing customs with the *carnet de baggage*[1] Terry drove behind the minibus, probably driven by Hooky, and remembers their arrival in Amsterdam: "We were driving round looking for the Paradiso. To us it was the biggest thing there, forget Ann Frank's house, forget the Reichs museum. All we'd known was the Paradiso because The Doors had played there. Ian was made up by that. Our first gig on a European tour was at a venue famous for Jim Morrison having been there. We were expecting the Paradiso to be a fantastic place but it turned out to be a shit hole of an ex-church. It was the only European gig we'd actually heard of. With it being Holland it had its own little coffee shop there so Rob and Steve were off. It was bitterly cold. Because we're in Amsterdam we have to go and walk round the red light district after we've done the gig and got the truck back to the hotel. Also more coffee shops because Rob just loved dope. It had been snowing and there was ice all over the place. Ian (and Annik) stayed behind."

It wasn't far to drive to the next day's gig and so everyone stayed in bed late before they headed off to the Trojan Horse at Den Haag, one of several local council funded venues in Holland. Terry: "The little league rock and roll hotel we stayed at was quite good. The guys running it were used to having bands stay there and they were cool about them staying up and when it got too late the owner just left us to the bar and said they'd charge us the next day. It was quite cool; they also made us breakfast whenever we

---

[1] A list of every piece of equipment.

wanted it the next day. It was freezing. I think we had to bump start the truck on that Sunday, it was that cold. Rob was at his most annoying on this tour, he was in his element, loaded up on lager and dope, he'd spend the nights just going around the room telling everyone what their faults were – Rob himself having no faults at all!"

Paul Morley saw this aspect of Rob's personality as part of his role: "I think he was the one the band looked to first of all to see that he believed in it. He was such a sort of blunt guy – if he went for something and decided that you'd done a good job, then you really must have done because he was very hard to pierce really. If you got enthusiasm from him and got kind of love from him, then you must be doing something. It was almost like he was their first layer of true criticism."

On January 13, Joy Division played at the Doornrood in Nijmegen, a Dutch town where three rivers, the Rhine, Maas and Waal, converged and where there were several bridges, one which featured in the 1977 war film *A Bridge Too Far*. Fortunately, Nijmegen was not too far from Den Haag in the south of Holland, and comprised only a short journey east. It was another council run affair and it was here, or so Terry believes, that Rob left his case containing all their money behind at the gig. After wandering off, they had to go back for it.

All the clubs on this tour were smaller than those the band had now become accustomed to playing in England. The capacity at most of them was between 350 and 500. Terry: "It was a bit like going back to a different level that we'd grown out of in a way – in London and Manchester we were good for 1,500 people. It was also weird because over there the vast majority of the audience wouldn't be punks. In Holland we'd got hippies with long hair and all sorts."

On January 14 the group drove into Belgium to play the King Kong in Antwerp. The hotels on the tour were organized, as part of the whole deal, by the local promoter and this particular gig was in a rough part of town. The promoter at this show knew that the group wouldn't get out of the venue until late and so, to save money, booked them into the local whore house. This meant that they couldn't check in until the brothel closed at 4 am as most of the rooms were in use until then. "The brothel had UV lights and portraits of topless women, speakers by the pillars and pubic hair on the pillows," says Terry.

Ian and Annik wanted to get away earlier than 4am and so Ian took the keys of the minibus to remove their bags and in doing so also removed Terry's bag which he accidentally left on the pavement from where it was stolen. Terry was left with only the clothes he was wearing until they got to

Rotterdam where Rob gave him £35 to buy some new clothes and a new bag. At that time, incidentally, £35 bought jeans, two shirts, a bag and socks. When Ian was made aware of his mistake the next day he apologized to Terry but, with everyone around, he had to make fun of it.

Annik recalls with a shudder the rooms at the brothel, with their red paint and dim lights. "We were supposed to go and sleep in some kind of hostel for prostitutes and I really didn't like it," she says. "It was horrible, gloomy, with horrible lights and very crude. I didn't feel well there. The band were having a laugh, they thought it was funny to stay in that kind of place but I really didn't feel happy there. Maybe also it made me feel like a prostitute and I wasn't one. Perhaps that's why I disliked it so much."

Annik remembered staying with Ian in Antwerp at the house of the concert promoter. "I remember the night staying at Raf's, the organiser of the concert. It was cold, we had tea and slept on some sofa or I think he gave us his bed."

It was disconcerting for Annik to be the only girl amongst so many young men, on the road, enjoying their freedom. "They were four or five funny lads, having a laugh like boys do at that age all the time," she says. "I was quite fond of them all, mainly Hooky who shared most sympathy for me, even for Rob who kept teasing me all the time. Suddenly the fact that there was a girl was a bit different – it broke up the atmosphere between them. I don't recall them being bad to me – never, no. I was honestly quite discreet. I was not the one to be all over Ian, not having him breathe, far from it. I was just there – watching them soundcheck, listening to them and having something to eat. They had their life as a group, we would go to sleep and then be travelling in the van. Sometimes it was tiring though."

The group had a lengthier drive to reach their next gig at The Basement in Cologne, in Germany, on January 15. This was another venue that was very hard to find – they were looking out for a club but in fact it turned out to be the basement of yet another church. That night Terry met a girl named Sandra Smith who was backpacking around Europe and she became a regular on his guest lists for the next few years.

The following night, on January 16, they were in Rotterdam, the Netherlands' second city, at a venue called Lantaren. Mike Pickering, who was living in Rotterdam as it was the home town of his Dutch partner Gonnie Rietveld[1], met up with Joy Division that night. Terry recalled that

[1] Mike and Gonnie formed the group Quando Quango and released several records on Factory in the Eighties. Subsequently Mike had success as a house DJ at the Hacienda and later enjoyed international mainstream success with the group M People.

Harry Demac picked up a Dutch girl that night who became a source of annoyance to the band and crew by hanging about and getting in everyone's way. "You don't want women about backstage. It's bad karma," he says. Terry was also doubtful about Annik. "At some time in the future Ian and Annik could have been a serious thing and then Annik might have become friends with, say, Sue (Barney's wife) and she'd have asked her what it was like in Europe," he adds, echoing the traditional wisdom of roadies sensitive to the ebb and flow of life on the road.

In this regard it seems Joy Division were no different from travelling musicians from decades past. The opportunity to meet agreeable, free-spirited girls has always been one of the perks of being in a band but such encounters are unlikely to sit well with regular partners back home. As a result, girlfriends and wives have never been popular on the road, not only because they would doubtless restrict the extra-curricular activities of their men but because they might report back on the nature of such activities to partners at home. Bands have imploded for less.

In Rotterdam the group were up nearly all night enjoying themselves with Mike and Gonnie. "It was a relatively posh hotel, probably two stars," recalls Terry. "Because it was Mike's home town he came round and showed us where to go to have breakfast which was like a tram drivers' café where we had the uitsmijters – ham & eggs done in a fancy way."

After a hearty breakfast and refuelling at the tram stop the entourage left for Brussels to play Plan K for the second time, after which Annik had to return to London and her job at the Embassy.

It was a short journey north, just over the border to the southern tip of Holland for the next day's gig at a faceless club called Effenaar in Eindhoven, the home of the massive Philips electronics company. "There was talk of going out to see the bridge (the one in the movie *A Bridge Too Far*) but I don't think we did cos it meant getting up and going out in the cold," says Terry.

The Minni Pops – with Wally Van Middendrop – were supporting, as they did for all the dates in Holland and Belgium. Terry thought that Hooky was trying to set him up with the girl in the band. "Didn't manage it," he admits.

The last gig in Holland, on January 19, was at the far northern tip of the country in a town called Gronigen, at Club Vera. Terry can recall how cold it was, with freezing snow, and how they actually had to climb a hill – probably the only hill in Holland – on the way to Gronigen. "It was a strange place," he says, "with some strange military surplus shops and some strange shoe shops. Three of us bought white shoes, the only colour they had, for about £3, but they were good quality. I was still short of clothes and feeling the cold, so I bought a big military brown leather coat. It could stand up on its own."

The next day's journey east from Gronigen to Berlin was long and arduous – "a bastard of a drive," as Terry put it. This was in the era of cold war Europe, with three transit corridor roads leading from the west, south and north, but the cheerlessness of their surroundings was dispelled somewhat by the extraordinarily low prices they found on the way. "There were some great services there called Intershops," says Terry, "and all they did was sell duty frees at prices you wouldn't believe, because they wanted to get hard currency in because they were all East German marks. We got a load of stuff from there. We were all on big cigars and bottles of everything."

The minibus was able to travel at around 90mph, but the truck could only do 55-60mph maximum. After stopping at the first service station the band in the minibus had no reason to drive so slowly on this long road to Berlin so they left Terry and Harry behind. Vehicles were not allowed off this road corridor which had a ditch alongside it with guards at every turn-off into the fields beyond. Terry: "We're going along and it's snowing when the truck is flagged down by East German police/military with light sticks or flares. We're pulled to one side thinking 'What now?' They made us – because we had a truck – put a toe rope on the back and pull out some East German cars – Trabants – that had come off the road into the ditch. They had guns so they could do whatever they wanted. So even though we'd left fairly early we got into Berlin just after midnight. Fortunately the pension we stayed in was easy to find and it was, near enough, right in the centre of Berlin near the old cathedral. We're in Mark Reeder's town. He'd met up with the band early on."

Mark had taken the band on a tourist circuit of the city and, before the gig the next day – January 21 – he took them over to East Berlin through Checkpoint Charlie. On the Communist side the group bought little badges (DDR) to take back with them. Terry recalls that the minibus got lost on their return because Mark was using a 1940 street map. Unable to find the venue Kant Kino – a venue in a cinema – Terry had someone from the venue come to meet them. Kant Kino is still there today.

Mark Reeder recalls that after this show, Ian discussed palm reading with him. "I remember Ian telling me about Lindsay Reade reading his palm while we were sitting drinking beer in a bar. He told me this with fascination – he was stroking and staring at his life-line – that she had said he was going to live until he was 80. You know, although this sounds really awful, at that moment I simply didn't believe it. I had a kind of flash. It was really weird.

"I'm interested in the subject of the supernatural but I'm a pretty sceptical person when it comes to things like palm reading – and even more so after this incident. Some of my friends and colleagues believe I possess some kind of clairvoyant tendencies, but I don't actually believe in such things and I always try and find some rational explanation for it when it happens. But there was something deep down inside me that said that that wasn't going to happen. At that moment, I just pushed that instant negative thought to the back of my mind, though it was always there. I can tell you it was the first thing I recalled, when I heard that Ian had committed suicide."

Ian wrote to Annik from Berlin on the back of a postcard of the Brandenburg Gate: *MISS YOU VERY MUCH. BERNARD AND I ARE VERY DEPRESSED AT THE MOMENT, THE GIG HERE WAS VERY BAD, WE PLAYED WELL BUT AGAIN THE SOUND WAS JUST NOT GOOD ENOUGH. BERLIN IS A VERY STRANGE CITY, YOU CAN FEEL THE TENSION EVERYWHERE. LAST NIGHT WE WENT TO THE BERLIN WALL AND SAW THE REICHSTAG AND THE BRANDENBURG GATE WHERE THE S.A. ONCE MARCHED THROUGH.*

Of all the members of the band, it seems that Ian had developed his closest relationship with Bernard. Annik: "Ian loved to write his songs and enjoyed the band and especially Barney."

Ian goes on to describe the earlier gigs that Annik had missed: *THE GIG AT EINDHOVEN WAS VERY GOOD ALTHOUGH WE HAD A BIT OF TROUBLE WITH A LOCAL GROUP OF "ROCKABILLY" FANS. GRONIGEN WAS ABOUT AVERAGE.*

In the early hours of the following morning, as soon as the Berlin gig was over, Terry, Harry and his Dutch girlfriend left straight away in order to be sure of catching the ferry home from Rotterdam which departed at 6pm on January 22. It was still freezing cold, and Terry recalls that instead of the usual gritters spraying salt there were trucks with men throwing big blocks of rock salt onto the road. "Moving vehicles then had to try and dodge hitting these things the size of breeze blocks," he says. "The band went to a hotel but I had to allow for the slower speed of the truck plus stop at every border and do the carnet. We got pretty well turned over leaving Berlin and when we got to the other end, crossing the border from east Germany to west, it was 'Was ist dis?' and they'd point to something on the carnet and you'd have to find it for them. So you'd be unloading the truck to show it to them. Then they were always looking to see if you had any bribes, any T-shirts, any stickers."

★　★　★

Shortly after his return from Europe – on January 29 – Ian Curtis sent a long letter to Annik from Barton Street. As always he wrote in capital letters: *THINKING OF YOU CONSTANTLY AND LOOK FORWARD TO SEEING YOU NEXT WEEK[1]. I'VE BEEN WORKING NON-STOP FOR THE PAST SIX HOURS (IT'S NOW 10PM) AND THOUGH I'VE WRITTEN A LOT THERE'S NOT MUCH I CAN USE IN THE WAY OF LYRICS FOR SONGS.*

I'VE BEEN PLAYING LOW *VERY QUIETLY IN THE BACK-GROUND AND THE TRACK 'SOUND AND VISION' SEEMS VERY APT AT THIS MOMENT AS THE ROOM I'M IN IS COMPLETELY BLUE; WALLS, CARPET, SETTEE AND ALL, EXCEPT FOR TWO RED LIGHT FITTINGS ON ONE WALL (THE BULBS ARE WHITE), IT'S THE ONLY ROOM IN THE HOUSE THAT I FEEL COMFORT-ABLE IN. IN FACT THIS AFTERNOON I TOOK MY WORK TO THE LIBRARY AND WORKED THERE FOR A FEW HOURS. IT WAS LIKE BEING BACK AT SCHOOL, WITH THE SILENCE AND A FEW STUDENTS THERE.*

MACCLESFIELD'S A REALLY STRANGE TOWN. SOME PEOPLE SEEM REALLY AWARE OF THINGS, OTHERS (MOST OF THEM) SEEM TO JUST DRIFT ON BY AS IF THEY ARE LIVING IN SOME KIND OF PAST EXISTENCE. WHEN I GO INTO TOWN I ALWAYS SEE SOMEONE I KNOW – EITHER SOMEONE I WENT TO SCHOOL WITH, PEOPLE WHO KNOW ABOUT THE GROUP OR PEOPLE I WORKED WITH IN THE DISABLEMENT RESETTLE-MENT SERVICE. THESE PEOPLE I ALWAYS FEEL REALLY SORRY FOR. ALWAYS AT A TOTAL LOSS WHAT TO DO, AND ALWAYS GLAD TO SEE YOU AND TALK TO YOU. I MET A YOUNG BOY TODAY AND TOOK HIM FOR A DRINK. HE'S BEEN LOOKING FOR WORK FOR YEARS BUT NO-ONE WANTS TO KNOW HIM. I TRIED FOR AGES, I JUST CAN'T STAND THE HOPELESSNESS. I ALWAYS THINK SOMEONE COULD GIVE HIM A CHANCE IF THEY WANTED, YET I CAN'T DO ANYTHING TO HELP HIM AND OTHERS LIKE HIM ANYMORE.

"He was truly the nicest and kindest man I ever met in my life," says Annik. "He had a whole world inside him, a true understanding of mankind. You know how compassionate he felt, especially for the weakest. He opened my eyes on being compassionate; he really opened my heart to others, even to people very different from me."

[1] A reference to the University College, London, gig on February 8.

The letter offers a glimpse of how Ian was maybe beginning to tire of the shallow nature of the music business. If only fleetingly, he seems to be looking back at his job with a sense of loss. At the employment exchange, in his role as a disablement resettlement officer, there was an opportunity to help people like this young lad. Ian had an empathy that in some ways may have been his undoing. He cared. Perhaps he cared too much.

Annik: "He felt a lot for others, for people who were poor or who didn't have a very interesting life or interesting job. He really felt for them. He was a very kind man, very polite, very soft spoken. That's why I didn't recognise him at all in that movie [*24 Hour Party People*] where he was speaking crudely and roughly and saying 'fucking' words. I think maybe when he was drunk – he would be acting in an extreme position – that I could well believe. Otherwise, I always saw him speak nicely to the fans and to the people in the hotel. He met a few of my friends at Plan K and he would shake hands very nicely and say hello and smile. Smoking his cigarettes very quietly. I'm really not exaggerating; he was a real nice person. He opened my eyes on feeling for others, to put myself in their place, to feel for the handicapped and the poor. Before him I was more blind."

At the close of this letter, Ian mentions his dog, Candy: *IT'S POURING DOWN WITH RAIN AT THE MOMENT AND I'VE GOT TO TAKE THE DOG FOR A WALK. I GOT SOAKED EARLIER ON TODAY AS I HAD TO BATH HER, SHE GOT HERSELF ABSOLUTELY COVERED IN MUD THIS MORNING CHASING A GREYHOUND. SHE KEEPS LICKING MY HAND AND THEN SITTING BY THE DOOR WITH THE LEAD IN HER MOUTH AND THEN FLICKING IT OVER HER HEAD, SO I'D BEST MAKE A MOVE.*

In his next letter to Annik, dated Sunday, February 17, at 1.15 am, he mentions the dog again: *IT IS VERY QUIET AND LONELY HERE TONIGHT, EVEN THE DOG IS ASLEEP BY THE FIRE.*

In between these two letters Joy Division played two gigs, the first on February 7 at the New Osbourne Club in Manchester. Terry: "Why we were playing another shit hole of a gig there with another ridiculous reason for doing it, I don't know. What sob story had Rob been given this time? You could see there was going to be trouble. The truck got broken into but we were in the gig so there was nothing in it."

The New Osbourne Club was just around the corner from the site of the Electric Circus and enjoyed the same level of decrepitude. The gig was intended as a benefit for *City Fun* fanzine. Rob Gretton had shown considerable interest in the 'zine and had attended a number of recent editorial meetings alongside Liz Naylor, Cath Carroll, Bob Dickinson, Jon Savage and Mick Middles. For some time he had been promising that Joy Division would play a gig to help support *City Fun*.

Unfortunately, despite a reasonable attendance, it was an evening of edginess, uncertainty and a muted performance from the headlining act. The truck wasn't the only vehicle to be broken into on that night. As the crowd crushed through the entrance, photographer Kevin Cummins could be seen hurrying out, red faced and angry, as his vehicle too had suffered from a smashed window. In short, the vibes were bad, despite the fact that many people claimed to have seen Iggy Pop in attendance, the blond leader of the Stooges having performed earlier that night elsewhere in Manchester.

Section 25 and A Certain Ratio supported Joy Division and both bands showed more enthusiasm than the curiously lacklustre main act. It could have been simple fatigue, which would have been understandable. It could have been the general dampening of spirits among a gang who still had heads in their European adventure. But it was also an evening that saw a detached Ian Curtis, for once reluctant to dance, fronting the band with little sense of performance.

Even die-hard Mancunian Joy Division fanatics noticed that something was amiss. Something just didn't feel right. They eventually filed out into an unwelcoming North Manchester night, feeling slightly deflated.

The next day everyone drove down to London for the gig at the University of London Union (ULU). Terry believes this was the one gig when Martin Hannett did the mixing: "[It was] the only one," he says. "We put an extra PA in the back of the hall and fed effects through it – not the standard sound coming off the stage but treated sound."

Terry also noticed what the fans were wearing. "Over the past few months there seemed to be a lot more kids turning up wearing macs," he says. "At this one three or four people had gone a step further and were wearing green macs with green tights, like the TV version of Robin Hood. It was a sign of how the fans were beginning to shape some of the legend as well. First of all they start aping what Ian was wearing and then they start going off and having their own version of it."

Paul Morley attended this show and wrote a review for *NME*. "I remember them playing a gig at the London YMCA or somewhere in London," he says. "I lived there and they played this gig and it was the first time I'd ever heard 'Love Will Tear Us Apart'. They played it live. I remember thinking 'Oh my God' – you kind of suddenly realise they were still doing it – whatever kind of chaos was going on. I remember having a drink with Ian afterwards and people often ask, 'What did you say to him? Did you say how great he was?' All the things I would say in print but no – you didn't say it. You just bought him a pint. I remember we were standing in the corridor. It was like a student gig and there were lots of people milling about and there was me and Ian. I wish that I could say … 'And we discussed this.' Do you know what I mean? But we didn't. We probably talked about football, we probably talked about 'When's the record coming out?' What do you pull away? I pull away with him and a pint glass. And a vague thing – isn't it funny he drinks pints? You think of a pint as being a bit gung ho – well I do cos I wasn't a pint drinker. It seemed such a huge volume of liquid for me. I remember Ian with his pint and I would have my vodka or whatever – a dainty drink, and I sometimes think that's why I wanted so much from an interview with him. You'd come away from this great two-hour interview with him but you came away with little half-hearted thoughts and little nervous laughters and we want to be good and we won't sell out. Vague generalisations and it was the same with this conversation which may well have been the last conversation I had with him – I bought him a pint. I remember him drinking it and we didn't say much to each other. I certainly didn't kiss his feet and tell him he was magnificent. And he certainly didn't thank me for giving him any good reviews."

Annik and Ian were able to meet again that night. Letters, phone calls and concerts were to be the main, if not only, points of contact for them in the future. His second long letter to her was actually written on a large post-card, on the front of which was a print of a painting by Cezanne, *Le pont de Mennecy*. Again Ian tells Annik how he has been thinking of her constantly and hopes that she will be able to come down on Wednesday – the date of a Joy Division gig at High Wycombe. He says that he hopes they will be staying in London that night as he would very much like to see Bauhaus – although, in the event, the group drove straight back to Manchester from High Wycombe.

Ian writes: *IF POSSIBLE I'M GOING TO TRY TO GET DOWN TO LONDON MORE OFTEN AS I CAN'T STAND SPENDING LONG PERIODS AWAY FROM YOU AND I THINK THE CHANGE WILL BE GOOD FOR ME.*

As Mark Reeder had observed, Annik was a kind of intellectual or creative sparring partner for Ian. They had films, art, books and music in common, matters in which she retains a huge active interest to this day. Ian's letter of February 17 makes mention of their shared interests: *I SAW* APOCALYPSE NOW *AT THE CINEMA TODAY. I COULDN'T TAKE MY EYES AWAY FROM THE SCREEN. IT WAS AMAZING TO HEAR THE DOORS' 'THE END' USED TO SUCH GOOD EFFECT, ONE*

OF MY FAVOURITE SONGS. WHEN I GOT HOME I COULDN'T STOP PLAYING MY OLD DOORS RECORDS AND ALSO STARTED READING POEMS FROM T. S. ELIOT. I'VE BEEN READING HIS BOOKS EVER SINCE WE STUDIED HIS WORK AT SCHOOL WHEN I WAS SIXTEEN. "THE WASTE LAND" AND OTHERS STILL HAVE A SPECIAL PLACE IN MY HEART.

In his next letter Ian referred back to the European tour, mentioning someone he knew from Amsterdam, called Jeff, who had phoned and told him he'd seen Joy Division on the TV, filmed at Rotterdam (although Ian didn't remember seeing any cameras there). Ian and Annik's shared love of music is apparent in the letter – he asks her how Simple Minds were (who she must have seen in Brussels in February). He goes on: *I HOPE THEY WERE GOOD. I BELIEVE THEY WERE PLAYING WITH THE ONLY ONES, I QUITE LIKE SOME OF THEIR SONGS, ESPECIALLY THE FIRST SINGLE "LOVERS OF TODAY". MARTIN HANNETT HAS PRODUCED SOME TRACKS ON THEIR NEW ALBUM, THEY'RE ONE OF HIS FAVOURITE GROUPS.*

On the back of the Cezanne postcard, Ian's choice of quote foreshadows the future, much as the cover to *Closer* eerily did:

Is it like this
In death's other kingdom
Waking alone
At the hour when we are
Trembling with tenderness
Lips that would kiss
Form prayers to broken stone

(T.S. ELIOT – 1925)

In a short second letter to Carole, Annik wrote that Vini Reilly of Durutti Column wrote a piece of music for Ian because he "felt a lot for him". The title was taken from the above poem, *Lips That Would Kiss*.[1]

---

[1] Annik later sent Ian's parents a 12-inch of this record. The track was produced by Martin Hannett and released on Crepuscule on a compilation *From Brussels With Love* as well as a 12-inch.

CHAPTER 16

Watching Love Grow

"You can never leave your kids and you can never have the woman you're in love with." – Tony Wilson

To those observing them from the outside – and there were many of them – Joy Division's progress seemed like the stuff of dreams. Here was a band at the forefront of post–punk British music, at the peak of their powers, with one critically acclaimed album already under their belt and, guided by the muse of Ian Curtis, an even richer seam of songs as works in progress. The prevailing feeling was that 1980 would be their breakthrough year with a new single and a second album to take the band beyond the spring. The roller-coaster was gaining momentum, just as it should do.

To those observing them from the inside – and there were about a dozen of them – Joy Division's progress wasn't quite as rosy as it seemed on the surface. The songs might have been forthcoming and the gigs were getting bigger but their frontman, the lynchpin on which everything depended, was all too well aware of his own frailty. The fits were getting worse and more frequent, he was torn between his wife and child on the one hand and his new love on the other, and everyone was relying on him to an extent that simply made everything, the pressure, the responsibility, the demands, so much worse with every leap forward. Something had to give.

On February 24, 1980, Joy Division returned to Strawberry for a one-day session to record a 12-inch version of 'She's Lost Control' for release in the US only.

Ian wrote about the session in his next letter to Annik, posted on Monday February 25: *DEAR ANNIK, I LOVE YOU. I FEEL VERY TIRED AT THE MOMENT BUT DO NOT FEEL LIKE SLEEPING. WE DIDN'T FINISH IN THE STUDIO UNTIL NINE O'CLOCK THIS MORNING, IT WAS ABOUT FIVE WHEN I DID THE VOCALS – I HAD TO WRITE A NEW VERSE WHILE I WAS THERE. THE SONG SOUNDS COMPLETELY DIFFERENT FROM THE VERSION ON THE ALBUM. I CAN'T MAKE UP MY MIND WHETHER IT'S BETTER OR NOT, I THINK I'LL HAVE TO LISTEN TO IT A FEW MORE TIMES YET.*

Superficially, Ian's letter seems typical for an average young man in love, sharing his feelings along with the small details of day-to-day life. Except that it was no ordinary life and, despite his youth, his situation deemed that his love for Annik could not be as simple as it appeared. He continued: *THERE SEEMS TO BE A FINAL REALISATION OF THE WAY THINGS ARE GOING AT HOME NOW. EVEN THOUGH, AS I'VE EXPLAINED (OR TRIED TO) TO YOU, IT'S BEEN LIKE THIS FOR WELL OVER A YEAR, WE'VE TALKED MORE OPENLY, AND I HAVE THIS HORRIBLE FEELING, A TOTAL NUMBNESS THAT I CAN'T REALLY DESCRIBE, A FEELING I'VE HAD AT OTHER POINTS OF MY LIFE WHEN THERE WAS CONFUSION ABOUT WHICH WAY TO GO, A KIND OF JOURNEY TO AN UNKNOWN DESTINATION, THOUGH THIS TIME I FEEL I'M BEING PUSHED TOWARDS A PATH I CAN SEE LOOMING OVER THE DISTANCE. ANYWAY ENOUGH OF THIS, FATE WILL TAKE ITS COURSE IN DUE TIME.*

Ian's confusion would stay with him to the end of his days, and went to the core of his being. The nature of this confusion was not so much 'I don't know the way to go', as much as 'I don't know but I should know or I need to know the way to go'. 'I don't know' is not, of itself, necessarily a bad thing, but with confusion there is a pressure that one ought to know.

This dichotomy – or split – is something to which many parents, especially fathers, may relate. Tony Wilson had two children with his second wife and experienced similar torment to Ian as this relationship disintegrated. "I have had the experience of being in a marriage that didn't have love or passion in it and that was on both sides," he says. "We married out of convenience and had children whom we adored. We were living neither happily nor unhappily – it was a friendship – but suddenly the moment came when I fell properly in love with someone else, Yvette, and I realised that I could never leave the marriage because it would mean leaving the kids. But I could also not live without Yvette. Therefore I had to leave. But I couldn't leave. I could never leave because of the kids. So suddenly you get this thing where there are two complete opposites which are both absolute. You can never leave your kids and you can't leave the woman you're in love with."

There were other pressures on Ian. His sleep pattern was disrupted and a tiring schedule was taking its toll on his health and increasing the likelihood of further fits. Joy Division played High Wycombe Town Hall on February 20, a 250-plus mile round trip, with Killing Joke supporting. The group journeyed down during the day and drove back that same night, leaving in the early hours.

On February 28 the group played The Warehouse in Preston with Section 25 again supporting. This gig proved something of a shambolic affair; a dozen songs performed while hovering on the edge of power and equipment failure. The opening three numbers – 'Incubation', 'Wilderness' and the fast improving 'Twenty Four Hours' – were played in the face of mounting technical problems which came to a head at the conclusion of the fourth song, 'The Eternal', which disintegrated into an embarrassed silence, leaving Ian to declare: "I would like to apologise… for everything…" Then he muttered something along the lines of "… allow the band to play around a bit…" and for a few edgy moments the most promising new band in Britain lapsed into a disharmonious tune-up against a background of shuffles and shouts from the audience.

Mercifully, the disintegrating atmosphere was repaired by a transcendent moment. The gremlins apparently banished, Ian ushered Joy Division into a gorgeous, lilting version of 'Heart And Soul', one of the more difficult vocal challenges in the Joy Division repertoire. It was the first time it had ever been performed to an audience.

Ian had written about this song to Annik in his letter of February 25: *AT THE MOMENT I'M JUST LEARNING THE WORDS TO A NEW SONG 'HEART & SOUL' WHICH HOPEFULLY WE'LL PLAY ON FRIDAY, IF ALL GOES WELL IN REHEARSAL TOMORROW.*

He was actually referring to a gig in London the following night, when he and Annik would next meet. Meanwhile, the Preston gig was salvaged by the new song and the evening concluded with an almost punkish 'She's Lost Control'[1].

---

[1] This show was released on the 1999 bootleg, *The Fractured Music Archive Volume 1, Preston 28 February 1980*. In 1988 Pete Hook referred to the gig as "… one of our very, very worst nights."

"[It was] shit – it had a tiny, postage stamp stage and next to no power," says Terry Mason of the Preston gig. In the absence of a dressing room, the group were given the use of the kitchen with one comfy chair. Problems and awful surroundings notwithstanding, Joy Division were still able to have a laugh. Terry: "We knew Rob would make sure that he'd get the comfy chair so we stacked it onto coke cans so you'd not notice. He came in, flops himself down and, of course, fell over. The cans collapsed underneath him."

One of Section 25's mates took up a challenge to eat a mountain of butter. "Bet you a fiver you can't eat all that butter, we said," says Terry. "This guy did it and then he pointed out, 'Oh that was easy' and said he'd become addicted to evaporated milk, that every day he was drinking pints of Nestles condensed milk – that made us feel a bit sick."

At this point in their evolution, Joy Division was able to command in the region of £500 just about anywhere they played. It seems, however, that to add to their frustrations at Preston Rob Gretton had not struck such a good deal and the promoter refused to pay any more than £150. This was despite the fact that his club was packed solid full of people all paying £5 a head or thereabouts. Terry: "Anyone sensible would want to make sure you come back in a couple of months' time but this guy was unflinching. Ian was really pissed off about money that night. It was like this guy was taking the piss out of us. So we stole frozen chickens out of a freezer. We all went home with chickens but Ian took two because he was more pissed off than anyone else."

With Ian having cause to be in a bad frame of mind after that night, Alan Wise, who has suffered from neurological driven 'Petit Mal' throughout his life, thinks this might have increased the likelihood of an attack in the near future. "Depression is more likely before a fit," he says. "The attack causes a fast release of energy in the brain and the mood is then generally lifted".

The band arrived back from Preston quite late and were up early for the long drive to London the next day. Steve used to pick everyone up – and would collect Ian first – so these two, starting out from Macclesfield and heading in the wrong direction for the first leg of the journey, always had a longer day when the group ventured south.

The London show, Joy Division's biggest gig to date, was at the Lyceum on The Strand. Perhaps it was the long drive or perhaps it was something to do with the frustrations of the previous night, but Ian had a grand mal epileptic fit that began on stage. Terry: "He also had the pressure of Annik being there – in the sense that he had to be 'Ian with Annik' as well as 'Ian with the band.'" Larry Cassidy of Section 25 noticed at several gigs, however: "Ian seemed twitchy in the dressing room. He was quite nervous. Annik had a good effect on him."

It is likely that the rapidly escalating success of the group was placing additional stress on Ian. The Lyceum in London was considerably more prestigious and bigger than the Electric Ballroom where they'd last played in the capital. It had just opened after a refurbishment and was now a seated theatre, situated close to Covent Garden where The Strand meets The Aldwych. The music press was out in force that night. The pressure was on. Perhaps Ian's concern following the problems experienced the night before, coupled with his constant fear of a recurrence of an epileptic fit was, in itself, a trigger.

Tony Wilson remembered this night well. "I was side stage," he says. "Normally I'm not, normally I'm on the mixing desk, watching Rob work, but I was side stage that night and again, the whole thing you think it's a great performance but you see Ian getting slightly more manic than ever and you see the other members of the group look at each other and looking at Ian and taking their minds off performing and beginning to concentrate on Ian cos they know it's about to go off and you can see Terry begin to get ready. At the end of a song Ian would slump against a mike and Terry would run on and drag him off. I then helped Terry – we dragged him to the side and then there were these typical stone stairs going up and up into the roof of the theatre. So we took him up three or four flights of stairs to get away from everybody into the dark and we're just holding him. The reason I remember it so well is that John Curd was the promoter and he was one of the toughest men in the music industry. He came round this corner hearing this noise and says, 'What the fuck's going on?' and he saw me and Terry and our lead singer and John Curd went white and he said, 'Oh sorry' and just vanished. I've never seen a grown man more scared in all my life."

Terry recalls: "It had been a shit night all round. The promoters didn't sort out a parking permit and so the Luton van was towed by the police. I had to spend most of early evening getting over to Elephant & Castle to get the truck out of the pound."

The only gig Joy Division played in March was on the 5th at Trinity Hall, Bristol. This was a Community venue that Terry describes as: "The equivalent of the Russell Club, an Afro-Caribbean club, but that night the crowd were mainly students. The chairman of the club wanted to introduce the band to the crowd which was fine."

Terry remembers that at the end of the set the MC had mistakenly thought the group wanted to 'milk' the applause before they would go back on stage – but the real problem was that Ian had yet another fit. Again, it occurred towards the end of his performance on stage, but now it had happened at two gigs in a row.

Annik was there that night and kept Ian's set list. Underneath she wrote 'Fit. Ian My Love'.

Ian also had a fit at home around this time, as he described on some postcards he sent to Annik the day after the Bristol gig: *THE ATTACKS OF EPILEPSY ARE BEGINNING TO FRIGHTEN ME, ESPECIALLY MONDAY NIGHT WHEN I CRASHED INTO THE GLASS DOOR. WHEN I AWOKE I WAS COVERED IN GLASS & STARED AT THE JAGGED PIECES STILL STUCK IN THE DOOR. SOMETIMES I'M AFRAID TO GO OUT SOMEWHERE AT NIGHT FOR FEAR OF HAVING A FIT IN A CLUB OR CINEMA. I GET MORE NERVOUS WHEN WE PLAY NOW FOR FEAR OF IT HAPPENING, IT SEEMS MORE FREQUENT. I DON'T THINK I COULD SET FOOT ON STAGE AGAIN IF I EVER HAD A FULL STAGE ATTACK WHILE PLAYING. IT GETS MORE WORRYING WHAT WITH THE AMERICAN TOUR AND LOTS OF OTHER DATES COMING UP. I KEEP THINKING THAT SOMEDAY THINGS WILL BE SO INTENSE THAT I'LL NO LONGER BE ABLE TO CARRY ON.*

The embarrassment and shame he felt was overwhelming. Ian must have believed the prognosis for his illness was poor and that his career was threatened, however promising it looked to the world outside his immediate circle. Privately, he was beginning to cast serious doubts over his future with Joy Division.

Annik: "He was very, very scared of getting sicker. Of not being cured and getting so sick he wouldn't be able to look after himself and of being an embarrassment."[1]

On March 12, Ian wrote to Annik: *I HAVE A FEELING THE EPILEPTIC CONDITION WILL WORSEN. IT FRIGHTENS ME. IT IS A LIE TO SAY 'I'M NOT AFRAID ANYMORE'. THERE IS NOTHING THE DOCTORS CAN DO BUT TRY TABLETS. THEY'VE TRIED SO MANY DIFFERENT COMBINATIONS. I'VE HAD ALL THE TESTS THEY CAN GIVE ME, BRAIN SCANS, ELECTRO-ENCEPHLAGRAMS AND THEY KNOW WHERE THE TROUBLE IS – FRONT LEFT OF TEMPORAL LOBE. BUT AS WITH MANY CASES THERE IS STILL NO OBVIOUS CAUSE. I STILL HAVEN'T*

---

[1] Matt Greenhalgh, the screenplay writer for the movie *Control*, watched a video from the National Society for Epilepsy which showed a film to an epileptic of himself having a fit and the young man wept openly.

TOTALLY ACCEPTED IT. I FEEL IT MORE AS I USED TO WORK WITH PEOPLE WHO HAD EPILEPSY (AMONG OTHERS) AND EVERY MONTH USED TO VISIT THE DAVID LEWIS CENTRE AS PART OF MY JOB. ALL THE VERY BAD CASES ARE THERE FOR TREATMENT OR JUST TO BE LOOKED AFTER. IT LEFT TERRIBLE PICTURES IN MY MIND – YOUNG BOYS AND GIRLS WEARING SPECIAL HELMETS AND PADS ON THEIR ELBOWS AND KNEES TO STOP THEM HURTING THEMSELVES WHEN THEY FELL. SUCH LOVELY PEOPLE IN SUCH A DESPERATE SIT-UATION.

I FELT I HAD TO TELL YOU THIS EVEN THOUGH IT MAY CHANGE YOUR FEELINGS FOR ME, I LOVE YOU SO MUCH AND DON'T WANT TO LOSE YOU, YET I FELT I MUST TELL YOU WHAT THIS CONDITION AT ITS WORST CAN DO.

He adds, on a note of hope but almost as an afterthought: *ON THE OTHER HAND THE FITS CAN SUDDENLY DISAPPEAR NEVER TO RETURN.*

Annik was witness to three or four fits which all took place at concerts, as well as one in a recording studio. Of all the references in Debbie's book to Annik, the one she found most distressing was the suggestion that she did not care when Ian had a fit and even rejected him because of it. This is entirely out of character for Annik. Ian himself refers to the comfort she brought him after a fit when he wrote to her about his health concerns the day after the Bristol gig: *THOUGH IT EMBARRASSES ME WHEN PEOPLE ARE THERE WHEN IT HAPPENS AND I FEEL BITTER AND AFRAID, I WAS GLAD YOU WERE THERE. I AWOKE TO SEE YOUR FACE AND FELT A LOT CALMER AND REASSURED. YOU HAVE THIS EFFECT ON ME. EVEN ROB SAYS YOU WERE GOOD FOR ME IN EUROPE. HAVING THIS AFFECT ON ME AND TAKING THE EDGINESS AWAY.*

Annik: "There is a limit to how much one can witness someone else baring their soul and seeing their utmost intimacy. When Ian had a fit it is true I felt like a 'voyeur' if I was getting too close and felt the band (and Rob and roadies) just wanted to cope with it themselves. I felt helpless maybe. You needed to be strong to be able to carry Ian. What was only prudency and shyness was misinterpreted for aloofness."

Annik was born under the sign of Libra, an air sign and she spoke more than once of the need for space, air to breathe. To respect this need in others is second nature to her. At the close of the many Joy Division gigs she attended Annik was never inclined to rush backstage immediately, as some are wont to do, but rather to hang back in the auditorium until she felt an appropriate amount of time had elasped. In fact she felt far from aloof: "I felt I loved him more than ever because he was utterly lost when it would take place. He looked in a panic and complete mental disorder and my blood would rise and turn for me to be near him and make sure he would not hurt himself and would try to take his pain away.

"When it happened he looked 'supernatural', just like he had some special vision and was taken above us. He was kind of glowing and was literally rising from the ground."

Ian clearly felt the responsibility and strain of Joy Division weighing down heavily upon him. In this same letter he writes: *I FEEL LIKE LEAVING THE GROUP. ROB IS BEGINNING TO ANNOY ME WITH HIS ATTITUDE, YET THE SONGS ON THE NEW ALBUM MEAN SO MUCH TO ME AND I MUST GET THROUGH THAT AND I FEEL SO MUCH FOR FACTORY — TONY, ALAN AND ALL. I FEEL LIKE GOING BACK TO MY OLD JOB AMONG REAL PEOPLE.*

He speaks of satisfying his restless spirit and asks: *IS SOME HAPPINESS AND FULFILLMENT TOO MUCH TO ASK FOR? YOU ARE THE ONLY THING THAT MAKES ME TRULY HAPPY AT THIS MOMENT, WHEN I'M WITH YOU, WHEN I'M NEAR YOU, WHEN I THINK OF YOU.*

Ian continues: *I AM PAYING DEARLY FOR PAST MISTAKES. I NEVER REALISED HOW ONE MISTAKE IN MY LIFE SOME FOUR OR FIVE YEARS AGO WOULD MAKE ME FEEL HOW I DO. I LIVE BEYOND OBLIGATION AND RESPONSIBILITY. OBLIGATIONS I KNOW I CAN NEVER KEEP YET ARE THERE IN FRONT OF MY EYES EVERY DAY. I STRUGGLE BETWEEN WHAT I KNOW IS RIGHT IN MY OWN MIND AND SOME WARPED TRUTHFULNESS AS SEEN THROUGH OTHER PEOPLE'S EYES WHO HAVE NO HEART AND CAN'T SEE THE DIFFERENCE ANYWAY, MINDS ARE DEAD AND ALL FEELING REDUNDANT. I THANK GOD I HAVE MY SOLITUDE (AS YOU CAN APPRECIATE) AND HAVE HAD EVER SINCE I WAS A CHILD AND CAN AT LEAST LIVE IN PART WITH MY OWN THOUGHTS AND WANDERINGS.*

He wrote a much more cheerful letter to Annik only the day before this. The general tone of the March 11 letter is optimistic compared to the somewhat pessimistic outlook on March 12. His opening paragraph on the 12th gives a clue that a phone conversation may have been part of the reason: *I DIDN'T MEAN TO UPSET YOU, IT HURTS ME SO MUCH WHEN YOU ARE UPSET OR SAD.*

Annik, ignorant of the fact that Debbie hadn't accepted her marriage was over, was still uncomfortable with the growing love between herself and Ian when he had a wife and child at home.

Annik: "Ian and I shared emotions and feelings but we did not spend much time together. We were full of respect for each other and cared a lot for each other. It was pretty melancholic when we met as we knew we would not be able to see one another for long. It was quiet and tender. We had in common some melancholy maybe, some deep need of absolute love and trust. He knew I was out a lot and meeting lots of people. He understood that my need for freedom was first a way of being open-minded and curious and wanting to see and hear all I could. I was hungry for life – mainly through music – but even very far away we felt close and committed. I knew he loved his daughter and never asked more than meeting whenever it was possible. I didn't realise at all that he felt trapped in a triangle situation."

Lindsay Reade: "It is perhaps ironic that Annik's surname is Honoré, and Ian's was Curtis (which he believed stood for the same code) – courtesy and honour. And knowing them both, I have no doubt that their standards were/are extremely high, yet here they were committing virtual adultery when they were both barely out of their teens.

"In a sense Ian and Debbie were both in the grip of the strongest feelings of a new love but circumstances deemed that Debbie's was 'right' and Ian's was 'wrong'. Can love, in its purest sense, ever be judged like that? Admittedly parental love and romantic love are leagues apart and I'm in no way implying that Ian didn't love his baby daughter. I have no doubt whatsoever that he did. However, I think he felt alienated because his illness dictated he couldn't be alone with her and tend to her in a practical sense. His career meant he was absent for most of the time. As anyone with a young baby would appreciate, that must have been really tough on Debbie. But then again the very thing that took him away meant that he was able to materially provide for his child, as his code of honour would naturally dictate. He may even have felt – as a lot of men of that generation and earlier generations did – that providing was the most important thing, that that was the way for him to give his love to his daughter."

Whatever the problems and however much Ian's conscience may have been troubled, his correspondence with Annik reveals, over and over again, not the faintest doubt of his feelings toward her. On Tuesday, March 11, he wrote: I'VE NEVER EXPERIENCED ANYTHING LIKE IT BEFORE, I CAN FEEL YOU NEAR ME ALWAYS AND ALL THE WEIGHTS I SEEM TO CARRY JUST DISAPPEAR, JUST LEAVING A

WONDERFUL CALM. I LIVE IN SPLENDID ISOLATION AND NO-ONE CAN TAKE IT AWAY, ONLY WHEN I'M WITH YOU AND FREE TO MOVE.

This sentiment was echoed by Annik when, in an interview with the authors, she spoke about love: "Love is the drug," she said.

Why is that? "It makes you feel alive."

What makes it happen? Where does it come from? "Deep down from the bottom of your heart. It touches something that's so deep in there when you see one person that you care for. Yes. It makes you tremble and it creates a bond between two persons. I remember when I was in Egypt or when Ian was on tour – I had him near me all the time. You are near even if you are miles away. You only get that with a few people. I can't explain it."

Annik had evidently been over to Belgium for a gig at Plan K before Ian wrote these letters. She was still the contact in London to invite groups to come over, discuss money and deal with travel and transport arrangements. Tickets, posters and advertising was handled in Brussels. Hence Ian added, on March 11: *IT SEEMS AN ETERNITY SINCE I LAST SAW YOU, EVEN THOUGH IT IS LESS THAN A WEEK... I HOPE YOU ENJOYED YOURSELF IN BELGIUM. HOW WERE THE SLITS AND THE POP GROUP? GOOD I HOPE, AND YOUR DOG AND YOUR PARENTS.*

Ian also refers to his own dog, Candy, regretting that whereas he was once able to walk her two or three times a day, this is no longer possible: *MY DOG IS LYING NEXT TO ME. I FEEL SO SAD THIS IS THE LAST WEEK I HAVE WITH HER. WHEN I COME TO LONDON SHE IS TO BE GIVEN AWAY. I CAN'T BELIEVE IT AND DON'T THINK I WILL UNTIL I RETURN. AND SHE DOESN'T GREET ME AT THE DOOR, TAIL WAGGING, "... TO SHED A TEAR FOR ALL THE DUMB CREATURES OF THIS WORLD..." (HUMANS INCLUDED).*

He sounds more optimistic than in his next letter about his future with Joy Division, talking of the impending album recording and also mentions: *THE COPIES OF 'SORDIDE SENTIMENTALE' HAVE ARRIVED, THE COVER'S INCREDIBLE, I'VE GOT YOU ONE AND WILL BRING IT DOWN WITH ME ON MONDAY.*

He also refers back to the recording of 'Love Will Tear Us Apart' on March 8 in Strawberry Studio: *WE STILL HAVEN'T FINISHED 'LOVE WILL TEAR US APART' THERE IS STILL A LOT TO DO, VOCALS, GUITAR, SYNTH DRUMS, WE'RE HOPING TO COMPLETE IT AT BRITTANIA ROW, IT'S CHANGED A LOT FROM THE PREVIOUS RECORDED VERSION. TONY CAME DOWN TO THE STUDIO ON*

SATURDAY, HE'D BOUGHT ME A FRANK SINATRA DOUBLE ALBUM, HE WANTS THE VOCALS DONE LIKE THAT. I PLAYED IT AND NONE OF THE OTHERS COULD STAND IT, THOUGH I THINK IT'S A GOOD LP. HE'S GOT A GREAT VOICE. WE WERE THERE FROM 6.00PM SATURDAY TO 12.00 NOON SUNDAY. EVERYBODY WAS SO TIRED.

Frank Sinatra wasn't exactly new to Ian – in fact Sinatra was a favourite of Ian's dad, Kevin, and Ian grew up listening to him. Tony Wilson thought that Ian's vocal phrasing might become influenced by Sinatra if he listened to the album and remembers being pleased to see it lying open on the floor of Strawberry Studios. Ian had obviously listened to it.

Tony Wilson: "I told Ian that the real emotion in the delivery of the lyrics of a song exist within the spaces in the syllables and if you spread the syllables you will find that's where the emotion will come in."

With this in mind, it's likely that the Sinatra influence played a part in the way in which Ian chose to sing the chorus in 'Love Will Tear us Apart' – "Love will tear us apaaaaaart again". The emotion sits over the aaaaaa(h) rather than over the short staccato syllables.

Nevertheless, Tony adds: "I don't like to talk about me giving Ian this album because it runs completely contrary to my ideas that the guys in suits should never have the temerity to tell musicians what to do with their music."

Like Annik, Wilson believes in giving the artist room to breathe. Though quick to say that he didn't think it was the job of record executives to give advice to their protégées, he nevertheless did talk to Ian about this and Ian did take his advice. How do we know? Listen to the two different versions of 'Love Will Tear Us Apart' – the first recorded at Pennine and the second at Strawberry. Although Tony was quick to make clear: "I always believe that the only creative thing we ever do – those of us without the talent that is – is push our musicians for better or worse towards the right or the wrong producer. I have got it both wrong and right."

Perhaps the reason Ian took on board what Tony was saying was because he wasn't telling him what to do with the music. It's possible that their intellectual/emotional natures made contact. As Pete Johnson says: "Ian was intellectually very sharp."

'Love Will Tear Us Apart' would become Joy Division's signature tune, the one song in their catalogue that is universally recognised as a timeless classic. Although it breached the Top 20 singles chart – the only JD record to do so – it spread outwards across the surface of the mainstream, drawing in fans hitherto unaware of the band, and has stayed the course, regularly appearing on published lists of all time greats. Paul Morley, musing on how Ian might view the enduring influence of Joy Division in the summer of 2005, notes: "The only clue I have in a way is trying to imagine a 20-odd year old me looking at it 25 or 30 years later. Cos I'm still around I'm constantly surprised by it. Part of me is dead impressed that you can walk in Virgin in Times Square in New York and they're playing 'Love Will Tear Us Apart' and it's just after Bowie and it's just before Led Zeppelin and you think they got there, they made it."

Whether or not 'Love Will Tear Us Apart' was, in artistic terms, Joy Division's finest moment is simply a matter of opinion… and all too often the opinion of those who have never heard Joy Division beyond the gateway of this song. Whatever, it was destined to ring out from classic rock radio stations down the generations, indeed taking its place next to the Zeppelins, Dylans and Bowies.

'Love Will Tear Us Apart' was born from pain. That much was always obvious. The song's posthumous release would make it absolutely clear, as ears first became addicted to those rising opening chords, just how much profoundly personal those lyrics actually were. It was a beautifully clipped and tailored lyric too, and showcased Ian's growing ability to throw evocative one-liners from the heart of the song.

"Why was the bedroom so cold?" asks Ian in a line that echoes Phil Spector's heartfelt masterpiece, 'You've Lost That Lovin' Feelin''; about the death throes of a relationship, sifting through the debris after infatuation has long since receded, two people sitting in silence, nothing left to say.

Part of the success of 'Love Will Tear Us Apart' was its omnipresent capacity to reach to all those who'd experienced this, but there was a touch of irony in the song's title insofar as it could be seen as a dark antidote to the Captain & Tennille hit, 'Love Will Keep Us Together', a fluffy confection by Neil Sedaka that had stuck like a globule of pink bubblegum to insipid radio play lists since emerging in 1975. It was Malcolm McLaren who actually did put the two songs together within the context of an as yet unreleased album. When Tony Wilson played Lindsay Reade this curious hybrid, it certainly left a lasting impression on her. "Tony played that song to me I thought it was a hit – shades of times past – and I felt, privately, quite moved by it," she says. "The reason – it seemed to give hope, to be optimistic even. It felt like a kind of message, that even torn apart we can be put back together, that none of us are lost or apart from love, that Ian was OK. Of course there is a paradox in both lyrics. And you're never sure which side of the border you're on. But whichever one it is it you can never be that far from the other."

★ ★ ★

Ian's next trip to London with Joy Division was to record *Closer* at Brittania Row Studios in Camden Town. While Ian was away Debbie and her parents made arrangements to find an alternative home for Ian's dog Candy, somewhere quite far away. It was also around this time that Debbie found out about Ian's 'affair' with Annik, and there are some in his circle of friends who feel that Debbie's decision to dispose of the dog might have been a way of hitting back at Ian for Annik. Then again, looking after Candy was an extra burden on top of other domestic chores, in particular looking after a small baby.

Terry Mason: "Debbie knew what the dog meant to him. He was really upset. He went about with a picture of the dog in his wallet. I think Debbie could see how she could really get to him – hurt him. She made him hand it over to someone in Irlam – miles away – so he couldn't see it."

Terry was sufficiently moved by the event to buy a dog of his own: "We had this conversation that after America I was going to get a dog and he could share my dog," he says. As it turned out Terry would actually collect this dog on the day of Ian's funeral.

CHAPTER 17

Closer

"That last track – the young men with the weight on their shoulders – was the way he was talking in his last days – with that same soft voice because he was so tired and confused and sad." – Annik

Breaking with the tradition of recording in or around Manchester, Joy Division and Martin Hannett elected to record the second album at the Pink Floyd-owned Britannia Row Studios in Islington, from March 17 to the end of the month. Even at this cut-off point, there would be little respite, for the band were obliged to remain in the capital at the start of April to perform four gigs in three days. The demanding schedule had to be maintained, even though they would surely be exhausted following intensive studio sessions.

Commuting to and from Manchester was clearly out of the question so to ease the pressure those who controlled the purse strings at Factory adopted a practical approach and the band stayed at two rented flats in York Street, off the north end of Baker Street, in London's West End. Even though, as ever, time and money were somewhat tight, this at least allowed them to enjoy the myriad distractions of central London. It was a world away from Stockport and was certainly symbolic of a band on the rise.

Having driven the group's equipment down, Terry returned to Manchester, leaving Dave Pils on hand as the London-based roadie. The two flats were occupied by the band and Rob Gretton while Dave returned to Walthamstow when he wasn't needed. At one point during the recording, Rob allocated £20 for each of the band's partners to buy a 'saver' ticket from Manchester to Euston, so they could visit. Ian's unease with this situation is reflected by Deborah Curtis in her book *Touching From A Distance*: evidently she called Ian but he failed to mention that suitable accommodation had been organised for the female contingent in the form of the two small flats, one of which was occupied by Ian and Annik. Although Annik did stay in the flat during this period, she also had her room in Parsons Green.

In other respects, the frugal budgetary demands placed on Joy Division were still in place. During the recording of *Closer*, they existed on £5 per day, sufficient for food and modest drink, though little more than that, not at London prices, even in 1980. A downbeat kebab house around the corner from the flats found itself serving these Mancunians chicken salads several evenings at a cost of £1.05p each, leaving enough per diem for a couple of pints in a local pub at the end of each session.

By contrast, Annik was relatively wealthy, and she recalls being gently chided by Rob on the subject of money. "I remember Rob sometimes being a bit rude to me," she says. "In London he made a comment about me buying clothes in Joseph – this was a big joke, buying expensive trousers. Because I was spending money when they didn't have any. But there was nothing so bad."

Terry Mason got the impression that Ian seemed to need more money than anyone else and was therefore willing to take on, as ever, extra work for pin money. Terry remembers the band telling him that Annik objected to Ian doing menial chores and apparently said, in her rounded Belgian vowels: "You should not be doing the i-ronn-ning. You are a genius!"

Terry thought that the suggestion in Deborah Curtis' book that Annik was ordering Ian about came from Annik's financial independence: "Rob paid Ian pin money for doing the ironing. Rob had the money, so he had the upper hand. If they were about to go somewhere they would wait for him, because of him having the money. But Annik had her own money and was independent of Rob. She didn't need to wait and would say to Ian 'Let's go now.'"

The band bowed to Martin Hannett's preference for working at night and seemed perfectly happy to accommodate this nocturnal activity. Terry recalls that Ian seemed "in a better situation" and, by all accounts, the recording of *Closer* was made by a fairly content band, happy, no doubt, to be staying in central London. Britannia Row was a comfortable environment in which to work, and there was a full-sized pool table on the premises, which helped keep the musicians away from Hannett's mixing desk when he wanted to work alone. Nevertheless, the *Closer* sessions were still fairly intense, with Ian apparently 'trance-like', scribbling lyrics on scraps of paper.

In the Joy Division tradition, the tension was relieved by a number of japes.

"It was always tense for people who were around Joy Division because you never quite knew what they were going to do," says Tony Wilson. "You just knew that something would happen. They were just that kind of band, especially Ian, who was a real practical joker. He loved that. I think it helped him relax and forget his worries. I tell a story about driving back to the band's flat, one night during the recording of *Closer*. When we got back to the flats, all the bands had to run off and check that their beds were in order... that no-one had smeared them with ketchup or something. They were always doing stuff like that."

Jeremy Kerr remembers that ACR were down in London with Tony at this time, doing a Peel session or a gig, and they visited Joy Division at their flat. ACR had put some cornflakes in one of JD's beds and in someone's socks, but that was nothing compared to how JD wreaked vengeance. When it came time for ACR to leave and JD were waving at them from the window, they all grabbed the door handles of the van to find them smeared with jam or peanut butter and barely had this had time to register before they were pelted with eggs hurled from the window by the group who were laughing their heads off. Wilson remembers seeing Ian laughing, standing looking out of one window with Annik by his side.

Genesis P-Orridge remembers going shopping with Ian near to the studios in Islington. "There were some shops hidden away," he says. "We looked at German memorabilia, iconography. Chris Farlowe[1] had a booth called Comrade In Arms or something, selling army uniforms, helmets, bayonets, badges, that sort of stuff. I was into camouflage designs."

Lindsay Reade recalls visiting the studios with Tony Wilson: "I remember thinking they must really be going places now they were recording in London but wishing all the same that they were still at Strawberry which seemed more like home. The building (35a Brittania Row) seemed a bit cold in comparison, like a school."

Although *Closer* would become generally known as one of the classic 'downer' albums, Lindsay Reade says that this wasn't necessarily evident at

---

[1] Singer who had a number one hit with 'Out Of Time', written by Mick Jagger & Keith Richards, in 1966.

the time, at least to those fairly close to the recording. Hannett utilised plenty of enhanced technology to 'freshen up' the basic Joy Division sound while the haunting quality of Ian's vocals and his intensely personal lyrics tended to pull the album in a more reflective direction. This is never more evident than on 'Isolation', in which a fairly light, almost 'pretty' melody is intensified by Curtis' performance; take the vocal away and it could almost be a pop song.

Tony Wilson thought that Martin created something revolutionary with this track: "The thing Martin did, which no-one gives him credit for, is he invents modern music. He invents digital music. He has this vision. He'd been working with early synthesisers and then with Joy Division and particularly New Order he begins to wire up and connect primitive computers to keyboards. Martin does this and for the first time ever in history there had always been rhythm and melody – on different instruments. You can hear this on the song called 'Isolation' by Joy Division. On 'Isolation' the beat comes from the keyboard. Everyone sees 'Blue Monday' as the changeover record but in fact its coming of age came from having learnt from Martin. 'Blue Monday' was the first record that New Order did without Martin."

Such lightness was only fleeting, however. Most fans came to this recording after this story's tragic conclusion and after first gazing at the album's 'tombstone cover' approached it as a dark and disturbing record even before the needle hit the vinyl. Thus, hearing *Closer* for the first time was an unforgettable moment for many. It was a record drenched in atmosphere and mystique, music you had to wade through, dark and sinister like a big dense forest, and it's no exaggeration to suggest that its posthumous arrival would carry a weight unprecedented in popular music. It was impossible to separate the awful reality of this story from the haunting voice on the album called *Closer*.

Ian Curtis took the record one step beyond a kind of post-punk howl, injecting an absolute reality that was genuinely unsettling; something that couldn't be dismissed as a grey industrial drone, the boyish moaning of a shallow twenty-something yet to experience any true depth in his life.

The fans knew it would be imbued with pain. And so it was. As Simon Reynolds notes, in his 2005 book, *Rip It Up and Start Again* "… it was as if the band had absorbed his [Curtis'] pain and recreated it sonically. Listening, it is like you are inside his head, feeling the awful down swirling drag of terminal depression." The irony here is that while this might prevent you from ever wanting to take the record from its sleeve, it is also an astonishing, almost unprecedented compliment.

In 1996, Peter Hook told Mick Middles: "We were pretty happy at the time of recording *Closer*. We knew we had a really good album. It was rare for a band to make a really good second album because they are usually cobbled together at speed, whereas the first can take years to bring together. But we were very confident. We knew our way around a studio. We felt comfortable with Martin. It was just... happening."

The young Irish band, U2, certainly thought so. On a television retrospective, Bono would famously refer to "... the holy voice of Ian Curtis..." and his band, fresh faced, new to London, addicted to *Unknown Pleasures* and about to embark on a recording career with Island Records, also wanted the services of Martin Hannett. In the event he did produce their debut Island single, '11 0'Clock Tick Tock', but when it came to their first album U2 chose Steve Lillywhite.

As Hooky revealed to writer David Thompson: "I can remember U2 coming to the studio when we were doing *Closer*. U2 were the best Joy Division copyists. They were very Joy Divisionesque. They were desperate to meet Joy Division and they would get Martin Hannett in to do their next record and they came to see us and, God, they were just like little kids. I was only 22 and they were like 16 and I would dismiss them. You forget about people and all of a sudden they are the biggest band in the world and... fucking hell, maybe I should have been nice to them."

Astute, perceptive and ferociously ambitious, U2 undoubtedly based their breakthrough recordings on the rockier side of Joy Division. Ironically perhaps, U2, for all their songwriting brilliance, initially lacked the innovative desire of Joy Division and the two band's musical paths would depart at the point where Joy Division began to experiment heavily with the possibilities of the synthesisers; indeed, with this new album being made at Britannia Row

Closer saw Martin Hannett flexing his muscles. He would later claim it was his most "mystical" and "cabalistic" recording. Somewhat unexpectedly he chose to soften the disco pulse beat used so effectively on *Unknown Pleasures* and stretch the new songs as much as possible, so they all attained a certain sense of grandeur. While some – amongst them Paul Morley – retained a greater fondness for *Unknown Pleasures*, others believed that few albums have ever attained such extraordinary intimacy as the aptly named *Closer* – closer to the heart, closer to the voice, closer to the soul, the centre of the music.

Hannett pulled Ian's vocals right to the top of the mix, enhancing the intimacy of *Unknown Pleasures* as in a heartfelt novel, where writer and reader enjoy moments of one-to-one intimacy. It was an effect that developed as the album progressed, and was less pronounced on the opener, 'Atrocity Exhibition', as on other tracks. This featured a hot, exotic Moroccan beat, perversely reminiscent of Can's 'Tago Mago', which rose and fell behind a Curtis voice that beckoned the listener towards the album; a warm, welcoming command: "This is the way, step inside."

'Isolation', by striking contrast, saw an ice-cold synth pushing Ian's vocal to a lonely, soulless fringe. With its detached prettiness – like an ice maiden – lost in solitude, it seemed as if Ian was gathering his thoughts. "'Isolation' reminds me of Kafka's *Metamorphosis*," wrote *Sounds* critic Dave McCullough. "Hannett brings the tone down a step, synths flower, references of 'Mother I've tried, please believe me', the song is short and bursts with action, though, typically for the entire album, at the very last moment, somehow ebbs away incomplete just as the very reverse seems assured. That, too, adds to the hopelessness."

In *Melody Maker*, Paulo Hewitt noted that Ian Curtis appeared to be facing a situation of hopelessness at every turn. Quoting Ian's lyrics to 'Colony' and 'Twenty Four Hours', he cites two separate moments where Curtis attempts to grasp contentment, only to see it slipping through his fingers. In fact 'Twenty Four Hours' provided the album's most heartbreaking moment, with Hooky's bass rising to a sudden height and powering the song forward, leaving the singer trailing in its wake. This song, blessed with a captivating ebb-and-flow, was seen by many as the true defining moment of the band's entire career.

Annik, who attended the sessions, shares a vivid memory of Ian in the studio, laying down the vocals for 'The Eternal' and 'Decades', which close the album. She clearly remembers Ian going into the booth to sing them, and that he "… had his eyes closed and his hands on his head."

She felt strangely embarrassed to be there, to be near him like this – almost as if he were naked. She said there was a sacred quality about it – as it there was some kind of inner, Holy Communion taking place. Listening to these songs again many years later, she said: "The voice and the music are just amazing. Steve was such a good drummer. I love 'The Eternal' and 'Decades' and remembered almost every word even though it had been maybe 20 years I had not heard them. I remember Ian singing them very late at night and concentrating and closing his eyes. I felt I was very privileged to be there sometimes and really left him to be the way he wanted and tried not to intrude and just observe more than to act. I always feel people want far too much from artists and should be thankful enough to receive the huge present of their music, book, painting or art in general. They need air and to breathe and their freedom.

"That last track – the young men with the weight on their shoulders – was the way he was talking in his last days – with that same soft voice because he was so tired and confused and sad."

Ian's studio technique had certainly improved. He'd developed an ability to latch onto the melody and write his way into the heart of the song, at times climbing straight onto the feel, as if the songs had been waiting for him, which was no easy trick. Peter Hook, watching Ian at work in the studio, would later refer to this ability as, "… the work of a master."

The fact that *Closer* was an album made by four rather unsophisticated lads in their early twenties belies its sheer elegance, which has not weakened with the passing of two-and-a-half decades. Martin Hannett's innovative effects have also stood the test of time. As with *Unknown Pleasures* he had taken a risk in relying heavily on the technology of the moment which often serves to date the music as that technology becomes outmoded. Escaping this trap was no easy feat – albums of the era from Teardrop Explodes, The Cure, Killing Joke and The Mekons were among many loudly applauded at the time, only for them to sound dated as time marched on. The contrast between many of these albums and *Closer* is far more evident during the intervening years as more and more young bands struggle to create something equally precious.

The band recorded 12 songs at Britannia Row, with three of them – 'Komakino', 'Incubation' and 'As You Said' – not making it onto the final album. The latter two remained unfinished instrumentals while 'Komakino' is notable as it contained the Ian Curtis line, "This is the hour when the mysteries emerge" which would have surely sat effectively on the album. These three oddities became famously collectable as Factory, in one of their more perverse moments, released them as a limited edition flexi-disc before *Closer* came out. The logic of allowing the public to listen to three tracks of a slightly lesser standard as a precursor to an album release remains difficult to grasp. By then, however, the entire Joy Division story had been darkened by tragedy.

Closer, of course, was clothed in one of the most chillingly evocative album sleeves of all time, a sleeve that perfectly evokes the grandeur and softness of the music within. It was all the more surprising that Factory designer Peter Saville had not heard the music prior to his commission.

Peter Saville: "Rob (Gretton) was fully aware that the visuals of Factory belonged to me. It's also true that the visual aspect was a huge part of Factory. Tony (Wilson) liked to be associated with that. By virtue of being in charge of Factory, he had a way of assuming that the powerful design or powerful sound had something to do with him. That wasn't really the case. He didn't tell Rob how to manage bands or Martin how to create sound.

Nor did he tell me how to produce the visuals. But it was fantastic because we were all given total freedom. Most of the time, with Factory, I just sent my artwork straight to the printers and neither the artists nor Tony would even see it until it arrived, completed. No other record company would be like that. And that's how we approached *Closer*."

Rob and the band arrived at Peter Saville's Portabello Road studio with apparently no pre-conceived ideas of how the artwork might look. "When Rob and the band came to discuss a sleeve for the second album, they just said, 'What have you got?'" says Saville. "I had not heard the album. I didn't know its title. I had no idea what the music would be like or what the band wanted."

Earlier that week, however, Saville had found himself profoundly affected by a collection of photographs published in an arty photography magazine called *Zoom*. Saville: "These images were the contemporary equivalent of Post Modernism in Architecture. They were by Bernard Pierre Wolf and had completely bowled me over. They were from a graveyard in Northern Italy and the local tradition there tended towards grandiose family tombs. The local families outdid each other by having more and more ornate tombs. It was so powerful to see contemporary pics evocative of 18th Century neo classical images."

Nevertheless, they seemed an unlikely subject for an album cover.

Saville: "I didn't think the band would like them for one minute but I showed them to them and, to my amazement, the four of them gathered around like animals feeding at the zoo. At that point I am certain that I would have looked at Ian to see if he liked them. I wanted to know if he was supportive of the idea and he certainly appeared more than enthusiastic."

Tony Wilson thought this indicated that Ian was the leader of the band: "Saville's got used to working with bands over the years and he says that when you offer artwork to a band you pretty soon ascertain how the mechanics of that particular group work and there is always someone who makes the decision. He says, for example, that when he presented those pictures of the graveyard in Italy[1] Ian said he liked them and he caught Ian's eyes and thought 'OK – so it's done'."

Saville continued: "Of course, I couldn't just nick them. So I asked Tony to get hold of Bernard Pierre Wolf, and the photographer immediately agreed. From that point, I took a typeface that I had found… it was from the second century, I think, apparently the first ever example of Roman

[1] They later became the 'Love Will Tear Us Apart' 12-inch as well as the *Closer* sleeve.

Lapidary lettering… obviously it was a few centuries out of copyright and in the public domain."

Saville's brief was, to say the least, vague: he asked Rob if the band wanted their name on the cover.

Gretton: "Not really."

He then asked if he wanted the name of the album on the cover:

Gretton: "Not Really."

Anything?

Gretton: "Not really."

Saville: "I just did what I liked. There is a theory that a lack of info makes the consumer feel like an initiate of a secret. I think that was true of Factory."

Unlike *Unknown Pleasures*, where the press reaction was mixed, *Closer* received glowing notices from all corners of the music press. Opinion was divided on the meaning of the album's ambiguous title. Most reviewers, at the time and in retrospect, believed it to be an album that was somehow 'closer' – nearer – to the soul or heart of the music. Another train of thought, equally believable, suggests that the album was 'closer' to the place where Joy Division wanted their music to be. Of the original reviewers, only Mike Nicholls, in *Record Mirror*, took the alternative meaning of the word and called it a 'closer', as in the closing of proceedings. He was derided for this at the time, but this interpretation is equally valid. Paul Morley thought this was the meaning of the title and spoke of Joy Division's career ending "with the cover of the album looking like it was a tombstone and of it being called *Closer* which can also be *Closer* – as in the final closer (closed). At the time I thought it was and I thought, 'How can you call it *Closer?*'. I said to Tony – don't call it *Closer* and he went, 'What do you mean? It's called *Closer*'. I thought they'd called it that as in this is the closer, the end."

In his *Sounds* review, Dave McCullough wrote the line: "… dark strokes of gothic rock…" and there is good reason to suppose that this was the first use of the word 'gothic' in a rock context, eternally nailing Joy Division's second album as an integral record in the Goth genre. Many fans beg to differ, believing the music of The Cure, Sisters of Mercy, The Mission, Cradle of Filth, Marilyn Manson etc., to be far removed from that of Joy Division.[1]

* * *

[1] In January 2005, the Reverend Marcus of St Edward King and Martyr Church in Peas Hill, Cambridge, instigated a 'goth' church service, which featured music by Joy Division as well as Depeche Mode and Sisters of Mercy. The special service made the national press as it celebrated its first anniversary in 2006.

Terry Mason returned to London on March 30 to help Section 25 with their gig at The Marquee on Wardour Street. Joy Division took that evening off from recording and wandered down to Soho to catch the set. Larry Cassidy: "We got on very well with Joy Division. No big deep conversations – we just got on all right. We shared some digs during a London spell. Annik was there, she was sharing a room with Ian. We were just going about being a group."

The following day Terry found himself running round London, picking up an extra flight case for Ian's white Vox teardrop guitar from Bulldog in preparation for Joy Division's forthcoming US tour, and he remained in London for a three-night residency at The Moonlight Club in West Hampstead on April 2, 3 and 4 that featured bands on the Factory roster. Joy Division were required to perform on each night, albeit at different times. If nothing else, this showcase would demonstrate to the London audience just how quickly the Factory roster had started to swell. The artists included Vini Reilly's Durutti Column, Section 25, Crawling Chaos, Kevin Hewick (a lonesome troubadour from Leicester), reggae outfit X-O-Dus, A Certain Ratio and The Royal Family. Factory's intention was to demonstrate the strength of their eclectic if somewhat unfashionable artists who were struggling to emerge from Joy Division's shadow.

March had proven to be a rewarding month for the band but their schedule was looking busier than ever. A huge effort was required from them and, in particular, from their troubled front-man. There seemed to be no return and no way out from the heavy responsibility and daunting schedule of gigs, all of which increased the possibility of his epileptic fits.

Genesis P-O'rridge recalls that he and Ian actually plotted an escape route for him around this time. "We had ideas of doing a band, there was a secret plan," he says. "We were planning a Throbbing Gristle/Joy Division gig at La Palace in Paris. Near the end there was going to be a jam with both bands together – say 'Sister Ray' and then at the end Ian was going to announce that he'd quit the band and so had I and we were going to work together."

Terry Mason likened Ian's situation to a scene from one of Ian's favourite films of the period, *Apocalypse Now*, where a snail is walking down the edge of a razor. The weight of the snail pulls it further down onto the razor: it cannot help but ultimately cause its own destruction.

CHAPTER 18

The Present Is Well Out Of Hand

"I actually meant it you know. Everyone thinks it was a cry for help but it wasn't a cry for help." – Ian

Unable to return to Manchester to rest following the recording of their second album, Joy Division remained in London to fulfil their various obligations, the first of which was the three-night stint at the Moonlight Club. 'Factory by Moonlight' might have sounded like a romantic proposition but, as is often the case, the fantasy and the reality were poles apart. A showcase for struggling Factory acts was all very well but Joy Division's revered status as darlings of the music press meant that in reality the success of the three nights rested fairly and squarely on their shoulders. Rob Gretton, now a partner in Factory Records, no doubt felt compelled to offer the services of his band to help raise the profile of the company in the relatively uncharted territory of the capital.

It is less easy to understand the reasoning behind Joy Division's appearance at the Rainbow Theatre on Good Friday, April 4, supporting The Stranglers, especially since this conflicted with the Friday night finale at the Moonlight, thus necessitating a race across town to fulfil both engagements. Certainly, an appearance at the Rainbow in Finsbury Park, a venue that held almost 3,000, carried some cachet, as did appearing with a 'name' act like

The Stranglers. The show was originally promoted as one in a series of nine that were sponsored by Levi Strauss, the jeans manufacturer, to celebrate the venue's 50th birthday. Other nights would see performances by heavy metallers Judas Priest, Iron Maiden and Whitesnake and soul stirrers the Average White Band, hardly appropriate company for the cutting edge disturbance of Joy Division.

The Stranglers had already committed themselves to playing two of the nine evenings when their singer/guitarist Hugh Cornwell was sent to Pentonville Prison for two months after losing an appeal against a conviction for drug possession. As such the gig changed shape and became a benefit gig for Cornwell, with a variety of singers waiting in the wings to take his place on lead vocals. They included Toyah Wilcox, Hazel O'Connor, Billy Idol, Phil Daniels, Nicky Tesco, Ian Dury, Richard Jobson, Peter Hammill, Robert Smith, Robert Fripp and many more. The Rainbow was sold out that night.

"Groups were turning up just to do it," says Larry Cassidy of Section 25. "They didn't have all that much time to play. We were supposed to go on and Rob came up to me and said JD had another gig on the other side of London and if they do the spot before The Stranglers they wouldn't be able to make it so did we want to do it? So I said yes. They went on before us."

Because most of their gear was at The Moonlight, Joy Division performed with a minimum of equipment on stage which was far from ideal for a venue as big as the Rainbow. Far more worrying was that Rob's request to the lighting technicians that they refrain from using strobes wasn't heeded.

Many of Joy Division's London-based friends made it to the Rainbow to witness a fractured set with varying intensity. It was undeniably more captivating than the recent Moonlight shows, beginning with a ferocious 'Dead Souls', followed by 'Wilderness', 'Shadowplay' and 'Decades'. By all accounts, including reviews in the music press, Ian's dancing appeared less rhythmic than usual, less effective perhaps; jagged, trance-like and unsettling. At the conclusion of 'She's Lost Control', the whole spectacle suddenly darkened: Ian was clearly having a fit as he staggered backwards into Steve Morris's drum kit.

"Some pillock turned the fucking strobe light on," says Larry Cassidy. "Rob always used to make sure that the lighting guy knew not to turn the strobe lights on because it sets off epileptic fits. This guy turned them on and not long after Ian ended up in the fucking drum kit. So he gets carted off stage – up all the corridors at the back to the dressing room and that was the fucking end of that. And then we had to go on."

Joy Division remained locked in the dressing room until Ian's seizure passed. Then they drove across town to West Hampstead for the final show at the Moonlight. "Ian was not in great shape but he believed that the show must go on," says Terry.

Back at the Moonlight Tony Wilson was unaware that Ian had had a fit at the Rainbow. "I wasn't there," he says. "I was at the Moonlight. I remember them arriving. He seemed all right. He was fine."

So Joy Division took the stage for the second time that night, only for disaster to happen a second time. It was about two thirds of the way through the Moonlight set – 25 minutes in – when Ian's dancing started to lose its rhythmic sense and change into something else entirely. With the band flashing nervous glances at each other, with Terry hovering by the side, the theatre that was a Joy Division performance turned into something verging on the grotesque. Ian was engulfed by another fit and the show collapsed to a halt. Some members of the audience believed it was all part of the act, but those aware of the situation knew all too well that this was the most violent attack that Ian Curtis had ever suffered in public.

Paul Morley had travelled across London that night, following the band from Finsbury Park to West Hampstead, and he remembers how the effort needed to make this journey in a short time was somewhat exhausting in itself, even without having to twice perform on stage. "Even for a healthy person it was very unlikely that they would do two shows of such intensity on the same night," he says. "You felt that it couldn't be helping that Ian was driving himself to such a peak of response to his own performance. And the fact it was happening more and more on stage toward the end seemed to suggest it was not the best way to try and treat that condition. It was just accelerating. In hindsight we could say it was accelerating to the suicide but there is a world where it didn't necessarily have to, it could have accelerated into a kind of weird peace where it all calmed down."

Terry Mason believes that the principal reason for doing a series of gigs in London was to try to put aside money to help fund the forthcoming American tour, but he finds it difficult to understand the events of this night. "I was wondering what we were doing there at all," he says. "We didn't have that much to do with The Stranglers that we needed to be at their benefit. The money at the Moonlight was split equally between the bands so it was not of much material benefit. We were just propping up Factory. It wasn't even important. Ian has just done two gigs that meant fuck all to him. It was a massive attack at the Moonlight and, afterwards, Ian looked crushed."

Tony Wilson concedes that this was an unusual night but doesn't feel the band's schedule was unusually stressful, as they were used to working hard. "I think in hindsight that was kind of normal for bands of that era," he says. "For bands in that position, on the way up the ladder, it was quite normal to play three gigs a week. I think the Moonlight period was peculiar. The Moonlight was a wacky idea… I think that was a bit extreme."

Ian and Annik were together for the duration of these London gigs and she left for Belgium on either Saturday April 5 or the day after. Terry thinks that Ian returned to London to stay with her after the Malvern gig on the Saturday but is probably mistaken as Annik certainly purchased her overland ticket to Brussels that day. She still has the receipt, purchased from a travel agency in Buckingham Palace Road and priced £11.70. On it she wrote: "I left Ian Saturday morning, he was still asleep, very tired after the concert at the Rainbow (fit) and the Moonlight Club – after many tears, embraces, kisses, depressions, breakdown till almost daybreak."

Later Annik wrote to Carole: "Obviously he was very tired and depressed after what happened at the Rainbow when he had a fit on stage in front of 3,000 people."

It would have been understandable if Joy Division had pulled out of their commitment to play at Malvern Winter Gardens on Saturday, April 6, the night after the Rainbow/Moonlight debacle. Nevertheless, with Section 25 in dutiful support, they took their place on stage and despite increasing concern over Ian's illness it appears to have been a more relaxed occasion. Indeed, Terry remembers this night as one of the happiest of them all. "It was a lovely sunny day, out in the fresh air, throwing stones and twigs in the streams," he says. "Everyone seemed happy, even Ian. It reminded me of the day of Ian's audition, when we interviewed Ian by taking him to the country. London was 80 miles away and this was a moment of light relief. Things had gone full circle. The gig was timed so that people could catch the last train to get back to London.

"We'd sort of got away from all the London thing that was around us and our little gang was back together, like a bunch of 15 year olds throwing stones in streams. Things like that were what you pick up on more than whether a gig was a classic gig. Thinking back on Malvern it would be quite a restrained gig cos we'd gone from the Moonlight which was tiny and claustrophobic to… this was like, it reminded me of the main hall at the school me, Hooky and Barney went to. A big bank of windows down one side. Basically all the problems of Good Friday had disappeared and it was just us lot again being the knob-heads that we were."

Larry Cassidy also enjoyed the night: "That [Malvern] was good – like the Winter Gardens in Blackpool but a bit more upmarket. It was dead good, the place, the atmosphere, everything. Obviously we knew these were Joy Division gigs but there was no sort of crappy 'we're bigger than you' shit. If you play well and people enjoy it, what more do you want? It was a good gig. Everything was fine."

Everything wasn't fine. The following day, Easter Sunday, April 6, Ian Curtis attempted suicide by taking an overdose of pills at his home on Barton Street. He then told Debbie what he had done, and she called an ambulance which took him to hospital to have his stomach pumped. In view of the circumstances, many of those around him assumed it was a cry for help. Somewhat shamefully, Ian telephoned Annik from the hospital.

Annik: "I think the first suicide attempt was somehow an accident. He had probably been drinking again but it was maybe a sign to show, 'Look I don't know which direction to take.' When he called… this is something I will never forget… he called me at work, during the day, from the hospital. He sounded really just like a little boy. He said he'd had an overdose of pills and he was here in the hospital and my heart sank. I said, 'Why did you do that? You must not do things like that.' He said he was lost and it was an accident and he'd never do it again and then he said I should visit and that we must never part because he wants to be with me. After he said all that, I said, 'Yes we must get together again and too bad for all the problems.' And he did write to me a few times in April after that suicide attempt. "It seemed obvious after that… it made things clearer after that first attempt that now he knew which way to go. That's the way it seemed to me. I thought it made things clearer for all of us but obviously not – it was more complicated."

Terry thought the reason Ian didn't go through with the suicide was for practical reasons. "Ian was panicking with regard to the pills because if you get it wrong you don't die, you just destroy your liver or your kidneys," he says. "And you're in pain for the rest of your life. We did know that maybe he'd looked it up somewhere and he knew you had to be careful about it. That you might not die but just wreck your body."

Ian referred to his suicide attempt in a letter to Annik that he wrote on Thursday, April 17, at 10.00pm: *IT'S BEEN VERY HARD THESE PAST TWO WEEKS TO COME TO TERMS WITH EVERYTHING AFTER LAST (BUT ONE) SUNDAY NIGHT WHEN ALL BALANCE WAS DESTROYED. JOY DIVISION IN ITSELF IS SUCH A GREAT RESPONSIBILITY NOT ONLY FOR MY OWN HEALTH AND PEACE OF MIND BUT THE FACT THAT ON ME RESTS THE FUTURE OF THE OTHERS AND MORE BESIDE. INDEED THE*

STRAIN HAD BECOME TOO MUCH. I JUST FELT LIKE RUNNING AWAY FROM EVERYTHING, HIDING IN A CORNER BACKING OUT OF RESPONSIBILITY AND DECISION.

Annik: "I would not blame Ian for committing suicide and I still believe he didn't do it for any of us. It added to the problem perhaps – the fact that it made it a bit complicated but he died mainly because it was an accident, it seems to me, because he was sick, very sick, and because he didn't know how to cope with his illness and the group and the trips and the recording and the concerts – it was all getting too much for him. I don't think he died for love. No. No. It was really a shame he was so sick. And the fact I think that he knew how it would end up at its worst – being an epileptic – frightened him. I remember in one of his letters he said there is no room for the weak and the emotive. And that's how he felt. Very weak. You are looked upon as weak when you show too much of your feelings on your sleeve."

In the same letter Ian seems to be going some way to explain his actions:

I WISHED I WAS LIGHT YEARS AWAY OR DIDN'T EXIST AT ALL AND BECAUSE OF THAT FEELING THAT IS EXACTLY HOW I EXISTED – I WAS RUNNING AWAY, I HID, THAT'S WHY I FOUND IT HARD TO EVEN TALK TO YOU, YET YOU WERE THE ONE THING I KNEW I REALLY WANTED, REALLY CARED FOR YET DESPITE THAT BECAUSE OF MY BEHAVIOUR I FELT YOU SLIPPING AWAY EVERY MINUTE AND THIS ONLY MADE ME FEEL WORSE. IT WAS LIKE CLIMBING OUT OF A PIT AND SEEING THE LIGHT AT THE TOP YET EVERY STEP I TOOK UPWARDS I SLID TWO STEPS DOWN. THE MORE I FELT LIKE THAT THE MORE I WANTED TO RUN. EVERYDAY I SPOKE TO YOU I COULD SEE YOU GETTING WORSE. I FELT SO RESPONSIBLE AND SO SICK WITH MYSELF I WANTED TO RETREAT FURTHER IN YET IN TRUTH I FELT LIKE CALLING OUT BUT JUST COULDN'T DO IT, IT WAS LIKE A NIGHTMARE, EVERYTHING GOT OUT OF HAND AND NOW I FEAR THEY WILL NEVER BE THE SAME AGAIN. I'VE NO RIGHT TO ANYTHING WHATEVER IT IS I WANT OR DESIRE THERE'S NO ROOM FOR THE WEAK OR EMOTIVE.

On Bank Holiday Monday, Tony Wilson, Lindsay Reade, Rob Gretton and Alan Erasmus drove over to Macclesfield to pick up Debbie Curtis and visit Ian in hospital, listening to the tapes of *Closer* as they did so.

"It sounded great, better than in the studio in a way, perhaps because it was now a complete album and made more sense as an entire work," says Lindsay. "I thought Ian should have felt extremely pleased with himself creating something like that. But poor Ian was in Macclesfield hospital as we listened to the most stunning achievement of Factory to date."

There was a feeling amongst those in the car that the quality of the music was completely at odds with the problems, domestic and otherwise, of Joy Division's lead singer. It didn't make sense to them that he would want to leave this world.

It was Lindsay's suggestion that after he was released from hospital Ian should stay with her and Tony to ease the pressure of his double life, and Tony agreed. "As I understood it at the time Debbie was threatening divorce unless he gave Annik up," she says.

"Meanwhile he was under another kind of pressure to be with Annik and it seemed there could be no peace in either camp. Perhaps he just needed some space. From the band as well, perhaps. I assumed it was a domestic problem though. I didn't realise how seriously the epilepsy was affecting him and it never occurred to me then that he may have felt he couldn't go on with the stage performances."

At the house on Barton Street the party were greeted by Debbie, looking shaken and pale but still quite strong. Lindsay stayed behind to look after young Natalie while Debbie and the others went to the hospital. Lindsay gave Debbie a card she'd made to give to Ian on which there was a quote by playwright David Hare next to a hand drawn picture of a cow surrounded by grass, flowers and a hill: "There is no comfort. Our lives dismay us. We have dreams of leaving and it's the same for everyone I know."[1]

When they arrived at Ian's room, he was sitting up looking slightly embarrassed. "He looked a bit pale," says Alan. "I remember thinking that Rob was being a bit too jovial for the occasion. It seemed a very serious situation – not that we should have been morbid or anything."

Meanwhile, back at the house Lindsay was babysitting Natalie and taking in her surroundings. Debbie was clearly a diligent housewife for it was clean and tidy, a reflection of the environment in which Debbie had been raised. An uneaten, whole, cooked chicken sat on a plate in the kitchen

---

[1] It's likely that Lindsay's mother thought this would be a suitable quotation. Some 25 years later Lindsay met Matt Greenhaulgh, the screenplay writer for the movie *Control*, who was particularly interested where this quote came from. She had no idea but after research on the internet discovered that it came from a BBC TV play by David Hare called *Dreams Of Leaving* which was aired on the *Play For Today* on January 17. 1980. "I know that my mum never missed the *Play For Today* so suddenly felt sure that it must surely have originated from her," says Lindsay. "I was probably the carrier bird. But I knew there was truth in these words and I wanted Ian to be reminded that he was not alone."

and seemed to Lindsay to symbolise the love that had grown cold in this house. "It was as though that chicken was announcing something bleak," she says. "I took it then to symbolise doom somehow. It had just been left to go cold."

At the hospital Tony put it to Ian that he should spend a week or so with Lindsay and himself and Ian agreed. It was arranged that he would begin his stay the following day, Tuesday, April 8, after the next scheduled Joy Division show at Bury.

The decision to go ahead with the council funded gig at Derby Hall, Bury, was apparently taken by Rob, even though he was aware there was a good chance that Ian wouldn't be able to perform. He was hoping that Ian might be able to make a quick, low-key appearance before handing the vocal duties over to someone else who would close the show. Because of the relative success of the 'Factory by Moonlight' gigs, with the Factory roster providing a disparate blend of artists, Tony thought it would be a good idea for a Factory medley to cover for Ian, and to this end the gig also featured Minni Pops and Section 25. Unfortunately, Bury Derby Hall wasn't like the Moonlight and most, if not all, of the crowd, expected a normal Joy Division gig, with Ian Curtis on vocals throughout, with normal support acts. Touts were loitering with intent outside the venue, selling £3 tickets for £7 and there were plenty of takers.

Staging a Joy Division gig without Ian Curtis was never going to be easy and the band took the precaution of inviting Crispy Ambulance singer Alan Hempsall along as a stand-in, a daunting proposition for anyone. "I received a phone call from Bernard," says Hempsall. "He told me that Ian was ill. That's all I knew. He told me that Ian couldn't do the gig because he was poorly and would I mind stepping in for him. It was one hell of a shock, I can tell you. I had no qualms at all. Immediately I said, 'Yeah, of course.' I was keen as mustard. I was simply thrilled."

Hempsall began diligently learning Joy Division lyrics, including the new song, 'Love Will Tear Us Apart', which they had recorded from the John Peel Session, aired in January.

Larry Cassidy recalls the build up to the gig: "We get to Bury – start setting up, come to soundcheck time, we do that – Ian wasn't there, the band were but he wasn't. They do their soundcheck and then after that you're in a sort of limbo until you play. Then, I must have asked Rob where Ian was. He said he wasn't very well – he'd had a funny turn and such and such. Then the next minute Alan out of Crispy Ambulance is turning up in the dressing room. It gets to gig time and Ian's still not around and I think it transpired that we got the news he wouldn't be able to come at all. So it was kind of – guys in the dressing room, 'What are we going to do?' They're all out there. We sort of collaborated with Joy Division that the best way out of this would be to kind of mix the sets up. Just use the one kit, so you don't have to change kits or anything. We'd go on and do a bit of us and then slowly turn to JD and Alan would do some vocals – cos he knew the words, being a big fan – and we might be able to smooth it over a bit."

Then Ian arrived. Alan Hempsall: "I didn't know what to expect and I remember being quite surprised to see Ian in the dressing room. But I wasn't about to ask questions. I had gone along to do a job and, as far as I was concerned, that is what I was going to do. So I kind of kept within that professional attitude. As the evening wore on, it became apparent that it was taking a different slant from a normal gig. The Minni Pops went on first and did a full 40-minute set. There was then a short break and Section 25 came on, but only to play for about 20 minutes. At the time, they were Vini and Larry, the two brothers... and Paul the guitarist, who was on their first album. They would play for 20 minutes and their last number would be the single, 'Girls Don't Count'. It all seemed fairly straight-forward at this point. When 'Girls Don't Count' started, myself, Hooky, Bernard and Steve all joined them onstage, and Simon Topping from A Certain Ratio. So Larry did the lead vocals while Simon and myself sang the backing vocals, which consisted of the two of us singing 'Girls Don't Count' over and over again. There were two drummers and, as Larry was doing the vocals, he left bass duties to Hooky."

This unlikely assembly went down well, but crowd was still expecting to see Joy Division.

Hempsall: "At the end of that song, Section 25 and Simon left the stage. So that just left me with the three members of Joy Division, a pretty scary moment, to be honest. For me, a Joy Division fan, it seemed positively surreal. Here I was, standing in Ian Curtis's shoes. Well, I knew I couldn't but I was determined to make a decent job of it. We did 'Digital', from *The Factory Sample*, followed by 'Love Will Tear Us Apart'. I don't think I could have possibly known the greatness of that song at that point. What a strange way to get to know one of the greatest rock songs of all time."

Backstage Ian had indicated that he was willing to perform two of the slower numbers from the new *Closer* material, 'Decades' and 'The Eternal'. He duly wandered onto the stage, leaving a relieved Hempsall to retreat into the wings. Ian's performance on the two songs, which were unknown to the majority of the audience, was low key, leaving some to question whether

Curtis had appeared at all. Even Larry Cassidy admits that he doesn't have a clear memory of Ian singing that night.

When Ian left the stage he was replaced by Cassidy, Simon Topping from A Certain Ratio and Hempsall. They launched into The Velvet Underground's 'Sister Ray', with Larry taking over lead vocals while the other two provided backing. Although there was an element of unrest in the crowd, all seemed well as they departed.

It was a lull before the storm.

Hempsall: "I remember, as we were leaving the stage… there was this great big beautiful crystal chandelier hanging above the stage. It must have been there for donkey's years. At that point, someone threw a bottle which went bang into the middle of the chandelier and the whole thing just seemed to explode. We got completely showered with shards of glass and bits of chandelier. That was the moment it just kicked off. We ran off the stage and locked the door behind us. All I could hear was all these bottles crashing against the door. I didn't know how we were going to get out of there, I really didn't. Twinny and Terry Mason were on stage, swinging mike stands around, trying to clock people with them… well, in self defence. They were just trying to keep the kids off the equipment. It was getting really nasty at this point. Twinny got smacked over the back of the head with a bottle or glass which gave him this big gash. This was the point when Hooky, being the good Salford lad that he is, decided that, 'We can take these guys…' He grabbed two empty beer bottles and thrust them in my hands then picked up two more and, 'Come on… let's have 'em.'"

Larry Cassidy: "And they start lobbing bottles over Steve Morris's head. Glass was tippling down and cans, half-full of beer. Then it turns into a fucking tirade. Loads of it. So all the musicians fuck off. For some reason I got left behind the curtain. They couldn't see me. They were fucking bottling the empty stage. It was a big thick curtain but I could hear them. The dressing room was just there and they were lobbing stuff at the dressing room door. It subsided a bit and Hooky got really upset about it – being the big, macho man that he is. He wanted to go out into the crowd and start tearing it up. Paul Wiggin held him back. But the funny thing about it that I saw – cos they came out through the door… there's Paul, who was a big, tall guy, looked like Clint Eastwood… he's got Hooky in an arm lock, holding him back. But you know like when two guys have a row in the pub and a friend gets hold of one of them and it's all a bit – it was like that 'Hold me back, where are you?'"

There was no holding back Rob Gretton, as Lindsay Reade observed: "I saw Rob's face completely changing. He had this fierce stone-like look about him, ready for a fight. I had never seen him like that before. He shouted out in disgust, almost like a war cry, as he jumped, without a nanosecond of hesitation, straight into the fray."

Terry Mason started lashing out with a microphone stand at those who had attacked Twinny with the pint pot. "I was a reluctant fighter," he says. "Twinny was having the shit beat out of him after he'd been potted. He'd jumped in to help Rob. Rob had decided to punch someone and it wasn't happening like in cartoons. There were a few more people and Rob was getting a battering, so Twinny went in to save Rob and he got potted again. I thought, 'Oh fuck, I'm really shit at this, don't know anything about fighting but I'm from Salford, I go drinking in the same pubs as Twinny, I could never show my face if I didn't go in.' Someone had to get Twinny out of there."

Alan Hempsall, likewise, didn't regard himself as a fighter. "When Hooky charged out there, he dragged me with him," he recalls. "Well Hooky might be a warrior but I am a bit of a pacifist, really. I have always felt discretion to be the better part of valour but we went out onto the stage to face the audience who had whittled down to the few hardcore trouble makers who were really warming to the notion of a riot by this time. There was a row of bottles in front of them and they just kept picking them up and hurling them onstage. Me and Hooky were covered in glass. Hooky started charging around like a bull in a China shop… literally like that. And there was Tony Wilson hanging onto him, trying to drag him backstage. Tony was screaming, 'Come on Hooky… it's not worth it.' Clearly Tony was correct. It wasn't worth it. We could have got murdered out there. But Hooky being strong was dragging Tony all around the stage. I suppose it was quite comic in retrospect, but it didn't seem very funny at the time. But somehow we all managed to get backstage again, intact and we locked ourselves in again."

Terry believes that those who caused the trouble were "Scally types" who moaned when they said they couldn't get tickets – though he didn't think the gig was a sell out – and, as a result, Rob had put them on his guest list. "A lot of people felt cheated," he adds. "The ones who'd paid, they wanted Ian Curtis singing songs and weren't going to take shit."

When peace was restored Lindsay Reade drove Twinny to hospital, where he received several stitches. The pair whom Terry had attacked with the mike stand were also in casualty, sitting silently waiting to be attended. "There was a bit of an uneasy truce," says Lindsay, "a bit like Christmas day in the trenches. One of these other two lads said to the other that he'd only seen A Certain Ratio the week before and it was seeing their singer out front instead of Ian that made him throw the first bottle (that hit the chandelier)."

"We won on stitches," says Terry," they needed three between them whereas Twinny only needed two."

More seriously, Ian was deeply upset by the riot. "The whole thing after Bury shook him," says Terry. "I think it was cos he realised that his actions were actually affecting other people. Ian wouldn't have liked that, he wouldn't have seen the glory in a riot when people actually got hurt. Twinny was there with a couple of stitches in his head from being potted. I was still bruised up from getting a battering helping Twinny. So it was involving others – not just Debbie and Annik and that. It was people that really didn't have anything to do with any of his goings on but physically hurt – not just emotionally hurt. That seemed to get to him."

Tony remembers finding Ian with his head in his hands after the gig, blaming himself for the trouble. In an attempt to comfort him, Tony reminded him of the riot at Manchester's Free Trade Hall during Lou Reed's Sally Can't Dance Tour. That had been a fractious affair – with Reed standing ice-cold in dark glasses and then refusing to return for an encore, a stance which was symbolic of an approaching punk attitude. In typical 'myth-maker' style, Wilson reminded Ian how great such gigs were full-on art events.

Yet however much Ian loved Velvet Underground, it is doubtful that he was much consoled by this. Had Ian Curtis been a different type of rock star, one with the kind of ego more suited to the job, he would no doubt have been gratified that his absence from a gig caused a near riot. But he wasn't and he didn't. He was a gentle soul with genuine humility who really didn't want to hurt anyone. And here he was in a position where he seemed to be hurting everyone close to him – his wife, his daughter, his girlfriend, his group, his friends, and even his fans.

CHAPTER 19

A Cry For Help, A Hint Of Anaesthesia

"I think we all assumed – obviously wrongly – that it was a cry for help, a plea for anaesthesia. Looking back on it, it was a pity that the stupid bugger put that line in one of his songs. It made it easier to believe that was what it was, when obviously it wasn't. We thought it was – that's how fucking stupid we were." – Tony Wilson

After the Bury gig, Ian travelled back with Tony and Lindsay for the first night of his stay at their home. He was quiet in the car, obviously lost in thought. Their house, in the village of Charlesworth, was fairly remote, so much so that visits by friends and family were few and far between. A two-up and two-down end terrace, its second bedroom, in which Ian would sleep, had a sliding door and was quite cosy, albeit spacious enough to hold only a single bed. The kitchen and bathroom were in a downstairs extension. Due to work commitments, Tony was unlikely to be there for most of the time, leaving Lindsay alone with Ian during the day and in the early evening. Tony was presenting *Granada Reports*, which was broadcast live from 6 to 6.30pm every weekday, and rarely made it back home before *Coronation Street* began, but that particular week calls on his time meant that most nights he didn't make it home until very late. He was and remains a very busy man.

When Ian agreed to stay with Tony and Lindsay, it's likely he was expecting Tony to be around so it would have been a surprise for him to have to spend so much time with Lindsay who'd recently given up working as a teacher and was generally at home during the day.

"I didn't think he'd accept the invitation," says Lindsay. "It was perhaps a reflection of the state of mind he was in that he did. He didn't know me at all really – I was just a young sweet girl who happened to be married to the company boss. I think he thought quite highly of Tony – they shared an intellectual acuteness. My hope was that it would be a convalescent time for him. I understood the need for resolution and closure on one of his relationships but it seemed, in view of the drastic step he had just taken, that he needed time out from the whole thing. Plus it required a decision and clarity that I thought he could better make away from both women. I was not mature enough at that time to relate to the torment when a child and family are at stake. Of course there is always the possibility – which I hadn't considered then – that his mind was already made up."

When they returned to the house it was late and all three went straight to bed. The next day Tony left after a breakfast of toast and coffee, leaving Ian and Lindsay alone for the first time. The furniture in the living room consisted of a settee, two armchairs, a wicker rocking chair – Tony's throne – and a large, low, polished wood coffee table. Ian assumed a position on the floor with his legs under this table and leant back against one of the armchairs. "That is how I see him in that room," says Lindsay. "It was probably for convenience since the ashtray was on the table and a cigarette was frequently in his hand."

The Wilsons' record player was on the other side of the room opposite where Ian sat, and Lindsay played records continuously during his stay. A typical morning would consist of music from Iggy Pop (*The Passenger*), David Bowie (*Heroes*), Velvet Underground, Lou Reed, Neil Young and Brian Eno, all music that they both liked. While Lindsay busied herself making cups of coffee, serving lunch and tea and doing general chores, Ian remained in his spot apart from visits to the bathroom. "I didn't think this especially significant or worrying," says Lindsay, "nor did I think it chauvinistic but I expect I would in these more modern times. He seemed lost in his thoughts."

Lindsay can't recall whether Ian accompanied her to shops nearby or in Glossop but suspects he stayed in with the record player. They talked desultorily but, while there was no hint of coldness between the pair, Ian didn't seem inclined to say very much. "It wasn't until the evening that I – or we – became aware of the need for a bit more conversation or entertainment," says Lindsay. "We suddenly really felt alone. I wanted him to open up to me.

I do remember one particular evening when Ian and I were left to our own devices – Tony had gone somewhere that meant he'd be late, like 2am. I felt a little bit shy and awkward since Ian was clearly a man of few words by nature. Not only that but we had never been alone together before this visit. I was driven to speak to him and to engage him in something. I really wanted to help and, probably naively, imagined that I could."

On the evening when they were alone together until late, Lindsay, who had an interest in hypnotism and palmistry, suggested she read Ian's palm, as she had done some months previously in a dressing room or during one of many endless nights in the studio. "I clearly remember reading Ian's palm after the suicide attempt," she says. "I can only assume I must have looked at it twice. That night, I remember looking with some concern to see if Ian had a suicide line. I had gone on learning what several of the lines and con-figurations meant and one of those recently learned happened to be the suicide line."

Lindsay was aware that a suicide line was one where the headline droops down and merges with the lifeline. A highly logical, mathematical mind has a straight headline but more commonly the headline slopes downwards, but doesn't connect with the life line, and this suggests more of an artistic bent. She was hugely relieved to see that the artistic bent to the headline was the only visible sign.

"You're going to be all right," she exclaimed naively to Ian. "You haven't got a suicide line."

Ian appeared to think this credible, though Lindsay isn't sure now whether she simply imagined this. "I don't think he said anything but he seemed interested in the idea. I really believed he was safe."[1]

As the evening wore on, at around 10 pm, Lindsay suggested that she try to hypnotise Ian and he brooked no objection. "He was totally open and malleable," she continues. "I'd had a practise but only in a big hall and had never actually seen anyone go under. But I knew the techniques. So it was a simple matter to try them on Ian. What really shocked me though was that when I got to the end of the techniques – actually even before I got to the end – Ian was quite obviously in a trance. I stared in amazement and watched him for what seemed like an eternity. He wasn't awake and he wasn't asleep. He was unaware of anything in the room. If I giggled or coughed or simply just waited, he didn't respond.

"I was trained to take people out of trance as well but had not had a single lesson in what to do with a person whilst under. Clearly Ian's brain

---

[1] Lindsay dropped her interest in palmistry from the day Ian died and has not resumed it.

was highly suggestible in that the suggestion of hypnotism was enough to make him go under. He had an affinity to trance. Here was a chance to suggest to his brain the most uplifting healing affirmations to help make a positive difference to his life. Unfortunately I hadn't heard of NLP or affirmations then – indeed did NLP even exist then? My confidence was a bit low. I was out of my depth. It has always been a source of regret to me that this opportunity wasn't used or followed up on."

Barney would hypnotise Ian not long after this, and Ian wrote about it in what was actually his last letter to Annik, on May 5, 1980: *LAST NIGHT WAS VERY INTERESTING. BERNARD HYPNOTISED ME AND PUT MY SUBCONSCIOUS MIND THROUGH A SERIES OF REGRESSIONS INTO PAST LIFE AND TAPED IT ON CASSETTE. I STILL CAN'T BELIEVE IT THOUGH I'VE HEARD IT MYSELF. HE STARTED GETTING ME TO TALK ABOUT MY CHILDHOOD AND THEN REGRESSED FURTHER TO A LIFE BEFORE THAT, AND THEN OTHERS. I STILL CAN'T BRING MYSELF TO LISTEN TO IT ALL. I JUST CAN'T BELIEVE IT, BUT THE PROOF OF IT IS ON THE TAPE. I JUST CAN'T FIND AN EXPLANATION BECAUSE I WASN'T AWARE AT THE TIME WHAT I WAS SAYING.*

Lindsay was too inexperienced in hypnotism to dig into Ian's past and didn't know him as well as Barney. "How are you feeling Ian?" was all she could think to ask in order to dig down to the bone of truth and, hence, the clarity. "Confused," was all he replied. She had hoped to help bring some clarity to his life but on hearing this she assumed he was confused to the core of his being. "You would think I would have had the sense to at least say to him something along the lines of 'When you wake your confusion will have vanished, you will have clarity and confidence and optimism', but I was very young. I didn't want to mess with his head in any way. I suppose I was a bit panicky as well in case I couldn't bring him back. I had once gone in a trance myself – not a hypnotic trance – it was, I believe, a case of astral travelling. I left my body – such that my vision was moving away from it – but my body itself was clearly not moving. It was a most terrifying experience and my biggest fear was that I would be unable to return to my body. I remained outside it for a few hours. This happened to me when I was 18 and now, eight years later, I was afraid it could be repeated with Ian and it would be my fault. So I decided not to pursue anything other than the directions for bringing him back."

Lindsay needn't have worried. Ian woke up immediately after he was told to. Back in the room again, his mood seemed little altered; still quiet and thoughtful and still, no doubt, deeply confused.

After he woke up he talked to Lindsay about the Bury gig the day before. "I was standing in the wings watching them play and I saw it all going on without me," he said. "[It was] as though I was looking down on it – they were just carrying on without me."

The full significance of this was lost on Lindsay at the time. "I dismissed it as simply how it must have felt to Ian then. In other words, that night, they actually were carrying on without him. Mind you the audience were none too pleased about that. So one would have thought that they wouldn't do too well without him. But there was something about the way Ian said this that was kind of mystical and clairvoyant. It remains etched on my memory as evidence of a certain kind of clairvoyance that he had – although we didn't know it. He was highly intuitive of course but I think he had a knowledge that went beyond even that. And sure enough the band has gone on without him. Another strange thing is that it was as if Ian had a fore-knowledge of the moment when he had a foreknowledge of something else when he wrote the following: 'Watched from the wings as the scenes were replaying, We saw ourselves now as we never had seen.'"[1]

The following morning Tony was up and out of the house by 10 am. Ian took up his usual position with his legs under the coffee table, records were placed on the turntable and Lindsay ferried food and drink to and from the kitchen. Ian was a bit more talkative than the day before, probably because he was getting to know Lindsay better and realised that she had no agenda. "I wasn't passing judgement or taking sides – not the wife, not the girlfriend, and not even the band," she says. "With hindsight I suspect he had sought safety in the music by agreeing to stay at the house of the record company boss. Or perhaps he felt his career was the only place of safety he had left. Where could he turn? There was I, in surrogate mother mode, attempting to help this guy back to his own life. It was a bit unreal really."

Later that day Ian confided to Lindsay about another intuitive moment in his life which was somewhat similar to his experience at the Bury gig. Suddenly he came over as strangely mystical and blurted out: "I knew before I married Debbie that there would be another woman. I knew without any doubt that I'd love someone else. I was dressed in my wedding suit, the wedding car was on its way, and I was looking out of the window thinking about this."

"What did you do?" asked Lindsay.

[1] Decades, 1980.

"I nearly didn't get in that car," replied Ian. "I didn't see how I could make the vows in church knowing that I wasn't going to keep them. It seemed wrong to swear to God something you know to be untrue."

"But had you met or even seen anyone else?" asked Lindsay.

"No, it wasn't that at all," he said. "I hadn't even looked at anyone. I just knew that there would be someone else."

Lindsay understood where Ian was coming from. A believer in premonition and prophecy, since she thinks that time is not essentially linear, she didn't doubt that Ian Curtis had an unusually intuitive grasp of what the 'future' would bring.

Around noon that day there was a knock at the door. Lindsay wasn't expecting anyone and, indeed, confirms that it was rare for her to receive an unexpected visitor, apart from the milkman or the local priest who hoped Tony's line of work might lead to a boost of the church funds. Most of the visitors to this house either came to stay or were invited for dinner and arrived by car in the evening, as expected guests. Few of their friends lived in the vicinity, but an exception was Tony Connolly, who lived in Gamesley in Glossop.

Connolly was a rough diamond – "an ex-convict with a heart of gold," according to Lindsay – who had befriended Tony (Wilson's) father, Sydney, who was homosexual.[1] Tony's mother died in 1975, leaving Sydney Wilson alone and lonely until he met Tony Connolly two years later, probably in a pub. They picked each other up for what had all the makings of a one-night stand, and stayed together until Sydney's death in 1997.

Ian was a bit taken aback by the arrival of Connolly, which wasn't surprising as he was both eccentric and slightly shocking. He liked a drink, had a working-class accent and tattoos on his hands and arms. Despite his close relationship to the Wilson family he was once thrown out of the Haçienda for erotic dancing, swirling his hips and sliding his pants seductively down his bum while spinning around one of the painted poles.

Soon after Connolly's arrival Ian announced he was going out to get some cigarettes. After he'd left Connolly turned to Lindsay and said: "That guy is really depressed."

---

[1] You may wonder how he came to father Tony but Sydney and Tony's mother had an arrangement that worked. She had lost the love of her life during World War II, and her marriage to Sydney appeared to be a compromise in her mid-forties. She actually gave birth to Tony at the age of 46. She lived with her brother as well as Sydney. It is thought that Sydney and her brother may have been lovers at some point. Whatever the arrangement they raised a boy who was only ever aware of being very much loved by three adults.

"Although perhaps this was obvious I have to say that it hadn't really occurred to me that Ian was so acutely depressed," says Lindsay today. "[He was] quiet, yes, thoughtful, yes. It may seem stupid in view of his suicide attempt only a week earlier but I thought he was OK – as in he was eating and sleeping. He hadn't made a single complaint. He smiled and was affable and polite. He simply wasn't showing the kind of behaviour I'd associate with depression. I assumed he was in recovery."

"He's really depressed," continued Connolly. "He'll commit suicide for certain."

Lindsay was shocked and, aware that Connolly was in the habit of shocking people wherever he went, was inclined to treat his statement as rubbish. "I did the same when Connolly told me my mum was seriously ill," she says. "In fact my mum and I even laughed about him saying this – only three months before her death as it turned out. Looking back over a 26-year friendship with the man I'd say Connolly was psychic. I can understand if you think it faintly ridiculous for a man who described Ian as suicidally depressed at this time to be called psychic. But, believe me, it wasn't obvious to me."

Nor, it would seem, to anyone else. And if it was, no-one was doing anything about it. It's no secret that depression acts as a repellent, and people tend to turn their backs on sufferers. Nonetheless Lindsay believes that if friends had realised the state Ian was in, or had thought he really had any serious intention to end his life, they would have given him more help and attention. Doreen, Ian's mum, said that she and Ian's dad, "didn't have any idea of the problems that were going on. We didn't know about the overdose."

When Ian duly returned with a fresh supply of cigarettes in hand, Lindsay looked at him rather differently. "I'd assumed he was all right even if he wasn't exactly having the best time. He'd put on a reasonable show up until then. That night we watched television. He seemed to be amenable to whatever was on the menu, be it Iggy Pop, *Coronation Street* or steak and kidney pie. He didn't show much of a preference for anything and was quite happy to leave things up to me. Probably he was indifferent. But that night I decided, not for the first time, that Tony Connolly was wrong, that Ian's life wasn't in danger. He just was having a domestic problem and he needed to rest and recuperate. He was doing that with us and everything was going to be ok.

"That evening Tony got back and sat in his rocking chair rolling a joint. As always he was cheerful and optimistic. There didn't seem to be any problems from where he was sitting. I probably told him what Connolly had said but he would undoubtedly have said that it was rubbish, like he always has done about anything faintly metaphysical that I have ever said."

Lindsay can recall little else of note that occurred the week that Ian came to stay. There were no further visitors, and Ian appeared content to simply listen to music, smoke cigarettes, eat and sleep, all the while communicating little about what was going on inside his head. Ostensibly Ian accepted that he was under orders to be alone, though in hindsight it seems that if any of Ian's friends or family had visited then this would have stimulated him and certainly helped lift the tedium he and Lindsay were under. Annik had wanted very much to visit Ian after his suicide attempt when he was staying at the Wilson house but was outlawed, as was Debbie. It seems this was one occasion when wives and girlfriends definitely weren't being made welcome. It was tragic that Annik could not give her support to Ian then since she seems to have been the person who came closest to understanding the state of mind he was in immediately before and after his suicide attempt, and was therefore probably the best qualified to bring him back from that particular brink.

In a letter to Ian's sister Carole, Annik mentioned a conversation they had on April 8: "He sounded very emotional and sad and confused. It took him a long time before he told me what happened and he said, 'Oh it is stupid, stupid, it is not worth talking about'. I was terribly upset and wanted to go and see him as soon as possible but he was a long way from London, staying with Tony Wilson in Glossop, having a rest and was to be left alone. Rob insisted very much that all he needed was calm, peace and not to see either Debbie or me for a while."

"It had seemed to me that he needed to be away from both women – from the pressures of making a decision – but what did I know?" says Lindsay. "Who were we to judge what he needed?"

Ian wrote to Annik in the letter of April 17: *IT REALLY STUNNED ME WHEN I REALISED ALL THE DECISIONS OTHER PEOPLE WERE MAKING FOR ME, THE THINGS THEY WERE SAYING OR DOING ON MY BEHALF AND EVERYONE'S VARIOUS OPINIONS ON MY CURRENT STATE OF MIND.*

"With hindsight I can see clearly that isolation was not what he needed at this time and was not helpful." continues Lindsay. "Isolation was one of the tragedies."

Vini Reilly, however, remembered calling Ian on the telephone that week and when he related the following story to Lindsay it jogged her own memory. She distinctly recalls Ian sitting in the little study which you had to walk through from the living room to reach the kitchen and bathroom. She had assumed then that this long private conversation was with Annik.

Vini: "The strongest memory I have of Ian is after his first suicide attempt and he was staying at yours and Tony's place. I asked Tony if it was all right to ring him up and he thought it would be a good idea to have a chat with him. We spoke for about two hours on the phone. We were just chatting. I knew from my experiences that the worst thing to do was to say, 'How are you?' and all that sympathy shit. Sympathy is absolutely a waste of time when you're feeling like that. What people need is stimulation and some sense of normality. I just made sure that we had a normal conversation. Like 'What you up to?', 'When's the album coming out?', 'What you recording next?' and stuff like that.

"The thing I remember most is asking him about his lyrics. I asked him where they came from and told him how I really struggle with lyrics. He tried to explain that he had lots and lots of lyrics and he didn't see what the fuss was about really. They were just lyrics. He didn't know if they were any good or not. But he confided that he quite often wrote about a person or about someone but what he was actually writing about was himself. It was a strategy he used. You'd think he was describing someone else but he was actually describing himself. The other thing he said was that a lot of what he wrote didn't mean what people necessarily thought it meant. He said he thought a lot of people misunderstood what he was singing about and didn't get it. I asked him to give me an example. He described the lines from a song off *Closer*, which hadn't been released yet so I'd not heard it. The lines were: 'Accept like a curse an unlucky deal, With children my time is so wastefully spent.'[1]

"That song is about this guy that he used to see near where he lived in Macclesfield who, at that time, we would call him mentally retarded. I think we both used the same phrase. He described a grown man who had the mental age of about four or five – there was obviously something wrong with him. This man hung out with the children in the park near where Ian lived. Ian used to watch this guy with the kids. The song was a description of this guy who he used to see quite regularly. This guy couldn't communicate with any other grown-ups, he could only communicate with children. Basically what Ian was saying was that every song, every single line or phrases had a specific meaning for him. It was actually about something very specifically. It wasn't a general vibe – they were very specific his lyrics

[1] The song is 'The Eternal'

and people didn't understand that. I was quite surprised. I didn't really understand what he meant until I heard the song on *Closer*. Of course most people wouldn't know that he was actually describing something that really exists in reality as part of Ian's life. He said that every lyric in every song was basically multi-layered and had many meanings and could be applied to either him or sometimes it was inspired by describing another person but most of the time, in fact a lot of the time, he was describing himself.

"I know at the start of that conversation – you know when someone is depressed – his voice was very quiet but at the end of the conversation he was very animated and excited about things and more positive. But he brought up the subject of his attempted suicide with me. I was surprised. I thought this was a subject to be avoided and to try and keep it positive because that is how I would have been with it. But he just said – basically: 'I actually meant it you know.' Everyone thinks it was a cry for help and Rob said it was a cry for help. And Ian just said to me, 'It wasn't a cry for help. – I actually want out.' And there was nothing I could say to it. That's when I lost the ability to really be helpful to him in that conversation. It had been a long conversation before he said that. He seemed quite happy about it. He didn't say it in some dreadful doomy voice it was just like he'd made the decision and it was a very clear one he'd made. Ian told me that Rob had said that, 'This is obviously a cry for help and you need help and we'll get you help.' And Ian was saying 'It wasn't, I did mean it.'"

There was a Factory gig for Joy Division at the Russell Club on the Friday night, April 11. Terry remembers that the Factory nights were good money, with the group earning between £750 and £1,000. "Rob had freaked, expecting the people from Bury to cause trouble so he brought in security," says Terry. "There was Corky – a mate from Wythenshawe days, who went on to work with New Order, and Robbo, who was the head bouncer at Checkers in Altrincham. Robbo and his door team were the first set of bouncers at the Haçienda. In the Henry Royce pub we had more security than we ever thought we'd need. Rob was spooked by Bury. Ian was very apologetic to Rob, myself and Twinny. I think Tony may have given Twinny extra money – £5 a stitch! Ian wasn't well from having his stomach pumped and full of guilt because of damage caused."

A gig scheduled at Bradford on Saturday, April 12, was cancelled.

Lindsay Reade doesn't recall much about the Factory night or the weekend that followed and neither does Tony. On either the Saturday or Sunday morning, however, the couple had an argument when Ian was present in the home, an incident which Lindsay deeply regrets. "I lost it and started a row with Tony in the kitchen," she admits. "I don't think I had realised it until this point but I was pretty depressed myself by the weekend. I felt suicidal even if Ian wasn't. I shouted at Tony. I was angry with him that I had been left alone with Ian the whole time with zero support. Why had it only been the two of us? He didn't seem to think support was needed. In fact – as it turned out – the instruction Ian was under was to be left in peace and quiet. But I was not the right person for him to be left alone with."

Subsequently, Tony would tell Debbie Curtis that Ian and Lindsay were both 'nutters' driving each other round the bend by being together all day. Amongst other things Lindsay said – probably with a raised voice – was that Ian had sat in the same position all week – almost catatonically – and hadn't even so much as taken a cup through to the kitchen to be washed. "As soon as this was out of my mouth I regretted it," she says. "I knew that Ian may have heard it and I knew that I'd lost him. I didn't want him to leave. I wasn't asking him to. I was just out of my depth. The thing I feel most terrible about is that I was thinking about myself – about how I was feeling rather than thinking about Ian. He seemed in a calmer state than me though and, ostensibly, he appeared to be in a better frame of mind. It seems crazy – there's this guy who had dramatic explosions in public but in this domestic setting he was as quiet as a lamb. And there's me having an explosion in the kitchen. I still have guilt about that. I don't get the feeling that Ian thinks I let him down but I always will. Probably he understood. We were both volatile maybe. But the timing of it was crucially bad. Ian needed a sanctuary that was neutral. That's why I had offered it. But I blew it.

"Tony's reaction to my explosion was to assume a masterly control, almost as if I was irrelevant to the proceedings in any case. Tony told Ian they were leaving and they got into his car and drove off. I was really upset and didn't want it to be left like that. I didn't know where they were going but assumed Tony was taking Ian away from me. We always parked our cars facing up the hill and, on departure, turned around close by to go back down the hill and past the house. As Tony's car was making its way down the hill I ran out in front of it. That wouldn't have been the first or last time I did that. My memory is very dim but I'm sure the car thing with Ian did happen because I remember it being relayed back to me that Ian had told someone about it – maybe Barney – that he couldn't believe his eyes – 'She just threw herself in front of the car,' he said. So much so that if he had written 'She's Lost Control' after that date and we didn't know that the song was about a girl he met when he was a disablement officer then I would have thought it could have been about me. Where they went I don't know.

But wherever it was I was surprised that they came back as soon as they did. I thought Ian had gone for good and that Tony might have been gone for the whole weekend. It rather took away from my dramatic and drastic plea of 'Don't go like this' for them to drive off and then return so soon.

"Tony seemed to want to make it up to me. Perhaps he thought, quite rightly, that I needed time away from Ian's mood. It was a bit like being with a young infant – 24 hours with no other adult company is simply too much."

That evening Tony took Lindsay to see a play in Stratford, leaving Ian behind and on his own in the house. "That was a bad move," says Lindsay. "Debbie recalls Ian complaining to her that Tony left him 'with a pile of Hendrix LPs and some dope'. Not what he needed. Ian needed help. Just because I couldn't give it/wasn't aware of it at that point didn't alter that fact. I didn't enjoy the play. But I knew I'd lost Ian anyway.

"I thought he might be relieved to have the house to himself. Then I thought that he either wouldn't be there when we got back or, if he was, he wouldn't stay into the next week. He was back but he didn't stay. He said he was going to go back to Debbie's. I hoped this was the resolution but I knew there was no resolution. He was just leaving us. Or me, rather. He didn't want to be any trouble. I attempted to plead with him to stay but met a wall. His mind was made up."

Ian left the Wilson home in such a hurry that he left some of his clothes in the washing machine. He came back for them two days later. "I thought that at least his intention must be to live if he thinks he will be needing the clothes," says Lindsay. "I felt awful. I remember he didn't seem to want to come into the house. I told him again that there was no need for him to go. But the last thing he wanted to be was a burden."

In the movie *24 Hour Party People* the Ian character is seen calling round the Wilson house but does not enter. There is therefore a grain of truth in this but – in the movie – he goes home and kills himself the same day. Although this is factually incorrect, it was how it felt to Lindsay.

After leaving the Wilson home, Ian went to Barton Street and then to Barney's house and later to his parent's home in Manchester where, according to his mother, he did not seem unusually depressed. Lindsay: "Pete (Johnson) said that people who are acutely depressed do not have enough energy to kill themselves, that the more dangerous time is when they have started to lift out of the depression and are feeling a bit better. This fits in with what Ian's mum said – she thought he seemed all right."

During that time Ian received two postcards from Annik in Egypt which, though a bit gloomy in one part – speaking about the prevalence of death in Egypt – must definitely have reassured him that she did, in fact, still love him.

"Someone said that the words 'if only' are two of the saddest words in our language," says Lindsay. "They played over and over again in my mind after Ian died. If only this, if only that. But Vini Reilly said that he thought it was Ian's time. Funny that. People often say that about natural deaths but I have never heard it said about a suicide. Perhaps there is comfort in that. Perhaps it was his time to go."

CHAPTER 20

Watching The Reel As It Comes To A Close

"Ian really was at the centre of a storm in a way." – Paul Morley

However confused Ian may have felt after his suicide attempt, and despite the fact that he initially returned to Barton Street from the Wilson home, it seems clear that some form of separation from Debbie subsequently took place. On leaving the Wilson's cottage in Charlesworth he stayed mostly away from Barton Street for five weeks, living either at Barney's house or with his parents.

Ian's letter to Annik on April 17 went some way to explaining his desperation but she may have felt that she was intruding on his life, for elsewhere in the letter he wrote: *I REALISE JUST HOW MUCH I'M UPSETTING YOUR LIFE AND WHAT I'M DOING TO YOU. I FEEL SO ASHAMED OF MYSELF AND IT UPSETS ME TO SEE YOU THIS WAY. LIKE I'VE SAID BEFORE IT'S ME WHO IS INTRUDING ON YOUR LIFE NOT YOU ON MINE. I FELT AS IF THINGS WERE BECOMING A BIT CLEARER EARLIER ON BUT CAN NOW SEE EVERYTHING FALLING TO PIECES BEFORE MY EYES … I NOW FEEL A DEEP SELF-HATE*

… YET YOU WERE THE ONE THING I KNEW I REALLY WANTED, REALLY CARED FOR YET DESPITE THAT BECAUSE

OF MY BEHAVIOUR I FELT YOU SLIPPING AWAY EVERY MINUTE AND THIS ONLY MADE ME FEEL WORSE.

As he was writing this letter he was listening to the soundtrack of *Apocalypse Now*. He mentioned the dialogue, the actor Marlon Brando reading T. S. Eliot's *The Hollow Men*: *"THE STRUGGLE BETWEEN MAN'S CONSCIENCE AND HIS HEART UNTIL THINGS GO TOO FAR, GET OUT OF HAND AND CAN NEVER BE REPAIRED. IS EVERYTHING SO WORTHLESS IN THE END? IS THERE ANY MORE? WHAT LIES BEYOND, WHAT IS LEFT TO CARRY ON."*

He also mentioned the new album, *Closer*, but even this was cause for sadness: *I LISTENED TO A TAPE OF THE NEW ALBUM WHILE I WAS AT MY MOTHER'S. SHE HAS A FAIRLY DECENT STEREO TAPE SYSTEM, IT SOUNDS REALLY GOOD. IT REMINDS ME OF YOU, THE THREE WEEKS IN LONDON, EVERYTHING. IT BREAKS MY HEART TO LISTEN TO IT KNOWING YOU ARE SO FAR AWAY AND ARE NOW FARTHER AWAY STILL. IT MEANS SO MUCH TO ME. I REALISE MY FAILINGS, MY WEAKNESSES AND HOPE YOU FORGIVE ME. WHATEVER IS LEFT OUT OF ALL THIS, WHAT- EVER CAN BE REBUILT OR RE-ARRANGED, AS I'VE SAID SO MANY TIMES I'LL LOVE YOU FOREVER. I NOW HAVE THE GIFT OF SOUND AND VISION, AND WHAT I SEE OF MYSELF – I HATE AND THE THINGS I HEAR ABOUT ME – I ALSO HATE, BUT I'M THANKFUL THAT THIS IN ITSELF IS AT LEAST SOME MOTIVA- TION, SOME DRIVING FORCE TO URGE ME ON INSTEAD OF HIDING AND SHRINKING AWAY. I LOVE YOU – WITH ALL MY MIND, HEART AND SOUL*

Annik's letter to Carole in 1980 confirms the times and places of the final two meetings between her and Ian, the penultimate one occurring, coinci- dentally, at the penultimate gig Joy Division would ever play: "Eventually we saw each other again on April 19 in Derby," she wrote, "where Joy Division were playing and we stayed together in Manchester for the weekend afterwards."

This Saturday night gig was at a venue called the Ajanta, an old cinema in Derby. "There was a sense of relief amongst the band as this was going to be one of the last gigs for a while," says Terry. "Ian was a bit more relaxed – he probably knew that gigs weren't particularly good for him and Twinny had his stitches out so Ian didn't feel as guilty. The mood was generally upbeat."

Annik can recall the hotel where she and Ian stayed for that and the fol- lowing night: the Elton Bank Hotel, Platt Lane, in Rusholme. "I remember a night at a B&B – a pretty flowery room, typically English, where we were holding each other tightly," she says. "There was a park outside and we walked there in the morning."

On the following day, a Sunday, Ian and Annik visited Rob Gretton in Chorlton, and Annik's 1980 letter to Carole continues: "That is when Debbie rang up Rob to find out where Ian was and we were there. Debbie was crying, I was crying, Ian didn't say a word, only a bit later, back at the hotel, he cried as well, trying to explain that is the way Debbie was, she wanted to know what hotel he was at, what we were doing, what colours the curtains were... We fell asleep and Monday early morning we went back to the station to take the train, Ian back to Macclesfield, and me back to London to my office."

Annik has kept the two bus tickets of this, their final journey into Manchester together on April 20. Early the same morning Tony Wilson happened to be travelling on the same train, and he saw the couple wandering about as he was driving near Piccadilly Station. He could not imagine a pair of more lovelorn creatures, he said. He wrote about this meeting in his book, *24 Hour Party People:* "Wilson knew that the fifteen minutes to Macc would be Ian and Annik's final moments for a while and left them to it. He saw Ian on the platform at Macc, waving goodbye to Annik. The grey raincoat, all-night exhaustion written on his face; or maybe the exhaustion at the emotions he was bombarded with, the ones he could or couldn't filter into his words, into his group. After a polite ten-minute interregnum, Wilson made his way back to where Annik was sitting in second class. Idle chit-chat with a sad-eyed lady. Until mention of the new album brought it out.

"'What do you think of the album then, Annik?'

"'I think it's terrible.'

"'The album?'

"'No, no, not the music, but what it is, don't you understand? He means these things, they're not just lyrics, they're not just songs. He means it.'

"'Means what?'

"'When he says, "I take the blame," don't you understand? He does exactly that, he thinks everything is his fault, it's just all too real.'

"Wilson nodded. And thought nothing. She was in love, she took the music too seriously. She was a Belgian, she took everything too seriously. It was just an LP. A great LP but not real, not life.

"Wrong.

"Totally fucking wrong."

★   ★   ★

Back in London, at her office, Annik received a phone call from Debbie. In her letter to Carole, Annik wrote: "That is when Debbie rang me to question me. I mainly listened to her as I could not speak very easily, my boss was there. I said she had to ask Ian, not me, it was easier. Two hours later Ian called me crying like a baby, saying it was too much, he was going away, he didn't want to stay there any longer. So Rob came to collect him and Ian stayed with Barney, the guitarist, for some days. Unfortunately I had to leave England on Saturday (April 26) to go back to Belgium and then leave for Egypt with my mother. I wish we never went there at such a time but my mother had booked the holiday two months before and everything was already paid."

Annik spoke about this phone call to the authors of this book before Carole showed them her private letter. "She once rang me at work at the Embassy screaming insults in my ear," said Annik. "Never has anyone spoken to me like that in my life. I felt so bad. It was then I realised Ian had not told the whole truth. Although it is hard for me to understand so much hatred from Debbie after all this time, I really forgive her. I should certainly ask for forgiveness too but I never felt I did something wrong except meet Ian in the first place. It seemed just so natural to get together and was all so innocent. I think he was very stressed from his family life and mainly from his illness and found some kind of peace by my side, some kind of refuge or escape."

Later, Annik said that until the phone call from Debbie she was "on a kind of cloud – like in a dream. Because I didn't realise that somebody was getting hurt from my relationship. I had not a single clue. That Debbie was there and upset – to me it was as if she... I did ask a few times about his wife. I was so surprised he was married so young. He would say that it was something from his previous life as a youngster and now he was a different person and it was not what he wanted now. Suddenly I realised I was hurting somebody. And the words she said to me – suddenly I felt dirty, going out with a married man. To me it was never like that in my head. I was a virgin. I was a young little girl. I was a tall girl and I was maybe 21 or 22 by then but I was a kid. I was a kid."

This same day – April 22 – Debbie's father called Ian's parents to discuss the problems their children were going through. Until now, Ian's parents had no idea of the problems Ian was experiencing. "We didn't know about the suicide attempt," says Doreen Curtis. "We were never told. Debbie had phoned me one night when Ian hadn't come back from London. But I was flabbergasted when Bob phoned me and said Ian had got someone else and that Debbie was staying with them. We went up to Macclesfield. The boys were there with Ian upstairs. He didn't want us to see him like that. We called up and said, 'If you want anything you know where we are.' He never wanted to trouble you, but he came to stay with us soon after that."

Carole also noted how Ian kept his problems to himself: "He was a very good actor, Ian. He'd mask his emotions. He never let you know what was really going on. He wouldn't want to upset you. I know it sounds ridiculous because he's upset everybody, but he wouldn't have wanted to upset anybody. If it was now [2005] they would have lived together, not got married but it wasn't the done thing then."

There can be no question that Ian felt deeply ashamed about the dilemma he had created. Terry: "He had shame about his epilepsy and his relationship with his daughter and divorce was one more shame. We were nice working-class people. We came from families where no one got divorced."

Annik also felt guilty at what had happened, and she called Ian to convey her feelings, telling him: "There was no way I could carry on like this and that he had lied to me. He cried and begged for forgiveness, saying it was not true. He knew I did not want any of the 'mistress' thing."

Then Ian wrote to Annik that same night: *PLEASE DO NOT THINK YOU ARE A PRESSURE ON ME. I WOULD DIE IF I DIDN'T SPEAK OR HEAR FROM YOU. EVERYONE SEEMS TO HAVE EVERY-THING WRONG & THEY'VE BEEN TOLD SO MANY TIMES BEFORE. I HAVE NO CHOICE TO MAKE. EVERYTHING WAS COMING TO AN END AT HOME AND THE ONLY THING WAS WHEN IT WOULD ACTUALLY END AND WHETHER I SHOULD GO BEFORE. AS IT IS THINGS HAVE NOW FINISHED AND THAT WORRY IS GONE. THESE PROBLEMS WERE AROUND LONG BEFORE I MET YOU EVERYONE KNOWS BUT SEEM TO WANT TO MAKE AN ISSUE OVER THEM BY LOOKING COMPLETELY OUT OF PERSPECTIVE INSTEAD OF FINALLY PUTTING IT TO REST.*

Without anything having been said, Terry Mason's role within Joy Division had changed since Ian's illness, and he was intelligent enough to realise exactly what was needed of him. "If the US tour had gone ahead I would have been Ian's minder," he says, "but not a 'thumping people' minder more the 'make sure you eat breakfast Ian' or 'early night for us two' type of thing."

It was in this capacity that he was now called upon to perform the most distressing task of his entire tenure as Joy Division's road manager: taking Ian to a mental hospital.

On the night of April 21 Ian stayed over at Rob and Leslie Gretton's house. Terry was under instruction to take Ian to the outpatients clinic at Parkside psychiatric hospital in Macclesfield the next day. He picked him up at the New Hormones office in town, getting a parking ticket in the process. Terry: "I drove him to the hospital. He and Debbie had separated, Ian had said it was over, but when we got there she was sat waiting for him. What was she doing there then? I was really shocked. Ian just shrugged, he didn't seem surprised. I was thinking, 'Is she mad? Or is he mad? Which one of us is mad and which one of us is driving people mad here?' They went in to see the doctor and I sat in the waiting room."

In the past he and Ian had once joked about Parkside. Now the joke had become a macabre reality. "We'd gone past Parkside ages before and laughed and joked about 'That's where you live that'," says Terry. "With Ian's epilepsy it had been a case of 'Are you still taking your tablets?' but now, going to a mental hospital stepped it up a gear. Reality is… this is a lot more serious than we wanted to imagine. We knew having the fits wasn't good but all of a sudden the reality of taking your mate into a psychiatric hospital brings it into a sharper focus."

Terry had been led to believe that Ian and Debbie were separated, that Ian had settled the issue in his own mind and made a final decision about what he was going to do. He thought that Ian seemed sure that he and Debbie were "completely done", that a divorce was being arranged and he would give her half of what he earned. He was also under the impression that Ian was looking forward to going to the States, and was no longer thinking about suicide. Indeed, the fact that Ian would be away for between four and five weeks would be a break from all of the anxiety and temporarily resolve the problem of where he best ought to stay. Furthermore, the band was planning a six-month sabbatical after America. They had signed a publishing deal with Zomba which included a reasonable advance, and money from this and recent gigs had been deposited into the band's bank account to help fund the upcoming tour. Although this had yet to translate into an increase in their own personal income there was certainly cause for optimism as far as their financial future was concerned. There was enough money in the kitty for them to take a lengthy break so they could figure out what to do next, and Terry believed all of this would have taken a load off Ian's mind.

Ian didn't mention his hospital visit in the letter he wrote to Annik that day but he did refer, presumably, to something that had transpired from the visit the two of them had made to Rob Gretton's house: *I DON'T KNOW WHAT ROB IS SAYING. I CAN'T UNDERSTAND. OBVIOUSLY HE*

DOESN'T KNOW HOW MUCH I FEEL FOR YOU. MAYBE I'M TO
BLAME. I KEEP MY OWN PERSONAL FEELINGS VERY CLOSE TO
ME AND ONLY TALK TO CLOSE FRIENDS AS ALL MY FRIENDS
ARE LONG GONE IT'S HARD FOR ANYONE TO SEE HOW I
REALLY FEEL. YOU ARE THE ONLY ONE WHO KNOWS THAT.
YOU SHOULD IGNORE THE THINGS HE SAYS IF IT HURTS YOU.
IT HURTS ME TOO. YET OUR FEELINGS FOR OURSELVES ARE
THE MOST IMPORTANT, WE ARE THE ONES THAT COUNT AND
NOTHING ELSE MATTERS. ANNIK I WANT YOU SO BADLY, I
NEED YOU, I CAN'T DO WITHOUT YOU. YOU ARE NOT A PRES-
SURE ON ME. YOU ARE EVERYTHING TO ME. JUST FORGET
ABOUT EVERYONE ELSE. THEY ARE THE ONES CAUSING THE
PRESSURE BY NOT LETTING YOU SEE ME, YET THEY DON'T
REALISE. PLEASE TELEPHONE ME WHEN YOU CAN. I WANT YOU
TO."*

Ian was staying at Barney's house when he wrote this letter and enclosed
the telephone number, mentioning that he didn't like to use Barney's phone
for fear of running up a bill. He asked Annik to ring when she could.
Clearly he was anxious about the tour in America for personal reasons as
well as professional, and went on to write: *WHEN I GET BACK WE
MUST DECIDE EXACTLY ON WHAT WE WANT TO DO FOR THE
FUTURE, SO WHILE I'M AWAY THINK HARD SO THAT YOU
KNOW EXACTLY WHAT YOU WANT TO DO. I'M SCARED IN
CASE YOUR FEELINGS FOR ME CHANGE DURING THAT TIME.
I PRAY THAT THEY DON'T.*

The seriousness of Ian's intentions becomes more apparent as he goes on:
*I FEEL SO LONELY SAT HERE WITHOUT YOU & YET I KNOW
YOUR [SIC] THERE CLOSE TO MY HEART. THESE PEOPLE WHO
MAKE ME DOUBT MY OWN REASON & SANITY, IT HURTS ME
DEEPLY. I KNOW WHAT I HAVE SAID TO PEOPLE, WHAT'S BEEN
EXPLAINED MAYBE THE MEANINGS WERE UNCLEAR, MAYBE
I'VE BEEN GUILTY OF EXPECTING THEM TO THINK THE SAME
AS I OR UNDERSTAND AS YOU WOULD, LIKE YOU TO ME YOUR
ACTIONS OR THOUGHTS ARE ALWAYS CLEAR AND ARE ALL
TOTALLY UNDERSTOOD. YOU ARE THE CLOSEST TO ME AND
FORM A VERY SPECIAL RELATIONSHIP THAT I'VE NEVER SEEN
BEFORE IN ANYONE ELSE. LIKE I SAID WE'RE MEANT FOR
EACH OTHER AND NOTHING WILL KEEP US APART.*

★ ★ ★

Heartbreakingly, Annik describes her final night with Ian in her letter to Carole. This occurred on Friday April 25 at yet another Factory night, this one held at the small Scala Cinema on Tottenham Street, off Tottenham Court Road in central London. Joy Division had pulled out of a previous commitment to play on this particular occasion but Ian came down to London to watch the show anyway.

"Ian came down to London on Friday night to say goodbye," wrote Annik. "We were not going to see each other for a very long time, as when I was back from Egypt he would have left for the States. That is the very last time I saw him. I'll never forget. He had a six-day beard – very soft. He seemed relieved having left home – he looked fit and beautiful. We met at the Factory night at the Scala in London. ACR, The Durutti Column, Blurt were playing and also Section 25 (the group he produced with Rob). Films were being shown as well. We became tired and left at five in the morning. I still had to finish my packing as I was leaving at 10. I remember he went to bed before me and he called me to sit near him, he was crying and he looked so sad. The sorrow on his face. We slept for a few hours then we had to rush to go to the station. We took a taxi, I got there seven minutes before departure, we said goodbye very quickly and sadly and I left. I saw his face for the last time alive. He was to go to Euston station to take the train to Manchester where he would go and stay with your parents or rather Barney I think."

Annik was in Egypt from May 2 to May 16. She wrote Ian a poignant letter from there. This lone letter, the envelope of which bore a stamp with a picture of two Egyptian boats on the Nile with an aeroplane overhead, began, "My only one". Sadly, Ian never received this letter. However, he did receive one letter from Annik in Egypt, written before this. Alan Erasmus later returned another two letters from Annik that Ian also never received, both of which had been posted care of the Factory office.

The day that Annik left England was also the day of the very last Joy Division gig, in Birmingham. This was to be the band's final show in Britain before they would depart for their short tour of the US, the next logical step in their steady upward progress. To outsiders and many of those quite close to the band, Joy Division's growth towards some kind of international recognition now seemed inevitable.

The Birmingham gig was a fast-paced affair which began with Ian singing an immensely evocative new song, never played on stage before, entitled 'Ceremony'. It evidently had no title at this stage since Ian had simply written 'NEW ONE' on his set list. Its lovely guitar interplay was a further indication of just how fast this band was moving in terms of songwriting and musicianship. Having the confidence to open their set with a song that was post-*Closer*, itself still two months away from its scheduled release, almost verged on arrogance. The last set the band would ever play also included 'Shadowplay', 'New Dawn Fades', 'Twenty Four Hours', 'Transmission', 'Digital' and ended with 'Decades'. Most of the songs were unfamiliar to the bulk of the audience, another sign of their brimming confidence which didn't appear to have been dented by the increasing problems of their lead singer.

Terry Mason recalls the gig for an unusual reason. As the band weren't keen on allowing journalists to get too close to them at this point – for obvious reasons – it was Terry job to distract and block them. "Running interference[1]" is how Terry describes it. One of the journalists in question was *NME*'s Danny Baker, the one time *Sniffin' Glue* fanzine editor who would later go on to mainstream television and radio stardom.

"We were on slowing down mode before we went off to the States," states Terry. "Ian hadn't been that well. This was the last gig before we had the break before the States and we were all quite relieved about that. Part of my job was seeing Danny didn't overly annoy people. Rob couldn't do it cos Rob was everyone's mate. It was good cop, bad cop."

Ian wrote to Annik about this gig and mentioned another journalist who was also at *NME* at that time: *I THINK ADRIAN THRILLS WAS A BIT UPSET THAT WE LEFT HIM. HE CAME TO BIRMINGHAM AND ROB AND HOOKY HAD AN ARGUMENT WITH HIM ABOUT INTERVIEWS. HE LEFT WITH ANDY I DON'T THINK HE GOT WHAT HE WANTED AT ALL. I FELT SORRY FOR HIM BUT THERE WAS NOTHING THAT COULD BE DONE ABOUT IT. THE GIG WAS QUITE GOOD, IT WAS THE BIGGEST CROWD THEY'D EVER HAD, APART FROM THE USUAL MISTAKES HERE AND THERE (LIKE ME FORGETTING THE LAST VERSE OF 'TRANS-MISSION'), EVERYONE ENJOYED IT. I THINK THE BEST NUM-BER OF THE NIGHT WAS THE ONE WE'VE JUST RECENTLY DONE.*

Tony Wilson recalls discussing the use of language with Ian backstage at Birmingham, specifically about a line in one of Ian's lyrics – "When all's said and done" from 'Passover' – which Tony mentioned had a very antique, 19th Century English construction to it. Tony, who graduated from Cambridge in English Literature, was interested in it and liked the fact Ian had used the

[1] A US grid football term.

phrase in the song. Apparently Ian listened to what Tony had to say but declined to comment.

In the immediate aftermath of the Birmingham concert Joy Division managed to book in one more session with Martin Hannett, specifically to record two songs, 'Ceremony', which they debuted at Birmingham, and the lovely, forlorn 'In A Lonely Place'.

This recording – the band's last – would later surface on the *Heart And Soul* box set. The extensive liner notes suggest that it was recorded at Graveyard Studio in Prestwich and bootleg tapes that surfaced in the early Eighties certainly claimed that that was the case. However, there is a counter claim that the taped versions were actually from a latter-day practice session. The confusion causes arguments among Joy Division devotees to this day, and it is eminently possible that two sets of tapes were produced which were subsequently released by bootleggers and official sources alike. No-one has ever confirmed the truth of the matter.

The 'Love Will Tear Us Apart' video, which begins and ends with an opening and closing door with the graffiti 'Ian C' scratched across the outside, was the last filmed recording of Ian Curtis.

Ian mentioned this film in one of his letters to Annik: *ALTHOUGH I HAVEN'T SEEN THE FINISHED VERSION OF THE FILM THE SOUND IS REALLY BAD, BECAUSE MAINLY HARRY LET US DOWN AND WE HAD TO BRING SOMEONE ELSE IN WHOSE EQUIPMENT WASN'T AS GOOD.*

"Rob had had an argument with Harry Demac following the taping of the Bury gig," recalls Terry. "It was something to do with money. Anyway, we managed to get the big room at T.J.'s and we had replaced P.S.L. (Demac's sound company) with a P.A. system owned by Geoff Muir."

On Sunday, May 4, Rob Gretton flew out to America to finalise arrangements for the forthcoming tour. Terry says that Rob had told him the tour was due to open at Snoopy's Roller Disco in Los Angeles[1], although this differs from the list of dates Annik had written down in 1980 and Ian's own belief that the group were to fly to New York, not California. Rob had a list of equipment to be picked up as the group planned to take only their guitars to America, and he and Miles Copeland, who ran the F.B.I. – Frontier Booking International – booking agency, went through the tour dates together. Terry thinks Rob returned the following Friday.

[1] Now Esprit on La Cienaga Boulevard.

On May 8 Joy Division were due to film a TV programme called *Celebration* but there was a technician's strike involving cameramen at Granada so, unfortunately, it didn't happen. Ian mentioned this in his last letter to Annik on May 5, stating that the two numbers they planned to perform were the new one, 'Ceremony', plus 'Heart And Soul'. He also said that Tony wanted him to go over the Factory Film script and thought that would be "a nice change and interesting too". There is no indication in this letter that Ian was planning to end his life. On the contrary, he sounds quite positive. He writes: *BY THE TIME YOU READ THIS, I WILL PROBABLY BE GETTING READY FOR OUR FLIGHT TO NEW YORK. I'M AT MY PARENT'S HOUSE AT THE MOMENT. I'M STAYING HERE UNTIL TOMORROW WHEN I'VE GOT TO GO TO MACCLESFIELD TO THE HOSPITAL FOR MY MONTHLY VISIT. I NEED SOME KIND OF CERTIFICATE IN CASE I GET STOPPED AT CUSTOMS AND THEY WONDER WHAT THE TABLETS ARE.*

I SEEM TO BE ABLE TO DO A LOT OF WRITING HERE, AT MY PARENT'S. I THINK I'LL COME UP HERE FOR A WEEK BEFORE WE GO. IT'S VERY QUIET ROUND HERE. IT'S BEEN VERY SUNNY AND THEY'VE GOT A FAIRLY BIG GARDEN SO I'VE BEEN ABLE TO SIT OUTSIDE OR PLAY WITH THE DOG AND THERE'S NO-ONE TO BOTHER ME. I'M QUITE LOOKING FORWARD TO GOING NOW, WE'VE GOT A WEEK ON THE WEST COAST AND ONLY TWO DATES, SO IT WILL BE A NICE REST. THOUGH I'D MUCH RATHER BE WITH YOU. I WISH YOU WERE GOING AS WELL. WE FLY BACK TO LONDON ON JUNE 10TH I THINK. I'LL CHECK WITH ROB FOR DEFINITE. IT SEEMS AGES SINCE I LAST SAW YOU, SPOKE TO YOU AND THERE'S STILL ANOTHER FIVE WEEKS. I CAN'T STAND IT. I HOPE I'M NEVER AWAY FROM YOU FOR THIS LONG AGAIN.

Despite his feelings for Annik, this letter seems to infer that Ian is making an effort to step back from his emotional life and get on with his career. The only hint of any distance he may have felt from the band is when he refers to the success of the Birmingham gig. It was, he wrote, the best crowd they'd ever had. Not *we*.

"With him [having the fits] on stage," says Doreen Curtis, "he might have thought this was the end of his career – in that respect – I mean he could have done other things with the group. He wasn't dumb was he? He'd know that he'd have to give the singing up. He'd know in his own mind to actually appear on stage... he couldn't have done it could he?"

★ ★ ★

Terry Mason saw Ian for the last time on Thursday, May 15, when he picked up Ian's passport and two passport photographs which were required for a US visa. He drove to Macclesfield with Rob and Barney and when he arrived Ian gave Barney a pair of jeans and Terry a cover for *Ideal For Living* as Terry had only a white label copy of this record in a plain sleeve. Ian also offered Terry his copy of the valuable Sordide Sentimentale record but Rob advised him not to. No-one thought this burst of generosity indicated in any way that Ian was thinking of ending his life. "He could have been having a sort out, making sure what happened to his things, he was like that anyway, he would give stuff away," says Terry. "He was about to become homeless and couldn't hang on to too much stuff."

Terry went by train to London to the US embassy in Grosvenor Square on Friday, May 16, to obtain the visas for the band's passports. "It was a lovely sunny day," he recalls. "On the way back, relieved to have collected the passports all stamped with their visas – there had been tales of other bands having their tours rescheduled due to visa problems – I remember thinking, 'This is it, we're finally on our way, what on earth can possibly go wrong now?'"

Carole Curtis was working in a hotel in Torquay in May 1980, employed as a chambermaid and waitress. That year, as she did for three summer seasons, she stayed in a caravan next to the hotel. She thinks that she probably spoke to Ian on the Friday: "I can remember I was standing in the foyer of the hotel and my mum said, 'Ian's here, do you want a word with him before he goes?', and I said to him, 'Have a nice time on Monday'. But I remember thinking that he wasn't excited about it. I came off the phone and I thought that it was strange him going to America and not being excited. He sounded very reticent."

In Egypt, Annik was exhausted. Like all fair-skinned tourists to the sun-baked land of the Pharaohs her daily routine involved rising at 4am to go sight-seeing before the midday sun became unbearably hot. She was reading *The Idiot* by Dostoyevsky and thinking deeply about her relationship with Ian. She was missing him greatly and was in no little torment at the quandary of not knowing where it would lead them.

On her return to Brussels there were a few phone calls with Ian. The details of the last three of these were outlined in her letter to Carole. On the night of Saturday, May 17, she was in Brussels preparing to travel back to London the following day. Later in the evening she went to a gig at Plan K where James White & The Blacks were headlining, along with Digital

Dance who were friends of Annik and were there either supporting or just hanging out backstage.

Ian spoke to Annik at Plan K on Saturday evening, causing her to believe that she was the last person to speak to him alive. "I rang him three times," she wrote in her letter to Carole, "Wednesday night, Friday morning and for the very last time Saturday, May 17, at 9 o'clock. The first two calls he was at your parents', we talked about what happened while I was away, the divorce, the States soon, my holiday. I let him talk about the divorce without saying anything, he sounded a bit reluctant to speak too much about it, still he said he was giving her everything, the house, the car and also all his salary (£40 a week) for Debbie not to work and so for Natalie not to go to the nurses. I can't remember very well what was said, I think he was quite shocked though and spoke in a melancholic tone. We were for one hour on the phone, I tried to cheer him up, saying we would go on holiday to ski next Christmas or Easter. Just the two of us, no Joy Division around, far from England. He said yes but didn't seem convinced. He sounded defeated. It is hard to say, just over the phone, how someone feels.

"We arranged that I would ring him again on Saturday evening to see if it was possible at all to meet before they left for the States. After all I was going back to London on Sunday afternoon and they were only to leave Monday morning. I desperately wanted to see him. Saturday night he was in Macclesfield to collect a few things and also he wanted to try and go to the dentist because he had broken a tooth the day before. Also I suppose he wanted to see Debbie and Natalie. We only spoke for 10 minutes this time as I was in a public place and it was noisy. I could hardly hear what he was saying. He said he was going to watch a Herzog film and stay there for the night, also that he didn't know yet if it was possible to meet each other. I was a bit irritated that he didn't know yet if it was possible or not to meet – also a bit fed up I suppose, why was it always so difficult to meet? Still it was arranged that I would ring him on Sunday evening at your parents' to find out. That is when I found out something else."

Ian had been staying with his parents prior to the group's scheduled flight to America on Monday, May 19. His mother says that he seemed OK during the time he stayed with them. He was going out and meeting up with the band. On Saturday, May 17, Ian received a letter concerning his divorce proceedings.

"There was a letter he got on the day he died," says Doreen. "I think that had a lot to do with it. That Saturday morning, it came from a solicitor. I opened it by mistake. It was addressed to Mr. I. K. Curtis. I didn't read it. I just saw the top. He was in bed. I asked him if something was wrong. He didn't tell me but he said he'd have to go to Macclesfield to sort things out. He said he wanted to say bye bye to Natalie. I'd got everything packed for him. He'd got all his tablets on the sideboard. He said he was going to Macclesfield and he'd be home tomorrow. The boys phoned me Saturday night and said 'Don't forget to get him up early on Monday', and I said I would, that everything was ready."

Like Annik, Ian's mother's last sighting of her son was at a railway station, symbolic of a departing journey. "I was going to the Eye Hospital and Kevin said he'd drop Ian off at Piccadilly Station. I can see him now walking up the approach. He always used to stand and wave until you got out of sight. That was the last I saw of him. That was it until the police knocked on Sunday morning."

There was another friend whom Ian may have spoken to that night. Genesis P-Orridge remembers a phone call that made him very worried: "I had known for some time that Ian was in danger of actually going through with the suicide bid. I had been there myself and I knew that it is a moment… it is just a moment and once you get through that moment you start to come out of the other side. I knew that Ian was in a situation where he couldn't find a way out of the band, let alone all the other stuff. He had already told me that he couldn't go to America. He had said that he would rather die than go on that tour. Those were his words. I don't know what it was about that Saturday though. I knew in absolute certainty that I had to get a call through to Ian. Ian was obsessed with the song 'Weeping'. He sang it down the phone.

"I really felt worried. I tried to contact people around him. I spoke to Jon Savage – he said he'd ring Rob. I rang someone else and the person I spoke to laughed and said Ian was always saying stuff like that. Someone just recently, asked me why I didn't call the police. I never even thought of that. They probably wouldn't have responded, though it would have been worth a try."

Rob Gretton was unobtainable that evening because he was attending Mick Middles' wedding. None of the group was at home because this was their last opportunity to enjoy a night out with their partners before the US tour.

Although Annik believed she was the last person to speak to Ian when he called her at Plan K, according to her book *Touching From A Distance*, Debbie saw Ian after this call. She had taken a job working behind a bar at a local disco called Silklands and was on duty that evening as she had been on the previous night. The arrangement was that she and Natalie would sleep at her parents' house that Friday and Saturday night so that her mother could babysit. Ian had asked her to bring Natalie to Barton Street on the Saturday night but Debbie says in *Touching From A Distance* that she didn't trust him and therefore decided to keep Natalie away. At Ian's request Debbie called to see him in the early hours but, after a discussion on their future reached no conclusion, she returned to her parents' house, leaving Ian to spend the night alone.

Neighbours, Kevin and Pam Wood lived a few doors away on Barton Street and recalled seeing Ian walk past a couple of times at tea time that Saturday afternoon. "We didn't know why he was back home because they (he and Debbie) were living separate lives," says Kevin. "Then he walked past again about seven or eight o'clock at night. In the early hours of the morning – we think it was about 12.30am or 1am – we heard Debbie's car draw up outside the house and it was there for half an hour or 40 minutes and then we heard the car go."

Sleep was a precious commodity in the twilight hours of Sunday May 18 for the other women in Ian's life. His mother, aunt and grandmother all suffered restless nights.

Doreen: "I woke up about 4–4.30 am. I came downstairs. I felt as if something had drained out of me. I stood at the sink in the kitchen and got a drink of water. I thought I saw a bird the next day, like a dove, flying off into the distance. I might have been wrong. I can't remember if I saw it or if it was in my imagination."

Barbara: "I woke up about 4am, I think. I'd had a dream. There was a wall there and a hand trying to reach me. I was trying to pull them through the wall. I didn't know if it was a man or a woman. 'I'll get you', I was saying. They didn't want to go, whoever it was. They wanted me to get them back here. I couldn't. When I woke up tears were streaming down my eyes. I woke Brian [her husband] up and I told him about it. He thought it was something I'd seen on TV or read. I remember saying to him, 'But I can't get them. They've gone'. The next morning I got up and we took the children to the park and when we got back after lunch the phone went and Brian took it. He told me I had to sit down. My mum had woken up [in the night] too. She said she didn't know why but she felt all funny and got up and made a cup of tea. She sat up in bed with it. We were all up."

CHAPTER 21

When All's Said And Done

"No words could explain, no actions determine, watching the trees and the leaves as they fall." – Ian Curtis

Deborah Curtis discovered Ian's body on Sunday morning. Neighbour Kevin Wood was outside washing his car on Barton Street in the spring sunshine while his wife was cleaning the windows at the front of their house. Her parents had taken their six-month-old baby son for a walk in nearby South Park.

"It was about 11–11.30am and Debbie came past in a Morris Minor Traveller," says Kevin. "She'd got her little girl in the back who was a similar age to our son. Normally she would take Natalie out and go into the house with her but, for some strange reason, this time she left Natalie in the car. She walked in and within a few minutes came running out of the house hysterical. My wife and I ran up to her and couldn't get a word out of her. I told Pam to take her into our house and give her a coffee. I knew Ian was epileptic and it ran through my mind that he might have been in the middle of a really bad fit and she couldn't handle it. I went into the lounge, there was a table with a couple of spirit bottles and an empty glass there. I glanced at the mantelpiece and I could see an envelope and I then looked into the door that led you into the kitchen and Ian was there, unfortunately hung. Not as people would probably imagine, he'd tied a rope to the old fashioned clothes rack on a pulley, but by this time the rope had stretched and cut into his neck and he was knelt on the floor as though he was praying.

"I said to him, 'What the bloody hell have you done that for you stupid bastard?' I panicked and ran to a neighbour's house and warned him what to expect. We both ran back in and I decided that we should cut him down because we didn't know how long he'd been there, although it was pretty obvious he was dead. I took a knife off the drainer and cut the rope but he never actually moved. I went home and phoned the police and ambulance. The ambulance driver put one hand on the body's shoulder and said, 'Rigor has well and truly set in.' Debbie's parents came very quickly and took her away. If I hear the tune 'Love Will Tear Us Apart'… even now 26 years later it sends a shiver down my spine and it all comes back to me."

At the time the body was discovered Annik was making her way back from Belgium to her rented flat and job in London. She took a hovercraft across the English Channel in the early hours of the morning and although it was a lovely clear day and the sea was calm, she was very sick. Having risen at 6am after a late night at Plan K, she had only had three hours' sleep but nonetheless she thinks her vomiting was due entirely to her sense that something was badly wrong. "[I was] so sad and so sick," she says.

Concerned, she rang Ian's parents on arriving in England. Ian's father answered the phone and told her, bluntly, 'Ian is dead'. He could say no more. On hearing his voice Annik realised at once that Kevin Curtis was completely devastated, that something inside him had broken which could never be repaired. Anxious to learn more, Annik rang Rob Gretton. His immediate response was that someone must be playing a very cruel joke on her, that it quite simply was not true – but a short while later he phoned and confirmed the fact and the circumstances.

As the shock waves rang out across Manchester and the sorrow struck home, some of those closest to Ian were, deep down, not really surprised that he had taken his own life.

In Torquay, Ian's sister Carole was out sunbathing, recovering from a hangover from the previous evening when they had been celebrating her friend's birthday. Her dad called her with the devastating news. "In my mind I never thought he'd get his pension," she says today. "I never thought he'd see past 30 to be honest. Weird that. But only like looking back on it now can you think [it]. When I found out that he'd done it, I… I agree with Debbie when she said he wasn't bothered [about America] because he knew in his mind that he wasn't going."

Ian had said years ago that he wouldn't live long. Not in any morbid or depressing way. He told his aunt Barbara that in passing and, of course, she told him, "Don't be so silly".

Vini Reilly said of that Sunday: "I was waiting for the phone call and I wasn't remotely surprised."

Annik made immediate arrangements to travel up north and stay with Tony Wilson and Lindsay Reade. By a rather morbid coincidence, she found herself sleeping in their small spare room where Ian had slept five weeks previously, and for the exact same number of nights.

Annik was completely devastated, distraught and heartbroken. She was unable to sleep and seemed to Lindsay to have gone beyond any kind of rest. Tony Connolly, who had visited when Ian was there, was helpful and gave Lindsay some medicine, a sedative, thinking that it would calm Annik down and help her to sleep. He thought it might even knock her unconscious but soon after swallowing it, she announced that she was going out for a walk. Concerned about her frame of mind, Lindsay offered to accompany her but Annik insisted on being alone. She returned after about an hour and her mood seemed to be entirely lifted; indeed, she seemed almost happy again. She told Lindsay that she had been with Ian, that while on the hillside there had been a strong light, sweeping up and breaking through the clouds. She knew it was Ian and that he was OK – that he had managed to find peace now.

At the time Lindsay thought this experience was imagined, but helpful nonetheless since it evidently comforted her. Today, however, she feels differently. "In light of the experiences I myself have had subsequent to death of loved ones in my family, I now accept and believe that this meeting took place," she says. "I believe that the deceased can, and do, make contact. People dismiss such events as a fantasy of the half-baked – as I did with Annik at the time. While this is understandable, once a person has experienced something like this for themselves their feelings on such matters alter."

Some 25 years later, Annik's encounter on the hillside is her one abiding memory. "I think it gave him some kind of final peace and harmony that he was desperately looking for," she says. "I think he needed really a lot of peace, I am sure."

Annik was upset that she was prevented from attending Ian's funeral. At first Debbie forbade her to see his body too, but it was later arranged that she could visit the Chapel of Rest and Tony drove her there with Lindsay in his Peugeot Estate. "I had disliked that car from the day he bought it," says Lindsay. "I had always called the car 'the hearse'. Of course he had got it because it was useful for ferrying groups of musicians about. But that morning as we set off for the Chapel it seemed as if it had really become a hearse. It felt to me that we had Ian's body – or spirit at least – in the car with us. Tony and I went in to pay our respects together. I looked at Ian and said, 'God bless you' and at almost the same instant Tony said, 'You daft bugger' in a fond and friendly way. Afterwards Annik went in and was alone with Ian."

Annik: "It felt important to me to see him one last time and the expression on his face – there he was lying looking like his skin was wax, his body obviously emptied of all life – just an empty envelope – Ian had gone."

Having said goodbye in the only way she could, Annik decided to leave England as soon as possible. She flew directly from Manchester to Brussels on May 23, the day of Ian's funeral, and returned later to collect her things from Fulham. The embassy was not best pleased that she didn't work her full notice, seeing it as a breach of contract to be fleeing her post. "How can you be so upset? You weren't even married," the Chancellor told her. Annik's doctor in Belgium helped by stating that she was sick and incapable of continuing her work. Annik knew instinctively that this was the end of her life in England, and that she had to go home. Tony Wilson bought her an air ticket to Brussels, using the name 'Annik Curtis' because he was unaware of her surname. Michel Duval, who ran the label Factory Benelux, met Annik on her arrival at Brussels airport.

Paul Morley, whose own father committed suicide in the late Seventies, described his visit to see Ian's body at the opening of his book *Nothing* and, despite stating at the close that this was not true, that it was in his imagination, he says now: "I did go in, I did see the body, yes. In a way what I did was replace Ian with my dad, who I didn't see, so it was just a metaphorical thing almost, as if I'd recreated now enough of my father. I never saw my dad's body. At the end of the book I am willing myself to believe that I'd seen my father's body – but I hadn't. I remember getting the train on my own to Macclesfield. Tony was stood outside the church. He was on his own. I was very uncomfortable and I took some flowers and I remember Tony looked at what I'd written on the card and I was really embarrassed because I hadn't done anything special. I think it was just 'Missing you' or something, but you know Tony, he was looking for some quote from Dostoevsky or something magnificent. Even though I got the feeling – in hindsight – that somehow he was plotting the myth even then and wanting material. It just seemed a very odd situation."

Wilson also took A Certain Ratio to the morgue to pay their last respects to Ian. Jeremy Kerr felt somewhat frightened of going in but Rob Gretton told him it would be all right. Afterwards ACR went on to play a gig at De Villes. Apparently it was a very sombre set.

Paul Morley: "Tony was doing day trips, wasn't he, he was selling tickets. It was a very odd scenario and I didn't understand why it was him doing it (showing me the body) and not Debbie, or someone more directly to do with Ian. It's true about the myth – what Tony said to me was – 'You're going to write the book on Joy Divison so you've got to be here to see this'. That's what I mean that he was already busying away at that. There was definitely a kind of truth to it in a way which at the time you don't think it but it was something that, I guess, Tony knew. He needed to make history and you make history by telling it yourself. I wasn't informed enough to know what was going on. I didn't think there'd be a book about Joy Division. At that time you just thought he was thinking too far ahead. They're going to be Pink Floyd, they're going to be Led Zeppelin – no, they're not – or The Doors was his big one – this is gonna be our Jim Morrison, we need to know this story and you're going to be the one that does it."

Ian Curtis was cremated on Friday, May 23. Out of respect to Ian's family, Factory decided to hold their own wake, at their offices at 89 Palatine Road, Didsbury. It was fitting, perhaps, that the occasion was marked with an ironic twist, specifically the screening of the Sex Pistols film, *The Great Rock'n'Roll Swindle*, in which the rock'n'roll impresario Malcolm McLaren claims to have orchestrated the entire rise to prominence of the Pistols. This is strongly disputed by the band's intelligent singer, Johnny Rotten, who claims the power lay with the talent, rather than the management. Whatever, it was certainly a curious choice for this particular afternoon.

There was a sense of unease in the atmosphere. "The mood in the room didn't seem especially negative, or gloomy though perhaps that was more male bravado," says Lindsay. "Men are good at covering their feelings. Annik had gone and I felt at liberty to cry through most of that afternoon. When anyone close dies there are inevitably feelings of guilt but when someone commits suicide the guilt is magnified hugely. I think a lot of my grief for Ian centred on guilt feelings along with a feeling that something or someone could have prevented his death.

"There was a line in the film we saw that jumped out at me – 'No-one is innocent'. I looked around the room and thought this statement was true – it wasn't *just* me that was guilty. I took some comfort from that at least. Shortly after that Hooky came over and spoke to me. I was still crying quietly. I think it probably annoyed him. I don't blame him. I'm sure his grief went deeper than mine. Hooky said something along the lines of,

Ian Curtis steals the show at the Futurama Festival in Leeds,
September 8, 1979. *(Kevin Cummins/Idols)*

Annik Honoré on holiday in Egypt,
May 1980. *(Courtesy Annik Honoré)*

Ian on stage at the Plan K Club
in Brussels, October 16, 1979.
(Philippe Carly – www.newwavephotos.com)

Sombre young men: Joy Division photographed in Paris,
December 1979. *(Pierre Rene-Worms)*

Paris, December 1979. *(Pierre Rene-Worms)*

On stage at Les Bains-Douches Club in Paris,
December 18, 1979. *(Pierre Rene-Worms)*

A family Christmas dinner in the Last Drop Inn, Bolton, 1976,
from left, Kevin Curtis, Doreen, Debbie, Ian, grandparents Les and Edith,
Uncle Brian, Aunt Barbara, Carole and her friend Gail Lyon.

Here are the young men; April 1980. *(Harry Goodwin)*

Ian Curtis, in Germany, January 1980. *(Mark Reeder)*

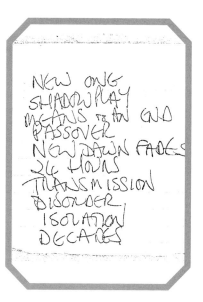
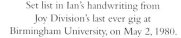

Set list in Ian's handwriting from
Joy Division's last ever gig at
Birmingham University, on May 2, 1980.

Ian's last photograph, taken in a Manchester
photo booth for the US visa he required for
Joy Division's aborted tour of America.

DEAR ANNIK,
    BY THE TIME YOU READ THIS, I WILL
PROBABLY GETTING READY FOR OUR FLIGHT
TO NEW YORK. I MISS YOU SO MUCH, YOU
WOULDN'T BELIEVE. EVEN BEFORE WHEN I
DIDN'T SEE YOU I COULD TALK TO YOU BY
TELEPHONE BUT NOW EVEN THAT PLEASURE
IS DENIED ME, I FEEL SO ALONE. YET
EVEN THOUGH YOU'RE SO FAR AWAY YOU'RE
VERY CLOSE TO MY HEART

        I'M QUITE LOOKING FORWARD
TO GOING NOW, WE'VE GOT A
WEEK ON THE WEST COAST AND
ONLY TWO DATES, SO IT WILL
BE A NICE REST, THOUGH I'D
MUCH RATHER BE WITH YOU, I
WISH YOU WERE GOING AS WELL.

Ian's last letter to Annik, written on May 5, 1980.
(Courtesy Annik Honoré)

Curtis at the edge; a compulsive, unsettling performer,
April 1980. *(Peter Anderson/SIN)*

'What you crying for?' I said something along the lines of it being such a waste, such a terrible shame. He replied, 'Well I think it's a shame that you never knew him'. I thought he sounded angry and was a bit taken aback. Another reason to be guilty – that I hadn't got to know Ian. Maybe I misinterpreted it. Maybe he came over because he wanted to comfort me. Hooky is like that really. He was right about me not knowing Ian that well though. It was a shame I didn't because I would have made a better friend. I don't remember anything else from that day. I can't say for sure who was there. Tony didn't even remember we had a wake."

Paul Morley, who didn't go to the funeral, certainly remembers that day. "Playing the film seemed really odd – everyone didn't know whether to take it seriously or to have a laugh. Which way to take it, you know. I think the atmosphere was deeply traumatised, it was very, very sad but everyone was trying to cover it up and that life goes on. It was a very, very weird mixture of energy. It was a big old house and so the room was very large and a lot of people could get in. I just know I was hugging the wall, one wall. I felt very uncomfortable being there really. I was very shy as well. I can't imagine me mustering up the energy to put myself in that situation, but there was something about me that also wanted to do it somehow."

Terry Mason attended the funeral along with the band. He recalls that he and Hooky hired two cars for the occasion – a Mondeo and a Cavalier – since their own were considered unsuitable, unfit to be seen. They all followed on to the wake at Palatine Road. "Cabaret Voltaire were there at both ceremonies," he says. "There were plates of sandwiches at Alan Erasmus' flat that afternoon – cut the posh way into a triangular shape."

He also remembers collecting his new puppy that same day from a breeder in Boothstown, along with Iris, Hooky's then girlfriend. "The hire car had to be back by 5pm since it was a bank holiday weekend and the car was hired out again at 5.30pm. The little dog became agitated and fouled the back seat, leaving no time for the car to be cleaned before it was re-hired."

Life for the bereaved continued though it would never be the same.

An inquest into Ian's death was held in June, attended by – amongst others – Kevin Wood. "I was treated like a criminal and questioned why I had cut him down if he was already dead," he says. "Everyone had thought that the envelope on the mantelpiece was a suicide note but it wasn't. It turned out to be a letter that he'd written to Debbie saying that when he got back from America he wanted to get back with her and to be part of a normal family again."

Kevin Curtis came down with diabetes very soon after his son's death and the rest of his life was blighted by declining health. Ian's mother was also unwell with migraine headaches. Kevin died from cancer in 1995. Doreen had the good sense to combat her loneliness somewhat by acquiring a stray cat, name of Muff, but she still cries in private over the son she lost so tragically. Carole, too, still cries when she is reminded of her brother. Life may have moved on but the peculiar thing about grief is that, underneath the layers of all the years, it remains somehow unchanged and undisturbed. Nevertheless, just as Ian himself did, these women who loved him also know how to laugh. "For all your ills, I give you laughter," said Rabelais.

Annik: "It must have been terrible for his parents. More than for anybody. More than for me or Debbie. Very hard for Natalie of course but for his parents to see their young son dying like that."

Carole and Barbara swear they've caught sight of Ian in the street sometimes. Carole: "With his great coat on. I've not had it for years now."

Barbara: "I used to think he'd gone away somewhere and he wants quiet for a few years and then he'd reappear. And he'd say, 'I'm sorry but I had to go away to sort myself out.'"

Annik: "I swear I would have given my life for Ian to remain alive. For him to look after his daughter, carry on with the group and write songs and poems. Be in peace. And maybe never meet him in the first place. Nobody can replace him. How I wish he was here – not dead, not dead."

Tony Wilson believed for many years that Ian's suicide was for altruistic reasons: "At the time, I always thought it was to do with the fact that he thought he was helping everybody. He thought he was messing everyone's life up – his daughter, his wife, his lover – so that's what I thought for eight years until my own experience with the kids and Yvette in 1990. Certainly in 1980 and for the following 10 years I thought it was to do with that, that he was helping everybody and he thought he'd do everyone a favour. But that changed to be the irresolvable problem was resolved. That's my personal explanation. I have no reason to think that I should be right and everyone else is wrong. Bernard may be right – that it was the medication."

Terry Mason: "Ian killed himself, because he was a nice guy that had got himself a ridiculous situation from which he couldn't see any way to resolve it. I know that seems overly simplistic and wrecks any grand stories that there may be, but that's it."

Paul Morley has a theory about Ian's life: "My theory is that it was almost a weird strange sense that he knew he only had so much time, because lyrically and what he said seems so mature and articulate that you couldn't believe it came from a 22 year old. That there was something about him that had lived his complete life. So he had the maturity at the end of his years that a wise person has at the end of their years. This was the extent of his life."

When Annik returned to Belgium she went to live with her grandmother, with whom she had always been close, in a tiny village in the middle of nowhere near the French border. She recuperated by walking in the woods with her dog and remained there until September 1980 when she again took an apartment with a friend in Brussels. Michel Duval and Annik became involved in releasing records by groups other than the Factory catalogue that Michel dealt with, and launched the label Les Disques Du Crepuscule. It was Annik's idea to name the label 'Crepuscule' which means twilight. She began to pick up the pieces of her life and found work a very useful distraction. She remains thankful to Michel for that to this day.

The love between Ian and Annik was essentially simple yet classically tragic. Whilst it is true that everything – ultimately – ends in tears, could there be any hopeful note to end their sad story on?

Annik: "We were always happy together. We had a good time. He was always smiling to me. Always. Honestly, I see him like the face of an angel. Always smiling, always happy."

He remains an inspiration to her. "You know… Ian was really an inspiration for me to be a good person," she says. "He was never mean or unkind."

Given the extent of their shock and grief, it was to everyone's surprise that the remaining members of Joy Division picked themselves up and carried on almost immediately. In spite of the tragedy, Bernard Sumner, Pete Hook and Steve Morris – strongly aided by Rob Gretton – made the decision to move forward towards a new kind of band. Without the charismatic drive of Ian Curtis, without his central position within the dynamic, this would be an entirely different prospect. Initially billed as 'The No Names', the band's first performance without Ian was on July 29, at The Beach Club in Manchester. They played an intense instrumental set, surprisingly based around newer and subsequently post-Joy Division material. Two songs however, 'Ceremony' and 'In A Lonely Place', were recognisable as Joy Division survivors. At some point during this evening, it was announced – to no little immediate controversy – that the band would be called 'New Order'.

Paul Morley remembers how the group continued: "Ian didn't just kill himself and it all just disintegrated and the whole thing fell apart – the group themselves picked themselves up and kept going which was extraordinary. I would never have thought it or that it could have happened so quickly – it was only a matter of weeks. We seem to think it was a couple of years but it was actually just a few weeks. Even before they were New Order they were New Order. They played a gig down the road – you'd think it must have been a long time but it wasn't. They pulled themselves together and I think that was through Ian. Not just for him but I think it's in there – as much as it's in spite of him, I think it's for him as well. We're not going to give up just because of you but also we're going to carry on because of you.

"Ian did give them something quite special that I think they then carried on – again, unexpectedly. It was very moving seeing the first New Order gigs because no one filled Ian's place. Barney didn't move across for quite a while. The first time I ever saw them Barney was still playing guitar at the side, Hooky was out there so there was no one in the middle, a sort of ghostly absence… a presence which I thought was incredibly moving."

POSTSCRIPT

Ian Curtis Day, May 18, 2005

It was the 25th anniversary of the death of Ian Curtis. In Manchester city centre, an outdoor event was scheduled to take place in the evening: a screening of Joy Division footage outside The Triangle, a cosmopolitan shopping mall situated in The Corn Exchange, a building that had once been both a grand piece of architecture and a hub of north-west commerce. By the late Seventies it was sadly redundant, the home of a downbeat flea market and low rent offices.

More significantly, Pip's Disco, the venue for Joy Division's first gig under that name had flourished in a cellar complex beneath the building. But Pip's had long gone by 2005, and Manchester had changed beyond all recognition.

During the day, many hundreds of Joy Division fans drifted into the city. They came from all across Europe, many of them experiencing Manchester for the first time. Some stopped off at Macclesfield, and wandered into the crematorium to pay their respects.

Lindsay Reade visited the crematorium that day, with members of Ian's family. "We drove into the crematorium and at first got a bit lost trying to find Ian's stone," she says. "Doreen remembered that it was near a water tap and in view of the chapel. I parked somewhere and Carole and Barbara walked one way and I followed Doreen the other. The mother's instinct was the correct one. As we rounded a corner we knew we were near. Within sight were three men and a woman standing around a stone. The tributes were lovely already – messages and flowers and his family had come with loads more. His mum had brought a bunch of yellow roses, Carole had some unusual varieties – 'different', which is how she always regarded her brother – but one of them was lilac which is the flower I always remember Ian by. Every year when I see lilacs in blossom I remember that this is the time of year when Ian died. Barbara had red roses from her two children, Ian's cousins, and a bouquet as well, and I placed just one flower from Annik – a white flower whose name I did not know.

"I felt like the way I do when I'm with Tony – aware that people are thinking the person I'm with is somebody important. Only now it was Ian's mum. The fans were a bit apologetic to be there but Doreen said she was touched that they were and they visibly relaxed. We placed the flowers in bowls that Doreen had brought. Somewhat awkwardly we began to speak to the people there. The first was a man called Ian who said that Ian Curtis had completely changed his life. He worked with another guy there, called Mark, and they ran the website Joy Division Central. The lady they were with gave Doreen a hug. What amazed us was that they had travelled from Bath and London for this.

"As we stood there some others wandered up. Amongst them was a 14-year-old-boy called Jonathan, with a crop of curly hair, and a friend, a girl called Cat – both of them wearing King's School uniforms. Jonathan seemed very intelligent and, well, different. He turned out to be a musician – there was something a bit special about him. We wandered down to the Book of Remembrance. En route we met a man wearing a picture of Ian across his chest who was carrying a bunch of plastic flowers."

The inscription in the book read: "Curtis, Ian Kevin. Died 1980, Aged 23. Just for one moment, I heard/Somebody call, looked beyond/The day in hand, no-one there at all."

Lindsay Reade: "On the way back to the car we saw a guy reading the stones – lost, the way we were. 'He might be looking for Ian,' said Doreen 'but you don't like to ask.' I knew what she meant. It would be awful if he weren't. Nevertheless, I asked the chap, 'Are you looking for someone?' 'Yes Ian Curtis' he replied. It was easy to point the way because there were people gathered around. We introduced ourselves and he asked Doreen if she minded that he was there. 'No, not at all, touched.' He was worried it might appear ghoulish.

"We went from there to lunch at the Brocklehurst Arms which is on the edge of Hurdsfield. Hurdsfield is within walking distance of Macclesfield and we planned to drive round all the old haunts.

"The first port of call was Balmoral Crescent which was not far up the road. There was the house, unchanged by all the changes that had taken place in the lives of the people who inhabited it. We drove around the block looking for Hurdsfield County Primary School. Carole thought it must have been knocked down but after driving around another block we found it. Next we drove past Hurdsfield C of E Church where Ian was confirmed. This church stands quite high up and is visible far and wide.

"We seemed to be taking the early route of Ian's life because we drove from here to the place where 11 Park View once stood on the edge of Victoria Park. We saw the park, home to many a happy hour of game playing, Ian and Carole's big back garden at the time of living there. Although Park View has been demolished there are now rather plush apartments in this same area.

"We passed by Carole's old school before moving on to Barton Street. There were a couple of people standing opposite the house looking up at it. The word 'tourist' came to my mind which was, perhaps, a tad unkind but it reminded me of the John Lennon tour in Liverpool.

"Nearing the end of our tour of Macclesfield we decided to go back to the crematorium. The crowd had grown from four to 10. They were all men, bar one woman and if I had to characterise the one thing all these men might have had in common it was, strangely, intelligence. I asked Carole what she thought they had in common. She said, 'Intense or a certain intensity'.

"We stared at the tributes, the gorgeous flowers. A young lad was sitting on the grass, holding a flowering plant and wearing a t-shirt of *Unknown Pleasures*. He'd had earphones on but unplugged them to listen to Ian's family greet his fans. Doreen was very friendly (as is her nature) and the visitors were clearly very touched and pleased to have met her and his sister and aunt. Carole joked yet again, as we walked back to the car that her mum was getting like the queen or the queen mother with her royal handshake and will need to put on white gloves next. We all gave out a howl of laughter and looked back at the serious faces of Ian's young men. Doreen said that Ian would have seen the funny side of it. They are a family who laughs – and it is that, I think, which has kept Doreen remaining so youthful. She says that she takes after her own mother in that way."

Mick Middles: "There was a strange and relaxed atmosphere in the city that afternoon. The influx of Joy Division fans had not seemed conspicuous, as they melted into hoards of regular shoppers, here and there an *Unknown Pleasures* t-shirt perhaps, but nothing particularly uniform. The truth was that they came in all manner of age, style, shape and fad. This became apparent as they started to drift towards The Triangle at 6pm. A disparate, gathering, in good humour, relieved that the forecasts of inclement weather had seemingly failed to materialise. For once, Manchester remained respectfully dry. Slowly a crowd formed, swelling back towards the moderne façade of Selfridges. Mostly they remained calm, focusing on the screen where, at one point, Anton Corbijn's dark, gothic 'Atmosphere' video was shown. In truth, the actual screening seemed secondary. For most, it was enough just to be there. In corners, old friendships – some very old – would be rekindled. Old Joy Division fans, a quarter of a century later, a flash of recognition. I met one myself, a man called Keith, latterly a successful professional working in Manchester. I had last glimpsed him at The Leigh Festival. He just felt that he had to pay his respects.

"'There's no one else quite like this since,' he stated.

"For a while, the 'Love Will Tear Us Apart' video galvanised the crowd. At this moment, a fan of more tender years, French, I think – short haired, black leather jacket, dark skin – rushed to the front of the crowd, sinking to his knees and noisily unleashing familiar lyric line from the song, lost in hero worship.

"But most just turned up because they... well, they felt they should. They knew they had been touched by something special, whether it had been back then, in one of the venues in which this very human drama had been played out onstage, or in later years, chancing across a copy of *Closer* perhaps, or finding themselves drawn towards that 'Love Will Tear Us Apart' video on MTV.

"Whatever, if the gathering outside The Triangle could be seen a cross section of the Joy Division audience of 2005, then it was certainly fitting for a band, and a singer, who defied the odds during their brief existence, and have continued to defy them over the years. Any tragedy of a significant rock figure, serves to freeze them to a youthful perfection. Joy Division will never age, never soften to the compromise of middle age, and never run out of ideas. Opinion is divided as to whether Ian Curtis would have been comfortable in the role of Major International Rock Star. Would he have grasped the role in the manner of Bono, or remained in a distant, enigmatic isolation? Of course, we will never know. As it turns out, he is still there... somewhere. His influence echoes resoundingly through to so much of the music of 2006, adding heart and soul to the performances of younger bands... and magic, too."

AFTERWORD 2009

The Icon Who Is Larger
Than Life

Three years have elapsed since the publication of *Torn Apart*, all of them busy years for Joy Division and busy years for Ian Curtis, the icon who is now larger than life. However, almost three decades have passed since the death of Joy Division, all of them decades of frenzied musical activity and rapidly unfolding technology as embraced by, among a thousand others, New Order. It would be reasonable to expect that the very sound of contemporary music, let alone the increasingly shallow elements of celebrity that often accompany it, would have moved us all firmly away from the often naïve music made by those four lost boys of Joy Division.

But this is not the case. On the contrary, the fact that modern music has advanced at such a pace is itself serving to preserve the special nature of Joy Division, rendering them truly untouchable, unreachable by all the musicians that now look to them as a major influence. There simply cannot be another Joy Division because that world has gone. That Manchester has gone. The context has shifted although the impact remains the same, if not more so.

The simple fact is that between 2006 and 2009 activity surrounding Joy Division reached frenzied levels. No longer are they a small but highly influential band of yesteryear, name-dropped by every earnest would-be young star of indie and dance. Far from vaporising in the wake of the post punk upsurge, as so many did, this band has truly evolved firmly into the contemporary era. They remain active. Ian Curtis, perhaps more than any other rock star of his era, also remains active in a realm all of his own. The remainder of the band have famously moved on but not so Ian, even if the industry around him has moved to a surprising new level.

It's likely that Ian Curtis would feel uncomfortable in the contemporary world. Weird things are happening. Fashion houses sell glammed-up girly tops, cheap glittery bling items featuring the logo that adorned *Unknown Pleasures*. Ian Curtis' haunting image is featured on hi-fashion t-shirts, albeit in the ironic manner of The Ramones a few years ago. They have become de rigueur, if only in the discos of Skegness and Ibiza.

The reason for this is the outpouring of films and books which have now set in stone the image of Ian Curtis as a romantic but doomed outsider figure, none more so than Anton Corbijn's 2006 movie *Control*. This book played its part too, helping to sway the second half of that film away from the course steered by its template, Debbie Curtis' memoir *Touching From A Distance*. In addition, there has been the acclaimed Joy Division documentary plus a variety of lesser hyped – though equally worthy – DVDs and television programmes.

To accompany this activity, myriad articles peppered the mainstream press, in particularly those corners of the broadsheets that are now the domain of silver-haired hacks who were once stalwarts of the great music inkies of the seventies, the pillars of the Joy Division fan base

As with The Fall's Mark E Smith, the second coming occurred partly because the original fans had risen to positions of importance within the media, but there were downsides, not least the news that someone had stolen Ian Curtis' headstone from Macclesfield cemetery. This was truly shocking, more a reflection of the godless values of 2008 than anything else, shallow celebrity culture at its most deadening. What? How? Why? One almost expected it to show up on eBay. Thankfully, those closest to the story helped secure a swift replacement.

There have been less worrying downsides. The sight of ageing New Order performing Joy Division songs – as is their right, of course – was witnessed by the authors of this book at Blackpool's Empress Ballroom. It seemed to stand completely against the truly progressive spirit that had famously fuelled that band in younger years. It just didn't seem right.

What was once refreshing and new now seemed plain old hat, with the band's celebrated lackadaisical onstage demeanour now reduced to a state of decaying dynamism. That summer had seen their album *Waiting For The Siren's Call* achieve reasonable reviews and gather enough new interest to make them a must-see sideshow on the festival circuit. However, the album soon became a dusty also-ran in many record collections. The context of this was apparent in the autumn of 2008, when re-mastered editions of five of the band's early albums, *Movement, Power Corruption And Lies, Low-Life, Brotherhood* and *Technique* all proudly emerged to rapturous critical accolades. Even within a period curiously cluttered with excellent albums across the genres, New Order's re-emergence, rather like that of Joy Division's, seemed strangely poignant, far more so than the final – if this be the case – sightings of the band themselves. In the aftermath of *Waiting For The Siren's Call*, a public and seemingly acrimonious split dulled the end of their glorious career.

Hooky's embittered remarks in regard to this howled from his Myspace blog. However, the bass player, never one to hang around in a sulk, was already working the 'wheels of steel' in Britain and Europe, seemingly thoroughly enjoying being a DJ. In addition, there was a stop-start-will-they-won't-they project, Freebase, in which Hooky would be joined by the other two Mancs of bass wielding glory, ex-Stone Rose and latter-day Primal Scream's Mani and ex-Smith Andy Rourke. In reality, it always seemed a rather dubious venture and, as we write, little of note has emerged beyond vacant rumour.

There have been a number of worthy books. Kevin Cummins' outrageously expensive *Juvenes* finally framed his iconic photographs in a setting of true class. Paul Morley's *Joy Division Piece By Piece* was more than a mere collection of articles and, given its skilful threading from the writer in retrospect, really did capture a flavour of the times; more so, in fact, than the sprawling retrospective archives in some of the more respected music papers which, in effect, were little more than PR exercises intended to heighten the impact of *Control*.

Control truly pushed the Joy Division industry to new heights, reaching out to a level way beyond anything the group had glimpsed in their heyday. For a while, in the media, you just couldn't escape Ian Curtis.

We – the authors of this book – chose to catch the film at Macclesfield Heritage Centre, which certainly seemed more apt and evocative than Cornerhouse where, frankly, mixing with the glitterati didn't really appeal. I emerged, two hours later with, at best, mixed feelings.

I certainly enjoyed the band performance scenes, apart from the dreadful and inaccurate depiction of the riotous Bury gig (where did those skinheads come from?), but, although beautifully shot, albeit in some kind of museum-like gritty northern dream-state, this version of the tale left gaping holes. Despite being two hours in length, huge chunks of story were missing and, worse, none of the characters or relationships were explored beyond a rudimentary level.

273

Ian Curtis, in reality amiable, talkative and intelligent, was pushed into a predictably slow downward spiral of doom. Nonsense. The relationship with Debbie barely rose beyond "D'ya wanna cup of tea, love?" and Annik was inevitably cast as a glamorous hanger-on lost in a state of fan-like adoration, initially at least. The relationship between Ian and Annik thankfully moved to a somewhat higher level with the inclusion of quotes from Ian's letters and I like to think that, in our humble way, our book helped pave the way for that.

However, there is a simplistic approach to Ian's relationships that feels strangely empty. A few days prior to seeing this film, I had watched *Atonement*, the film of Ian McEwan's critically acclaimed novel, which elegantly brings very sensitive emotions to the surface. Anton is an excellent surreal pop promo director who does not, as yet, have the skill to achieve this.

Tony Wilson's portrayal was, again, pathetic, insultingly so, with the hapless character reminding me of a geography teacher from the *Kes* era; badly dressed, humourless, sexless, witless and drab, in no way resembling the man himself. The scene where he signs the contract in his own blood before fainting spectacularly is straight out of Daffy Duck. I was beyond embarrassment at that point.

Almost as irritating was the sight of Joy Division manager Rob Gretton reduced to a state of laddish cliché. I cannot believe that anyone who knew Rob would be comfortable watching that. I found it (again) insulting and am stunned that the members of New Order allowed it to slip though. Rob had his moments but, in the main, he was a considered and quiet man whose obvious intelligence transcended an arguably overstated period as a football hooligan. Interestingly, back in 1983 I shared a van with New Order, Kevin Cummins, Chris Bohn and Anton. Rob was strangely aggressive towards Anton and I never fully understood why. Perhaps Anton never really forgave him. Who knows?

This is just a snapshot of my feelings, for what they are worth, but there is so much more. The film does, of course, have some highly commendable scenes. The band performance shots – apart from Bury – are simply astonishing and the use of music in general is superb. Nevertheless, it lacks a sense of the evolving scene, from ragged punk to the new sophistication of postpunk. Legendary London gigs, the European tour and the Buzzcocks shenanigans are all ignored or were left on the cutting room floor. There is a scene near the end where my friend Lindsay is seen hugging Annik, Who? How? Why? It's just a small point, but there are loose ends all over the place, including the mystery of Candy, Ian's dog, a hugely important, glaring and, one senses, deliberate omission.

With *Control* still hovering in the media, and Joy Division seemingly outpacing New Order – among many others – in the curious musical maelstrom of 2007, the timing of the release of Grant Gee's Joy Division documentary carried the risk of overload. After all, *Control* had itself centred on part of a story already covered in *24 Hour Party People*. In addition, albeit in the shadows, there had been two other Joy Division and Factory DVD based documentaries, James Nice's *Shadowplayers* which gathered together most of the old Factory hands to produce a rather jumbled history of the label, and *Joy Division Under Review*, which was hardly groundbreaking but more charming than the title suggested.

It was becoming crowded out there, especially as two books – this book and Debbie Curtis' memoir – had also closely charted what was essentially the same story.

Like *Control*, the Joy Division documentary, *Joy Division, Their Own Story In Their Own Words*, enjoyed 'premiers' in London, Sheffield, Liverpool, Manchester and elsewhere. More often than not, the screening would be followed by elongated talks on the subject featuring several of the film's collaborators. This didn't seem particularly odd at the time, although it remains difficult to imagine the same thing happening with documentaries on other bands. Grant Gee's previous music film, Radiohead's *Meeting People Is Easy*, proved a splendidly paranoid on-the-road affair but despite Radiohead's elevated international status – far bigger than Joy Division in terms of sales, if not esteem, and even that would be a close run thing – the film wasn't received with anything like the same fanfare.

Once again, the authors of this book, one of whom – Lindsay Reade – featured in the film, did not attend the more glamorous showings. That said, catching it at a Salford Quays opening in October 2007, we were treated to an after-show question and answer session with Hooky and Steve Morris. It passed without serious incident although Hooky was hard pressed to recall if any unreleased Joy Division recordings remained in some distant and dusty archive. The conclusion was a fairly non committal, "Not really, although there might be some live stuff."

During another screening, at Sheffield, Hooky was joined by an ebullient Jon Savage who confessed that watching the documentary, which he largely scripted, "makes me feel like dancing."

The documentary was made just in time to feature Tony Wilson commenting on the musical upsurges of Manchester as well as his most enigmatic charges. This was fortuitous as without Wilson on board a gaping hole would have appeared at the heart of this story. Most evocative of all, however, was the city of Manchester itself, captured in a jumble of cleverly segued reportage. Admittedly, through these aged lenses, it did seem rather grim. On the film, the story – *this story* – unfolds skilfully, the stack of spliced interviewees being, in the main, the usual suspects of the band, Pete Saville, Paul Morley, John Robb and, mercifully, Annik Honore and, as mentioned, Lindsay Reade. The absence of Deborah Curtis is both striking and refreshing. Once again the enigma that was Ian Curtis was featured in lengthy broadsheet articles that dissected his legacy, his lyrics and his life. Would people ever tire of this? It seems not. All the films, all the books, all the records continue to gather in sales momentum.

The Joy Division and Ian Curtis industry continues to throw up the occasional unexpected oddity. Is Ian Curtis' voice heard on the somewhat bizarre *Martin Hannett Personal Mixes* album, an unofficial compilation of outtakes from the *Unknown Pleasures* sessions at Strawberry Studios? It is an intriguing collection of clanging sound effects, in-studio banter and alternative versions of songs. Although uneven and difficult to listen to, it was eagerly devoured by the most devoted of fans before re-emerging in several other formats, on vinyl and in double album CD under the title *In The Studio With Martin Hannett*.

It's impossible to even speculate on quite what Ian Curtis would make of the Manchester of 2008. It's now a city of mass and, at times, rather bullish regeneration, with angular industrial chic flat blocks rising on, it often seems, a weekly basis. Today, of course, it is bright, smart, teeming and as profoundly cosmopolitan as any city in Europe. It remains famously a city with a thriving music scene even if, given the large proliferation of venues of all shapes and sizes, rather fragmented and lacking the village atmosphere that polarised the forces of Manchester punk. The paradox is that, while on any given night you might discover three new bands with musical skills way beyond Joy Division, it remains highly unlikely that any will attain the same degree of cultish longevity. Even perennial outsiders Elbow, 2008 winners of the Mercury Prize, might produce a stream of classic albums and yet, as they are not and can never be in the moment, they can never be Joy Division. In their wake emerge bands from every corner of every genre, from elder statesmen like Doves to brash Salfordian popsters The Ting Tings, from breakthrough acts such as The Courteeners to Fraser King, Twisted Wheel, Exile Parade and others, and echoes of Joy Division can be heard in so many of them.

The nature of rock music in the 21st Century is such that after a respectable period of time its foremost practitioners and historical precedents are elevated to Heritage Status. Nowadays you can purchase Factory mugs in the Urbis shop, and in this same museum for much of 2007 the spirit and feel of The Hacienda was recreated as an exhibition, complete with Hacienda trainers selling for an eye-watering £245 alongside rolling footage of A Certain Ratio. In addition, as Lindsay notes in her afterward, an excellent event in memory of Anthony H. Wilson brought eager young-sters face-to-face with many of the main Factory characters.

Which is as it should be.

Mick Middles, November 2008

Although this is an addendum to our book about the life of Ian Curtis and its aftermath, it would be inappropriate not to begin my contribution with anything other than an acknowledgement of the passing of the much loved Tony Wilson. Ian Curtis and Tony Wilson shared a like-minded, high intel-lect and a political philosophy that touched every area of the Factory mindset. Tony was unquestionably Ian's principal mentor, not least in the guidance he offered during the recording of Joy Division's music, an example of which can be found on page 205 of this book which describes how Tony influenced Ian's vocal on what remains their best known song, 'Love Will Tear Us Apart'.

Tony was young and still had much to offer, which for those he left behind in Manchester and elsewhere made his death all the more difficult to accept. He was more philosophical about it. "The readiness is all"[*] he quoted more than once, adding that his life had been so wonderful and perfect that he was quite prepared for it to be taken away. When his illness was diagnosed his positivism remained uppermost. He remarked that having cancer was an "adventure" and campaigned widely to make the drug sutent available on the NHS, making headlines on the subject eight days before he died.

For all Tony's achievements – and they were many and I don't belittle them by saying this – what I admired the most was the way he handled his illness and final journey, the business of dying in effect, a business we all have to attend to sooner or later. He told me that he was just getting on with it and he did, in much the way he got on with living, bravely treading his own path and proving beyond all doubt that he was, when 'all's said and done', indeed a truly exceptional human being.

[*] "If it be now, 'tis not to come; if it be not to come, it will be now; if it be not now, yet it will come: the readiness is all." Hamlet

The interest in Joy Division, Factory and the Hacienda seemed to accelerate with the release of *24 Hour Party People* in 2002. It was certainly a funny and interesting film, even if I did take exception to my character being portrayed as participating in the sex aspect of its inevitable "sex, drugs, and rock'n'roll" theme – probably because I was one of the few females around at the time. Nonetheless it was one of many fine movies from the Michael Winterbottom stable. Tony used to like to quote Springsteen's early song 'Rosalita' – "Someday we'll look back on this and it will all seem funny". With the help of Steve Coogan it did!

Mick Middles and I began research for this book soon after the film's release because it came to the attention of Omnibus editor Chris Charlesworth that there was no biography of Ian other than his wife's memoirs which were not entirely objective. Although we had another, more generalised Factory book in mind when we met with Chris, he saw Ian as the central figure in it all and proposed instead that we write about his life, which we did.

It was at this point that I became aware how much public interest in Ian and Joy Division was already gathering speed. There was a website devoted entirely to Factory Records, Cerysmatic Factory, and a specific Joy Division website, Joy Division Central, with almost daily updates and lists of books, records and films, a detailed reference to satisfy even the most eager fan. Our book was not the first on the related subjects, nor was it the last as there followed a plethora of books and exhibitions at Urbis, DVDs and more which all culminated in the volcanic explosion of two films that can currently be found quite easily in any local DVD store. Now, of course, there is an element of saturation, but there will always be other stories to be told. We hope.

Long before the release of *Control*, Amy Hobby had been developing the concept of a film about Ian's life and had optioned Debbie Curtis' book, *Touching From A Distance*. However, when her option expired and needed renewing things went awry.

Shortly after she had finished working on her film of *Hamlet*, in 1999, Amy was approached about an Ian Curtis movie by a young writer named Michael Stock. In the spring of 2000 she met with Debbie Curtis and her boyfriend to discuss the project. "We had a lovely long dinner and drinks at a big pub somewhere outside Manchester and either on this trip or a subsequent trip Michael and I met with Tony Wilson," she says. "I really enjoyed spending the day with him – he was smart and wicked funny."

Amy Hobby's original option agreement was signed and paid for in June 2000, after which Michael Stock began work on the script. "In the spring of 2001 we started taking meetings," she says. "We wanted to get moving! We weren't happy with the script and I remember long meetings with Michael ripping it apart and creating new outlines while in I was in LA for the shooting of *Secretary*. Music supervisor Beth Rosenblatt, who I had worked with on *Hamlet*, came on board in a producer capacity. Beth and I met with Tom Attencio, Danny Bramson, as well as someone from Zomba who controlled much of the publishing for the songs. We pitched the project to a number of places but really it came down to the script and the fact that Michael was attached to direct and he didn't really have any feature directing credits."

It seemed the script was the stumbling block to this project. "In 2002 we went back to the script [but] we should have brought on another writer at this point, and this is my failure as a producer," admits Hobby. "I was being loyal to Michael since he had the original idea but maybe I was not doing what was best for the project. There can be a point in the screenwriting process when a writer is so lost that they will never deliver a workable draft. Also, Michael was going through some things in his personal life that seemed to keep seeping into the script. The right writing partner might have done the trick.

"In November of 2002, we invited Debbie and her daughter (with Ian) to the *Secretary* premiere at the London Film Festival. We had a nice coffee with them and they seemed to enjoy themselves and everything seemed cool. While in London, my producing partner and I met with everyone in town on the project… Pathe, Film Four, you name it. But the commercial viability of the project remained dubious. Without a 'name' English director or 'name' leading actor, we weren't really getting anywhere. I was working to convince Michael that it would be better for the project if we could get somebody else to jump on board as director in an effort to get some juice behind the project. At the same time my company was dissolving. I was splitting with my long time producing partner (and friend) and it was a devastating and exhausting process."

In the midst of all this, the option renewal for Debbie's book came up, and Amy's business partner was unwilling to pay the renewal fee on behalf of their company. The payment thus became delinquent. "In the 'divorce' the project became mine," continues Amy, "because it was obviously my passion project. Because the company/partnership that optioned it no longer existed, I didn't want to pay out of my own pocket in order to have the project still owned by the now non-existent company. Anyway, I wrote to Deb and Annie and asked to have the option put into my new company name (which was just me). I got a sort of wall of anger, then silence that I never understood. I think I must be missing some information about what really happened. Further letters and emails were never answered."

In 2005 Amy brought in a new partner, Neal Weisman, and re-thought the project. "Did we need the book?" she says. "Could we scrap the script we never really liked? Could we start totally anew somehow? But it would be good to have some underlying material to base the project on. In my new company, I began working with a new producer named Russ Stratton. He was passionate about Joy Division and was obsessed with certain ideas about Ian, hypnosis and a different take on the story. He convinced me it was worth a go."

At this point Amy was put in touch with me and discussions centred round using *Torn Apart* as a basis for the movie. However, by this time, a rival project, which turned out to be *Control*, was happening elsewhere. "I was reluctant to revisit the project that had been so hard and hurtful but somehow just talking about it got me excited again," says Amy. "We knew there was another project but we decided to proceed anyway. We had a brand new script written from scratch working from *Torn Apart*. Tom Browne came highly recommended from our new director Jamie Thraves. We were talking with Jamie Bell about playing Ian. Neal and I travelled to Manchester to have lunch with the band and Rebecca [Boulton, from New Order's management]. With our new package we were beginning to have some good meetings [but] there was this sort of competition that arose with the other project and lots of bad feelings expressed by Debbie and Tony. Rebecca ultimately asked us to let 'the other guys' make their movie. We didn't want to make a movie without permission from the band, so we gave up."

The first I (Lindsay) had heard about it all was when Tony told me of his disappointment that Debbie hadn't received her option money. He took a moral stance on the issue and decided therefore that his position was to "fuck off the rogue film". Personally I wasn't so sure that *Control* wasn't the rogue film. In fact, in view of Amy's account, I would say that it was but dividing lines between 'official' and 'rogue' can easily become obscured, especially when the subject of a film or book has passed away and is in no position to authorise anyone to do anything.

I was disappointed that Amy's film, provisionally titled *All The Time*, was never made. I had every faith in the integrity of the contributors and, after all, it was they who had originally developed and worked so hard on the idea. But, such is life. It was not to be.

Nonetheless, I tried to view *Control* from an objective viewpoint and can see why so many fans enjoyed it. The fact that it irked me does not undermine its merit. It was probably because I knew all the people involved and felt their portrayal on screen was wide of the mark, especially Tony Wilson who in reality was a sexy, vibrant guy and not the wally on screen who seemed to be based on Steve Coogan's Alan Partridge-esque portrayal in *24 Hour Party People*. Nor were the Joy Division gigs remotely like my memories of them. I felt that the girl that played Annik had something about her that rang true, and it was quite poignant that this actress (Alexandra Maria Lara) and the actor that played Ian (Sam Riley) apparently fell in love in real life. I failed to understand why it was shot in black and white but Annik and Ian's sister Caroll spoke well of Anton Corbijn. Whereas *24 Hour Party People* may have been, as Tony once remarked, "a collection of lies that manages to tell the truth", *Control* was, in my opinion, more a collection of truths that somehow told a lie. Also, it was clear to me that indirect use had been made of this book. Still it had a powerful impact and audiences were gripped.

Personally I was distressed as being portrayed as Tony's 'girlfriend' rather than wife, which I felt was a deliberate slight because of my initial support for the Amy Hobby project. Marriage obviously meant a great deal to Ian. I believe he was religious at heart and took his marriage vows extremely seriously. Ian had said he knew he would love another woman after Debbie, and even told me he 'saw' this on the day of his marriage as the wedding car arrived. Even so late in the day, being the honourable person he was, he seriously considered calling the wedding off – not getting into that car – because he didn't want to break his vows to Debbie, and this was four years before he even met Annik.

The Joy Division documentary had more impact on me and I preferred it to *Control*. It was vividly real and had more depth, I felt. I even watched it twice which is something I would not do with *Control*. Once was enough or, as someone once observed about the Indian city of Calcutta, "I'm glad I've seen it because now I don't have to see it again."

I'm sure that anyone who saw Annik interviewed in this documentary would conclude that, far from being the predatory husband snatcher that some have implied, she is a deeply sensitive and beautiful woman who has been much maligned. I thought this film left people to make their own minds up about Ian's life and suicide but *Control* went for the obvious, powerful and dark though that may have been. There can be no question that style triumphed over truth.

The Tony Wilson Experience, a 24 hour interview marathon held on midsummer's day of 2008 at the Urbis museum in Manchester was a delightful and fitting accolade to him and to the artistic endeavours of all his associates. One of the attendees astutely observed that it was "shambolic enough to be useful". It certainly was. It had a spirit of craziness, colour and intelligent rambling that perfectly captured the spirit of Tony's extraordinary life.

Lindsay Reade, November 2008.

APPENDIX 1

Where Are They Now

Carole Baguley lives in Manchester with her husband and daughter, Lucy.

Kevin Cummins is a noted rock photographer, living in London.

Deborah Curtis is an author living in Cheshire. In addition to Natalie she has a son, Wesley, from her second marriage to Roger Boden.

Doreen Curtis lives in Manchester. Her husband Kevin died in 1995.

Natalie Curtis lives in Manchester and works as a photographer.

Alan Erasmus co-founded the Hacienda nightclub in Manchester and continued as a director of Factory until its bankruptcy in 1992. He lives in Manchester with his family.

Rob Gretton went on to manage New Order, and was also a co-founder of the Hacienda. After forming Rob's Records he worked with a band called Sub Sub, who were later known as Doves. He died of a heart attack aged 46 in 1999.

Martin Hannett continued as a record prodyucer and although he was involved in a lawsuit against Factory and Tony Wilson in 1982 he subsequently came back to the fold and produced The Happy Mondays amongst many other groups, mostly from Manchester. He died of heart failure aged 42 in 1991.

Annik Honore lives with her son, Bertrand and daughter, Sasha, within commuting distance of Brussels, where she works. She returned to England a few times after Ian's death to visit Macclesfield cemetery, and is sure she could still find the lane where there is small stone marked "Love will tear us apart". She remains a passionate fan of music and culture.

Peter Hook, Steve Morris & Bernard Sumner regrouped with Gillian Gilbert on keyboards and became New Order.

Pete Johnson manages a regional Home Office team working on drugs and crime, based in a government office in Birmingham, where he lives.

Barbara Lloyd is married with a son and daughter.

Terry Mason spent several years working and touring with New Order. He has now forged a successful career in the world of IT, and has a 16-year-old daughter called Sian.

Paul Morley lives in London, where he is an esteemed broadsheet music journalist, author and television arts pundit.

Genesis P'Orridge lives in America. He spent the Eighties running Psychic TV and still performs with Throbbing Gristle.

Mark Reeder lives in Berlin and works extensively within the European music industry.

Vini Reilly still records and performs with Durutti Column. He lives with his girlfriend in Manchester.

Peter Saville's sleeve for New Order's *Power, Corruption And Lies* was nominated as a Great British Icon in 2006. Manchester City Council appointed Peter Creative Director for the launch of the new branding for the city in 2006?

Pete Shelley & Steve Diggle both still perform as Buzzcocks.

Tony Wilson died in August 2007. Such was the esteem in which he was held in the city that the Union Jack on Manchester Town Hall was lowered to half mast as a mark of respect. As with everything else emanating from Factory, Tony's coffin was given a Factory catalogue number – FAC 501.

Alan Wise has worked for many years as a Manchester music promoter. He is currently working with the Fall, among others.

APPENDIX 2

The Writings Of Kevin Curtis

When the authors of this book first discovered that Ian's father, Kevin, had harboured aspirations to became a writer, it was difficult to know quite how seriously to take it. Many people, if not *most* people, find themselves duly inspired, at one point or another during the course of their life. Mostly the aspiration fades to a fleeting dream, or becomes trapped in some rambling manuscript, to be kindly read by the immediate family before being carefully stored at the back of the wardrobe. For the most part, the exorcism of writing is, itself, enough. Only a small minority are fired with enough belief to take it to the next level.

Kevin Curtis was a busy man. A heavy work schedule and a hectic family life must have made the task of sitting down, researching and completing a number of articulate works, particularly difficult. Especially as, in the late Fifties and early Sixties, artistic expression was generally less encouraged than it is today.

However, when we were privileged enough to be shown three examples of Kevin's work, it was immediately obvious that he had taken his writing very seriously indeed.

His play, *For Those In Peril,* had been professionally presented. It also proved to be a highly articulate work by a writer who had given much thought, not just to satisfying a distant ambition, but to seriously seek publication. More than that, it also proved to be a powerful wartime story, a work in which he had taken a great deal of care and consideration to bring to such a professional level.

It isn't feasible to publish the complete play here, nor would it be particularly apt but what follows is Kevin's own synopsis, which he had neatly presented at the beginning of the play.

There were two other examples of his work. One, a complete story, is printed at the foot of this synopsis. There was also a complex and fascinating piece of non fiction; a tale of police forensics in the early Sixties, although naturally outmoded by the tremendous scientific advances made in the time since, proved to be an intriguing historical essay.

Perhaps more importantly, and more relevant to this book, all three are the work of a man with an intelligent, analytical and aesthetic mind.

SYNOPSIS

For Those in Peril – By Kevin Curtis

The section of the play covers five days – from late evening of Saturday 12 September 1942 until late evening Thursday 17 September, 1942. Two sets are needed: one the Operations Room of the German U-Boat Command, Paris, the other being the office of the Commander-in-Chief, U-Boat command.

On the evening of Saturday 12 September, 1942, Lieutenant Commander Werner Hartenstein, on U-156, torpedoed and sank the British Troop Transport *Laconia*, just north of the Ascension Island in the South Atlantic. The *Laconia* was bound for the UK with approximately 3,000 people on board, including women and children and 1,500 Italian prisoners of war. Commander Hartenstein on his own initiative and, no doubt because of the Italian allies amongst the shipwrecked, commenced rescue operations and requested assistance from U-boat Command, Paris.

Vice Admiral Donitz, Commander-in-Chief, U-boat Command – at that time a man of 50 years of age, and a German sailor who had spent most of his service in the U-boat arm, decided – against the wish of the remainder of his staff – not only to allow the rescue to continue but also to despatch two more German U-boats and an Italian submarine to assist. Donitz also had units of the French fleet sent from Dakar to collect the survivors picked up by the submarines. As a result, some 800 British men, women and children and 450 Italians were saved.

During the rescue Hartenstein's U-boat was bombed by an American Liberator bomber while towing four lifeboats full of survivors. The following day Wurdemann's U-boat was also bombed. Despite this, and the antagonism from his staff, in particular Godt and Hessler – who were younger men and therefore more fervent Nazis – and despite repeated warnings from Hitler's GHQ not to risk the safety of the U-boats – Donitz persisted with the rescue.

While Donitz was found guilty at the Nuremburg Trials of 'Crimes against the peace' and 'war crimes' – it was stated that the evidence did not establish that he had deliberately ordered the killing of shipwrecked survivors – and there was, in fact, only one reported incident during the war of a German U-boat shooting shipwrecked survivors.

Though the play is based on fact and the signals given were in fact transmitted – also Captain Godt and Commander Hessler were on Donitz's staff – the play was purely the author's interpretation of what may have taken place during those five fateful days, and the author's effort to illustrate a little known episode of the 1939–45 war.

It should be added that the author served in the Royal Navy operating in the Western Approaches Command on anti-submarine patrols.

★ ★ ★

The story that Kevin wrote had no title but Lindsay Reade thinks it appropriate to call it by a phrase he used in the last line. Lindsay: "Carole was looking over the manuscript before she handed it to me and said that she'd just got a shiver when she read that one of the characters in the story is called Hooky. I lovingly re-typed this. War has never interested me but this tale held me in its grip. The reason I felt so inspired by this was because of its, well – I'll let the title say what it is:

That Unknown Quality

by E.K.Curtis

Crawley was mesmerised by the water streaming into the quickly flooding compartment. It was now up to his chest and felt to him as if he were encompassed by a band of steel – crushing life from him. He climbed higher up the steel ladder that led to the upper deck and safety, but the hatchway at the top had been jammed by the force of the explosion and, try as he would, he could not open it.

There were now six rungs of the ladder still above the scum covered water and he estimated he had twenty minutes left; twenty minutes of a very short life. Trapped in the flooding compartment of his sinking ship.

So this was it, thought Crawley, after the months of uncertainty that had filled him with anguish, it had happened. Now he could laugh. He wanted to laugh because it was all over. Yes, over in a matter of minutes – after what had seemed like a lifetime of torture. Why? He asked himself, why had he been afraid? Why had the thought of what had just happened caused him so much mental pain? So many sleepless nights? He looked down at his hands. They were steady. His mouth was dry and his lips parched, but that was understandable, even justified in the circumstances. Then what had made him fear this moment? This he must find out. But how? Think back, that was it. Relive the fear. Remember what had led up to it – and then conquer it. He looked at his watch, 7.25 p.m. Now he forced himself to concentrate. Letting his thoughts drift back an hour in time – to what seemed to be another life on a different world.

In his mind's eye he could visualise what had been taking place an hour previously. Crawley could see himself seated on the mess-deck table. His shoeless feet resting on the long cushion-covered wooden form. He was trying to read, but not succeeding.

As he sat there he was vaguely conscious of the other off-watch stokers; their voices mingling with the dull, ever present throb of the engines and the creaking of the various gear, as the ship ploughed her way through a north Atlantic night. Crawley read the same line over and over again, unable to get further into the novel, as Yorky, who was forever whittling a piece of wood – that never seemed to take the shape of their frigate – was telling the mess in general: "Wun day," he was saying, "Wun day, this 'ere model'll be on't mantelshelf back in Batley, an I'll look at it an tell children… now when I were in't Andrew…"

"Stow it Yorky," interrupted Jan, "or you'll have us all sea sick with the lamps swinging too much."

Just beyond Yorky were the two 'Stripeys' playing their nightly cribbage contest, their voices growing louder and louder as the fate of the stake, twenty duty-free cigarettes, became more apparent.

"Fifteen two, fifteen four, fifteen …"

"That's enough. You can't see anymore, you've counted the Jack twice already."

"What do you mean, I've counted the Jack twice? I…"

Further argument was curtailed by the noisy entrance of Snowy White as he clattered down the steel ladder into the mess.

"I've just heard the buzz…"

"Can it Snowy," shouted Hooky. "Every time you hear a buzz we finish up round Russia, and I'm not that fond of Uncle Joe."

"No, honest. It's straight up this time Hooky." continued Snowy. "I've just heard 'Jimmy the one' telling 'Guns'. After this trip, he says, after this trip we're going in for a tiddley refit. Twenty four days leave each watch. How about that? Twenty four days up the line. Wine, women, and more hootch."

"Aye. An you'll be glad t'get back to th'ole sardine can," added Yorky. "Fags are as short as hell in't civvy street."

At that moment the 'tannoy' began to crackle into life, and the mess deck fell silent. The men detailed as cooks of the messes began preparing the tables, anticipating the call "Cooks to the galley", for supper. That call was never piped. In its place was the urgent voice of the officer of the watch with a very different order.

"Stand by action Hedgehog. Depth charge party set one patter 'A' for Able, fifty feet. Gun crews close up."

The order was followed by the high-pitched scream of the anti-submarine action station siren.

Why the devil does it have to happen at meal times? Crawley asked himself, as he hurriedly pulled on his laceless oil stained boots. Feeling in his boilersuit, he took out a cigarette packet, counted twelve and told himself he would have sufficient to last until the secure was sounded. He then slung his deflated life-belt over his shoulder, after first checking to see that the red coloured survivors' light, attached to the belt, was in working order. Satisfied he began to make his way aft', becoming aware of the other hurrying forms of his messmates, as they went with a sure speed of months, and even years, of practice to their respective action stations.

On reaching the bulkhead door, Crawley unfastened the securing dog clips, waited until the ship had almost completed a starboard roll, and, letting the roll of the ship open the heavy steel door, he stepped smartly over the breakwater plate. The port roll of the ship closed the door and he slammed the dog clips into the locked position. He was now in the seamen's aft' mess deck and as he made his way through he saw that the damage control party were at their station.

"Shake a leg, Crawley," the leading stoker in charge urged him in a sarcastic tone. "You're not on a blasted pleasure cruise now and you should have been closed up two minutes ago. If it happens again you'll get your cap on and have words with the owner."

The remainder of the control party added a few choice remarks of their own and then quickly forgot about him in the urgency of their tasks.

Crawley passed through another bulkhead door into the canteen flat, and through yet another door leading into the last compartment space of the ship – the aft' steering compartment – his action station. After entering this confined space, he secured the bulkhead door with the dog clips, unhooked the telephone head and mouth pieces from the bulkhead, plugged the long wire lead into the circuit and reported himself closed up to the damage control officer on the bridge. The formalities over, he sat down on a box of spare parts for the long, lonely wait until the secure was sounded, or he was relieved at 8 pm for the first watch in the engine room.

Sitting there, headphones over his ears, Crawley let his gaze wander about the compartment. The electro-hydraulic steering gear, with the large wheels for manual operation in case of emergency. The maker's instruction card for operating the gear, which he had read at least a hundred times, during previous spells of duty in that compartment. Though wearing the headphones, he could still hear the continual whirr of the "Hele-shaw" pump, as each turn of the wheel, by the quartermaster on the bridge, was transmitted through the telemotor to the steering gear, and oil was supplied to the four hydraulic rams to move the twin rudders situated just beneath his feet, on the underside of the hull. Almost in the centre of the compartment was the steel ladder leading to the watertight hatchway that opened onto the upper deck, from where, at that moment, he could hear the sea booted feet of the seamen as they set the depth charges, under the directions of 'Jimmy the one', the first Lieutenant.

The loud hailer crackled into life again.

"This is the Captain speaking. It seems we have pinged one this time, so we shall do a depth charge run and then a pattern of hedgehogs. Set depth charges 'A' for Able, fifty feet."

The voice of the 'Gunnery' officer then took over.

"Stand-by depth charge party – 300 yards – stand-by."

Now, as the twin screws thrust the ship along with maximum revolutions, Crawley felt the dreaded feeling returning. His stomach muscles tightened and his mouth became dry. He cast a swift glance towards the hull and wondered if it was the thought of the thin plates, separating him from the sea that made him feel that way. No, he was not afraid of the sea, he had been in the compartment scores of times during exercise action stations and never worried about the sea engulfing him. Perhaps, he thought, it is because the compartment was at the stern of the ship, and would be the first to be hit should an acoustic torpedo – which is attracted by the sound and vibration of the screws – be fired at the ship. No, he told himself, not that – then what?

"Stand-by depth charge party – fire."

He was again conscious of the voice, and then the muffled explosions as the depth charge throwers were fired, coupled with the rumbling sound as other charges were rolled over the stern of the ship. The heavy drums, ten of them, filled with amotal set to explode at a predetermined depth – in this instance fifty feet – were now falling through the murky sea to the unseen, but, thanks to asdic, not unknown U-boat. Crawley, alone in the steering compartment, braced himself for the expected explosions of the charges, knowing that though the ship was still going ahead at full speed the force of the explosions would shake the ship as if she were the attacked and not the attacker. Seconds later the deadened honk of the depth charges detonating sounded to Crawley as if they had gone off under the stern. The lights flickered momentarily as the shock vibrated through the ship.

The frigate now slewed round at full speed, and as the asdic picked up contact again, the engine revolutions were increased for the hedgehog attack. Twenty-four depth bombs, fired from a multiple thrower over the bow of the ship, which would explode on contact. As the ship slowly rolled and lurched at slow speed ahead into the attack, Crawley asked himself if he were afraid of death. He did not want to die, at eighteen life should be beginning, not ending, but he did not think that caused the sickening feeling. The gunnery officer's voice again came over the 'tannoy'.

"Stand-by action hedgehog – 100 yards – stand-by – fire."

Crawley felt the ship jump forward, increasing to full speed and swinging to starboard to be clear of the explosions that might follow and to prepare for the next attack. He imagined the 24 bombs up in the air, now hurtling down into the depths to strike the underwater menace. He listened, his mouth slightly open, straining his ears as if he could actually hear the bombs gliding through the water of the north Atlantic. It seemed hours to him since the order to fire had been given and then came a series of muffled thuds in quick succession – hits had been scored on the U-boat.

The ship was still heeling over as she slewed round to go in for another depth charge run. Suddenly, a loud explosion, that seemed to burst Crawley's ear-drums, thundered and echoed in the confined space of the compartment, and the plates vibrated as the ship came to a shuddering stop as if it had hit a sand bank. Crawley closed his eyes and instinctively dropped down on his knees, with his arms shielding his head, to ward off some unseen attacker. Seconds later, when he opened his eyes, there was an oppressing darkness, and he realised the lights must have failed. He stumbled round in the darkness until he found the emergency light, switched it on and as the blue glow lit up the compartment, he considered his next move.

Knowing that the power had been cut off by the explosion, which must have been caused by a torpedo hit from a companion U-boat to the one they had been attacking, he began to assemble the hand steering gear, the last resort for steering the ship. After fitting the lever to the hand pump, he next tried to contact the bridge, only to find that the telephone circuit was off the board too. The only course left open for him now was to go to the upper deck and report the facts to the first Lieutenant and ask for further instructions.

Crawley climbed up the steel ladder and, grasping the wheel, fitted on the watertight hatchway to release the dog clips, he tried to turn it, but it would not move. He returned to the deck plates, picked up a wheel-spanner and once more climbed the ladder and attempted to open the hatch, but without success, it was buckled. He banged on the deck head with the wheel-spanner in an effort to make the depth charge party hear him. This too was unsuccessful and he came to the conclusion that the seamen must be busy elsewhere. Returning to the deck plates, he decided to go through the bulk-head door and report to the damage control party in the seamen's mess and it was then that he saw the water streaming in the compartment from the canteen flat. He was fascinated at first; noticing each successive mark the scum covered water left on the whiteness of the bulkhead as the ship rolled, only to disappear again as the water rose higher and higher. Then the full implication came home to him. The canteen flat must be flooded and in a short time the bulkhead would collapse, allowing the water to rush unchecked into the steering compartment. Even now the bulkhead frame was warped and the water infiltrating in – and he was trapped.

He rushed blindly back to the ladder. Unmindful of the blood streaming into his eyes from a cut on the forehead he received when he bumped into the hand lever of the pump. He just wanted to escape from the steel tomb the compartment had suddenly become. He hammered on the deck head plates with his bare hands, until they too were cut and bleeding, praying that someone would hear him and release the hatch. The icy water was now up to his waist, pulling at him. Beckoning him to let go his hold and sink into its depths. And still he beat with clenched fists on the steel plates. The noise echoed around the compartment, mocking him and his feeble attempt to get free. Then his panic receded as the fruition of his naval training came to the fore, and his calmness returned.

He was brought back to reality when the roll of the ship caused him to involuntarily swallow a mouthful of the scum covered water, which had now reached his neck. He began to cough and retch and his mind returned to the present. It was now 7.45 pm and he knew he was going to die. There were no sounds of the men on the upperdeck and he surmised that they must have abandoned ship, not knowing he was alive, trapped like a rat in the flooded compartment. The ventilating fans were now submerged and the air was fouled and reeked of oil fumes. Still he wanted to laugh, because he had conquered the unknown fear and his mind was at peace for the first time in so many months. He now knew what had troubled him. It was not the thought of dying. Rather the thought that he might let his shipmates down, and all that it would entail. At eighteen he did not know, and could not know, how he would react when put to the test. And it was this thought, the fear of being a coward. Of deserting his post. Bringing shame to his family, and seeing the scorn on the faces of his messmates. This had caused the fear. The sleepless nights. Now he knew he would never be troubled again. He had met the test and had carried out his duties until the end and he was happy.

But now, as the surging water extinguished the emergency light and his life, no one would know the price he had paid to find, that unknown quality – that is man.

APPENDIX 3

Joy Division Discography

9/6/78: *Short Circuit – Live At The Electric Circus* (Virgin Records VCL 5003) 10″ LP: 5,000 blue vinyl (the rest in black), 300 orange vinyl (promo issue only)

    1)   At A Later Date

This is a compilation album of live tracks from the Electric Circus, October 2, 1979 featuring also The Fall, Steel Pulse, The Drones, John Cooper Clarke, Buzzcocks

6/78: *An Ideal For Living* EP (Enigma PSS 139) 7″ EP: 1,000 only. Fold-out sleeve designed by Bernard Sumner.

    1)   Warsaw
    2)   No Love Lost
    3)   Leaders Of Men
    4)   Failures

10/78: *An Ideal For Living* EP (Anonymous ANON1) 12″ reissue: 1,200 copies only. Sleeve design by Steve McGarry; photography by DB Glen. This reissue was prompted by the poor sound quality of the 7″.

    1)   Warsaw
    2)   No Love Lost
    3)   Leaders Of Men
    4)   Failures

1/79: *A Factory Sample* (Factory Records FAC 2) 2x7″ singles produced by Martin Hannett. Shrinkwrap sleeve with five stickers (Joy Division = a ventriloquist's dummy). Design by Peter Saville.

    1)   Digital
    2)   Glass

Compilation featuring also The Durutti Column, John Dowie and Cabaret Voltaire.

5/79: *Unknown Pleasures* (Factory Records FACT 10) 12″ LP produced by Martin Hannett. Sleeve design by Peter Saville.

1) Disorder
2) Day Of The Lords
3) Candidate
4) Insight
5) New Dawn Fades
6) She's Lost Control
7) Shadowplay
8) Wilderness
9) Interzone
10) I Remember Nothing

10/79: *Earcom 2: Contradiction* (Fast Products FAST 9b) 12″ EP. Produced by Martin Hannett. Sleeve design Bob Last.

1) Autosuggestion
2) From Safety To Where…?

Compilation featuring also Thursdays and Basczax.

10/79: Transmission/Novelty (Factory Records FAC 13) 7″ single produced by Martin Hannett. Sleeve design by Peter Saville. Rereleased on 12″ with new cover as FAC 13.12 12/80

3/80: *Licht Und Blindheit* (Sordide Sentimental SS33022) 7″ single, produced by Martin Hannett, 1,578 numbered copies. Gatefold colour booklet and text by Jean-Pierre Turmel (English translation by Paul Buck) front cover illustration by JF Jamoul and collage by Jean-Pierre Turmel.

1) Atmosphere
2) Dead Souls

4/80: Flexidisc (Factory Records FAC 28) Produced by Martin Hannett. Initial pressing of 10,000 copies. Free giveaway.

1) Komakino
2) Incubation
3) As You Said

4/80: Love Will Tear Us Apart (Factory Records FAC 23) 7″ single. Produced by Martin Hannett. Sleeve design by Peter Saville. Rereleased on 12″ with a new cover FAC 23.12 27.6.80

1) Love Will Tear Us Apart
2) These Days
3) Love Will Tear Us Apart (Pennine version)

7/80: *Closer* (Factory Records FACT 25) 12″ LP produced by Martin Hannett.
Sleeve design by Peter Saville. Photography: Bernard Pierre Wolfe.

1)   Atrocity Exhibition
2)   Isolation
3)   Passover
4)   Colony
5)   A Means To An End
6)   Heart And Soul
7)   Twenty Four Hours
8)   The Eternal
9)   Decades

2/9/80: Atmosphere / She's Lost Control (Factory Records FACUS 2/UK) 12″
Single. Sleeve photography by Charles Meecham; typographics by Peter Saville.

8/10/81: *Still* (Factory Records FACT 40). 2x12″ LP. Sleeve design by Peter
Saville. First 5,000 with Hessian cloth cover. Compilation including many
unreleased tracks, produced by Martin Hannett.

1)   Exercise One
2)   Ice Age
3)   The Sound Of Music
4)   Glass
5)   The Only Mistake
6)   Walked In Line
7)   The Kill
8)   Something Must Break
9)   Dead Souls
10)   Sister Ray
11)   Ceremony
12)   Shadowplay
13)   Means To An End
14)   Passover
15)   New Dawn Fades
16)   Transmission
17)   Disorder
18)   Isolation
19)   Decades
20)   Digital

Tracks 11 – 20: Joy Division's last ever concert at Birmingham University, 2 May
1980.

11/86: *Peel Sessions* (Strange Fruit SFR 13). 12″ EP.

1.   Exercise One
2.   Insight

3. She's Lost Control
4. Transmission

Recorded January 31, 1979. Produced by Bob Sargeant, first broadcast on John Peel radio show February 14, 1979.

5/87: *Peel Sessions* (Strange Fruit SFR 33). 12″ EP.
1. Love Will Tear Us Apart
2. Twenty Four Hours
3. Colony
4. Sound Of Music

Recorded November 26, 1979 Produced by Tony Wilson, first broadcast on John Peel radio show December 10, 1979.

6/88: Atmosphere (Factory Records FAC 213). Sleeve: Plus en Min (detail) by Jan Van Munster; art direction by Peter Saville; design by Brett Wickens, Peter Saville Associates; photography by Trevor Key.
7″ Single 1)Atmosphere 2)The Only Mistake
12″ Single 1)Atmosphere 2)The Only Mistake 3)Sound Of Music
Cassette Single 1) Atmosphere 2)The Only Mistake 3)Sound Of Music
CD Single 1)Atmosphere 2)Love Will Tear Us Apart 3)Transmission, live at the Factory, Manchester

7/88: *Substance: Joy Division 1977–80* (Factory Records FACT 250). Sleeve: Energie-Piek ijs (detail) by Jan Van Munster; art direction by Peter Saville; design by Brett Wickens; Peter Saville Associates; photography by Trevor Key. Compilation of various releases.
LP: 1) Warsaw 2) Leaders Of Men 3) Digital 4) Autosuggestion 5) Transmission 6) She's Lost Control 7) Incubation 8) Dead Souls 9) Atmosphere 10) Love Will Tear Us Apart
CD: 10 tracks of the LP + Appendix: 11) No Love Lost 12) Failures 13) Glass 14) From Safety To Where…? 15) Novelty 16) Komakino 17) These Days

1/90: *Peel Sessions* (Strange Fruit SFR 111). Sleeve design by Peter Saville Associates; photography by Anton Corbijn.
1. Exercise One
2. Insight
3. She's Lost Control
4. Transmission
5. Love Will Tear Us Apart
6. Twenty Four Hours
7. Colony
8. Sound Of Music

Tracks 1 to 4: recorded January 31, 1979. Produced by Bob Sargeant, first broadcast on John Peel radio show February 14, 1979.

Tracks 5 to 8: recorded November 26, 1979. Produced by Tony Wilson, first broadcast on John Peel radio show December 10, 1979.

7/95: Love Will Tear Us Apart 1995 (London Records YOJX1). Designed by Howard Wakefield, Art direction Peter Saville
12″ Single: 1) Love Will Tear Us Apart (original version) 2) Love Will Tear Us Apart (radio version) 3) Love Will Tear Us Apart (Arthur Baker remix) 4) Atmosphere (original Hannett 12″)
Cassette Single: 1) Love Will Tear Us Apart 1995 (radio version) 2) Love Will Tear Us Apart (original version)
CD Single: 1) Love Will Tear Us Apart (radio version) 2) Love Will Tear Us Apart (original version) 3) These Days 4) Transmission (live)

8/95: *Permanent* (London Records 8286242). Sleeve design by Peter Saville and Howard Wakefield; photography by John Holden. Compilation of various releases.
1. Love Will Tear Us Apart
2. Transmission
3. She's Lost Control
4. Shadowplay
5. Day Of The Lords
6. Isolation
7. Passover
8. Heart And Soul
9. Twenty Four Hours
10. These Days
11. Novelty
12. Dead Souls
13. The Only Mistake
14. Something Must Break
15. Atmosphere
16. Love Will Tear Us Apart (Remix by Don Gehman)

12/97: *Heart & Soul* (London Records 8289682) 4CD boxset. Designed by Peter Saville, Jon Wozencroft and Howard Wakefield.

Disc One
1. Digital
2. Glass
3. Disorder
4. Day Of The Lords
5. Candidate
6. Insight
7. New Dawn Fades
8. She's Lost Control
9. Shadowplay

10. Wilderness
11. Interzone
12. I Remember Nothing
13. Ice Age
14. Exercise One
15. Transmission
16. Novelty
17. The Kill
18. The Only Mistake
19. Somethink Must Break
20. Autosuggestion
21. From Safety To Where…?

All tracks produced by Martin Hannett, 1 & 2 Recorded at Cargo Studios, Rochdale, 3–18 & 20–21 Strawberry Studios, Stockport. 19 Central Sound, Manchester.

1 & 2 released on *A Factory Sample* (1-79), (3-12) *Unknown Pleasures* (5-79) 13,14 & 17-19 *Still* (10/81). 15 & 16 7″ vinyl (10-79). 20-21 *Earcom 2: Contradiction* (10-79) 1,2,15,16,20 &21 *Substance* (7/88). 13,14,17,18 & 19 With added post production.

Disc Two:
1. She's Lost Control 12″
2. Sounds Of Music
3. Atmosphere
4. Dead Souls
5. Komakino
6. Incubation
7. Atrocity Exhibition
8. Isolation
9. Passover
10. Colony
11. Means To An End
12. Heart And Soul
13. Twenty Four Hours
14. The Eternal
15. Decades
16. Love Will Tear Us Apart
17. These Days

All tracks produced by Martin Hannett. 1 & 16 Strawberry Studios, Stockport. 2 & 17 Pennine Sound Studios, Oldham. 3 & 4 Recorded at Cargo Studios, Rochdale. 5-15 Britannia Row, London.

1 released on 12″ vinyl (9/80). 2 & 4 *Still* 9(10-81). 3 & 4 *Licht Und Blindheit* (3/80). 3 12″Vinyl (9/80), 5 & 6 7″ Flexi (4/80), 7-15 *Closer* (7/80), 1, 3, 4, 5, 6, 16, 17 *Substance* (7/88).

Disc Three:
1. Warsaw
2. No Love Lost
3. Leaders Of Men
4. Failures
5. The Drawback
6. Interzone
7. Shadowplay
8. Exercise One
9. Insight
10. Glass
11. Transmission
12. Dead Souls
13. Something Must Break
14. Ice Age
15. Walked In Line
16. These Days
17. Candidate
18. The Only Mistake
19. Chance (Atmosphere)
20. Love Will Tear Us Apart
21. Colony
22. As You Said
23. Ceremony
24. In A Lonely Place (Detail)

1-4 produced by Warsaw, 5-7 John Anderson, Bob Auger, Richard Searling & Joy Division. 8 Bob Sargeant. 9-11 & 14 Martin Rushent. 12,13,15, & 22 Martin Hannett, 16-19 Stuart James, 20 & 21 Tony Wilson.
1-4 & 16-19 recorded at Pennine Sound Studios, Oldham, 5-7 Arrow Studios, Manchester, 6, 8, 20 & 21 BBC Studios, London 9-11 & 14 Eden Studios, London. 15 Strawberry Studios, Stockport, 12 & 13 Central Sound, Manchester, 22 Britannia Row, London, 23 & 24 Graveyard Studios, Prestwich.
1-4 released on *An Ideal For Living* 7″ Vinyl (6/78). 12″ Vinyl (10/78) & *Substance* (7/88). 5-7, 9-19, 23 & 24 previously unreleased. 8, 20 & 21 broadcast 2/79, 12/79 & *The Peel Sessions* (90). 22 7″ Flexi Disc, uncredited track (4/80) 7 & Video 586 12″ Vinyl (9/97).
5, 6 & 7 RCA demo. 16-19 Picadilly Radio Session. 9, 10, 11 & 14 Genetic Records Session. 8, 20 & 21 *John Peel Session*.

Disc Four:
1. Dead Souls
2. The Only Mistake
3. Insight

4. Candidate
5. Wilderness
6. She's Lost Control
7. Disorder
8. Interzone
9. Atrocity Exhibition
10. Novelty
11. Autosuggestion
12. I Remember Nothing
13. Colony
14. These Days
15. Incubation
16. The Eternal
17. Heart And Soul
18. Isolation
19. She's Lost Control

1-10 recorded live at The Factory Hulme 11 Prince of Wales Conference Centre, YMCA, London. 12-14 Winter Gardens, Bournemouth, 15-19 Lyceum Ballroom, London.

6/99: *Preston 28th February 1980* (FACD 2.60). Designed by Howard Wakefield and Paul Hetherington, Art direction by Peter Saville.

1. Incubation
2. Wilderness
3. Twenty For Hours
4. The Eternal
5. Heart And Soul
6. Shadowplay
7. Transmission
8. Disorder
9. Warsaw
10. Colony
11. Interzone
12. She's Lost Control

Recorded live at the Warehouse, Preston February 28, 1980.

7/00: *The Complete BBC* (Strange Fruit SFR 094). Designed by The Peter Saville Studio, Photography Jon Wozencroft.

1. Exercice One
2. Insight
3. She's Lost Control
4. Transmission
5. Love Will Tear Us Apart
6. Twenty Four Hours

7.   Colony
8.   Sound Of Music
9.   Transmission
10. She's Lost Control
11. Interview

Tracks 1 to 4: recorded January 31, 1979. Produced by Bob Sargeant, first broadcast on John Peel radio show February 14, 1979.

Tracks 5 to 8: recorded November 26, 1979. Produced by Tony Wilson, first broadcast on John Peel radio show December 10, 1979.

Tracks 9/10: recorded live for *Something Else*, September 15, 1979

Track 11: recorded for Radio One in '79 interview of Ian Curtis and Stephen Morris by R. Skinner

4/01: *Les Bains Douches 18 December 1979* (FACD 2.61). Designed by Howard Wakefield and Paul Hetherington, Art direction by Peter Saville.

1.   Disorder
2.   Love Will Tear Us Apart
3.   Insight
4.   Shadowplay
5.   Transmission
6.   Day Of The Lords
7.   Twenty Four Hours
8.   These Days
9.   A Means To An End
10. Passover
11. New Dawn Fades
12. Atrocity Exhibition
13. Digital
14. Dead Souls
15. Autosuggestion
16. Atmosphere

1–9 Recorded live at Les Bains Douches, Paris, December 18, 1979.

10–12 Recorded live Amsterdam, January 11, 1980

13–16 Recorded live Eindhoven, January 11, 1980

APPENDIX 4

Joy Division Film & TV Appearances

20/9/78: Granada Studio 2, Manchester
Performance: Shadowplay
Broadcast on *Granada Reports*, with negative offcuts from the *World In Action* about the CIA, chromakeyed behind the group.

14/3/79: Bowdon Vale Youth Club
Three songs filmed by Malcolm Whitehead as part of a 17-minute Super 8 film which also included: material shot during *Unknown Pleasures* rehearsal at TJ Davidson's, an interview with Rob Gretton recorded 23/3/79; and part of a speech by Manchester's then Chief Constable, James Anderton.
A version of this film was shown at the Scala Cinema in London on 13/9/79 – an event given a FAC number, FAC 9.

19/7/79: What's On: Granada 2
Performance: She's Lost Control
Version recorded live in the studio and broadcast on Granada 2.

15/9/79: Something Else, BBC2
Performance: Transmission, She's Lost Control
Interview with Steve Morris and Tony Wilson.

30/9/79: No City Fun
A 12 min. Super 8 film by Charles Salem; text by Liz Naylor (based on an article in *City Fun*) and music from *Unknown Pleasures*.

16/10/79: Plan K, Brussels
Performance: Love Will Tear Us Apart, Wilderness, Disorder, Colony, Insight, 24
Hours, New Dawn Fades, Transmission, Shadowplay, She's Lost Control, Atrocity
Exhibition, Interzone
There is some slow motion footage on *Here Are The Young Men* (FACT 37). The
rest of the concert is unreleased, some excerpts were shown as part of the 25th
Anniversary of the death of Ian Curtis in May 2005 by Ikon &.

27/10/79 – 28/10/79: Apollo, Manchester
Performance (27/10/79): Dead Souls, Wilderness, Colony, Auto-Suggestion, Love
Will Tear Us Apart, Shadowplay, She's Lost Control, Transmission
Performance (28/10/79): Sound Of Music, Shadowplay, Colony, Day Of The
Lords, Twenty Four Hours, Disorder, Walked In Line, I Remember Nothing,
Transmission
Both nights at the Apollo were videotaped in full (on ½ inch tape) by Buzzcocks'
manager Richard Boon. Some songs were released on the Factory video, *Here Are
The Young Men* (FACT 37)

18/01/80: Effenaar, Eindhoven, Holland
Performance: Digital, Colony, New Dawn Fades, Autosuggestion
Filmed on Super 8.

28/4/80: Love Will Tear Us Apart promo video
Several versions of this video were edited out of this performance at T.J.
Davidson's rehearsal studios. It was directed by Stuart Orme, and first shown on
Granada's Saturday morning children's programme, *Fun Factory*, on June 26, 1980.
Manchester DJ Ray Teret introduced the clip thus: "Joy Division isn't a female
vocalist, it's a band."

Video Compilation

8/82: *Here Are The Young Men* (FACT 37) (VHS)
1) Dead Souls
2) Love Will Tear Us Apart
3) Shadowplay
4) Day Of The Lords
5) Digital
6) Colony
7) New Dawn Fades
8) Auto-Suggestion
9) Transmission
10) Sound Of Music
11) She's Lost Control

12) Walked In Line
13) I Remember Nothing
14) Love Will Tear Us Apart
Tracks: 1,2,3,& 11 Manchester, Apollo Theatre 27/10/79
Tracks: 4,9,10,12 & 13 Manchester, Apollo Theatre 28/10/79
Tracks: 5,6,7 & 8 Eindhoven, Effenaar, The Netherlands 18/1/80
Track 14: not credited on the sleeve but official promo video

APPENDIX 5

Joy Division Concert Listing

1977
As THE STIFF KITTENS
29 MAY Electric Circus, Manchester
As WARSAW
31 MAY Rafters, Manchester
1 JUN The Squat, Manchester
2 JUN Newcastle
3 JUN The Squat, Manchester
16 JUN The Squat, Manchester
30 JUN Rafters, Manchester
JUL The Squat, Manchester
27 AUG Eric's, Liverpool (afternoon)
14 SEP Rock Garden, Middlesbrough
24 SEP Electric Circus, Manchester
2 OCT Electric Circus, Manchester
7 OCT Salford Technical College, Salford
8 OCT Manchester Polytechnic, Manchester
13 OCT Rafters, Manchester
19 OCT Piper's Disco, Manchester
24 NOV Rafters, Manchester
31 DEC The Swinging Apple, Liverpool

1978
As JOY DIVISION
25 JAN Pip's, Manchester
14 MAR Bowdon Vale Youth Club, Altrincham

28 MAR Rafters, Manchester
14 APR Rafters, Manchester
20 MAY The Mayflower Club, Manchester
9 JUN The Factory I, Manchester
15 JUL Eric's, Liverpool
27 JUL The Fan Club (Roots Club), Leeds
28 JUL The Factory I, Manchester
29 AUG Band On The Wall, Manchester
4 SEP Band On The Wall, Manchester
9 SEP Eric's, Liverpool
10 SEP Royal Standard, Bradford
2 OCT Institute Of Technology, Bolton
12 OCT Kelly's, Manchester
20 OCT The Factory I, Manchester
24 OCT The Fan Club (Branningan's), Leeds
4 NOV Eric's, Liverpool
14 NOV The Odeon, Canterbury
15 NOV Brunel University, Uxbridge
19 NOV Bristol
20 NOV Check Inn Club, Altrincham
26 NOV New Electric Circus, Manchester
1 DEC Salford College Of Technology, Salford
22 DEC Revolution Club, York
27 DEC The Hope And Anchor, Islington, London

1979
10 FEB Bolton
16 FEB Eric's, Liverpool
28 FEB Playhouse, Nottingham
1 MAR The Hope And Anchor, Islington, London
4 MAR The Marquee, London
14 MAR Bowden Vale Youth Club, Altrincham
17 MAR University Of Kent, Canterbury
30 MAR Youth Centre, Walthamstow, London
3 MAY Eric's, Liverpool
11 MAY The Factory (Russell Club), Manchester
17 MAY Acklam Hall, London
23 MAY Bowdon Vale Youth Club, Altrincham
7 JUN Fan Club, Leeds
13 JUN The Factory (Russell Club), Manchester
16 JUN The Odeon, Canterbury
17 JUN Royalty Theatre, Holborn, London
22 JUN Good Mood, Halifax

25 JUN Free Trade Hall, Manchester
28 JUN The Factory I, Manchester
3 JUL Free Trade Hall, Manchester
5 JUL Limit Club, Sheffield
11 JUL Roots Club, Leeds
13 JUL The Factory (Russell Club), Manchester
27 JUL Imperial Hotel, Blackpool
28 JUL The Fun House (The Mayflower), Manchester
2 AUG Prince Of Wales Conference Centre, YMCA, London
8 AUG Romulus Club, Birmingham
11 AUG Eric's, Liverpool (two performances)
13 AUG Nashville, London
22 AUG Youth Centre, Walthamstow, London
27 AUG Leigh Open Air Pop Festival
31 AUG The Electric Ballroom, London
8 SEP Futurama One Festival, Queen's Hall, Leeds
22 SEP Nashville Rooms, London
28 SEP The Factory I, Manchester
2 OCT Mountford Hall, University Of Liverpool, Liverpool
3 OCT Leeds University, Leeds
4 OCT City Hall, Newcastle
5 OCT The Apollo, Glasgow, Scotland
6 OCT Odeon, Edinburgh, Scotland
7 OCT Capitol, Aberdeen, Scotland
8 OCT Caird Hall, Dundee, Scotland
16 OCT Plan K, Brussels, Belgium
18 OCT Bangor University, Bangor, Wales
20 OCT Loughborough University, Loughborough
21 OCT Top Rank, Sheffield
22 OCT Assembly Rooms, Derby
23 OCT King George's Hall, Blackburn
24 OCT The Odeon, Birmingham
25 OCT St. George's Hall, Bradford
26 OCT The Electric Ballroom, London
27 OCT Apollo Theatre, Manchester England
28 OCT Apollo Theatre, Manchester England
29 OCT De Montfort Hall, Leicester
30 OCT The New Theatre, Oxford
1 NOV Civic Hall, Guildford
2 NOV Winter Gardens, Bournemouth
3 NOV Sophia Gardens, Cardiff CANCELLED
4 NOV Colston Hall, Bristol
5 NOV Pavilion, Hemel Hempstead

7 NOV Pavilion, West Runton
9 NOV The Rainbow Theatre, London
10 NOV The Rainbow Theatre, London
8 DEC Eric's, Liverpool
18 DEC Les Bains-Douches Club, Paris, France
31 DEC Woolworth's, Oldham Street, Manchester

1980
1 JAN Piccadilly Gardens, Manchester
11 JAN Paradiso, Amsterdam, Holland
12 JAN Paard Van Troje, The Hague, Holland
13 JAN Doornroosje, Nijmegen, Holland
14 JAN King Kong, Antwerp, Belgium
15 JAN The Basement, Cologne, Germany
16 JAN Club Lantaren, Rotterdam, Holland
17 JAN Plan K, Brussels, Belgium
18 JAN Effenaar, Eindhoven, Holland
19 JAN Vera, Groningen, Netherlands
21 JAN Kant Kino Music Hall, Berlin, Germany
7 FEB The Factory II (New Osbourne Club), Manchester
8 FEB University Of London Union, London
20 FEB Town Hall, High Wycombe
28 FEB The Warehouse, Preston
29 FEB The Lyceum, London
5 MAR Trinity Hall, Bristol
2 APR The Moonlight Club, London
3 APR The Moonlight Club, London
4 APR The Rainbow, London
4 APR The Moonlight Club, London
5 APR The Winter Gardens, Malvern
8 APR Derby Hall, Bury
11 APR The Factory I (Russell Club), Manchester
19 APR Ajanta Theatre, Derby
25 APR Scala Cinema, London, CANCELLED
26 APR Rock Garden, Middlesbrough, CANCELLED
2 MAY High Hall, Birmingham University, Birmingham
8 MAY The Astoria, Edinburgh CANCELLED

APPENDIX 6

Two Songs About Ian Curtis

MISSING BOY

Vini Reilly (Durutti Column) never plays a gig without performing 'Missing Boy' – Ian's tune. He's performed it at every single gig since Ian died.

There was a boy
I almost knew him
A glance exchanged
Made me feel good
Leaving some signs
Now a legend

Try to capture
As the light began to fail
Shapes to compose
Shadows of frailty
The dream is better
Dissolves into softness
But the end is always the same

I don't believe in stardom
Machinery in action
Like a dead bird in the dirt
Like a rusty can on the ground
Same old order

There was a boy
I almost knew him
Leaving some signs
Now a legend

Words & Music by Vincent Reilly
© Copyright 1981 Movement Of the 24th January Publishing. Zomba Music
Publishers Limited.
All Rights Reserved. International Copyright Secured. Used by kind permission.

I.C. WATER

Genesis P-Orridge wrote and dedicated this song to Ian Curtis. It was released by
Psychic TV.

And I see much more clearly everyday
And I sense I can see you play
And there's always some truth
And there's always something I should say
There's always someone there to give me water everyday

Water
Water I hear you say
And I know
And I feel
What you say is far too real
And everything
And everywhere
And everything you say you care for
Water
I need some water

You tell me things and they're things I should have known
Where your tears are now they're not quite your own
And at night you lie in dreams you haven't flown
And we spin in circles that look so blown
And the tears stream down from the sky
Each tastes bitter
The salt of asking "Why?"
And your words come down and fall over me
Each one is a friend
And each one is the rain
And each is the sea
And worlds are so close they're inside my heart

Falling, falling, falling
Ripping me apart
Like water
Water everyday
Water
Water I hear you say
Water
What a strange sound
Water, what a strange sound
Water, what a strange, strange sound.

Words and lyrics used with kind permission of Genesis P-Orridge
© Copyright 1990/2006 Porridge With Everything Inc, New York, USA
All Rights Reserved. International Copyright Secured.

APPENDIX 7

Bibliography

In additional to their own personal knowledge and interviews with those mentioned in the Acknowledgements at the front of this book, the authors have drawn information from the following sources.

Books:
Curtis, Deborah. *Touching From A Distance* (Faber & Faber 1995)
Diggle, Steve, and Rawlings, Terry. *Harmony In My Head* (Helter Skelter, 2003)
Edge, Brian. *Pleasures And Wayward Distractions* (Omnibus Press, 1984)
Ford, Simon. *Wreckers Of Civilisation: The Story of Coum Transmissions And Throbbing Gristle* (Black Dog, 1999)
Haslam, Dave. *Manchester. The Story Of A Pop Cult City* (Fourth Estate, 2000)
Johnson, Mark. *An Idea For Living* (Proteus, 1984)
Lee, CP. *Shake Rattle And Rain* (Harding Simpole, 2000)
Matlcok, Glen, and Silverton, Pete. *I Was A Teenage Sex Pistol* (Virgin, 1990)
McGartland, Tony. *Buzzcocks: The Complete History* (IMP, 1995)
Middles Mick. *From Joy Division To New Order: The Factory Story* (Virgin, 1996)
Morley, Paul. *Nothing* (Faber & Faber, 2000)
Nolan, Dave. *I Swear I Was There. Sex Pistols And The Shape Of Rock* (Milo, 2001)
Ott, Chris. *Unknown Pleasures* (Continuum, 2004)
Reynolds. Simon. *Rip It Up And Start Again (Post Punk 1978-84)* (Faber & Faber 2005)
Savage, Jon. *England's Dreaming* (Faber & Faber 1991)
Thompson, Dave. *True Faith: An Armchair Guide To New Order, Joy Division, Revenge, Monaco And The Other Two* (Helter Skelter, 2005)
Wilson, Tony. *Twenty Four Hour Party People* (Channel Four, 2000)
Wood, Lee. *Sex Pistols Day By Day* (Omnibus Press, 1988)
Magazines & Periodicals
NME, Sounds, Melody Maker, The Face, City Life, City Fun, Shy Talk, Ghast Up, Penetration, Girl Trouble, Out There, Mojo, Record Collector, Spin Magazine.

Index

Singles releases are in roman type and albums in italics

315